THE DUCHESS OF MALFI

John Webster

for the King's Men at Blackfriars and the Globe

Edited by

LEAH S. MARCUS

THE ARDEN SHAKESPEARE

LONDON • NEW YORK • OXFORD • NEW DELHI • SYDNEY

THE ARDEN SHAKESPEARE
Bloomsbury Publishing Plc
50 Bedford Square, London, WC1B 3DP, UK
1385 Broadway, New York, NY 10018, USA

BLOOMSBURY, THE ARDEN SHAKESPEARE and the Arden Shakespeare
logo are trademarks of Bloomsbury Publishing Plc

First published in Great Britain 2009
Reprinted 2012, 2013, 2014, 2015 (twice), 2016 (twice), 2017, 2018, 2019, 2020 (twice)

Bloomsbury Publishing Plc does not have any control over, or responsibility for,
any third-party websites referred to or in this book. All internet addresses given
in this book were correct at the time of going to press. The author and publisher
regret any inconvenience caused if addresses have changed or sites have ceased
to exist, but can accept no responsibility for any such changes.

A catalogue record for this book is available from the British Library.

A catalog record for this book is available from the Library of Congress.

ISBN: HB: 978-1-4081-1948-8
PB: 978-1-9042-7151-2
ePDF: 978-1-4081-3813-7

Series: Arden Early Modern Drama

Printed and bound in India

To find out more about our authors and books visit www.bloomsbury.com
and sign up for our newsletters.

The Editor

Leah S. Marcus is Edwin Mims Professor of English at Vanderbilt University. Her previous publications include *Childhood and Cultural Despair* (1978), *The Politics of Mirth* (1986), *Puzzling Shakespeare* (1988), *Unediting the Renaissance* (1996), two co-edited volumes of the writings and speeches of Queen Elizabeth I (2000, 2003) and a Norton Critical Edition of *The Merchant of Venice*. At present she is completing a Norton Critical Edition of *As You Like It*.

CONTENTS

LIST OF
ILLUSTRATIONS

GENERAL EDITORS' PREFACE

Arden Early Modern Drama (AEMD) is an expansion of the acclaimed Arden Shakespeare to include the plays of other dramatists of the early modern period. The series publishes dramatic texts from the early modern period in the established tradition of the Arden Shakespeare, using a similar style of presentation and offering the same depth of information and high standards of scholarship. We define 'early modern drama' broadly, to encompass plays written and performed at any time from the late fifteenth to the late seventeenth century. The attractive and accessible format and well-informed editorial content are designed with particular regard to the needs of students studying literature and drama in the final years of secondary school and in colleges and universities. Texts are presented in modern spelling and punctuation; stage directions are expanded to clarify theatrical requirements and possibilities; and speech prefixes (the markers of identity at the beginning of each new speech) are regularized. Each volume contains about twenty illustrations both from the period and from later performance history; a full discussion of the current state of criticism of the play; and information about the textual and performance contexts from which the play first emerged. The goal of the series is to make these wonderful but sometimes neglected plays as intelligible as those of Shakespeare to twenty-first-century readers.

AEMD editors bring a high level of critical engagement and textual sophistication to their work. They provide guidance in assessing critical approaches to their play, developing arguments from the best scholarly work to date and generating new perspectives. A particular focus of an AEMD edition is the play as it was first performed in the theatre. The title-page of each volume displays the name of the company for which the play was written and the theatre at which it was first staged: in the Introduction the play is discussed as part of a company repertory as well as of an authorial canon. Finally, each edition presents a full scholarly discussion of the base text and other relevant materials as physical and social documents, and the Introduction describes issues arising in the early history of the publication and reception of the text.

Commentary notes, printed immediately below the playtext, offer compact but detailed exposition of the language, historical context and theatrical significance of the play. They explain textual ambiguities and, when an action may be interpreted in different ways, they summarize the arguments. Where appropriate they point the reader to fuller discussions in the Introduction.

CONVENTIONS

AEMD editions always include illustrations of pages from the early texts on which they are based. Comparison between these illustrations and the edited text immediately enables the reader to see clearly what a critical edition is and does. In summary, the main changes to the base text – that is, the early text, most often a quarto, that serves as the copy from which the editor works – are these: certain and probable errors in the base text are corrected; typography and spelling are brought into line with current usage; and speech prefixes and stage directions are modified to assist the reader in imagining the play in performance.

Significant changes introduced by editors are recorded in the textual notes at the foot of the page. These are an important cache of information, presented in as compact a form as is possible without forfeiting intelligibility. The standard form can be seen in the following example:

31 doing of] *Coxeter;* of doing *Q;* doing *Rawl*

The line reference ('31') and the reading quoted from the present editor's text ('doing of') are printed before the closing square bracket. After the bracket, the source of the reading, often the name of the editor who first made the change to the base text ('*Coxeter*'), appears, and then other readings are given, followed by their source ('of doing *Q;* doing *Rawl*'). Where there is more than one alternative reading, they are listed in chronological order; hence in the example the base text Q (= Quarto) is given first. Abbreviations used to identify early texts and later editions are listed in the Abbreviations and References section towards the end of the volume. Editorial emendations to the text are discussed in the main commentary, where notes on emendations are highlighted with an asterisk.

Emendation necessarily takes account of early texts other than the base text, as well as of the editorial tradition. The amount of attention paid to other texts depends on the editor's assessment of their origin and importance. Emendation aims to correct errors while respecting the integrity of different versions as they might have emerged through revision and adaptation.

Modernization of spelling and punctuation in AEMD texts is thorough, avoiding the kind of partial modernization that produces language from no known period of English. Generally modernization is routine, involving thousands of alterations of letters. As original grammar is preserved in AEMD editions, most modernizations are as trivial as altering 'booke' to 'book', and are unworthy of record. But where the modernization is unexpected or ambiguous the change is noted in the textual notes, using the following format:

102 trolls] *(*trowles*)*

Speech prefixes are sometimes idiosyncratic and variable in the base texts, and almost always abbreviated. AEMD editions expand contractions, avoiding confusion of names that might be similarly abbreviated, such as Alonzo/Alsemero/Alibius from *The Changeling*. Preference is given to the verbal form that prevails in the base text, even if it identifies the role by type, such as 'Lady' or 'Clown', rather than by personal name. When an effect of standardization is to repress significant variations in the way that a role is conceptualized (in *Philaster*, for example, one text refers to a cross-dressed page as *Boy*, while another uses the character's assumed name), the issue is discussed in the Introduction.

Stage directions in early modern texts are often inconsistent, incomplete or unclear. They are preserved in the edition as far as is possible, but are expanded where necessary to ensure that the dramatic action is coherent and self-consistent. Square brackets are used to indicate editorial additions to stage directions. Directions that lend themselves to multiple staging possibilities, as well as the performance tradition of particular moments, may be discussed in the commentary.

Verse lineation sometimes goes astray in early modern playtexts, as does the distinction between verse and prose, especially where a wide manuscript layout has been transferred to the narrower measure of a printed page. AEMD editions correct such mistakes. Where a verse line is shared between more than one speaker, this series follows the usual modern practice of indenting the second and subsequent part-lines to make it clear that they belong to the same verse line.

The textual notes allow the reader to keep track of all these interventions. The notes use variations on the basic format described above to reflect the changes. In notes, '31 SD' indicates a stage direction in or immediately after line 31. Where there is more than one stage direction, they are identified as, for example, '31 SD1', '31 SD2'. The second line of a stage direction will be identified as, for instance, '31.2'. A forward slash / indicates a line-break in verse.

We hope that these conventions make as clear as possible the editor's engagement with and interventions in the text: our aim is to keep the reader fully informed of the editor's role without intruding unnecessarily on the flow of reading. Equally, we hope – since one of our aims is to encourage the performance of more plays from the early modern period beyond the Shakespeare canon – to provide texts which materially assist performers, as well as readers, of these plays.

PREFACE

It has been nearly half a century since the last full-dress edition of *The Duchess of Malfi*, by John Russell Brown, appeared in 1964. When Suzanne Gossett asked me whether I would like to edit this magnificent play, I jumped at the chance. Little did she know how much labour she had condemned herself to as the Arden Early Modern Drama General Editor responsible for supervising my work. Every Arden edition is a collaboration among many diligent people, and this one is no exception. My primary debts, gratefully acknowledged, are to Richard Proudfoot, who helped me think outside the box when wrestling with Webster's metrics; to David Kastan, who convinced me in a dark moment that the book would, one day, be published; and to Suzanne Gossett, whom I affectionately term my 'handler', and who sacrificed weeks of golden summer in Italy to correction and proofing. Suzanne read every word and notation symbol multiple times, improving the edition every time. I also owe warm thanks to John Jowett, who made several crucial interventions, particularly in his wonderful suggestions about early staging. The series publisher, Margaret Bartley, has been helpful at every point through difficult times of transition. Linden Stafford is the most wonderful and sharp-eyed copy-editor anyone could reasonably hope for. She has also doubled as my expert on French spelling and British ornithology – not an insignificant matter in a play full of references to birds and bird life. Jane Armstrong, Hannah Hyam and Damian Love have saved the edition from numerous errors. Charlotte Loveridge and Anna Wormleighton located and prepared many of the illustrations.

I also owe thanks to a number of other colleagues who contributed to the project along the way, especially Lynn

Enterline, who taught me about melancholy and hyenas, Kathryn Schwarz, Holly Tucker, Katharine B. Crawford, and the rest of the Vanderbilt GEMCS crew, who patiently endured much exposure to material from the edition in our seminars over the years and offered many insights. Laurie Maguire, Tiffany Stern, Carolyn Dever and Michael Neill supplied me with their research and advance publications just when they were needed. David Gunby, whose name occurs many times in this volume to record my debts to his edition of Webster, read and critiqued the Introduction. Cynthia Cyrus of the Blair School of Music at Vanderbilt offered enormously valuable advice about the musical setting for the song in Appendix 3. Her student Christine Smith ably prepared the final version of the song text.

I also owe a considerable debt of gratitude to my own graduate students, those who kept freshening my thinking about the play over the years and those who intervened more concretely as research assistants. Donald Jellerson helped prepare the playtext in its early stages and did the first transcriptions of the texts in Appendices 1 and 2. Jennifer Clement helped with research. Both of them will find themselves credited in the commentary for suggestions I adopted. Bethany Packard checked all the textual notes, and Jane Wanninger checked the commentary. For any errors that remain I am, of course, responsible, and promise never, ever to attribute even one mistake to them.

Research for the edition was done primarily at the Harry Ransom Center of the University of Texas, the Bodleian Library, the British Library, the Morgan Library in New York, the Houghton Library at Harvard, and the New York Public Library. I owe special thanks to all of the library staffs for help above and beyond the call of duty. Special mention also goes to the Vanderbilt Interlibrary Loan Office, which has the magical ability to conjure up manuscript microfilms and even eighteenth-century books at very short notice. My thanks also to the editors and publishers of *Shakespeare Studies* for permission to reprint, in revised form, several paragraphs from my article 'The author and/or the critic', in *Shakespeare Studies* Forum: The Return of the Author, ed. Patrick Cheney, *Shakespeare Studies*, 36 (2008), 90-100. I would also like to thank Vanderbilt University for granting me leave time and money to carry out research for the edition.

Finally, as always, I would like to thank my family: my daughters Emily, who was luckily already off at university when the real work began; and Lauren, who lost much quality time because of notes and collations; and my husband David, who offers emotional support and, even more crucial, fixes dinner. This edition is dedicated to my own private Duchess, my great aunt Dr Mary Leah Cook of Waynesville, Ohio (1869–1964), who was an old woman before I was born and nevertheless transformed my life. She was a teacher, physician, writer, amateur botanist, zoologist, farmer and philanthropist whose cheerful practicality, high intelligence and strength of character touched all who knew her. In small-town America, as at the court of Amalfi, though there is a vast difference in scale, 'Integrity of life is fame's best friend, / Which nobly beyond death shall crown the end.'

INTRODUCTION

John Webster's *The Duchess of Malfi* is the most frequently performed of all non-Shakespearean plays of the early modern period. It has its share of violence and of intriguingly strange props – a poisoned holy book, a severed human hand. But it also has as its central figure one of the most luminous and charismatic of all early modern stage heroines. The Duchess who dominates her eponymous play is never called by any name other than her title, but she is far from being a stereotypical aristocrat. She breaks the social rules and evades her aristocratic brothers' attempts to control her by contracting a daring clandestine marriage and managing to keep it secret through a number of years and the births of two children.

The Duchess's brothers are so corrupt that they verge on the ludicrous – a melancholy Cardinal who flouts his vows of celibacy and openly keeps a mistress; a duke, Ferdinand of Calabria, who suffers from a strangely incestuous attraction for his sister and eventually goes mad, believing himself to be a wolf-man. But their vices are chilling as well as ludicrous and the two brothers are very dangerous, sending their spy Bosola to pry out the Duchess's secrets and surrounding her with an atmosphere of suspicion and paranoia. The miracle is that she manages to build and sustain a happy and productive life for herself even as spies and corruption swirl around her. She is unquestionably a proto-feminist in her evasions of her brothers' attempts to control her, yet she places such a low value on the power tactics by which they attempt to enforce their will upon her that she refuses to use similar tactics even to save herself and her family. The Duchess of Malfi is only one of many unforgettable characters with which John Webster has filled his dramatic masterpiece.

She starts out as a charming, witty woman who lights up the play with her love of life whenever she comes onstage; she grows over time and persecution into a figure of almost superhuman courage and endurance as her brothers attempt (with a singular lack of success) to break her spirit, reduce her to madness and depravity, and turn her into one of themselves.

WHO WAS JOHN WEBSTER?

The 1998 film *Shakespeare in Love* portrays John Webster around 1593 as a terrifying lad who enjoys torturing small animals. While dangling a mouse before a hungry cat, Webster informs Shakespeare that he acted a part in *Titus Andronicus* in which he was beheaded. That most macabre of Shakespearean plays has evidently shaped Webster's aesthetic sense: he confides, 'I like it when they cut heads off. And the daughter mutilated with knives.' The implication is that Webster as a dramatist in later life will remain mired in adolescent fantasies of blood and dismemberment while Shakespeare moves on to greater things.

For casual viewers, perhaps, *Shakespeare in Love* offers a fair enough characterization of Webster's work, or at least of his best-known plays, *The White Devil* and *The Duchess of Malfi* (hereafter referred to as *Malfi*). In *Malfi* alone, we are treated to a severed hand, a waxworks display of corpses, a parade of madmen and a courtesan murdered by kissing a poisoned Bible, in addition to the standard Jacobean complement of deaths by sword or dagger. But the film portrait of Webster, however hilarious as parody, is far removed from the historical figure, who was as much an idealist as he was a specialist in violence, and whose major tragedies evoke bizarre images of mutilation and death as part of a carefully calibrated response to specific Jacobean issues and problems.

Before 1976, when researcher Mary Edmond put the two figures together, we had known of a John Webster (died 1614) who was a wealthy coach-maker in London and of a younger

John Webster (born *c.* 1580 and died *c.* 1626–34) who was a dramatist and man of letters, but we had not known that the two men were father and son. Webster the elder was an influential member of the Merchant Taylors Company, one of the largest and most powerful of the London livery companies, which could boast among its honorary members the heir apparent to the English throne, Prince Henry, made free of the company in 1607, and many other notables. John Webster the younger was evidently the elder of at least two sons. A second son, Edward, devoted his life to running the family's coaching business, which left John free to follow other pursuits.

John Webster the playwright probably attended the Merchant Taylors' School, which was run by his father's company. Its famous headmaster, Richard Mulcaster, was no longer there by Webster's time, but it was still one of the best of London's grammar schools, and would have given Webster a top-class humanist education, with strong emphasis on Latin and Greek language and literature. Perhaps John Webster the elder intended his first-born son for the law. We find in the records of New Inn, Chancery, a note of the 1598 admission of a 'John Webster of London' who was 'son and heir apparent of John Webster of London, Gentleman'. This may not be John Webster the playwright, since Webster was a common name, but the dates are right, and throughout his life Webster held close ties with members of the Inns of Court (Forker, 31–56). In any case, legal training would have served Webster well if, as Muriel Bradbrook has speculated, John worked in the white-collar, legal and record-keeping side of the family's coaching business while his younger brother ran the manufacturing side. During the many decades of his activity in the London theatre, John Webster was probably also active in the family's flourishing transport enterprise.

The mainstay of the business was the manufacture, rental and sale of coaches and 'caroches' (large coaches), which were elaborately fitted out with upholstery (hence the link to the Merchant Taylors). Coaches were newly fashionable in London and clogged the city streets; in plays of the period there were running jokes about their wild popularity and also their potential, when curtained for privacy, to serve as brothels on wheels (see 4.2.103–5n.). The Websters also dealt in horses for posting long distances at great speed and built carts used for a variety of purposes, from the rough conveyances used to display scolds and sexual malefactors about the streets of London and carry the condemned to the gallows, to the much heavier vehicles that bore the elaborate pageants in the annual Lord Mayor's Show and James I's 1604 royal entry into London (Bradbrook). Given Webster's background in the coach and carting business, it is amusing to recognize his plays' many references to coaches, caroches and post-horses as a seventeenth-century version of product placement – inspiring desire for the sumptuous vehicles referred to (but not as a rule displayed) onstage.

It was quite common for leading actors and playwrights to have membership in the London livery companies: actor Edward Alleyn was probably a freeman of the Worshipful Company of Innholders, like his brother; Robert Armin and John Lowin were both free of the Goldsmiths; Ben Jonson was (infamously) a Bricklayer; James Burbage and possibly also his son Richard Burbage were Joiners; John Heminges was a Grocer, and so on (Kathman, 'Freemen'). But John Webster's connection to the Merchant Taylors was closer than that of most actors and playwrights to their respective livery companies and he appears to have been quite proud of it, at least by fits and starts. After his father's death in 1614, he was made free of the company by patrimony. In 1624 he wrote and staged the London Lord Mayor's Show for John Gore, a Merchant Taylor who had just been elected Lord Mayor. The printed version of Webster's show, *Monuments of Honour*, called a 'Magnificent Triumph' on its title-page, was printed by his neighbour Nicholas Okes, who also printed several of Webster's plays. The title-page announces that the show was '*Invented and Written*' not by John Webster Poet but '*by* John Webster Merchant-Taylor' (Webster, 3.253).

4

What did it mean in Jacobean London to be both an active member of a livery company and an active participant in the world of the theatre? For one thing, Webster's dual career no doubt accounted at least in some measure for the intermittence of his record as a playwright. He usually worked collaboratively, as was standard for the period, writing around 1602 with a varied group of dramatists: Michael Drayton, Thomas Dekker, Thomas Middleton, Thomas Heywood and others. With the exception of *Westward Ho* and *Northward Ho!*, both collaborations with Dekker printed in 1607, and Dekker's *Sir Thomas Wyatt* (1607), which reworked another collaboration, all of these earliest plays are lost. We do have Webster's 1604 revisions of John Marston's *Malcontent*, which are adroitly designed to relocate the play from the playing conditions of an Elizabethan boys' company to those of a Jacobean adult company, the King's Men. The fact that Webster was the dramatist who did these revisions suggests that he was already regarded as someone familiar with the London theatre and the requirements of its different venues; Webster's additions include an Induction in which five actors from the King's Men, among them Richard Burbage and John Lowin, amusingly play themselves (Webster, 3.309–56). For several years after 1607 we have nothing, then in a great burst Webster's single-authored plays *The White Devil* (1612) and *The Duchess of Malfi* (1613–14), a published verse tribute on the death of Prince Henry called *A Monumental Column* (1613) and prose additions to Sir Thomas Overbury's enormously popular *New and Choice Characters* (1615), including a Character of '*An excellent Actor*' explicitly aimed at defending the profession of actor against a defamatory earlier character by an Overbury imitator who had called actors ignorant rogues (Webster, 3.483; Forker, 546–7, n. 33).

There follows another quiet spell from 1615 to 1623, during which Webster may have composed *Guise*, which is lost; *Anything for a Quiet Life* with Middleton (*c.* 1621); and one more single-authored play, *The Devil's Law-Case* (1617–19). Significantly, this period of relative inactivity in the theatre followed Webster's 1615 inauguration into full membership in the Merchant Taylors Company. Then from 1623 onwards Webster again became active in the theatre, publishing two of his three surviving single-authored plays that had not previously been published, writing his Lord Mayor's Show and beginning a renewed career of collaboration with William Rowley, Thomas Heywood, Philip Massinger and others that lasted at least until 1626, the last year in which we have reliable records that he was still alive (Webster, 3.xl–xli). Given the infrequency with which he wrote as a single author, it is a remarkable tribute to Webster's formidable talent that his name stands in the canon alongside or above those of dramatists who were much more prolific than he.

Unlike Shakespeare but like Ben Jonson, Webster has left a body of critical commentary about his work as a dramatist and man of letters. His dual career also probably accounts for a certain defensiveness we can sense in these critical pronouncements. Most of the theatre people who were also members of livery companies tended to conceal or at least downplay their membership, since it was likely to detract from their claim to the status of gentleman. A satiric poem, 'Notes from Blackfriars' (printed in 1618), describes Webster, among other frequenters of Blackfriars theatre, as 'Crabbed (*Websterio*) / The *Play-wright, Cart-wright: whether? either? ho –* ' implying that his dual professions undercut one another and make him impossible to categorize (*Certain Elegies*). Another satire of 1615 glances derisively at the family business by referring to Webster's style as 'dressed over with oyle of sweaty Post-horse' and guilty of 'hackney similitudes' (Stephens; see also Forker, 546–7, n. 33). If anything, Webster's constant need to negotiate between two professions, one of them more frankly and grittily commercial than the other, appears to have made him more sophisticated than most in understanding that drama had to be marketed like any other commodity and in articulating tensions relating to the playwright's need to accommodate the tastes of various audiences, both in stage performances and in print.

Lukas Erne's study of *Shakespeare as Literary Dramatist* cites Webster repeatedly to explicate the seventeenth-century shift by which control and 'authority' over playtexts gradually shifted from the dramatic companies that owned them to the authors who had written them. For Erne, Webster is effectively a critic who articulates what Shakespeare should have written about the printing of his plays but didn't. Already in his preface to the 1612 edition of *White Devil* Webster explains that he has taken the '*liberty*' of publishing the play not to '*affect praise*' but to redeem his work from a poor performance at the Red Bull theatre, where it was deprived of a '*full and understanding Auditory*'. He warns readers not to expect the play to conform to the classical rules and corresponding *gravitas* of a '*true Drammaticke Poem*' because of his need to fit it to the scruffy venue of its performance. He also defends himself against the charge of slow composition: 'Alcestides *objecting that* Eurypides *had onely in three daies composed three verses, whereas himselfe had written three hundred*,' Euripides retorts, '*heres the difference, thine shall onely bee read for three daies, whereas mine shall continue three ages*' (Webster, 1.140). The self-comparison to Euripides is based on more than habits of composition, and has been discussed by critics at least since Thomas Campbell and Swinburne (see Moore, 49–51; Swinburne, 297). Like Euripides, the last of the three great classical Greek dramatists, Webster overturns classical convention by focusing in a realistic mode on women and women's issues, creating low-born characters who sometimes exceed their betters in intelligence and acuity, and displaying the weaknesses of 'heroes' whose exalted status is not matched by personal worth (see also Loraux).

In his preface to *The Devil's Law-Case* (printed 1623) Webster struggles with the conundrum of representing dramatic action in a literary text designed for readers: '*A great part of the grace of this (I confesse) lay in Action; yet can no Action ever be gracious,*

*where the decency of the Language, and Ingenious structure of the
Scene, arrive not to make up a perfect Harmony'* (Webster, 2.78).
This statement nicely balances a recognition of the power of
action onstage and the power of a competing *'grace'* of inferred
action, poetry and structure as communicated in a literary text
for readers (Erne, 77). When Erne discusses the distinction
between a 'play', which is staged, and a 'poem', which is read, he
again calls upon Webster, whose preface to *Malfi* (1623) insists
on calling the published text a 'poem' destined to last 'when
the poets themselves were bound up in their winding-sheets'
(p. 122). The title-page specifies that the version offered readers
is 'The perfect and exact copy, with diverse things printed that
the length of the play would not bear in the presentment' or
performance. If we put preface and title-page together, we can
infer that in Webster's view 'plays' are likely to be shorter and
'poems', their printed versions, longer and more elaborate,
designed to be perused by succeeding generations of readers
who can linger over felicitous details in a way that audiences
in the theatre cannot (Erne, 145). At the same time that he was
being chided by contemporary wits for his ignoble participation
in the world of London manufacturing, Webster, like Ben
Jonson, was also in the process of defining a new literary role for
the playwright as publishing critic and man of letters.

We have come a fair distance from the Webster of *Shakespeare
in Love* and his alleged fixation on stage dismemberment
and strange images of death. The historical John Webster's
critical pronouncements do not sound like those of one who is
particularly invested in such matters; indeed they sometimes
express Jonsonian scorn for the lumpish bottom strata of London
viewing audiences, whose tastes ran to mindless violence and
noise. The two plays that have earned Webster his reputation
as connoisseur of the bizarre are also his acknowledged
masterpieces, *White Devil* and *Malfi*, both of which were written
and performed around 1612–15, during the brief, incandescent
period of Webster's most concentrated literary output. His

literary productivity during those years was at least in part a response to political crisis that he also demonstrably experienced as a deep personal loss. The final, climactic tableau of Webster's 1624 Lord Mayor's Show focuses on Prince Henry as a paragon of virtue and accomplishment, a pattern to the livery company of which he was an honorary member and to London at large – and this despite the fact that Prince Henry had at that point been dead for twelve years (Webster, 3.247). Both the Lord Mayor's Show of 1624 and Webster's earlier verse tribute to Prince Henry published in 1613, shortly after Henry's death, use striking images for the dead prince that Webster also applies to another virtuous dead 'prince', the Duchess of Malfi (Neill, 334–8). The verse tribute refers to Henry as a paragon whose 'beames shall breake forth from thy hollow Tombe, / Staine the time past, and light the time to come' (Webster, 3.383); in the play, Antonio describes the Duchess as someone whose 'worth' 'stains the time past, lights the time to come' (*Malfi*, 1.2.127). In creating his Duchess, Webster was also evoking a set of ideals that appeared to many in England to have died with Henry.

To tie Jacobean stage 'melancholy' to broader crises of the time is by now a critical platitude. And yet the images of fragmentation and dismemberment that characterize Webster's *Malfi* are prominent in other plays of the period as well, and link up with contemporary issues like Protestant fear of engulfment by Catholicism and Londoners' perception of a growing estrangement between court and city. Balanced as he was between his two professions of 'playwright and cartwright', Webster may have felt this estrangement more keenly than most. The court was a natural magnet for those involved in the London playhouses, providing them with income, patronage and visibility and at least nominally underwriting all of their activities, since James I on ascending the English throne had made the drama a royal monopoly and attached each of the London dramatic companies to a member of the royal family. The City was another magnet, increasingly estranged from the court. The work of its 'industrious sort of people' (Hill) provided the primary source of Webster's family income and prestige. London was a centre of manufacturing and civic pride, a laboratory for emerging values that challenged royal prerogative powers in the name of citizens' liberties.

WEBSTER AND JACOBEAN NOSTALGIA

In 1603 James I came down from Scotland and claimed the English throne to nearly universal applause and a collective sigh of relief. After the final years of the reign of Elizabeth I, which had seen widespread famine, war with Spain and an increase in the perennial anxieties over the childless Virgin Queen's refusal to name a successor and thereby secure the nation's religious status as Protestant rather than Catholic, Londoners in 1603 were treated to the sight of a married monarch already blessed with an heir and a spare in Princes Henry and Charles, apparently staunchly Protestant, and offering an implicit promise of national renewal and vitality. As is the nature of sudden bursts of political euphoria, the enthusiasm quickly began to fade, particularly among the more militant Protestants. James made peace with Spain in 1604 and showed no interest in continuing the Continental wars in support of beleaguered Protestantism that Elizabeth, who had defeated the Spanish Armada in 1588, had continued to tolerate during the 1590s by offering them some financial support. James delivered a mixed message on Protestantism, appearing to favour broader tolerance of Catholicism, at least until the uncovering of the Catholic Gunpowder Plot conspiracy in 1605 forced him to retrench. To critics, he appeared to continue to show undue preference to pro-Catholic factions at court. He developed a reputation for bounty – great generosity towards his favourites and seemingly limitless spending at court – that gradually soured his relationship with London and Parliament, who were expected to support his financial largesse. His relatively open erotic attachment to male favourites and his tolerance for drunkenness and debauchery at court also helped to alienate the more strait-laced among his subjects.

While for many in England James I represented a break with the Elizabethan past, his heir apparent Prince Henry offered elements of continuity with the goals of Elizabethan Protestantism. Henry was particularly popular with strongly anti-Catholic elements at court and in the City; he was a militant Protestant, at least by comparison with his father; a good sportsman whose projection of an aura of virile masculinity suggested a contrast with his father's appearance of effeminacy, a 'Renaissance man' whose many talents and interests appeared poised upon his succession to reunify the nation. But in 1612 Henry died – so suddenly and unexpectedly that many suspected poison.

Much has been written about the Jacobean cult of Elizabeth that, particularly after the death of Prince Henry, began to flourish among those who were becoming alienated from the Stuart regime. With the loss of the prince, the one remaining member of the royal family who appeared to carry a continuing dedication to the goals of the militant Protestants was Henry's sister Elizabeth, who married the staunchly Protestant Frederick V, Elector Palatine, shortly after Prince Henry's death. The fact that she was named after Elizabeth I perhaps encouraged a conflation of the two figures in the public mind. At any rate, Princess Elizabeth was celebrated as Elizabeth I *rediviva* and many of the symbols associated with the reign of the dead queen were applied to her: poets lauded her as Astraea, goddess of justice, a second phoenix, and so on. At the same time, Elizabeth I's shortcomings as a monarch were retrospectively forgotten or at least placed in altered perspective, and militant Protestants and others disaffected with Stuart rule came increasingly to focus on her reign as a lost golden time of military triumph and goodwill between monarch and people.

An increased interest in female protagonists in drama of the Jacobean era can be correlated with nostalgia for the reign of Elizabeth I and values she had posthumously come to represent

(Watkins; Shepherd; Hageman and Conway). The most obvious case is writer Thomas Heywood, who produced a number of literary works in various genres that took their inspiration from the portrayal of Elizabeth I as Protestant martyr in John Foxe's *Book of Martyrs* (1563) and emphasized the dead queen's role as a unifying symbol for her subjects and as a bulwark against Catholicism. The two plays of Heywood's popular sequence *If You Know Not Me, You Know Nobody* (1604–5) commemorated Elizabeth by replaying high points of her reign and tying her to a fantasy of London liberty and autonomy that the historical Elizabeth would, no doubt, have repudiated. Thomas Dekker's *Whore of Babylon* (1607) brings Elizabeth onstage in another guise as the heroically virtuous 'Titania the Faerie Queene', who battles victoriously against the '*inveterate malice, Treasons, Machinations, Underminings, and continual blody stratagems, of that Purple whore of* Roome', the eponymous Whore of Babylon (Dekker, 2.497). Critics have linked even the skull of Gloriana in Middleton's *Revenger's Tragedy* (1606) with a combination of Jacobean nostalgia for a lost world of virtue associated with the Virgin Queen, for whom 'Gloriana' had been a frequent epithet late in her reign, and rage over the sad truth that such a glorious figure had, in the end, died and decayed (Mullaney; Allman; Hyland).

Webster was working closely with Middleton, Heywood and Dekker on other projects when they produced these plays. Of course artistic proximity is no guarantee of political commonality. But if we look at Webster's dramatic career over time, we see his plays repeatedly advocating citizen as opposed to courtly values, portraying Catholic rituals and institutions as inherently corrupt, and valorizing individual probity as opposed to inherited rank as a guarantor of personal worth. Simon Shepherd has identified *Malfi* as the last and most eloquent in a series of plays written and staged around 1610–13 centring on virtuous, heroic women who challenge corrupt men that attempt to assert political and sexual dominance over them: George Chapman's *The Revenge of Bussy d'Ambois* (1610–11), Middleton's *The Lady's Tragedy* (1611), Dekker's *Match Me in London* (1611–12), Cyril Tourneur's *The Atheist's Tragedy* (1611) and finally *The Duchess of Malfi* (1613–14). All of these works at least implicitly replay elements of Jacobean nostalgia for Elizabeth by associating female autonomy with virtue, and domination by courtly males with corruption and oppression. Of course, as Andrew Gurr has noted, some of the new stage emphasis on women can probably be attributed to a shift in audience sympathies as more women attended plays (Gurr, *Playgoing*, 71–2). But men in Jacobean audiences were also drawn by the new theatrical emphasis on women's issues; arguably, they too could potentially identify with political subjects who were abased and implicitly feminized as a result of tyranny. The 1610–13 plays that Shepherd has noted as leading up to *Malfi* carry an element of muted political critique in which female autonomy calls up associations with the lost court of Elizabeth I, and male sexual and political dominance resonates with the corruption and absolutist ideology of the court of James I.

Of course, Webster's Duchess of Malfi, as a wife and mother of several children, departs strikingly from official images of the sterile Virgin Queen. In Webster's play we are in the realm of the cultural imaginary: the Duchess's fecund, happy life as a wife and mother enacts a fantasy of Tudor dynastic succession that Elizabeth had obstinately refused to fulfil. There had, however, been persistent rumours of Elizabeth's sexual dalliances, of her secret affairs or marriages, of children born surreptitiously while she went on progress; there were also aspirants to the throne who claimed to be the queen's natural children (Levin). The clandestine marriage of Webster's Duchess recalls these rumours and redeems a female ruler from the most scurrilous of them in that her children are born in wedlock; at the end of the play, the eldest son of the Duchess and Antonio is poised to succeed her. The Duchess also sometimes echoes the language of Elizabeth I. Like the monarch, she frequently refers to herself as 'prince' rather than the more gender-specific 'princess'; the Duchess also refers to witchcraft practices against herself that parallel forms of witchcraft actually used against Elizabeth (4.1.61–4 and n.; Marcus, *Puzzling*, 53–105); and Webster's contemporaries may also have sensed echoes of Elizabeth's excommunication by the Pope in the scene of the Duchess's banishment (3.4). Some of the pathos of *Malfi* comes from the fact that it offers a vision, albeit fleeting, of a radiant female ruler who has used her sexuality productively – kept her virtue and authority intact and still managed to produce heirs, as Elizabeth I never did. Early in the play, Antonio offers an idealized image of what a court could be: 'a common fountain, whence should flow / Pure silver drops in general' to nurture and sustain both courtiers and commonwealth. The Duchess's brothers exemplify Antonio's contrasting vision of a corrupt court, polluting the 'common fountain' and spreading 'death and diseases' through their 'cursed' example (1.1.11–15). Only the Duchess and those closest to her somehow manage to escape the worst of the general contamination.

Webster's later writings continue in the same vein of guarded anti-court sentiment. A decade after its initial composition, the 1623 First Quarto edition of *Malfi* reiterates a critique of traditional aristocratic hierarchy across several layers of its printed text (see Quarto Paratext, pp. 114–26). In Webster's dedicatory letter to '*George Harding, Baron Berkeley, . . . Knight of the Order of the Bath to the Illustrious Prince Charles*', the playwright discounts these courtly connections, 'The ancientest nobility being but a relic of time past and the truest honour indeed being for a man to confer honour on himself, which your learning strives to propagate and shall make you arrive at the dignity of a great example.' Webster's dedicatory letter is echoed within the play through the Duchess's marriage to Antonio, a man of low birth, and her repeated statements that it is not rank but virtue that counts. Thomas Middleton's commendatory poem printed in the 1623 edition strikes a similar note, claiming that individual merit rather than royal and aristocratic connections is the best guarantor of artistic worth:

> ... for every worthy man
> Is his own marble; and his merit can
> Cut him to any figure and express
> More art than death's cathedral palaces,
> Where royal ashes keep their court.

(p. 123)

Anyone reading Webster's play a year after its publication in 1623 would receive an even stronger political message from the Middleton endorsement. Middleton's *A Game at Chess* (1624) satirized James I and Prince Charles's enormously unpopular machinations for a marriage between Charles and the Spanish Infanta. William Rowley, who also contributed a commendatory poem to the 1623 *Malfi*, probably played the fat Archbishop of Spalato in the same production of *A Game at Chess* (Middleton, 2.293). The play was a phenomenal box-office success, but was shut down as seditious after a nine days' run and Middleton himself was forced to go into hiding. He never wrote another play. After the debacle of *A Game at Chess*, Webster went on to further collaborations with Heywood, Dekker, Rowley and other dramatists whose work had long been associated with critique of the Jacobean court.

All of which is not to suggest that *Malfi* can be reduced to the status of an anti-Catholic or anti-Jacobean tract. Were the play no more than that it would scarcely have survived to fascinate subsequent readers and critics across a very wide spectrum of political and social prejudices from the seventeenth century to the present. But to place the play within its first historical milieu, however provisionally and speculatively, is to become attuned to resonances that can help us understand why it was so important to its contemporaries. *Malfi* places relatively good people (the Duchess, her husband Antonio, his friend Delio) in a nightmarish stew of Italian political and ecclesiastical corruption characterized by a peculiar devotion to bizarre displays of madness, fragmentation and truncation. Although the Duchess and Antonio do not manage to survive to the end of the play, Webster offers the Duchess as an exemplar of heroic constancy in a twisted world that incarnates Protestant England's worst fears about Catholicism.

THE PLAY AND THE HISTORICAL SOURCES

Thanks to the research of Barbara Banks Amendola, we now know a great deal about the historical Duchess of Malfi and her immediate family. She was born into the glorious world of the Italian Renaissance, which was also the cut-throat world of Niccolò dei Machiavelli. The historical duchess was Giovanna d'Aragona, Duchess of Amalfi from 1493 until her disappearance some time after 1511. She was of royal blood, a daughter of the Spanish House of Aragon, which ruled the Kingdom of Naples more or less continuously between 1442 and 1501. The Duchess's grandfather was Ferrante I of Naples, who attained that title in 1458 and hung on to it tenaciously for thirty-six years. Her father, Enrico d'Aragona, was the eldest son of Ferrante I, but illegitimate. He was well regarded by his father, despite his irregular birth, and given the title of Marquess of Gerace. The Duchess's mother was Polissena Centelles, the daughter of Baron Antonio Centelles, a renegade magnate in a perennial state of rebellion against the House of Aragon. The marriage of the Duchess's parents was part of a peace treaty during which the rival families united against the threat posed by French invaders. Shortly after the wedding, however, Antonio Centelles was arrested and imprisoned by Ferrante I and his son Enrico, the new bridegroom, who would go on to become the Duchess's father. Baron Centelles was never heard from again. The Duchess's father ultimately reaped an appropriate reward for his Machiavellian tactics against his father-in-law. He was poisoned, probably by his own half-brother, a few weeks before the Duchess's birth. She was the elder of fraternal twins born in 1478; her elder brother Luigi, who inherited his father's title but went on to become a Cardinal and aspirant to the papacy, had been born four years earlier.

The Duchess herself probably received a good education, since humanist learning was highly valued by the House of Aragon. At the age of twelve she was married to Alfonso Piccolomini, son of the Duke of Amalfi, who succeeded his father as duke in 1493. At the age of fourteen, therefore, Giovanna became Duchess of Amalfi. She had two children with Piccolomini, a girl who died at the age of eight in 1498 and a boy born the same year who eventually succeeded his father as Duke of Amalfi. Meanwhile, the Kingdom of Naples had been plunged into turmoil by the French invasion of 1495; the Duchess's husband was wounded in battle and died three years later, probably as a result of lingering ill health brought about by his war wounds, and several months before the birth of his son and heir. Upon the birth of her son, the Duchess of Malfi was named regent, and held the Duchy of Amalfi until her disappearance around 1511.

Giovanna Duchess of Malfi was young and beautiful; a portrait attributed to the workshop of Raphael and titled *Giovanna d'Aragona* probably represents her (Fig. 1; Amendola, 194–206). So far as we know, she avoided the sexual profligacy that characterized the behaviour of some of her close relatives and led an exemplary life, even as a widow – until she became front-page news in Italy and indeed around Europe as a result of the revelation of her scandalous secret marriage. A Neapolitan chronicler reported:

> On Sunday November 17th 1510, it was common talk throughout the city of Naples, that the illustrious Signora Giovanna d'Aragona, daughter of the late illustrious Don Enrico d'Aragona, and sister of the most Reverend Monsignor Cardinal of Aragon, having let it be known that she wished to make a pilgrimage to Santa Maria of Loreto, had gone thither with a retinue of many carriages and thence departed

1   Portrait of Giovanna d'Aragona (oil on canvas), attributed to the workshop
    of Raphael

with Antonio da Bologna, son of Messer Antonino
da Bologna, and gone with the aforesaid, saying that
he was her husband, . . . leaving behind her one male
child of ten, who was Duke of Amalfi.[1]

1   Cited and trans. from Notar Giacomo della Morte, *Cronica di Napoli*, in Amendola,
    149.

This initial account apparently came before there was public knowledge of the Duchess's children with Antonio da Bologna. We do not know the exact date of the Duchess's secret marriage – perhaps late 1505 or 1506. By the time she made it public in 1510, she and her husband had had two children whom they had miraculously managed to keep secret and she was pregnant with a third, who was probably born in 1511. After their public announcement the couple fled to Siena, trying to evade capture by agents of the Duchess's family. She and her two younger children were intercepted on their way from Siena to Venice and imprisoned in Amalfi; they were never heard from again. Her husband escaped to Milan, where he was murdered by a Daniele da Bozzolo in 1513, very likely at the behest of Cardinal Luigi d'Aragona, the Duchess's elder brother.

The story of the Duchess of Malfi captured the imaginations of many writers and readers even generations after her death and exists in a number of versions, beginning with the narrative of a Dominican friar, Matteo Bandello. Bandello appears to have known Antonio personally in Milan in the few years before his murder; Bandello wrote a novella in 1514 about the love story of Giovanna and Antonio in which Bandello himself figures as Antonio's friend Delio. This was a fictionalized account, not a historical narrative, and Bandello's rendering of Antonio, whom he actually knew, squares better with what we know from archival sources than his account of the Duchess and earlier portions of her story. Bandello is quite sympathetic to the lovers, lamenting the 'great cruelty' of the sexual double standard by which

> we men always want to satisfy every whim that comes to our mind, and we do not want poor women to satisfy theirs . . . It seems to me a great stupidity that men consider that their honour and that of their house be vested in the appetite of a woman. If a man makes a mistake, however great, his relations do not lose their noble status . . . There was, for example, that

19

count (I will refrain from giving his name) who took a baker's daughter for his wife, and why? Because she had a great deal of property, and no one reprimanded him. Another count, noble and rich, took for his wife the daughter of a mule driver without even a dowry, for no more reason than it pleased him to do so, and now she has the place and rank of a countess and he is still a count as before.

(Bandello, trans. in Amendola, 111)

The earliest retellings of the tale of the Duchess of Malfi were those of the so-called 'Corona manuscripts' (Amendola), which circulated widely in different versions and largely repeated Bandello, but with some additions. In later life, Bandello lived in France in close proximity to the court of Queen Margaret of Navarre. One of her protégés, François de Belleforest, made a loose translation of Bandello's *Novelle* into French. The 'Unfortunate marriage of Seigneur Antonio Bologna with the Duchess of Malfi, and the piteous death of both' appeared as the first story in the second volume of his *Histoires tragiques* (Paris, 1565). Belleforest added long speeches and passages of moralization and was much more critical of the Duchess than Bandello had been. John Webster's main source of the story was likely William Painter's rendition of Belleforest into English in *The Palace of Pleasure* (see Appendix 1). The Spanish dramatist Lope de Vega also created a play based on the Duchess's story, *El mayordomo de la duquesa de Amalfi*, at about the same time as Webster's, though it is unlikely that the two dramatists knew each other's work (Garcia).

Painter's version of the story follows Belleforest in blaming the Duchess for her fate. Painter puts her in the same category as the Babylonian Queen Semiramis, who, he claims, is remembered not for her princely exploits but for her shameful record of 'vice', sexual licentiousness and cruelty. Similarly, the Duchess is a modern exemplar of the destructiveness of unbridled lust:

> Thus I say, bicause a woman being as it were the Image of sweetenesse, curtesie & shamefastnesse, so soone as she steppeth out of the right tracte, and leaveth the smel of hir duetie and modestie, bisides the denigration of hir honor, thrusteth hir self into infinite troubles and causeth the ruine of such which should be honored and praised, if womens allurement solicited them not to follie.

> (Appendix 1, p. 347)

Painter's account of the Duchess and Antonio casts her as the courtly seductress and him as the largely innocent victim who, after serving Frederick of Aragon during his exile in France, had retired to his house 'to live at rest and to avoyd trouble, forgetting the delicates of Courtes and houses of great men, to be the only husband of his owne revenue' until he was fatefully recruited as head of the Duchess's household (p. 348). Her folly and shameful lust drove her to seduce him, and both were destroyed by their passion. 'Who wold think that a great Ladie wold have abandoned hir estate, hir goods and childe, would have misprised hir honor and reputation, to folow like a vagabond, a pore and simple Gentleman . . . like a female Wolfe or Lionesse . . . and forget the Noble bloud of Aragon'? (p. 372)

Mapping Painter's rather simplistic value system on to Webster's play, some critics have viewed Webster's Duchess as a cautionary example of the destructive power of lust, particularly in a high-born woman who can bring down the lives of others along with her own. But Webster's portrayal of the Duchess is much closer to Bandello's version: by wishing to marry, she is not demonstrating some monstrous illicit passion, 'like a female Wolfe or Lionesse', to quote Painter, but instead containing her sexuality in a productive way within marriage. Webster relocates the monstrous lust excoriated in Painter to the Duchess's brothers instead: the Cardinal is a sexual connoisseur, flaunting his disregard for his vows of ecclesiastical celibacy; Ferdinand burns with incestuous lust for his sister and actually becomes a 'Wolfe' through his lycanthropy by the end of the play. The evidence we have of the play's impact in early performances suggests that audience sympathy was solidly with the Duchess. The play was a success onstage, revived probably twice before it saw print in 1623 and several times thereafter (see pp. 91–6). Middleton's commendatory verse calls the play a '*masterpiece of tragedy*' and asks rhetorically, 'who e'er saw this Duchess live and die / That could get off under a bleeding eye?' (p. 123): that is, who could see the Duchess onstage without weeping at her fate? A manuscript poem by William Heminges, son of John Heminges, a shareholder in the King's Men, the company that had staged Webster's play, wittily refers to continuing sympathy for the Duchess around 1632, when the play had recently been revived. Heminges's poem is a mock elegy mourning the 'death' of poet Thomas Randolph's little finger, which had been severed during a brawl. Heminges quips that the company of London poets wishing to give the finger proper burial applied to Webster's brother Thomas for coaches, only to find that all had been conscripted for the funeral of the Duchess of Malfi:

> but websters brother would nott lend a Coach:
> hee swore thay all weare hired to Convey
> the Malfy dutches sadly on her way
>
> (Smith, 12)

Webster's version of the Duchess's story makes use of Painter and also revises him; Webster may well have had access to Bandello, Belleforest or other versions of the story that were available in print (see Boklund; Forker; Amendola). But, like all playwrights of the period, he freely altered his source texts when it suited his dramatic purposes. Yet, mysteriously, in several instances he seems to have had access to historical information not in the published materials. Webster's play includes the detail that the Duchess and Antonio's eldest son survived them – a fact mentioned in none of the printed sources but only in some of the Corona manuscripts. Similarly, Webster posits that the Duchess and the younger of her two brothers were twins – something that is likely to have been true, but is mentioned in none of the sources. Finally, Webster gives the Cardinal, the Duchess's older brother, a mistress named Julia. Cardinal Luigi d'Aragona did in fact have a mistress named Giulia – yet another mysterious correspondence, since her name is not given in any of the major retellings of the story (Amendola, 176, xxii, 114). Perhaps Webster had access to oral reports by travellers returning from Italy or written sources of information that have not yet been uncovered. Or perhaps he was so preternaturally attuned to the Duchess's story that he 'invented' circumstances that were, unbeknownst to him, supported by the historical record.

THE ARAGONIAN BROTHERS

Webster also altered numerous elements of the Duchess's story, usually to intensify the horror that surrounds her. His portrait of her elder brother the Cardinal deviates from the sources by having Luigi d'Aragona murder his mistress as well as his sister: the episode in which he disposes of Julia by means of the poisoned Bible in 5.2 appears to be Webster's own concoction. Similarly, Webster has the Cardinal in 3.4 formally divest himself of ecclesiastical authority through an elaborate religious ritual so that he can take up arms alongside the Pope. The historical Cardinal had no need to compartmentalize his life in that way. He had started out as a secular aristocrat, but gave up his wife and title as Marquess of Gerace for a bishopric and then a cardinal's hat in the hopes of ascending to the papacy and consolidating the House of Aragon's power over the Papal States. He was, after his ordination, a man of the church but also a man of action, putting on armour over his cardinal's robes to sally into battle. He was also a bon vivant – one of the secular young cardinals of the period who doffed their ecclesiastical garb when it suited them and devoted themselves to high living, women and song.

Castiglione's *Courtier* shows the illustrious Luigi d'Aragona playing practical jokes at carnival time along with a merry band of tricksters (Castiglione, book 2, 87).

Webster's character is instead a brooding figure whose corruption is darkly corrosive rather than light-hearted, a 'melancholy churchman' whose apparently youthful face is 'nothing but the engendering of toads' (1.2.75–6). Webster portrays the Cardinal's use of ecclesiastical objects and rituals as vehicles for his own vice: he orchestrates the elaborate rite at the Shrine of Loreto to justify his abandonment of his cardinal's hat and office; he employs a Bible or some other sacred text to poison his unwanted mistress. Horatio Busino, a Catholic priest who served as chaplain to the Venetian ambassador in London in 1617–18, witnessed a performance of *Malfi*, probably in early 1618. The English, he complained, 'deride our religion as detestable and superstitious, and never represent any theatrical piece . . . without larding it with the vices and iniquity of some Catholic churchman, which move them to laughter and much mockery.' At the performance of *Malfi* they

> represented the pomp of a Cardinal in his identi-
> cal robes of state, very handsome and costly, and
> accompanied by his attendants, with an altar raised
> on the stage, where he pretended to perform service,
> ordering a procession. He then re-appeared familiarly
> with a concubine in public. He played the part of
> administering poison to his sister [Busino's error for
> 'mistress'; his diary had earlier complained that it was
> difficult for him accurately to describe distant things
> because of his short-sightedness (Busino, 138)] upon
> a point of honour, and moreover, of going into battle,
> having first gravely deposited his Cardinal's robes on
> the altar through the agency of his chaplains. Last of
> all, he had himself girded with a sword and put on his
> scarf with the best imaginable grace. All this they do

in derision of ecclesiastical pomp which in this kingdom is scorned and hated mortally.

(Busino, 145–6)

As Gibbons has suggested (3.4.0.1–2n.), the 'altar' may have
(daringly) displayed a statue reproducing the Black Virgin of
Loreto and Child – in which case the image would resonate with
the wax bodies of 4.1 and doubtless increase the scene's anti-
Catholic frisson.

Webster's portrayal of the Duchess's twin brother Ferdinand
also departs from the historical record in order to intensify
the threat he represents. Ferdinand is Webster's fiction. The
Duchess's twin brother was named Carlo, and was not directly
implicated in her death along with his elder brother, Cardinal
Luigi; the historical Carlo was married rather than single and
also not, so far as we know, incestuously inclined, nor given
to madness and lycanthropy (Amendola, 158). The name
'Ferdinand' instead evokes another member of the House of
Aragon, Ferdinand d'Aragona of Spain; he and his queen
were the Ferdinand and Isabella who sponsored Christopher
Columbus's voyages to the New World in 1492, two years after
the Duchess of Malfi had married her first husband. But the
Spanish Ferdinand was better known for his shrewdness and
unscrupulousness as a political operator. Machiavelli praises him
for his great and extraordinary successes:

> Always in the name of religion, he resorted to a pious
> cruelty, despoiling the Marranos and driving them
> from his kingdom. There could be nothing more piti-
> ful or unusual than this. Under the same cloak of piety
> he attacked Africa; he undertook his Italian campaign;
> and lastly he has made war on France. Thus, he has
> always planned and executed great things which have
> filled his subjects with wonder and admiration.

(Machiavelli, *Prince*, ch. 21)

This was, in other words, the Ferdinand who expelled the Jews and Muslims from Spain and set in motion an elaborate system of rules by which his countrymen eventually had to demonstrate *limpieza de sangre* – purity of blood from Moorish or Jewish admixtures – in order to assume any type of government post (Sweet). The historical Ferdinand's emphasis on the purification of Spanish blood resonates strongly with Webster's Aragonese brothers and their obsession with the purity (and corruptibility) of their own and their sister's blood:

> CARDINAL   Shall our blood,
>   The royal blood of Aragon and Castile,
>   Be thus attainted?
> FERDINAND   Apply desperate physic.
>   We must not now use balsamum, but fire –
>   The smarting cupping-glass, for that's the mean
>   To purge infected blood, such blood as hers.
>   (2.5.21–6)

For even slightly paranoid Protestants among Webster's contemporaries, the stage evocation of a territorial magnate descended from the House of Aragon may also have resonated with the reign of the Catholic 'Bloody Mary' Tudor, whose mother was Catherine of Aragon and who had claimed sovereignty over Naples by virtue of her marriage to Philip of Spain, also a descendant of the House of Aragon.

Unlike the Cardinal in the play, however, Webster's Ferdinand appears to have no sexual outlet beyond incestuous yearning for his sister. His many expressions of narcissistic involvement in his sister's body have been interpreted differently over time. During the heyday of Freudian criticism, Ferdinand was commonly understood as suffering a displaced Oedipal attachment to her (Lucas; Murray, 161–5). Other critics have explained his seemingly incestuous desires as displaced homoerotic attachment to the 'strong-thighed bargeman' and other male lovers he fantasizes his sister in bed with (2.5.42–5; see Calbi, 1–31) or as an expression of dynastic exclusivity: the only blood worthy of the 'royal blood of Aragon' is his own, as represented in his sister (Whigham). This last interpretation resonates with scandalous rumours out of Italy: the infamous Lucrezia Borgia, a relative by marriage of the historical Duchess of Malfi, was reputed to have slept with her brother Cesare in an attempt to secure the papal succession for the Borgias (Amendola, 112–13). Webster's play repeatedly associates Ferdinand with an arbitrary political tyranny that turns out to be inseparable from the tangled web of his illicit sexual desires. He is proud and autocratic: his courtiers may laugh only when he does (1.2.42–4), but his laughter is dangerous – 'Like a deadly cannon / That lightens ere it smokes' (3.3.53–4). He deploys fragmentary objects in a way that suggests the Catholic use of sacred relics as objects for display – the severed hand, the mutilated waxwork bodies revealed through the opening of a curtain (4.1.54 SD), even the Duchess's body, which, she complains, he wants to keep 'cased up like a holy relic' (3.2.137). As the play progresses, Ferdinand's madness is increasingly associated with rituals of the Italian (and English) courts. Indeed, Antonio interprets the spectacle of ambitious suppliants at court as nothing more than an unusually well-furnished madhouse that is 'lunatic beyond all cure' (1.2.331–5). As if to underscore Antonio's point, in early performances of the play, when Ferdinand sends actual madmen to torment the imprisoned Duchess (4.2), the madmen onstage doubled the courtiers who had sycophantically surrounded Ferdinand in acts 1 and 2.

As has frequently been noted, the structure of 4.2 up to the Duchess's death constitutes a mordant parody of the Jacobean court masque. Court masques under James I were elaborate and hugely expensive holiday extravaganzas consisting of dances, songs and allegorical tableaux. Typically they comprised an initial 'antimasque' allowing temporary licence to undesirable negative elements – vices to be dispelled from the kingdom or from the royal self-representation – followed by a main masque in which the negative elements are banished and the king is celebrated in a series of apotheoses that successively reveal his divine virtues and power. The 'masque' engineered by Ferdinand in *Malfi* features the dancing madmen as 'antimasque', then parodies the structure of the 'main masque' at the Stuart court by displaying the Duchess's virtues of fortitude and constancy magnificently in the progressive stages of her spiritual ordeal at the hands of a masked Bosola, who takes on a sequence of different roles as her tormentor and spiritual counsellor (Ekeblad; Coddon, 40–2). But these displays in *Malfi* operate in counter-motion to the ascending pattern of the Jacobean main masque in that the central figure is not apotheosized but extinguished. Ferdinand's 'Masque of the Duchess' ends in her execution.

As Ferdinand gradually descends into lycanthropy after his sister's death, he takes on subhuman attributes that Reformation Protestant culture associated with Catholic spiritual predation. Twentieth-century researchers have speculated that legends about predatory wolf-people may have stemmed from frightening encounters with rabid wolves or with human victims of porphyria, a disease that is associated with photosensitivity and night wandering, skin discoloration from jaundice, and self-mutilation (see Illis; and Fig. 2, which carries little scientific authority but illustrates the type of disfigurement associated with the disease). Wolves had been eradicated in England by the sixteenth century, but they were still active in some heavily wooded areas of Europe, and where there were wolves there were also stories about wolf-men – humans who as a result of witchcraft or direct demonic intervention took on the bodies of wolves and began to murder and dismember their fellow humans.

Stories of lycanthropy were popular in England as well: interestingly, one popular account of a German lycanthrope named 'Stubbe Peter' (Peter Stubbe in the original German) asserts that Stubbe committed incest with his sister while in the shape of a wolf (see Appendix 2). Webster makes Ferdinand's lycanthropy, similarly, a reification of his lust for his sister, but

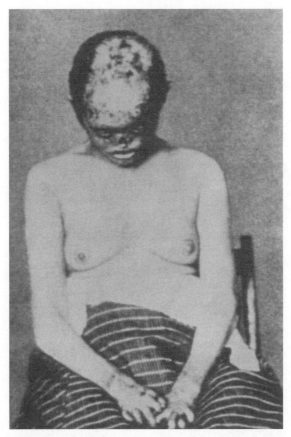

2 Twentieth-century photograph of a lycanthrope, from W. Hausmann (1923),
reprinted in Charlotte F. Otten (ed.), *A Lycanthropy Reader: Werewolves in
Western Culture* (Syracuse, NY, 1986), 198

it also resonates with images of spiritual predation, particularly
in Protestant demonizations of Catholicism. Fig. 3 shows Lucas
Cranach the Elder's woodcut (1510–15) of a wild man, probably
a werewolf though still in human form, carrying off a human
child and surrounded with the severed limbs of his previous
victims. A book of emblems from 1595 (Fig. 4) shows a wolf
in a similar pose devouring a lamb and explains that the image

3   Lucas Cranach the Elder, *Cannibal or Werewolf*, woodcut, Saxony (1510–15),
     Metropolitan Museum of Art

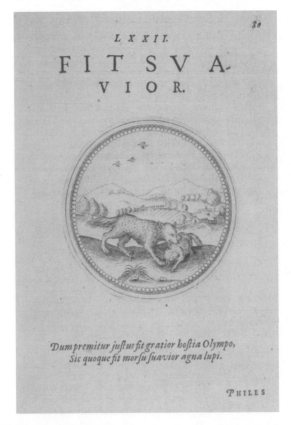

4   Wolf destroying the Christian sheep, from Joachim Camerarius, *Symbolorum et emblematum ex animalibus* (1595)

symbolizes the devil's destruction of the Christian sheep. In Protestant polemic, echoing Christ's teachings in the Sermon on the Mount about wolves in sheep's clothing (Matthew, 7.15), the wolf is specifically associated with Catholicism: cf. the 'grim Wolf with privy paw' who devours the helpless sheep in John Milton's *Lycidas* (lines 125–9) or, for a text closer in time to Webster, Thomas Adams's sermon on 'Lycanthropy, or the wolf worrying the lambs' (*c.* 1615). Adams, like Milton, associates the lycanthrope not only with Catholic prelacy but also with the emerging Laudian wing of the English Church – that is, the followers of William Laud (1573–1645). Laud promoted a highly ritualized form of Anglican worship that would be called 'high church'; he was associated with a number of repressive measures against more moderate Anglicans and Puritans; and he was eventually removed from his position as Archbishop of Canterbury, tried and executed (see pp. 85–6).

In Protestant invective, the Pope himself is not infrequently figured as a wolf or other terrifying beast-man, as in Machiavelli's description of Pope Sixtus IV, ally of the Aragonese against the Florentines, as 'a wolf rather than a shepherd' (Machiavelli, *History*, 371); such ideas lie behind Melchior Lorsch's engraving from around 1545 with a text by Martin Luther (Fig. 5). Webster's unforgettable portrayal of Ferdinand's lycanthropy is his own wildly original contribution to the Duchess's story. Within the play, Ferdinand's lycanthropy is associated primarily with melancholy, the most medically credible diagnosis available at the time. But, like many other elements of the play, for contemporaries it may well have resonated with the wolf in anti-Catholic and anti-Laudian tracts.

CLANDESTINE MARRIAGE

Webster's portrayal of Antonio is fairly close to the sources in that the playwright makes him attractive, accomplished and well spoken. But Webster departs from the sources in lowering Antonio's status, so that the social distance between him and the Duchess is accentuated. The historical Antonio was a gentleman from a distinguished family that had gradually decayed. His grandfather had been the illustrious humanist man of letters Antonio Beccadelli, 'Il Panormita', who had been raised to noble status in the court of Naples as secretary and adviser to King Alfonso V d'Aragona. In Naples he belonged to the prestigious governing body, the Seggio del Nido, all of whose

5   Melchior Lorsch, *Der Papst als Wilder Mann* ('The Pope as a Wild Man'),
    engraving by Melchior Lorch, with text by Martin Luther, Germany
    (after 1545)

members were aristocrats. Il Panormita's son married a wealthy
noblewoman who died young but left one son, the Antonio who
eventually married the Duchess of Malfi. Antonio had a palazzo
in Naples, part of which is still visible in the old section near the
House of Aragon's Castelcapuano, where the Duchess lived as
a child. Antonio inherited his grandfather's place in the Seggio

del Nido, which was still considered exclusively aristocratic; another member was Alfonso Piccolomini, the Duchess's first husband (Amendola, 97–9). The historical Antonio was not, therefore, hopelessly below the Duchess in rank, although he was her social inferior. Painter describes Antonio consistently as a 'gentleman', a 'gentle person, a good Courtier, wel trained up, and wise for government of himself in the Court and in the service of Princes' (see p. 348). When in Painter the Duchess of Malfi asks Antonio to serve as the master of her household, she apologizes to him that the office is 'unworthy for your calling' and appeals to him on the basis of his loyalty to the House of Aragon, since he had previously served King Frederick of Naples (pp. 348–9).

In Webster's play, by contrast, much is made of Antonio's low birth: Ferdinand calls him a 'slave that only smelled of ink and counters / And ne'er in's life looked like a gentleman, / But in the audit time' (3.3.70–2) – the implication being that Antonio spruces himself up on formal occasions but is otherwise to be defined as one of the 'industrious sort of people' demeaned by daily contact with money and household accounts. Even the two pilgrims in 3.4, who seem sympathetic to Antonio, are shocked to find that 'So great a lady would have matched herself / Unto so mean a person' (3.4.24–5). By lowering Antonio's social status, Webster accentuates the Duchess's contempt for rank as a trustworthy indicator of worth. She chooses him because she has fallen in love with him, but that love is grounded in her perception of his accomplishments and virtues as a 'complete man' (1.2.346). As the play progresses, it becomes evident that Antonio lacks some of the fearless readiness for personal combat that Ferdinand and even Bosola display later on: Antonio is mysteriously out of reach when the Duchess is threatened by her brother Ferdinand in 3.2, and he parts with the vulnerable Duchess with what has seemed to many readers to be unseemly alacrity in 3.5. But his failures of aristocratic *virtu* are to some extent redeemed by his tender uxoriousness and his talent for domesticity. By selecting as her husband a man with no independent claim to class status, the Duchess is able to satisfy her desire for a sexual partner and family without compromising her position as ruler of Amalfi; she is also able to evade, at least for a time, her brothers' claustrophobic aristocratic possessiveness, which causes them to view her as family property to be disposed in marriage as they please.

Was the Duchess's clandestine marriage legally valid? In Italy, before the Council of Trent, which was first convened in 1545 to enact measures defending the Catholic Church against the inroads of Protestantism and which tightened the rules governing marriage as part of this effort, customs varied from region to region. In Florence, as apparently in Amalfi, marriage was almost entirely domestic and non-ecclesiastical. A marriage was considered complete if the couple had exchanged vows and rings and then consummated the marriage. The Duchess and Antonio take these two steps in 1.2, moving from an exchange of vows directly to the marriage bed. However, even in pre-Tridentine Florence, where marriage practices were less ecclesiastical than in some other parts of Italy, a key element of valid marriage was that it be publicly acknowledged (Klapisch-Zuber, 178–212). The Duchess's marriage fails on that count, because Cariola is its sole witness and it is not made public until years later, after the births of three children. According to some of Webster's sources, the Duchess and Antonio eventually had their union blessed by a priest, and the Duchess in Webster's play may (or may not) refer to such an event when she protests to Ferdinand that in calling her children bastards he blasphemously violates 'a sacrament o'th' church' (4.1.38).

In early seventeenth-century England, marriage was similarly difficult to define: one's attitude towards clandestine marriage would depend on one's attitude towards established ecclesiastical authority. Before 1604, there was no question that clandestine marriage was valid, even under canon law, so long as the two partners exchanged vows in the present – not 'I will marry you in the future' but 'I marry you now' *per verba de presenti*. So in England before 1604 the Duchess would have been absolutely correct when she states, echoing the actual legal formula defining marriage, 'I have heard lawyers say a contract in a chamber / *Per verba presenti* is absolute marriage' (1.2.385–6). But after 1604 matters became more confused. In that year James I, in consultation with key bishops, put in force newly clarified canons requiring that marriage be preceded by the announcement of banns on three consecutive Sundays or the procurement of a valid licence from a bishop, and that it be performed by a duly licensed cleric in the parish church of one of the partners. But the new rules were resisted in many quarters. Like the Council of Trent in Catholic Europe, the 1604 canons in England sought to clarify the definition of marriage by taking it out of private hands and requiring it to be validated by ecclesiastical ceremony. By the time Webster wrote *Malfi*, English opinion had bifurcated on the topic, with supporters of James I and the bishops allied against those who considered the new canons on marriage an inroad upon their traditional privilege of marrying outside the direct control of ecclesiastical authorities. Opposition to the new canon law was particularly prevalent in strongly Puritan parishes, where there was resistance to the use of rings and to the ceremonialism of Anglican marriage ritual.

The Duchess is no Puritan by seventeenth-century London standards – she does, after all, give Antonio a ring. But some characters in the play refer to Antonio as 'precise' (2.3.65), a code descriptor for Puritans in the period. He is a more innocent, intelligent and successful version of Shakespeare's Malvolio in *Twelfth Night*, who is also a puritanically inclined household steward, but whose marriage to his mistress is never more than the stuff of ambitious dreams. The Cardinal considers Antonio an atheist because he does not go to mass (5.2.121–4). Perhaps he can be understood instead as a crypto–Protestant (Empson). He and the Duchess steer clear of the ecclesiastical ceremonies that define the corruption of other characters in the play; indeed, their secret marriage represents a haven of innocence from the political world of the Cardinal and Duke Ferdinand. In 1.2, before she proposes to Antonio, the Duchess refers to her marriage as a heroic act, a 'dangerous venture' like that of soldiers in battle, a solitary journey through a pathless wilderness (1.2.259–63, 274–6). She is doing something rare and unusual, not only because she is defying the wishes of her brothers and marrying beneath her station, but also because, in so far as she is understood within the context of London controversy, she is acting outside the ecclesiastical framework that claims the authority to define what counts as marriage.

The 'heroics of marriage' articulated by the Duchess was a prominent seventeenth-century theme, particularly though not exclusively associated in literature with Protestants who opposed the rituals of the Church of England (Rose, 93–176). Early audiences who interpreted the play's treatment of rituals and 'relics' as blatantly anti-Catholic were also likely to see the Duchess's marriage not as a scandalous violation of social norms but as a retreat into virtue (Allman, 40). Even Bosola, whose language on most topics is profoundly and corrosively equivocal, seems to approve of it. There was a parallel to the Duchess of Malfi at the Stuart court: Lady Arbella Stuart, James I's cousin, who was in the line of succession to the throne and remained unmarried for years while she waited fruitlessly for James to find her a match, then bravely took matters into her own hands and secretly married William Seymour. She and her husband were imprisoned but managed to escape, whereupon James I had Arbella recaptured and incarcerated in the Tower of London. Despite strong popular sentiment in her favour, she was never released. By 1614, when Webster's play was probably first staged, Lady Arbella was reportedly going mad and she died in prison in 1615 (Lever; Steen). To be sure, it had long been considered treasonous for royals in the line of succession to marry without the monarch's consent. But, to many observers of Arbella's fate, the king's treatment of her smacked of tyranny – the illegal use of royal prerogative powers. The Duchess, similarly, dares to choose her own husband and is cruelly punished for it – not because she deserves to be punished but because her brothers have arrogated to themselves the power to punish her. However, she, unlike Lady Arbella, retains her dignity and self-possession throughout her brother's drawn-out attempts to deprive her of her reason.

As critics have noted, *Malfi* is, among other things, a retelling of the story of Patient Griselda – the young wife who is tested by her husband and found steadfast despite the loss of her children, her status and even her marriage. David Wallace has shown how the story, as told and retold by Petrarch, Boccaccio and Chaucer, was interpreted in the fourteenth and fifteenth centuries as an analysis of political tyranny. Griselda's husband, like a political tyrant, deprives her of everything in his power to take away from her, but is unable to deprive her of her self-possession, her will and her agency, because she never says no to him and therefore never allows him to override her own wishes (Wallace, 261–93). Griselda therefore deconstructs the power of the tyrant by showing it to be without limits. Similarly, paradoxically, the Duchess preserves her identity and self-mastery precisely through her constancy and her acquiescence in her brothers' long list of torments in 4.1 and 4.2: 'I am Duchess of Malfi still.' But it is noteworthy that, in Webster's version of the Griselda story, tyranny is not exemplified through marriage. Quite the reverse: the Duchess is happily married in a relationship of mutuality and trust; it is her brothers who play the role of Griselda's infinitely demanding husband. They are sexually transgressive and perverse. Their tyranny is displayed in its full colours when they vicariously punish their own unacknowledged appetites by tormenting her.

BOSOLA

Bosola in the play is also largely Webster's invention. Unlike his historical counterpart, the mercenary assassin Daniele da Bozzolo, who was hired specifically to kill Antonio in Milan some two years after the Duchess's death, Webster's Bosola enters the story even before her secret marriage to Antonio as a household spy in the pay of her brothers. He speaks more lines than any other character in the play and appears in all but five short scenes (2.4, 2.5, 3.4, 5.1 and 5.3). Both structurally and morally he ties the play together: in some complex scenes such as 4.1, 4.2 and 5.2 he serves as an important thread of continuity onstage as other characters bustle in and out. In his mercurial and self-contradictory speeches he expresses, as though they all exist in solution within himself, virtually every moral attitude expressed by another character in the play, from cynicism and misanthropy to efficient pragmatism, to tenderness and high idealism. He betrays everyone, most cruelly and repeatedly himself. He is at once quaintly principled and strangely amoral or even, to our modern eyes, atheistic and existentialist. He plays a multitude of roles: disaffected academic satirist, ex-convict, 'intelligencer', bodyguard, stage manager for Ferdinand's spectacles of horror, satirist, grave-digger, bellman, priest, executioner and avenger. To these roles we can add that of art critic: in 4.2 he complains of the new style of tomb design becoming popular in early seventeenth-century England, in which the effigy no longer looks heavenward but props itself up on one elbow and looks straight out towards the spectator, as if it had 'died of the toothache' (4.2.152 and 149–55n.; see Figs 6 and 7). Like another of Webster's splendidly unsettled characters, the mercurial Flamineo, who has a similar role in *White Devil*, Bosola alters his disposition with alarming swiftness, and his violent mood swings are signalled through strangely unsettled, unanchored language (see p. 83; and Berry).When he dies, though he has much to say about the matter, we don't know whether he is saved or damned.

Bosola is based on a recognizable English type – the unemployed university graduate whose lack of employment has made him cynical about those in high places, yet drawn to power like a moth to flame. In the sixteenth and early seventeenth centuries, Oxford

6   Tomb of Elizabeth I at Westminster Abbey, showing the position for effigies
    approved by Bosola

and Cambridge had expanded their enrolments to accommodate
the need for new clerics to replace ousted Catholics and other
churchmen deemed incompetent, but the supply of graduates
quickly outstripped the demand, and there were many Bosolas
among the over-educated and under-employed. Frank Whigham
has usefully characterized him as suffering from a crisis of
inauthenticity – what Georg Lukács described as the 'reified
employee's general deformation': 'His qualities and abilities are no
longer an organic part of his personality, they are things which he
can "own" or "dispose of" like the various objects of the external
world' (Whigham, 219–20; Lukács, 100).

Were it not for Bosola, Webster's play might come across,
like some of Dekker's, as rather simplistic anti-Catholic and
anti-Stuart propaganda, albeit considerably better written. But
Bosola's perspective is anything but simple. He hates himself
for the ease with which he can be bought and made complicit

7 Tomb of Elizabeth Drury, showing the newly popular 'toothache' position
for effigies

with things he despises, but he seems unable to curb his own
obsessive enactment of the desires of those who pay him
until it is too late. Bosola's repeated self-condemnation over
the moral compromises he makes through his duties as secret
'intelligencer' for the Cardinal and Ferdinand figures a similar
complicity with the play's spectacles of violence on the part of
the audience and the playwright. Webster's play uses theatre to
expose the moral bankruptcy of various types of quasi-liturgical
theatrical show – the iconic display of mutilated bodies, the
courtly antimasque of madmen, the Cardinal's ritual divestment
at Loreto – but the very enactments that expose the corrupt
origins of spectacle also exploit its potential to entertain the
audience. The play comes close to endorsing contemporary
Puritan anti-stage invective, which was based on arguments
for the corrupting power of theatrical spectacle, except that

Webster's play, like the reluctantly parasitic Bosola, depends for its life on the very corruption that it simultaneously holds up for revulsion. We love to watch and hate ourselves for loving it, and we owe our recognition of the contamination of our response in large part to the self-contemplation of Bosola, who is curiously modern in his insights even as he also spouts platitudes of old-fashioned morality.

Bosola's cold ability to see the emptiness of meaning even as he seeks to embrace it finds echoes in critical pronouncements by Webster himself: in response to an anti-theatrical argument about the moral turpitude of acting on the stage – playing a part that 'lies' because it is not the expression of one's own identity – Webster contended in his Character 'An excellent Actor' that the 'Precisian' who condemned plays on the basis of Puritan principle was acting a part just as surely as the actor himself:

> All men have been of his occupation: and indeed, what hee doth fainedly that doe others essentially: this day one plaies a Monarch, the next a private person. Heere one Acts a Tyrant, on the morrow an Exile: A Parasite thus man to night, too morrow a Precisian, and so of divers others.
>
> (Webster, 3.483)

One day a Parasite and the next a Precisian. There could be no better capsule definition of the riven consciousness of Bosola, whose mercurial and self-conflicted perspective casts *Malfi* into a mode of intellectual complexity and self-interrogation that helps to account for its enormous power and fascination for readers and theatrical audiences.

LANGUAGE AND ACTION

Malfi is a play full of echoes, even a play tormented by echoes. The Duchess's voice is heard onstage in the haunting Echo scene (5.3), and several scenes echo one another through their structure (Luckyj). Most prominently, the secret marriage scene from 1.2 reverberates through the play like a Freudian return of the repressed. It is echoed in the loving exchange between the Duchess and Antonio followed by Ferdinand's horrific intrusion with a dagger (3.2), then again in Ferdinand's torments of the Duchess with the gift of the severed hand and the wax figures of her husband and children (4.1). The marriage scene is travestied in Bosola's 'love scene' with the almost-dead Duchess (4.2), and in 5.2's seduction scenes, first between Julia and Bosola, then between Julia and the Cardinal with Bosola as hidden witness. In several of these cases, the arras at the back of the stage serves to conceal unseen auditors. Similarly, Antonio's entry with drawn pistol in 3.2 is echoed by Julia's entry with pistol drawn in 5.2. The parallel structures serve, among other things, to focus attention on similarities and dissimilarities between their various aspects: Julia the promiscuous mistress echoes the Duchess's brothers' fantasies about their sister's sexuality; Bosola the social climber and adventurer becomes an all too visible echo of ambitions that Antonio fears in himself (1.2.331).

Webster frequently uses stage properties to echo and reinforce the language of the play. Some of his properties are emblematic: that is, they serve as visual symbols of and links with abstract ideas or sentiments expressed by persons in the play (McLuskie and Uglow). For example, early in the play a member of Duke Ferdinand's retinue awards Antonio a jewel as prize for his victory in the jousting (1.2.8). The Duchess later compares herself with a jewel (1.2.215–16), perhaps unconsciously echoing the biblical 'pearl of great price' (Matthew, 13.46). In the same scene she gives herself to Antonio in marriage, echoing Ferdinand's earlier gift of the jewel to Antonio, except that in this instance Ferdinand is emphatically not the giver. Later on, during the childbirth scene (2.2), the Duchess's jewels are alleged to have been stolen, and in act 3 Antonio is also called a 'jewel' by an only half-hypocritical Bosola (3.2.249). The jewel's connection with the Duchess's body reverberates through the play.

Similarly, the theatrical prop of the key to the Duchess's bedchamber is a repeated motif that gradually takes on emblematic status: both in 3.2 and later in 4.1, Ferdinand acquires a surreptitious key to the Duchess's 'closet' or private chamber. In 3.2 while she is in her private chamber she mentions the key to her heart, a commonplace idea in love poetry of the period. She thinks she is addressing Antonio but is possibly overheard by Ferdinand, who has used his secret key to enter her room undetected. If he has heard her speech and applies it to himself, it no doubt fuels his secret desires (3.2.60–1 and n.). Even something as small as the Cardinal's setting aside a book of devotion can take on emblematic status in the play. Scene 5.5 begins with the Cardinal musing on the book and then discarding it, saying of its author, 'Lay him by' (4). This echoes the larger sense in which he has already 'laid by' his ecclesiastical robes onstage during the Loreto scene (3.4) and similarly abandoned any pretence of interest in the spiritual dimension of his holy office. Scene 5.5 ends, shockingly, with the Cardinal applying the same language of discarding to himself. His dying words are 'let me / Be laid by and never thought of' (87–8). A small emblematic action comes to define the sum total of his life.

Some of Webster's emblems function relatively simply in the play. When the Duchess and Antonio exchange wedding vows, Antonio specifically mentions the marriage 'emblem' of the palm trees that can only bear fruit when they are planted in close proximity (Fig. 8):

> That we may imitate the loving palms,
> Best emblem of a peaceful marriage,
> That ne'er bore fruit divided.
>
> (1.2.392–4)

Similarly, musing on the vanity of human ambition, Antonio likens it in traditional fashion to bubbles blown by children (Fig. 9): 'Like wanton boys whose pastime is their care, / We follow after bubbles blown in th'air' (5.4.64–5).

44

VIVITE CONCORDES.

I.

KOmt hier mannen en ghy wijven,
    Die, wanneerje zyt gepaert,
Dickmaels ſijt gewoon te kyven,
    Dickmael toont u wrangen aert;
Leert hier van de boom-gewaſſen,
    Leert hier uyt het woeſte wout,
Leert op u geſelſchap paſſen,
    Siet! dat doet het quaſtigh hout.

Let op deſe Dadel-boomen,
    Die met beeken afgeſneén,
Sijn als bruggen op de ſtroomen,
    Mits ſy hellen tegen een.
Echte lieden, lieve paren,
    Soo ghy in den Echten ſtaet
Liefd en Eendracht kunt bewaren,
    Niet dat u té boven gaet.

Batillius:

PAlmarum hinc illinc pontis ceu fornice ducto,
    Amuem intermedium fœmina maſque tegunt,
Ultro dum oppoſitos mas inde, hinc fœmina ramos
Curvantes, ſibi ſe conſociare petunt,
Iré & in amplexus exoptatoſque hymeneos,

Quâ frondoſi oculi ſunt in amore duces.
Jam mihi non aliæ firment connubia flammæ,
Præferat his omnem non aliunde puer.
Pronuba jam caſtos palma una accendat odores,
Cedat & ipſa ſuas ſpinea tæda faces.

Greg. Richterus in Epiſtola dedicatoria axiom. Ecclef. ad matrimonium myſticum Chriſti
& Ecclefiæ, hoc ipſum Emblema non minus pie, quam argute tranſtulit.

De naturâ hujus arboris videndus omnino

Plin. lib. 13. cap. 4. Johan. Rerum lib. hieroglyph. 50. cap. 10. ubi
Diophanem autorem Græcum, & Georgica Florentini citat, qui
multo de Palinæ amore conſcripſit, eamque contabeſcere maris de-
ſiderio, quod, modò radices verſus eum porrigendo, modò verti-
cis in eum proclinatione, aliisque affectuum ſignis non obſcure
profitetur.

8   'Loving palms', emblem of peaceful marriage, from Jacobus Cats, *Emblemata
    moralia et oeconomica*, in *Alle de Werken* (Amsterdam, 1658)

9   Boys with bubbles as an emblem of vanity, from John Hall, *Emblems with Elegant Figures* (1658)

Antonio's relatively straightforward adoptions of the emblem literature may signal poverty of imagination on his part, for other characters can be more creative. Bosola, for example, uses a standard Platonic and Christian image of the immortal soul trapped in the mortal body: cf. Fig. 10, from the very popular *Emblems* of Francis Quarles (1643), where the soul is depicted as a child locked within the ribcage of a skeleton and glossed with the biblical citation 'O wretched Man that I am; who shall deliver me from the body of this death?' (Romans, 7.24). In Bosola's version, the soul is instead a bird trapped in the

10   The soul trapped in the body, from Francis Quarles, *Emblems* (1643)

oversized birdcage of the world: 'Didst thou ever see a lark in a cage? Such is the soul in the body: this world is like her little turf of grass; and the heaven o'er our heads, like her looking glass, only gives us a miserable knowledge of the small compass of our prison' (4.2.125–9 and n.; cf. Quarles's emblem of the imprisoned soul in a birdcage: Quarles, 284).

With similar inventiveness, the Duchess, grieving over the wax image of a dead Antonio that she believes to be real (4.1), uses a striking image from Virgilian epic that had made its way into emblem literature, but adapts it to express her own sense of loss. In Geoffrey Whitney's *Choice of Emblems* (1586), Whitney evokes the tyrant 'vile Mezentius', who practises a unique mode of execution, binding a living person with a dead one so that the living person is forced to 'imbrace' the corpse until he is dead himself (Fig. 11). For Whitney, the image illustrates the misery of 'unequal marriage', by which unsuitable partners are forcibly yoked together for life, to the exquisite misery of both. Whitney's verse explanation condemns 'hard' parents who force their child into an unwanted marriage as 'tyrauntes' – a telling term in relation to our earlier discussion of the Duchess's brothers and their attitudes towards her remarriage. In her lament for the 'dead' Antonio, the Duchess picks up on the emblem's association with unequal marriage but makes it positive, wishing nothing more than to be bound for ever, as in wedlock, to the 'lifeless trunk' of Antonio – a (stage) 'property' that her 'tyrant' brothers can put to good use if they will only fulfil her wish, 'bind me to that lifeless trunk, / And let me freeze to death' (4.1.64–7).

LANGUAGE AND SOURCE

Particularly during the early and mid-twentieth century, Webster's editors and interpreters were fond of castigating the playwright for over-derivative language. R. W. Dent, who ransacked the writings of Webster's contemporaries for borrowings, summed up the previous half-century's work by complaining, 'The man worked strangely, his creativity receiving some written stimulus at almost every turn. Sometimes he appears strikingly original, occasionally merely commonplace, but almost always – unless our present evidence is very misleading – he worked from sources' (Dent, *Webster*, 11–12). Now we would be likely to say that this description applies in varying degrees to all writers of Webster's

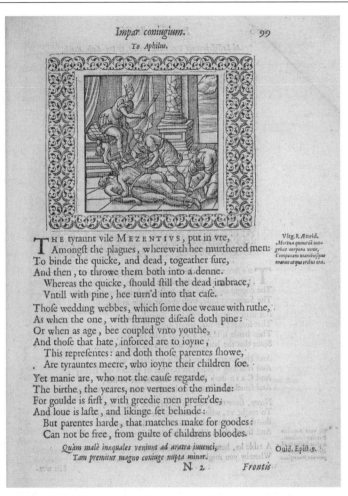

11 Binding the living to the dead, from Geoffrey Whitney, *Choice of Emblems* (1586)

period, or indeed of any period. Dent's assessment was based on an essentially Romanticist notion of artistic creativity as springing fresh and intact from the writer's brain. During the same period that they were busy reducing Webster's texts to a lamentable tissue of borrowings, twentieth-century 'disintegrationists' were also at work on Shakespeare, questioning the authenticity of much of the language in his plays and pointing out echoes from various sources that challenged the Bard's single authorship of all but the most highly regarded of his plays (Chambers). But the early twentieth-century assault on allegedly derivative language worked differently in the way scholars treated the two authors: while Webster was portrayed as generally lacking originality, Shakespeare was splintered into the 'authentic' bits that were original versus the 'inauthentic' bits that were borrowed from other authors: Shakespeare, in Foucauldian terms, was assumed to represent a 'constant level of value' whose inferior texts had been corrupted by others (Foucault, 151); Webster was defined as one of the 'others' who lacked 'true' originality and ignobly scraped their writings together by plagiarizing the work of those who were more inventive.

It is undeniably the case that Webster liked to borrow. He even liked to borrow from himself, as in imagery shared between his funerary elegy on Prince Henry and his portrayal of the Duchess of Malfi (Neill; see also p. 9). But that borrowing had profound significance, suggesting a kinship of spirit between two figures who were in many ways quite different. Like Hamlet (1.5.107) and many actual contemporaries, Webster likely kept 'tables' where he noted down important ideas from his reading and from his hearing of plays: the frequent word-for-word accuracy of his verbal echoes suggests that he reproduced them from written notes rather than from memory. Webster almost always borrowed in a highly strategic way, echoing but also altering his sources or their context so that the echo, if recognized, would create additional reverberations of meaning within his own text rather than showing its impoverishment. Indeed, the early printed editions of *Malfi* specifically mark a number of concluding rhymed couplets as commonplaces by means of either italics or quotation marks – as though to invite readers to consider a character's seemingly conventional statement in the light of its potential sources (see p. 89). But Webster plays elaborate games with these passages marked as commonplaces: some of them are apparently Webster's own invention, since they cannot reliably be traced to sources; some contradict other elements of the speech or scene they seem designed to sum up (see Goldberg).

We might, as an example, consider the last scene of the play, where Bosola's final dying couplet states, 'Let worthy minds ne'er stagger in distrust / To suffer death or shame for what is just' (5.5.101–2). Delio, in the play's concluding couplet marked as a commonplace, is a bit more sanguine, stating 'Integrity of life is fame's best friend, / Which nobly beyond death shall crown the end' (5.5.118–19). Which statement is more credible? Are worth or integrity of life rewarded or not, and if so in what way? Webster's use of conflicting moral adages at this late point in the play throws us back into consideration of Bosola's moral choices and the degree of Delio's understanding of the complexities of those choices – into whirling uncertainties that the play does not fully resolve, except perhaps through the figure of the Duchess, of whom both shadings of the adage are true. Moreover, Delio's comment extolling 'Integrity of life' recalls Horace's famous *Ode* 1.22.1–2, which begins *Integer vitae*: 'He who is upright of life and free from crime does not need the javelin or bow of the Moor' – lines so familiar to Renaissance schoolboys that in Shakespeare's *Titus Andronicus* even the brutal Goth Chiron recognizes the Latin passage and says he 'read it in the grammar long ago' (*Tit* 4.2.23). However, Horace's ode goes on in lines 9–12 to state, in what might retrospectively look like over-optimistic complacency, that even the wolf flees from the man of integrity – a sentiment that Webster's play, with its portrayal of the devastation caused by the lycanthrope Ferdinand, notably fails to confirm (Gurr, *Playgoing*, 100).

The commentary records Webster's most important borrowings so that readers can evaluate the functioning of his most significant textual echoes; with some of the less familiar texts, the notes also credit (in parentheses) the commentator to whom I am indebted for having noticed the borrowing. But the notes cannot go beyond a mere suggestion of the complexities of meaning we encounter if we start from the premise that the playwright borrowed strategically and intelligently rather than out of an inability to generate his own materials.

Another important purpose served by borrowing in the period was to define a social, political and/or intellectual group: Webster frequently echoes other texts in this way. As Dent has noted, he borrows with great frequency from Sir Philip Sidney's *Arcadia* and from Sir William Alexander's *Monarchic Tragedies* (1607). Alexander was connected to Prince Henry as a gentleman of Henry's Privy Chamber and also to the Sidney circle, having allegedly written his book of tragedies for Sidney's sister, the Countess of Pembroke; he also went on to write a continuation of the *Arcadia*. Penelope Rich, also connected with the Sidney circle as the 'Stella' of Sidney's sonnet sequence *Astrophil and Stella*, was the Websters' next-door neighbour, since her palace adjoined their coachyard. Rich had wedded Charles Blount in a scandalous secret marriage that defied James I's 1604 canon on marriage; she had had many children with Blount before marrying him. In her magnanimity and defiance of convention, she was another likely prototype for Webster's Duchess of Malfi. Penelope Rich was also the dedicatee of John Florio's translation of Montaigne, to which Webster is also strongly indebted (Bradbrook, 50–68). Florio had helped publish the original *Arcadia*. The dead warrior Sidney was, like Prince Henry, a rallying figure for the ultra-Protestant, pro-war, anti-Catholic faction to which Webster himself was also linked. And so we could build the connections ad infinitum. Suffice it to say that, for Webster's contemporaries, his many echoes of writings associated with a specific political or social group, however loosely defined, may have served as yet another sign of his own religious and political allegiances and carried special reverberations for, or in relation to, that group.

Another contemporary writer whom Webster frequently echoes was the minister Thomas Adams, called 'Puritan Adams', who preached a number of eloquent and highly influential sermons at Paul's Cross and elsewhere during the same years that Webster was writing his most famous plays. Webster may have known Adams's sermons by hearing them in person and/ or by reading them in manuscript or print. In some cases, we don't know who came first – Webster or Adams – since either could have borrowed from the other or even from a third source. It is interesting, though, that the most direct echoes of Adams's sermons in *Malfi* come out of the mouth of Bosola and are all from the same sermon castigating would-be courtiers for their lack of values and tellingly titled *The Gallant's Burden* (preached in 1612, printed in 1614): trees 'that grow crooked over standing pools' (1.1.49–52n.), the devil's quilted anvil (3.2.325n.), the 'many ways that conduct to seeming honour' (5.2.290–1n.), security as the 'suburbs of hell' (5.2.321–2n.). What does it mean that Webster chose to have his most spiritually torn character internalize Adams's well-known sermon so thoroughly? Surely this is more strategic echoing that adds to the moral complexity of the play. In close proximity to the period of Webster's greatest creativity as a playwright, Adams delivered and published a number of other sermons that probably either echoed or inspired Webster: *The White Devil* (1612), *Mystical Bedlam, or the World of Madmen* (1615) and *Lycanthropy, or the Wolf Worrying the Lambs* (preached in 1615; published in Adams).

All of which is not to suggest that Webster only made use of writers who shared his ideological bent. He borrowed frequently from John Donne, for example, especially, as might be expected, from Donne's anti-Jesuit satire *Ignatius His Conclave* (1611; see the commentary notes on 2.4.18, 3.1.31–5 and 3.5.40). Somewhat less predictably, he also borrowed from Donne's First and Second *Anniversary* elegies, published in 1611 and 1612, on the death of Elizabeth Drury. T. S. Eliot numbered Webster, like Donne, among the 'metaphysical poets' (Eliot, 'Metaphysical', 60). Like

Donne, Webster was fond of imagery that ties wildly disparate things together: as Donne has his twin compasses as a simile for two lovers in 'A Valediction: forbidding Mourning', so Webster's Duchess speaks of the doors of death that move 'on such strange geometrical hinges, / You may open them both ways' (4.2.213–14). Bosola is particularly given to extended 'metaphysical' imagery, likening a wounded war veteran's crutches to the geometrical compasses of a military tactician (1.1.61ff. and 64–6n.) and an assassin in danger of capture to a physician's leech with cut tail (5.2.299–303). Probable echoes of Donne's *Anniversaries* in *Malfi* include Antonio's remarks on creation *ex nihilo* (3.5.80–1 and n.), the Duchess's image of the over-charged cannon that may burst asunder (3.5.103–4) and Bosola's description of human flesh as mere 'crudded milk' (4.2.122 and n.).

Also like Donne in the *Anniversaries*, Webster was interested in the artistic problem of representing the disappearance of goodness and order from the world. Donne's *Anniversaries* associated the death of Elizabeth Drury, a 'rich soul' who had departed this life in 1610 at age fourteen, with the sickness and death of the whole world. Echoing the early seventeenth-century praises of the departed Elizabeth I, Donne's *First Anniversary: An Anatomy of the World* calls the dead queen's namesake Elizabeth Drury a 'Queen' who, having 'ended here her progress time', departed to her heavenly court (lines 7–8) and left the world bereft of order and coherence. Some of Donne's contemporaries were shocked. To Ben Jonson's complaint that Donne's poems were blasphemous for making such extravagant spiritual claims for the young daughter of a patron, Donne reportedly responded that he described 'the Idea of a Woman and not as she was' (Jonson, 1.133). Arguably, *Malfi* attempts something similar, but with greater credibility and rather less extravagance. Critics have long complained about Webster's decision to kill off the Duchess before the end of act 4, so that act 5 becomes, in the perception of some, a mere roiling mass of unfocused violence or a machine of destruction that slowly grinds to a halt. But that, surely, is Webster's point: this is another of the many cases in Webster where linguistic echoes lead to a perception of meaningful structural echoes. The Duchess is not flawless, but she carries with her a capacity for light, joy and love that enlivens an otherwise festering world. By showing how the play is emptied of light and reduced to madness and chaos once she is gone, Webster makes large claims for the power of virtue in general. By anchoring his point in the figure of an admirable and sympathetic woman, he out-does, or out-donnes, Donne.

MELANCHOLY AND DETERMINISM

Webster's play also echoes contemporary medical texts. The most precise of these echoes is the doctor's description of Ferdinand's lycanthropy (5.2.8–19), taken from accounts of lycanthropes collected in Simon Goulart's *Admirable and Memorable Histories*, published in Edward Grimeston's English translation in 1607. Goulart divides lycanthropes into two types: those whose severe melancholy causes them to believe that they are wolves; and those actually transformed into wolves by Satan (Goulart, 386–9). Ferdinand belongs to the former category, 'in whom the melancholike humor doth so rule, as they imagine themselves to be transformed into Wolves', and who spend their nights lurking in 'Church-yardes, and about graves'. One such madman encountered by Goulart was, much like Ferdinand, carrying 'upon his shoulders the whole thigh and the legge of a dead man'; another of Goulart's madmen averred, parallel to Ferdinand's claim to be hairy 'on the inside' (5.2.18), that 'Wolves were commonlie hayrie without, and hee was betwixt the skinne and the flesh' (Goulart, 387). The first of Goulart's lycanthropes was successfully cured of his disease; the second died a few days after his capture, before a cure could be effected.

According to the classical Galenic doctrine of humours that still dominated medicine during Webster's time, physical and mental ailments were not fully separate entities, but existed on the same continuum from body to mind. There were four chief bodily fluids or 'humours': blood, phlegm, yellow bile or choler, and black bile or melancholy. If the body produced too much of any one humour, the physical condition also manifested itself as mental imbalance. Gail Paster cites Thomas Wright (see also MacDonald):

> me thinkes the passions of our minde, are not unlike the foure humours of our bodies, . . . for if blood, flegme, choler, or melancholy exceed the due proportion required to the constitution and health of our bodies, presently we fall into some disease: even so, if the passions of the Minde be not moderated according to reason (and that temperature virtue requireth) immediately the soule is molested with some maladie.
>
> (Wright, in Paster, 150)

Melancholy was therefore understood as a physical condition, not only a state of mind. The word melancholy in Greek literally means 'black bile'. According to Galenic doctrine, it is a humour linked to earth and therefore cold and dry.

Nearly every character in Webster's play suffers from transient melancholy at one point or another: Antonio refers to his 'melancholy' during his banishment in France (1.2.310), and Julia is said to have been trapped on a 'melancholy perch' before her sexual awakening by the Cardinal (2.4.28). But the play's chief melancholics are three: Ferdinand, the Cardinal and Bosola. In its milder forms, as we see in the case of Bosola, melancholy is recognizable through the sadness and inertia that we now associate with depression. Bosola's melancholy was apparently brought on by chronic underemployment and a consequent lowering of self esteem: as Antonio says, 'want of action / Breeds all black malcontents' (1.1.80–1). Once Bosola is employed, his melancholy becomes more act than reality, or so Ferdinand seems to suggest, calling upon him to keep his old 'garb of melancholy' as a cover for his new profession of 'intelligencer' (1.2.178, 195). As Bosola untangles himself from the Aragonian brothers and solidifies the goal of avenging the Duchess's murder, he banishes his 'melancholy' inertia and becomes a man of action.

The Cardinal's melancholy is more severe than Bosola's: he is called a 'melancholy churchman' from early in the play (1.2.75) and becomes delusional by the final scene, when he sees a terrifying avenging image in the pond (5.5.5–7). How does melancholy lead to hallucinations (assuming that his vision was not, as some seventeenth-century spectators may well have interpreted it, an actual demonic visitation)? Seventeenth-century physicians might argue that the Cardinal's decline into hallucination happens because, as his melancholy increases its dominance over the other three bodily humours, it causes a build-up of black bile that literally chokes off the clarity of his perceptions.

His volatile brother Ferdinand is a much more serious case of hallucinatory humoral imbalance. For most of the play the Cardinal acts as an intermediary between Ferdinand and the saner characters, calming him and curbing the most florid of his fantasies. Though Ferdinand is associated at various points with melancholy or 'black bile' (see, for example, 5.2.8–10), his primary 'humour' in the play is overwhelming rage or choler. His body is over-dominated by yellow bile, which is hot and dry. His melancholy is much more severe and of a different physiological origin from that of the other characters – contemporaries would have called it 'melancholy adust' – a by-product of his choleric nature, which, to use humoral language, has a tendency to burn itself out, leaving behind the ashes of his ceaseless anger and combustion. Hence the play's references to Ferdinand in terms of explosives: 'wild fire' or a 'deadly cannon' that goes off with dangerous unpredictability (2.5.47, 3.3.53). The ashes of his choleric combustions thicken and beget 'many misshapen objects' in his imagination, just as a slimy polluted pond was believed to engender toads (Paster, 141; Otten, 129–33; see also 1.2.76, where similar language is used of the Cardinal). Because of the extreme combustibility of his nature, Ferdinand is even more clogged with bilious refuse than the Cardinal, which helps to account for his overwhelming susceptibility to disabling hallucinations like lycanthropy.

To what extent would it be reasonable, in terms of seventeenth-century humoral theory, to expect characters like the Cardinal and Ferdinand to be able to control their disease? In theory, human reason was supposed to allow an individual to curb his or her own excesses and keep the humours in proper balance, as in Thomas Wright's reference to reason's moderating of the 'passions of the minde', cited above. In practice, that volition was overwhelmingly difficult to achieve (Paster, 20–2; see also Burton). Through its use of humoral psychology, *Malfi* enacts a secular determinism that much resembles the Calvinist doctrine of predestination that many critics have seen operating in Webster's work: in fact, Bosola's image of human beings as tossed like the 'stars' tennis balls' may derive from Calvin's *Institutes* (Cecil, 66–8; Sinfield, 121–2). Webster balances the play on a fine line between faith and nihilism. His portrayal of the tyranny of the Cardinal and Ferdinand recalls seventeenth-century political theory by which the tyrant was defined as weak rather than strong – a victim of his own failures of will, which made him unable to resist the inroads of destructive humoral passions and unable to restrain himself from acting them out on a grand scale through the mechanisms of state (Bushnell).

Malfi appears remarkably modern in its recognition of the power of what psychoanalysts call 'projection' – the belief that other people have feelings or traits that we are unwilling to acknowledge in ourselves. As the Cardinal says of Julia, 'You fear / My constancy because you have approved / Those giddy and wild turnings in yourself' (2.4.10–12); similarly, Delio reassures Antonio about his premonitions of danger, echoing Lady Macbeth from the banquet scene (*Mac* 3.4.60) and suggesting that Antonio's perception of dangers to himself is only the externalization of his own fear. Lynn Enterline has shown how Webster makes Ferdinand's melancholy an effect of his non-recognition of difference from his twin, the Duchess: 'Webster defines the relationship between sexual difference and melancholia in this play according to visual trauma: male perception of itself as reflected back through female bodily difference becomes a wounding event that decisively changes the very eyes doing the looking' (Enterline, 262). A Galenic physician might critique Enterline's account on the grounds that, according to humoral doctrine, interpenetration of the individual and his or her surroundings is the rule rather than the exception. But the physician would probably accept the point she goes on to make – that melancholy in powerful people is a contagious disease that spreads its own violations of 'signifying boundaries' through other elements of the culture. In *Malfi*, if we accept seventeenth-century medical theory, Ferdinand's humoral imbalances can be seen as contributing to a broad corruption not only of the body politic as portrayed within the play but also of the theatrical medium by which that imbalanced, diseased body is communicated to the audience. On this reading, melancholia and humoral theory more generally serve both as internal generators of the play's pervasive echoes and also as corrupters of them, so that the audience is hard pressed to distinguish clear originals from contaminated copies.

In terms of humoral theory, the Duchess would be described as sanguine – warm and moist – a disposition associated in the period with blood, and with courage, hope and love. The three siblings in the play can therefore be recognized as enactments of three of the four elemental conditions recognized by Galenic medicine: melancholia, choler and sanguinity. The similarity of the siblings in appearance belies their contrasting natures in terms of humoral predominance, as Antonio notes: 'You never fixed your eye on three fair medals / Cast in one figure of so different temper' (1.2.106–7). Arguably, the Duchess's warm, sanguine temperament helps to trigger Ferdinand's fits of rage: he misrecognizes her warmth as sexual wantonness and allows it to increase his own choleric heat. But the Duchess, unlike her brothers, appears to have the desired ability to regulate her passions and thus to serve, against the deterministic bent of the play, as an exemplar of free will, even though this freedom from dominance by internal passions does not in any way save her from destruction. She experiences choler and melancholy in the course of her drawn-out torture at the hands of Ferdinand and Bosola, but she overcomes these emotions and dies in a state of serene intactness that carries political ramifications and represents the play's answer to her brothers' tyranny: 'I am Duchess of Malfi still' (4.2.137).

Like humoral theory, the language of witchcraft pervades the play, helping to create an aura of paranoia like that experienced, for example, by Antonio when he vacillates between fate and mere chance as explanations for his sudden and unpropitious nosebleed (2.3.41–3). As would be expected, the play's chief purveyor of witchcraft paranoia is the ever-infectious Duke Ferdinand: he considers his sister to be a witch, and her 'rank blood' to have the power to bewitch him all on its own (3.1.78). Similarly, Julia, the Cardinal's mistress, claims to believe that she has been bewitched into loving Bosola by 'Love powder' (5.2.145) and even the Duchess, when she recognizes in 4.1 that the cold hand her brother has given her has been severed from a dead body, fleetingly associates Ferdinand with witchcraft (4.1.53–4). The dead hand may be a *main de gloire*, a specially prepared mummified hand used by witches and other malefactors to guarantee the efficacy of their enterprises. According to Kathryn Rowe, the name is etymologically linked via Old French with mandragora or mandrake, a mysterious anthropomorphic plant reportedly generated by and subsisting on human blood, particularly blood that dripped from the gibbets of hanged men. Mandrake was believed to cause madness in humans, as Ferdinand claims has happened to him: 'I have this night digged up a mandrake . . . / And I am grown mad with't' (2.5.1–2 and nn.; Rowe, 97–104). Ferdinand's madness is therefore over-determined in relation to its potential agents within the play; by flailing about to discover an external source, he avoids recognizing his own monstrous appetites and the guilt that accompanies their unrestrained indulgence. In general, the play's more trustworthy characters dismiss witchcraft as mere superstition – a scepticism shared by many literate people in Jacobean England (Thomas). But the play's numerous witchcraft references link up with its anti-Catholic and anti-Laudian rhetoric to create a reverberating metalanguage of danger that increases, even as it interrogates, the play's remarkable power as theatre.

THE TEXT

Malfi was first published in the same year as Shakespeare's First Folio and about a decade after the play was first performed on the stage. The 1623 title-page (see Fig. 21) calls the play 'The Tragedy of the Duchess of Malfi' and includes important information about performance: 'As it was presented privately at the Blackfriars and publicly at the Globe, by the King's Majesty's Servants' – Shakespeare's company, the King's Men. The title-page also tells potential readers something about the nature of the text they will be encountering, though this information is perhaps not as immediately credible as the information about performance: 'The perfect and exact copy with diverse things printed that the length of the play would not bear in the pre-sentment', that is, onstage. Last but not least, the title-page proudly announces the author, in larger type than the preceding information about copy: 'Written by John Webster', along with a Horatian tag daring readers to find any better piece of literature to occupy their time.

It is unusual in the period for a quarto title-page to offer information that differentiates the printed text so explicitly from a shortened version used in performance (see p. 8). And in other ways the First Quarto of *Malfi* is unusual as well. It is the first English playtext to give a fairly complete cast list along with the names of the actors, in some cases not only for one but for two different early performances of the play (see Fig. 22). There are other elements of the edition that show care on the part of author, printer or both: the dedication letter from Webster to the 'Right Honourable George Harding, Baron Berkeley', three commendatory poems by fellow dramatists and a printed text in which all act and scene divisions are clearly and accurately marked. This last was almost certainly a feature of the printer Nicholas Okes's copy for *Malfi* rather than his own contribution: the First Quarto of Webster's *White Devil* (1612), also printed by Okes, contained no act or scene divisions whatever.

Nicholas Okes, active between 1606 and 1636, was a prolific and eclectic businessman whose list of authors included John Stow, William Camden, Francis Bacon, Sir Walter Ralegh, Rachel Speght of the *Hic Mulier* controversy (see pp. 70–1), Ovid and Lucan in translation, travel writers and religious writers of sermons and treatises, many of whom were Puritan-leaning divines. Okes also printed a number of dramatic texts, beginning with the Pied Bull quarto of Shakespeare's *King Lear* (1608), and going on to include plays by (among others) Ben Jonson, Thomas Dekker, Francis Beaumont and John Fletcher, John Ford and Thomas Heywood. Heywood's *Apology for Actors* (1612), to which Webster contributed a commendatory poem, closes with an epistle praising Okes for being 'so carefull, and industrious, so serious and laborious to doe the Author all the rights of the press' (*Apology*). Peter Blayney has challenged this characterization (Blayney, 28–9), but it seems not unfair by the standards of the time. At least twenty-nine copies of Q1 *Duchess of Malfi* survive, which is on the high side for quarto playbooks of the period.

The First Quarto text of *Malfi*, which is the only substantive text of the play, shows clear signs that its author was involved in at least one stage of the printing process beyond the production of the front matter. Editors of Elizabethan and Jacobean plays have long debated the extent to which authors concerned themselves in the process of publication: did they supply the manuscript, or at least look it over before surrendering it to the printer, who would typically be expected to discard it once the printed version had been produced? Play manuscripts could reach a London printer from a variety of sources – the author, the dramatic company who had performed the play and owned the officially licensed manuscript, or even patrons, copyists or individual actors. Assuming that authors were involved in the printing process at all, did they actually read proofs, most likely by visiting the printshop during the process of production? For most dramatists of the period, evidence is very scanty and editorial assertions of authorial involvement in the correction of printing-house copy are therefore highly conjectural. In the case of *Malfi*, there is still some conjecture, but there is concrete evidence of Webster's involvement. I have reproduced two versions of pages from the inner H forme (typeset pages locked together to be printed off as a single sheet) – the H1^v and H2^r opening in their first and second states (Figs 12 and 13) – so readers can see the evidence for themselves.

The first state of the quarto, usually designated Q1a (Fig. 12), is relatively straightforward.[1] On the left-hand page (H1^v) appears the beginning of 3.4, in which two '*Pilgrims to the Shrine of our Lady of* Loreto' witness the Cardinal's ritualized transformation from churchman to military commander and his public disavowal of the Duchess's marriage, all of which is described in the play's most elaborate stage direction – nine lines long – at the bottom of the page. The catchword at the foot of the page (a device printers used to help them correctly match up consecutive pages) is 'The', and the first words below the running title at the top of the right-hand page (H2^r) match the catchword, 'The Hymne'.

---

1   My discussion here is based on the thorough analysis of the printing process by formes in Gunby, 576–80.

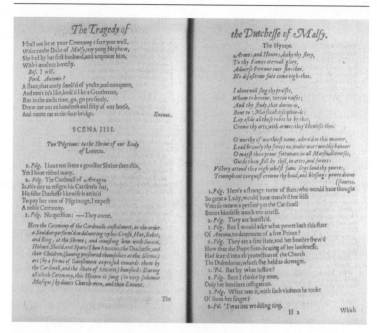

12 Q1a version of the beginning of 3.4, BL Ashley 2207, sig. H1ᵛ–2ʳ

In the second state of the quarto, usually designated Q1b
(Fig. 13), several things have changed. The stage direction at
bottom left has obviously been partially reset, since it now spills
over into a tenth line to accommodate '*Exeunt.*' The catchword
'The' remains, but it is more crowded because of additions to the
stage direction, and it has lost its function because the title 'The
Hymne' has now been removed from the top of the right-hand
page and the first words there after the running title are now
'*Armes, and Honors, decke thy story*'. Someone in the printshop
has deliberately stripped the 'Hymne' of its title. An added note
to the right of the text of the 'Hymne' suggests it is now to be
understood as a 'Ditty': 'The Author disclaimes this Ditty to
be his.' In Q1a, the 'Hymne' is so designated in the eighth line
of the stage direction as well; in Q1b that designation has been
replaced by 'Ditty' – a term that seems little in keeping with

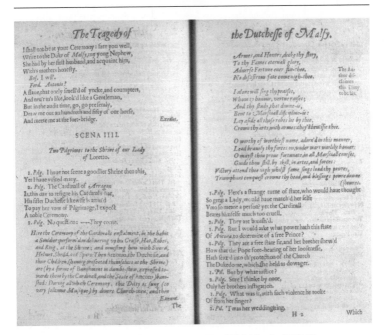

13 Q1b version of the beginning of 3.4, BL 644 f. 72, sig. H1ᵛ–2ʳ

the solemnity of the religious ceremony being acted onstage, to which the sung verses, by whatever name, serve as musical accompaniment.

What happened between Q1a and Q1b? Editors who have assimilated post-structuralist ideas about the nature of the literary text have become uncomfortable with an earlier generation's readiness to assume unquestioningly that, in making emendations, the editor's own sense of artistic decorum and aesthetic value would inevitably match those of the author, and that if the editor was convinced that something in the text was an error the author would necessarily have agreed (for a recent summary, see Marcus, 'Textual', 143–59). But here we have material differences that quite readily generate a narrative of authorial involvement. The most likely sequence (though there could be others) is that Webster came into the printshop of his neighbour Nicholas Okes to check on the copy, noticed in horror that someone else's verses were being printed as his with the grand title of 'Hymne' and insisted that the printer add a note to the right of them scornfully repudiating authorship of what he would only term a 'Ditty'. Although we do not have certain evidence, it is quite likely that the 'Hymne' was performed along with the dumb-show in early stagings of the play, perhaps to enliven and complicate the Loreto scene by introducing an auditory element that enhanced the song's praises of the Cardinal and thus worked against the devastating visual message of the Cardinal's vile public rejection of the Duchess's marriage. In disavowing the 'Hymne' through a printed marginal note, Webster was doing as much as was feasible to express his displeasure with its inclusion on aesthetic grounds, but perhaps also for religious reasons, since to use a sacred name in connection with a scene that satirized Catholicism might have struck him as blasphemy. The objectionable verses themselves had to be preserved in order to avoid massive resetting of copy, but at least he could register a disclaimer and deliver an implicit judgement through the scornful but religiously neutral term 'Ditty'.

This conjectural scenario is reinforced by the fact that a number of other highly informed changes are made to the same opening. In the first line of the long stage direction, '*order*' in Q1a is changed to the more specific '*habit*' in Q1b; and in line 6 '*forme of Banishment*' is augmented helpfully to '*forme of Banishment in dumbe-shew*'. In Q1b, that is, readers are specifically informed that the actions described in the stage direction had been performed in mime. In addition to several more minor changes, another page from the same forme (H4^r) shows a speech prefix corrected from 'Antonio' (Q1a) to 'Duchess' (Q1b) and an important stage direction added: '*Enter Bosola with a Guard.*' Either of these corrections could have been made by an alert in-house proofreader who noticed that the compositor had used the wrong speech prefix and omitted a marginal stage direction. But, given the number and type of corrections made to this forme, it seems highly likely that Webster examined it himself, successfully insisting on changes that made the text more accessible to readers while also downgrading the 'Hymne' to a 'Ditty' and thereby pointing to the printed text's composite origins. It is also reasonable to infer that Webster was not the one who supplied the text from which the printers had been working, since he appears to have felt so strongly about its inclusion of verses he considered inferior to his own. Q1a and Q1b of *Malfi* give us an uncharacteristically close view of changes to a playtext made, or at least alleged in its own language to have been made, at the insistence of the author himself. If, as Roland Barthes wittily suggests, the author is to be allowed as a guest into his text (Barthes, 78) then this is one place in which we can allow ourselves to recognize his shaping presence during the process of revision.

How much of the Q1 playtext did Webster examine in the printshop? The strong probability that he worked closely on the H1^v–H2^r scene opening does not necessarily mean that he corrected the entire text with equal care. As Peter Blayney has noted, printshop correction was a laborious process involving almost as many repeat trips to the shop as there are formes in any given edition, since formes were printed off at the rate of perhaps three or four per week and printers rarely had a sufficient store of type to keep more than a few formes in type simultaneously. Proofsheets could also be delivered to authors, although they too would probably have arrived at the rate of one sheet at a time over several weeks (Blayney, 60–88, 188–218). Q1 outer formes A and G show three stages of revision, the third of which is termed Q1c. For Webster to have corrected those formes, he would doubtless have been obliged to conduct not one but two checks of the proofsheets. Most of the emendations to *Malfi* were probably made by proofreaders or even revising compositors in the printing-house, and carry no particular authority. There are changes to one or two formes besides inner H that could be authorial – especially the addition of another crucial stage direction, '*Ferdinand giues her a ponyard*' at F4ʳ. But that addition, like any of the other added stage directions, could have been made by the printer or proofreader to rectify a compositor's failure to include a marginal notation found in the printing-house copy. There are also many changes to the rest of the playtext that are fairly neutral, such as 'ta'ne' in Q1a becoming 'taine' in Q1b, or 'what troope' in Q1a becoming 'what a troope' in Q1b, or 'Liuory' in Q1a and Q1b becoming 'Liuery' in Q1c. These changes probably reflect the tastes of the in-house proofreader rather than intervention by the author.

In a few cases, the 'corrections' seem to make matters worse, by which I mean that they seem to work against the push towards specificity and aesthetic discrimination that appears to associate elements of Q1b specifically with Webster. The most obvious of these is the change from 'pewterers' (Q1a) to 'painters' (Q1b) in G4ᵛ. This occurs at 3.3.19, where the despised Count Malateste is described by his fellow soldiers as having gone to war only in the comically indirect sense that he has hired 'pewterers' to make toy soldiers so that he can consult the news sheets for details of military engagements and then reproduce them as 'battles in model'. 'Pewterers' is far preferable in its quirky specificity to the revised, much vaguer 'painters' (Q1b) and accords better with the play's many other references to metal objects and mechanical devices – bullets, pistols, chained cannonballs, wire-drawers, 'enginous wheels' (see 3.2.176n.). But 'painters' is the reading adopted by every noteworthy editor of the play after Alexander Dyce (1830) with the exception of Martin W. Sampson (1904) on grounds that replacing 'pewterers' with 'painters' must be Webster's own revision. 'Painters' could, perhaps, have represented a failure of nerve on Webster's part, but it is more likely to reflect a failure of comprehension on the part of a proofreader or revising compositor. Similarly, at 3.2.201 Q1a reads 'A-loath' ('A-loth') while Q1b reads 'As loath' ('As loth'). 'As loath' sounds more modern and therefore, to modern ears, more correct. But the word 'as' occurs again later in the same sentence, creating awkwardness in the diction, and the dialectal form *a-* at the beginning of a word occurs at several other points in the play (*a-cold*, 1.2.338; *A-many*, 4.2.194, etc.). This case is somewhat murkier, and obviously we cannot assume that our own aesthetic judgements of the variants will replicate the author's. But, if we measure the two readings against the type of revisions we know he had a hand in, 'A-loath' is more likely to be Webster. Strong evidence of the author's participation in one stage of the proofreading process is no reason to credit him with all of it.

My base text for this edition is British Library 644.f.72 – a good copy that consists largely of pages in their revised Q1b and Q1c states but is also one of only eight extant copies to preserve the original Q1a state instead of the questionable Q1b alterations that I have just argued should be rejected. This copy also has the advantage of being widely available to readers who would like to compare my edition against the original, since it is the copy reproduced on EEBO, available through major research libraries and many universities. As is characteristic of other recent editors with a strong interest in book history and the material form of early printed texts, I follow the language of my base text very closely – some will complain slavishly – giving it the benefit of the doubt in all uncertain cases and emending only very reluctantly, when I cannot make sense of its readings. Because the stages of revision are of particular interest, my textual notes record all the Q1a, Q1b and Q1c variants except for obvious corrections of typographic errors; however, it is important for readers to bear in mind that these notations do not refer to specific copies of Q1 but rather to stages of revision that exist almost at random among printed copies because corrected sheets were freely mixed with uncorrected sheets in assembling the complete quarto. A full list of the press variants as they exist in twenty-nine copies of Q1 is given in Gunby, 576–80 (see also Brown, 'Printing' 1 and 2).

From the perspective of recent scholars interested in the material book, editors of Webster have, in general, been too quick to emend readings of the play that may initially appear to be errors but that, in their very eccentricity, can serve as clues to interpretation. A case in point is Ferdinand's statement, in conversation with his sister the Duchess at 3.1.38–40, 'I'll instantly to bed, / For I am weary. I am to be – bespeak / A husband for you.' Previous editors, beginning with the printers of the play's Second Quarto (Q2, 1640), have altered 'be – bespeak' to 'bespeak', assuming that the preceding word 'be' simply represents a false start on the part of the compositor. I preserve the Q1 reading on the grounds that it may well offer the deliberate record of a slip (of the type that we now call Freudian) by Ferdinand. At many points in the play, whether we happen to be Freudians or not, there is strong evidence of Ferdinand's strong incestuous attraction for his sister (see 2.5.47n., 2.5.63–6n., 3.2.59 SDn., 4.1.33n. and 4.2.249n.). The passage in which he says he'll go to bed, then that he'll be, or rather bespeak, a husband for her is one of those points, and deserves not to be edited out of existence.

Similarly, at 1.2.6 and 123 Antonio is called by the name's feminine form 'Antonia'. In both cases the printers of Q2 emended to 'Antonio', a reading followed in modern editions. At 1.2.123–4, Antonio's friend Delio reproaches him for waxing too fulsome in his praise of the Duchess: 'Fie, Antonia! / You play the wire-drawer with her commendations.' Is 'Antonia' a mere compositorial error, or is Delio making a point about Antonio's lack of masculinity in his evident adulation of the Duchess, a point that would resonate strongly during later portions of the play in which Antonio seems vacillating or evasive? The other case at 1.2.6 is less obvious in its gender implications: Ferdinand asks who won the tilting and Sylvia replies, in Q1, '*Antonia Bologna* (my Lord)'. But even here the feminized form of his name may be a clue to the courtiers' subtle deprecation of Antonio, the outsider, onstage. Q1 was published when the *Hic Mulier/Haec Vir* controversy – a battle of books between misogynists and defenders of women – was at its height.[1] The same Nicholas Okes who printed *Malfi* in 1623 had also printed the proto-feminist Rachel Speght's 1617 book, *A Mouzell for Melastomus*, refuting the anti-feminist John Swetnam's *Arraignment of Lewd, Idle, Froward and Unconstant Women* (1615). Questions of gender definition were very much in the air at the period. Indeed, Webster's play, with its valorization of a 'woman on top', could well have been viewed by contemporaries as a dramatic contribution to the debate, and the gender anomalies of its text are therefore worth preserving in our modern editions. The name 'Antonia' in 1.2.6 subtly (or blatantly) detracts from Antonio's victory in the tilting even as he is honoured for it. There are other cases when I have similarly gone against recent editorial tradition in preferring Q1 readings; these are recorded in the textual notes and many are also discussed in the commentary.

Another area in which I have been unusually faithful to my copy-text is in my preservation of Q1 act and scene divisions. Most editors follow these quite precisely, with one prominent exception: where Q1 creates a second scene in act 1 at the point (after 1.1.82) where the Duchess's courtiers come onstage and Delio says, 'The presence 'gins to fill' (1.2.1), most modern editors treat Q1's second scene as a continuation of the first on the grounds that the stage has never emptied and a scene break is therefore not required. As rationale for this emendation, editors have typically argued that either the compositors or the transcribers of the copy they were working from could easily have mistaken the entrance of a number of characters together for a mass entrance like those that characterize scene openings in the Q1 text (Brennan, 118 [1.2n.]; Gunby, 587, n. 77.1). (A 'mass entrance' is a list at the beginning of a scene of all the characters

---

1 For background on the controversy, see Katherine Henderson and Barbara F. McManus, *Half Humankind: Contexts and Texts of the Controversy about Women in England 1540–1640* (Urbana: University of Illinois Press, 1985).

who will appear in it, as will be discussed below.) This argument by previous editors, however, sits uncomfortably alongside their fidelity to Q1b's verbal emendations on the basis that Webster himself is likely to have either approved or initiated them. If the author was alert enough to recognize and call for alteration of so many other misreadings, even going to the trouble of disavowing some of the verses and inserting stage directions himself, would he not have caught something as blatant as an erroneous scene division? The page in question could easily have been corrected, if it were necessary, without troubling the typesetting of the rest of the forme in which it appeared. It is true that 1.1 ends without any indication of an '*Exeunt*' by Antonio and Delio, but that omission in 1.1 cannot be taken as significant evidence, since missing exits are one of the commonest omissions in early modern play quartos. Q1 2.3 similarly closes without a marked exit for Bosola, even though the following scene begins with an entirely different set of characters.

All of the early quartos of *Malfi* call for a new scene at 1.2 – even the Fourth Quarto (Q4, 1708), which claims to print the play as it was performed in 1707 and records numerous cuts and added stage directions that give us a fairly clear picture of the play in performance at that time (see p. 96) The editorial practice of combining 1.1 and 1.2 into a single scene appears to date only to the nineteenth century, where both of Alexander Dyce's editions (1830 and 1857) make the change without comment. The first nineteenth-century revival of the play, a wildly popular adaptation by R. H. Horne performed by Samuel Phelps's company at Sadler's Wells in 1850–1, follows Dyce in combining the two scenes into one, and Horne's text was gradually codified through the rest of the nineteenth century (McLuskie and Uglow, 24–31, 75n.; Horne). However, the fact that Q1 of *The Duchess of Malfi* is divided into acts in its earliest printed text suggests that it, like other King's Men plays written after the company took over the Blackfriars theatre in 1609, was designed with five-act performance in mind rather than the continuous, uninterrupted performance style that had characterized earlier King's Men plays written for the public theatre. At Blackfriars theatre, there were musical intervals between acts, and after 1608 this convention gradually extended to the public theatres as well. As Gary Taylor convincingly argues, after 1608 the earlier public-theatre 'law of re-entry', requiring an actor who had exited at the end of one act not to enter at the beginning of the next in the interest of dramatic verisimilitude, no longer applied (Taylor and Jowett, 3–50). A similar release from earlier restrictions appears to have obtained between scenes within a single act, as can be seen in Shakespeare's *Winter's Tale* (1610), where Camillo and Archidamus first enter together to comment on the court of Sicily, then exit at the end of 1.1 and immediately re-enter along with the rest of the court at 1.2 (Brown, 14, n. 82.1).

The Q1 scene break between 1.1 and 1.2 in *Malfi* serves important theatrical functions and should therefore be preserved as a clue to early performance. There are a number of points in the play where Antonio and Delio, who are close friends and confidants, serve as a chorus, establishing in conversation with each other a perspective that often differs markedly from those of other characters onstage and is usually quite trustworthy. Their choric comments similarly initiate acts 3 and 5. Having 1.1 and 1.2 both begin with the entrance of Antonio and Delio as commentators helps to establish this choric function for the audience at the very beginning of the action. Then too, in the Q1 arrangement of 1.1 and 1.2, as in *Winter's Tale*, the change in scenes signals a change in perspective. First in 1.1 the audience sees the pair of friends as outsiders looking in on the Duchess's court from a distance and shares their point of view, watching the parade of courtiers heading for court and hearing Antonio and Delio's caustic moral commentary on each as the courtiers pass by. Then the two friends exit and the stage empties. In 1.2, by contrast, we are in the thick of things, in the Duchess's crowded audience chamber, and see Antonio plunged into the midst of the court, interacting with the Duchess's courtiers and her brother Ferdinand.

Any argument relying on the timing of entrances in *Malfi* is, however, bound to be conjectural because the Q1 text, probably based on a transcript by Ralph Crane, has only mass entrances listing all the characters at the beginning of each scene rather than individual stage directions indicating each character's entrance as it would have occurred in performance. These mass entrances list with a fair degree of accuracy all the characters who will be present onstage during the scene, but with no clue other than the order in which they are listed as to the precise points at which they will enter. Ralph Crane was a theatrical scrivener whose activities we can document from 1618 to the mid- to late 1620s. His copy for *Malfi* has not survived, but the characteristics of Q1 are so similar to playtexts for which Crane transcriptions have survived that recent editors, myself included, feel fairly confident in attributing the copy behind Q1 to him – or to someone with a strikingly similar set of habits, one of which was a frequent preference for mass entrances.

We do not know certainly why Crane liked mass entrances. Perhaps he thought they made the playtext more accessible to readers; perhaps, basing himself on editions of classical dramatists and also printed plays of John Lyly and Ben Jonson, he thought mass entrances gave the texts an aura of artistic distinction in keeping with the rising status of the theatre and its textual afterlives during the early decades of the seventeenth century (Howard-Hill, 20–1). At any rate, the mass entrances in Q1 *Malfi*, along with a paucity of stage directions of all kinds, give modern editors and performers much mystification and also much freedom.

It would be fair to say that no two editors of *Malfi* are in precise agreement about the timing of entrances and exits beyond those of characters who initiate each scene and those whose exits are specified in Q1, and productions of the play also vary widely in their placement of entrances and exits.

Traditionally, editors have felt obliged to create a definitive version of the play, specifying stage action quite closely, even though their textual basis for doing so was, perforce, somewhat shaky. Like other revisionists, I have tried for a bit more openness, accompanying my own directions for entrances and exits with commentary notes indicating how other editors and performances have conceptualized and timed them differently, to a variety of theatrical effects.[1] Since the field of possible editorial choices is so wide and eclectic, it has not proved practical to record all variant stage directions in the textual notes. Beyond the early quartos, I list only the most influential stage directions in the textual notes and discuss the rest in more general terms in the commentary.

Malfi is a play that thematizes suspicion, paranoia, whispering, the 'whispering room' (a favourite image: see 1.2.249 and 3.2.259), spying and 'information'. The subject of who hears (or overhears) whom is therefore of particular interest to readers or producers of the play. In the absence of marked Q1 entrances, the only way we know for sure that any given character has entered is if he or she speaks, is spoken to, or is referred to as present by another character already onstage. At several points in the play a character enters, but we can't be certain how much of the speech preceding his own initial words he has been able to hear. For example, at 3.2, when Ferdinand surprises the Duchess alone in her bedroom, editors have varied widely in timing his entrance, and the precise language on which he enters can be crucial for fine-tuning readers' or spectators' understanding of his state of mind (see 3.2.59 SDn.). Similarly, in an action that parallels Ferdinand's surprise entry in 3.2, Bosola enters unseen by the Cardinal at 5.4 and overhears the Cardinal plotting his death. But how much does Bosola hear? By the degree to which editors specify where a given character is at the moment that others speak, and precisely who speaks to

---

1   See also McLuskie and Uglow, which contains a text of the play with useful running commentary on details of a number of performances.

whom, they can regulate and to some extent dampen the play's pervading atmosphere of paranoia and uncertainty. In keeping with the Arden emphasis on theatrical practices, I prefer to leave many of these scenes open and undecided, eschewing as much as possible stage directions of the type that clarify the flow of speech and information, except in so far as I discuss them in the commentary. For example, most recent editors have Antonio and the Duchess exit together at the end of 1.2, before Cariola's final lines lamenting the Duchess's combined 'greatness' and 'madness' in contracting her secret marriage with Antonio. But Q1's final stage direction '*Exeunt*' suggests that all three of them leave together. Much is to be gained by leaving open the possibility that Antonio and the Duchess hear, or overhear, or hear in part, what Cariola has to say. The only exceptions I make to my preference for openness relate to stage directions that I include because they resonate strongly with the use of props at other points in the play, as discussed above (pp. 43–4): Antonio's jewel, Ferdinand's stolen key, the Cardinal's discarded book.

For the same reasons, I do not indicate theatrical asides in my text of the play, except by following the Arden practice of using dashes to indicate a change in addressee. To mark a speech in a stage direction as a formal 'aside' is to make a number of assumptions about the specificity and exclusiveness of human communication that *Malfi*, with its emphasis on spying, 'intelligence' and the loss of personal boundaries, fails to confirm. There is only one place where the Q1 text may indicate through punctuation something like what we understand to be a theatrical aside – where Antonio, speaking to Bosola, says, 'This mole does undermine me' (2.3.14), a phrase set off by parentheses in Q1. The first marked asides in printed editions of the play do not appear until Q4, and even in that relatively late text there are only four – three by Bosola, at 2.1.152, 2.1.160 and 2.2.35–6; and one by Antonio, 'This fellow will undo me', at 2.3.29. In reading or staging the play we need to imagine ourselves in a world in which our modern assurance of civilized boundaries between people does not reliably exist, and in which the conventionalized luxury of the aside – speaking onstage without the possibility (or suspicion?) of being overheard by others onstage – is available to none of its characters.

Another characteristic feature of Crane transcriptions that has created problems and opportunities for editors is that, however carefully they have been produced, many of the surviving Crane copies are unclear about the distinction between prose and verse. Typically, as was common in manuscript materials of the period, Crane did not capitalize the initial word of verse lines, so that one potential typographic marker of verse is simply unavailable to readers. A sequence of long verse lines in a Crane transcription can look sufficiently like prose for it to be distinguishable as verse only by its metre. In addition, Crane was casual in transcribing short lines – even in an otherwise polished transcription often it is impossible to be certain whether short lines are meant to be prose or verse, or whether Crane even cared.

If Crane failed to capitalize initial words of verse lines, the Q1 printers over-compensated by capitalizing the initial word of nearly every first line, irrespective of whether it is verse or prose. By my count, if we exclude stage directions and the horoscope read by Bosola, which is clearly prose, there are only twelve lines in the play that are printed with initial minuscule as opposed to majuscule letters – just enough to convince us that the compositors understood the functioning of initial capitals in theory, but not enough to remotely approximate consistency in practice. In addition, there are many run-on lines of verse, and even cases where varying line lengths within a given speech appear to signal a shift from prose to verse or vice versa, but without any perceptible correlation between the printed line breaks and the metrical structure that verse would require. When it comes to lineation and versification, Q1's printing practices are sufficiently chaotic for me to be willing to depart radically from my base text, particularly if doing so will illuminate aspects of Webster's habitual practice that modern readers will have difficulty hearing unless they are made evident on the page.

With the exception of Ben Jonson, most dramatists of the period seem to have been fairly indifferent as to how their language was arranged on the printed page. Hamlet referred to 'hearing' a play, not seeing it: the sound of the verse was clearly highly significant to the spectator's experience of a play. But, as numerous dramatists complained, the printed playtext could be no more than a mere skeletal after-image of what John Marston called the '*soule of lively action*' possessed by the play onstage, in part because the printed text had lost the sound of the words in performance.[1] It seems that most dramatists of the period – and, if Ralph Crane is a representative example, most copyists as well – did not consider it crucial or perhaps even possible to require the printed record of the play to conform to a notational scheme that precisely reproduced the rhythmic patterns of the language as read or acted. The job of the editor in cases like the Q1 *Malfi* is therefore to create a lineation that captures for modern readers as much as possible the rhythmic brilliance and variety of Webster's language as it might have been heard by theatre-goers of his own time – people for whom a printed quarto text was at best little more than a plodding and de-animated afterlife of what had sounded onstage.

John Webster was highly experimental in his versification, as in most other aspects of his flamboyant, eccentric achievement as a dramatist. Thomas Middleton's commendatory verses to Q1 praise him particularly for his plain style: 'Thy note / Be ever plainness – 'tis the richest coat' (p. 123). By 'plainness' he did not mean monotony; every bit as much as John Donne, Webster

---

1 John Marston, *The Malcontent* (1604), sig. A4ʳ. Webster himself supplied an 'Induction' and other additions to the play that appear in this edition. See Webster, 3.315–56. For other contemporary sentiment like Marston's, see Marcus, *Unediting*, 160–8.

deserved hanging, as Ben Jonson put the matter, for not 'keeping of accent'. Webster regularly introduces hexameter lines into passages that would otherwise represent fairly regular iambic pentameter (see, for example, 3.2.320, 3.3.19, 4.1.76–7). He has a distinct fondness for sudden lines of anapaestic (more rarely, dactylic) pentameter or hexameter, which speed up or retard the pace of the verse as in Bosola's 'Sure, your pístol holds nóthing but pérfumes or kíssing cómfits' (5.2.150). Sometimes lines that are mostly anapaests are shared among speakers, giving an almost Molièresque brilliance to repartee onstage, as in a witty exchange between the Duchess and Antonio during the marriage scene (1.2.302–4):

ANTONIO
    I'd have you first provide for a good husband:
    Give him all.
DUCHESS   All?
ANTONIO   Yes, your excellent self.
DUCHESS   In a winding sheet?
ANTONIO
    In a couple.
DUCHESS   St Winfred! That were a strange will!

Another of Webster's characteristic tricks is to deliberately deprive a line of one or more metrical feet to allow for stage business, create special emphasis or indicate a change of emotional direction. Quite frequently, particularly in interchanges between speakers, these missing feet correspond to what we would now call one or more theatrical 'beats', creating tense pauses that, in the particular context of this play, can intensify our perception of nervousness or even paranoia onstage. Frequently lines are shared between speakers in a way that calls attention to missing metrical units. And, as if these effects were not enough, Webster also intermingles rugged verse with highly rhythmic prose in a way that makes a clear dividing line between verse and prose arbitrary at best. Sometimes we can see him sliding gradually from verse into prose: the initial line of a prose speech will match the iambic pentameter of verse lines that have gone before it, then the speaker will, as it were, tumble into prose. And Bosola, master change-artist that he is, can switch between prose and verse more than once within a single speech.

Most previous editors have been cautious in attempting to render the sound of Webster's language, resorting to prose when confronted with highly irregular verse which is, nevertheless, verse. Much of the most metrically irregular verse comes from Bosola, but occasionally, as though by contagion, it spills over into the speech of other characters. Modern readers tend to perceive Webster's prose as rhythmically flatter than his verse, and we certainly have difficulty with the interactions between characters who seem to speak in a rhythmic no man's land between prose and verse (as in largely satiric passages such as 1.2.1–65, 2.1.1–68 and 3.2.208–76). In order to keep as much as possible of the tension between an expectation of metrical regularity and Webster's metrical experimentation alive for readers, I have kept as much of the play as reasonably possible in verse. Some of the verse is brilliant and quick, some of it is lumbering and ungainly, but we have the best chance of perceiving Webster's astonishing metrical range if we see his verse passages arranged on the page as verse.

Here is an example from one of Ferdinand's 'mad' speeches from 5.2.41–5, printed by most previous editors as prose but also capable of being heard as verse. This is how it appears in Q1:

> *Ferd.* *T*o drive six Snailes before me, from this towne
>   *To Mosco*; neither use Goad, nor Whip to them,
>   But let them take their owne time: (the patientest
>   man i'th' world
>   Match me for an experiment) and I'll crawle after
>   Like a sheepe-biter.

In Brown's edition it appears in prose:

> *Ferd.* To drive six snails before me, from this town to Moscow; neither use goad nor whip to them, but let them take their own time:– the patient'st man i'th' world match me for an experiment – and I'll crawl after like a sheep-biter.

This edition uses verse lines as follows:

> FERDINAND
> To drive six snails before me from this town
> To Moscow, neither use goad nor whip to them,
> But let them take their own time (the patientest man
> I'th' world match me for an experiment!)
> And I'll crawl after like a sheep-biter.

As prose the passage moves fairly quickly; as verse it is irregular but clearly recognizable as iambic pentameter; it has an eerie suspension and deliberateness that go along with mad Ferdinand's claim of 'patience'.

Such a judgement is, of course, highly subjective, but there is some evidence that our own frequent puzzlement over Webster's irregular metrics has been shared by earlier readers and performers. Here are three versions (Q1, Norton and Q4) of part of a famous speech by Bosola which is occasionally printed as prose, but which most editors, throwing up their hands in despair, print as verse, following the lineation in Q1. That is the tactic adopted in the present edition. Bosola is describing Antonio's virtues to the Duchess in 3.2.244–8 – telling the truth but with lying intent, since his goal is to seduce her into trusting him.

> *Bos.* Sure he was too honest: *Pluto* the god of riches,
> When he's sent (by *Jupiter*) to any man
> He goes limping, to signifie that wealth
> That comes on god's name, comes slowly; but when he's sent

One the divells arrand, he rides poast, and comes
   in by scuttles:

(Q1)

BOSOLA. Sure, he was too honest. Pluto, the god of
riches, when he's sent by Jupiter to any man, he goes
limping, to signify that wealth that comes on God's
name comes slowly; but when he's sent on the Devil's
errand, he rides post and comes in by scuttles.

(Norton)

Bos. Sure he was too honest. "*Pluto* the God of Riches,
   "When he is sent, by *Jupiter*, to any Man,
   "He goes limping, to signify that Wealth
   "That comes on God's Name, comes slowly; but when
      he's sent
   "On the Devil's Errand, he rides Post, and comes in
      by Scuttles.

(Q4)

Q4 prints the full passage, but the double quotations around all
the words after 'Sure he was too honest' indicate that they were
omitted in performance in the early eighteenth century, as were
most of Bosola's other highly irregular lines from the same scene
and other metrically difficult passages elsewhere in the play. The
penultimate line in the excerpt can be understood as a mix of
iambics and anapaests, with major accents on 'comes', 'God's',
'slow-', 'when' and 'sent'. But the final line is harder to cram into
reasonable anapaests with major stresses on 'De-', 'Er-', 'Post',
'in' and 'Scu-'. It is almost as though Bosola were testing the
limits of the line.

   By the time of Q4, it would appear, theatrical companies
were sufficiently uncomfortable with some of Webster's most
daring breaches of metrics that they were willing simply to
excise the offending lines. It would be unwise to contend
that uncouth metrics was their only reason for doing so, since

they cut many metrically regular lines as well. However, the lurching metrics of the verse lines fit well with the vexed musings of the unreliable Bosola, whose verse in the play is often so irregular that it hovers on the brink of prose or even spills over into it. By being required to read the passage as verse we are forced to cope with the tension between its expected and its actual metrics. In the case of Bosola, Webster uses this tension to suggest a similar lack of congruence between language and intent. Which is not to suggest that Webster offers any sort of easy equivalence between moral compromise and irregular versification – only that his metrics are one of the many areas of the play in which he flouts conventional expectations to keep readers and viewers off balance in productive ways.

If Webster's verse often sounds like prose, his prose is often almost indistinguishable from verse. In order to preserve the gradual 'falling into prose' effect I referred to above, I have occasionally printed the first lines of otherwise prose speeches as verse in order to indicate how easily they can be heard as verse. Cf. 'One would suspect it for a shop of witchcraft' (2.1.40), 'Give me leave to be honest in any phrase' (2.1.92) or 'With all your divinity, do but direct me the way to it' (1.1.41) – a near-perfect line of anapaestic pentameter. Readers will readily find lines, particularly in the borderline areas between verse and prose, where they disagree with my judgement and would prefer a different arrangement of words to capture Webster's rhythmic effects on the page.

The matter of missing beats is also worth illustrating, though here the point of contention is not between prose and verse but rather between lines of speech shared by two or more characters. Not infrequently, a verse line shared between characters lacks one or more metrical feet. Sometimes the apparent lacuna allows time for stage business, as in 2.4.39, where a missing beat between Julia's speech and the Cardinal's reply appears to provide a break for offstage knocking.

JULIA

And spake like one in physic.   [*Knocking*]

CARDINAL

Who's that?

Another example occurs at 1.2.8, where a missing beat within Ferdinand's speech allows time for one of his followers to give Antonio the jewel he has won in the tilting: 'Give him the jewel. [beat] When shall we leave'. Sometimes Webster uses missing beats between speakers to indicate shock, as in the two missing feet between the Duchess's 'Whom? and Ferdinand's 'Call them your children' during the tense scene in which he is about to give her a dead man's hand and then display the children as corpses (4.1.32–4). I have freely parcelled out part-lines between speakers in order to indicate this tension, which is lost or at least attenuated if the speeches are set out merely as two separate short lines. Here is the interchange between the Duchess and Ferdinand treated in both ways so readers can see whether they detect a difference:

FERDINAND

For I account it the honourablest revenge,
Where I may kill, to pardon. Where are your
cubs?

DUCHESS

Whom?

FERDINAND   Call them your children;

(two part-lines, as printed in this edition)

FERDINAND

For I account it the honourablest revenge,
Where I may kill, to pardon. Where are your
cubs?

DUCHESS

Whom?

FERDINAND

Call them your children

(rejected alternative of two short lines)

Webster's missing 'beats' can suggest unease, shock or deep thought. They are key elements in his ability to generate emotional power.

Beyond the 1623 quarto, there are three other significant early texts of *Malfi*: the quartos of 1640, 1678 and 1708. All are of some interest, though none carries any particular textual authority. The Second Quarto (Q2) of 1640 advertises the play as 'approvedly well acted at the Black-Friers / By his Majesties Servants' and keeps the First Quarto's claim to include passages 'that the length of the Play would not beare in the Presentment'. The year 1640 was a time of national crisis, a year that many would date as the actual beginning of the English Civil War. In April Charles I was forced to recall Parliament after an eleven-year gap, to finance the Bishops' Wars (1639–40) against the Scots in his attempt to impose episcopacy and the new Anglican Book of Common Prayer upon Scotland. Instead of being granted the funds, he faced such a flood of petitions against royal abuses of power that after three weeks he dissolved what was subsequently named the Short Parliament. The episcopal policies of William Laud (see p. 32), the anti-Puritan, high-church Archbishop of Canterbury, were increasingly under fire in England, and Laud would be impeached and arrested the following year. When Charles called what later became known as the Long Parliament in November 1640, to raise money after the defeat of the English army against the Scots, Parliament passed legislation limiting royal prerogative powers and lifting traditional Stuart mechanisms for censorship of printed texts. The 1640 quarto of *Malfi* is the only one not to associate the play closely with specific performances through roughly contemporary cast lists: it simply reprints the cast list and actors' names from Q1. It was, I contend, published at that particular time largely for political reasons. Its printer, John Raworth, and his wife Ruth, who succeeded him after his death, were closely associated with the parliamentary cause, printing its ordinances, John Knox's history of Scotland and a number of other politically charged works, later including some by John Milton. By 1640, the play's portrayal of the Cardinal and his poisoned book doubtless resonated with the public outcry against Archbishop Laud, the imposition of the Book of Common Prayer and what were perceived by the more radical Protestants as a series of crypto-Catholic outrages against 'the godly'.

As it happens, Q2 contains 'errors' that might encourage a specifically anti-Laudian and anti-absolutist reading of the play. In all the early quartos it is Antonio, not the Duchess, who urges the adoption of the French fashion of keeping hats on before the prince (2.1.125ff.) – a comment that could easily have resonated with growing English and Scottish disrespect for Charles I. But there are other strategic Q2 omissions from the Q1 text that suggest a heightened disrespect for 'authority' in the 1640 text. Q1 has Bosola exclaiming at 3.2.279–82, 'Can this ambitious age / Have so much goodness in't as to prefer / A man merely for worth, without these shadows / Of wealth and painted honours?' Q2 drops 'A man merely for worth, without these shadows' and thus reads as a sardonic indictment: 'Can this ambitious age / Have so much goodness in't as to prefer / Of wealth and painted honours?' Castruccio's speech at 1.2.10–11 urging Ferdinand, 'you should not desire to go / To war in person', reads instead in Q2, 'you should desire' – an alteration that does not relate in any meaningful way to Ferdinand within the play, but perhaps instead reflects the increasing militancy of radical Protestants in 1640. Taken together, these 'errors' and others like them may be deliberate alterations by the printer that move the 1640 text even further than Q1 in the direction of anti-ecclesiastical, anti-absolutist and pro-war Protestant sentiment. So that interested readers can examine the evidence for themselves, I include all of Q2's verbal variants in the textual notes.

Q2 also exists in a second issue (Wing 1222), with remaining sheets of Raworth's 1640 text and a new title-page which does not offer a date but must be from some time in the early 1660s (when *Malfi* was revived on the Restoration stage) since it describes the play as printed 'As it was Acted by his late Majesties Servants at Black Fryers with great Applause, Thirty Years since. / And now Acted by his Highnesse the Duke of *York*'s Servants'. This reissue, at least in the Harvard Houghton Library copy that I have seen, does not include the cast list that had been reproduced in 1640. It sold, according to the title-page, for one shilling.

The third edition, Q3, followed in 1678, calling the play on its much abbreviated title-page 'The Dutchess of Malfey: A Tragedy. / As it is now ACTEED at the Dukes Theater' and specifying that it was to be sold in Covent Garden but nowhere mentioning the author's name. Q3 reproduces Q2, preserving almost all its variant readings, albeit with the usual number of corrections and misprints. It is of interest now for its contemporary cast list, which reworks the list from Q1 and Q2 to put Ferdinand first (where Bosola was before) and gives the names of Restoration actors who performed in the play during the early 1660s, including Mr and Mrs Betterton as Bosola and the Duchess respectively (see pp. 95–6). The textual notes record Q3 readings only occasionally, where they form part of a noteworthy pattern of revisions among the first four quartos.

The Fourth Quarto, Q4 (1708), is of considerably more interest, since it offers a new, alternative, title bringing in Ferdinand and the Cardinal, but in a way that casts the Duchess clearly as their victim – 'The *Unfortunate Dutchess of* Malfey, or The Unnatural Brothers: A Tragedy'. Q4 offers a new cast list with actors' names, so that through the four quartos we can trace the play's early performers with an unusual degree of detail. Q4 also features a thorough reworking of the text, with many alterations in wording, most of them to avoid sexual references that were seen as too explicit and other breaches of politeness, or to update the language: Q4 reads 'thing' instead of Q1's 'ruff', since ruffs would no longer be worn on the stage in the early 1700s, 'surgeons' instead of 'Chyrurgeons', 'sparks' instead of 'gallants', 'speaks' instead of 'speaketh', 'camp' instead of 'leaguer', 'informer' instead of 'intelligencer', 'fiddle' instead of 'lute-string', and so on. In addition, we can clearly trace two stages of revision in Q4. The playtext is much shortened, omitting many lines and passages, particularly irrelevant joking among courtiers, and a whole scene (3.4). In addition, on the page titled 'The Actors Names' it also offers a note on performance: 'Those Lines which were omitted in the Acting, by reason of the Length of the Play, are marked with (").' Between that second set of omissions from performance and the numerous added stage directions, the most famous of which is the comical evocation of the doctor in Ferdinand's mad scene (5.2) as taking '*off his four Cloaks one after another*' in order to do battle with the madman, Q4 offers unprecedentedly full evidence of one shape the play took in performance.

Q4 does not give us an authoritative text if by 'authoritative' we mean in any way endorsed by the author or based on some authorial document. But it is intriguingly possible that the omissions from Q4 provide clues to Q1's omissions in performance, which are referred to on the Q1 title-page but nowhere indicated within the playtext itself. At the very least, the Q4 omissions allow us to track two levels of priority, showing which parts of the play were considered indispensable in performance. Quite possibly, given the regularity with which *Malfi* was staged during the seventeenth century, the Q4 omissions could register a performance history going back before the Interregnum and perhaps as far back as the earliest productions of the play. The theatres were closed from 1642 to 1660. After the Restoration in 1660, William Davenant acquired the right to stage *The Duchess of Malfi*. At any point between the 1630s, when he began to make his mark on the London theatrical scene, and the death in 1653 of John Lowin, who had played Bosola in early productions of the play, Davenant could have been in close contact with Lowin. According to Restoration tradition, Davenant picked up many ideas about staging Shakespeare and other pre-war dramatists directly from Lowin (Gurr, *Company*, 205–9). Because of the extraordinary interest of Q4 readings for theatrical historians and anyone else interested in the shape the play took on the seventeenth- and early eighteenth-century stage, I have recorded all the significant textual differences between Q1 and Q4 in the textual notes. Materials omitted from the text as published are recorded in the textual notes as '*om. Q4*', and materials present in the Q4 text but marked there as omitted in performance are recorded as '*om. in performance Q4*'.

As already noted, *Malfi* is a play full of echoes – not only the literal Echo of 5.3 but the 'echo' of stolen information and numerous 'echoes' in the action onstage, in which one scene repeats another with variations to powerful effect (see pp. 42–4). Webster also includes a number of *sententiae* or commonplaces that may well have been recognized as such and therefore as a form of echo by early readers or spectators. Most of these appear at the end of speeches by major characters or at the end of scenes, and they often take the form of rhymed couplets, as in Antonio's 'The great are like the base; nay, they are the same / When they seek shameful ways to avoid shame' (2.3.51–2). These *sententiae* are punctuated in Q1 by double quotation marks at the beginning of each line, by italic type, or by both. Among the first four quartos there are interesting variations in the treatment of such passages. Q2 will frequently follow Q1, Q3 will sometimes leave the passages unmarked, while Q4 will mark them with italics or use double quotation marks to show that they were omitted in performance. (We can only hope that Q4's creators were consistent in their usage and did not at any point inadvertently preserve double quotation marks from an earlier quarto for a passage they wished to mark as a commonplace rather than as a passage omitted in performance.) Here, I indicate a number of the variable treatments of *sententiae* across the early quartos in the textual notes. In the text, I use single quotation marks for all the passages marked in Q1 as *sententiae*, whether Q1 punctuates them with quotation marks or with italic type. I also depart from Q1 in using quotation marks rather than italics for Echo's speeches in 5.3 in order to highlight the similarities between her speeches and the 'echoing' commonplaces elsewhere in the play that make it a veritable 'whispering room'.

Everywhere in the edition except in the textual notes and in references to them, I have modernized u/v and i/j in citations. In this edition I have tried to make the textual notes as accessible as possible for readers not familiar with the arcana of textual notation. Original spellings in Q1 readings are recorded, according to standard Arden practice, in italic parentheses. Frequently repeated Q1 spellings are signalled only at their first occurrence and marked with a plus sign. All the abbreviations in the textual notes are listed along with other abbreviations on p. 405. Ralph Crane had the habit of using hyphens between words in his transcriptions, particularly at the end of rhyming lines. I have recorded these in the textual notes where they seemed to me to be significant, but not otherwise. Crane also had the habit of using many apostrophes, particularly for words ending in '-ed'. I have recorded in the textual notes the Q1 words containing apostrophes that are not preserved in the modernized text only in cases where the Q1 spelling may give us important clues about pronunciation of the words and therefore also about metre and lineation. Similarly, I preserve aberrant forms of names where they seem to influence the metrics. If, for example, 'St Winfred' (1.2.304) elides the 'i' in 'Winifred', that may signal that the name was pronounced onstage as a disyllabic. Such evidence can never be conclusive, but it is suggestive enough to be worth documenting. My textual notes do not ordinarily record Q1 punctuation, but, if my modernized text departs from Q1 punctuation in a way that significantly influences meaning, I indicate the original punctuation in the notes. Generally in the textual notes a failure to document variant readings from all the first four quartos indicates that the readings remain the same, or substantially so. I hope readers will find relatively few cases in which important omissions are instead a result of my own error. As Bosola complains in the play, though in a rather more portentous context, the best intentions do not necessarily guarantee the best outcome.

EARLY PERFORMANCES AND AFTERLIVES

We are not certain precisely when *Malfi* was first performed, but it must have been before the death of actor William Ostler, a shareholder in the King's Men, who appears in the Q1 cast list as having played the part of Antonio. Ostler died in December 1614, possibly while the play was still in its first run, in which case he may have been replaced immediately by Robert Benfield, who is listed as the second to take on the role. The Q1 cast list, the first to appear in a play quarto in England, informs us that the play's three main female roles were played by three boy actors, at least one of whom also doubled male roles (see notes on pp. 119–20). These 'boys' were not mere children, but adolescents of at least twelve or fourteen years of age (Kathman, 'Boy actors'). However, Richard Sharpe could not have played the Duchess in the play's first run, since he did not join the company until 1616. David Carnegie has plausibly suggested Richard Robinson as the first Duchess, since he was playing women's roles in the King's Men during the period in question (Gunby, 425). In early performances the King's Men's most famous and versatile actor, Richard Burbage, played the part of Ferdinand, which suggests that his role rather than Bosola's may have been regarded as the leading male character in the play. Bosola, the other contender for leading man, was played by John Lowin, another well-known member of the company, who went on to become principal actor after Burbage's death (see notes on p. 119). The same cast list also gives us information about doubling, confirming that it was often used for metadramatic purposes. We are not forced merely to speculate that courtiers in the play doubled as madmen, for we know this to have been the case, assuming the list is accurate, since the two madmen listed – Nicholas Towley and John Underwood – also played Forobosco and Delio respectively (see notes on p. 119).

The play, according to its title-page, was presented both at Blackfriars and at the Globe theatre, quite likely during the same year, since the Globe was used during good weather and Blackfriars during late autumn and winter. The new Globe would not have been available until 1614, when it was rebuilt after a fire. The production may have started out at the indoor Blackfriars theatre, then moved to the rebuilt Globe in spring 1614. Although Blackfriars theatre was smaller and more intimate than the Globe, with space for about 600 auditors as opposed to five times that number for the Globe, recent research suggests that playing conditions at the two venues may have been more similar than earlier theatre historians had thought. Both playhouses had stages that were largely bare of props and scenery. The play calls for an altar for the Loreto scene (3.4), possibly also for a tomb for the Echo scene (5.3), which may have been available from an earlier King's Men production of *The Lady's Tragedy* (Brown, xxxv), a throne for the scene in the Duchess's audience chamber (1.2) and perhaps also a kneeler of some kind for the Cardinal (5.4; see 5.4.43n.). Both stages had upper playing areas, used for the courtiers, who talk of going 'down' to the Cardinal at 5.5.21, and a curtained or screened 'discovery space' at the rear that was used to hide Cariola in 1.2 and possibly also Bosola in 5.2. In 1.2 the covering for the discovery space is called an 'arras', while in 4.1 the discovery space is hidden by a 'traverse'. 'Arras' and 'traverse' were, so far as we can determine, different terms for the same covering, which could be opened easily and perhaps without visible agency. The discovery space was used for the highly theatrical revelation of the wax bodies (4.1) and could also have been used to indicate small spaces – like the gallery or the Duchess's closet in 3.2 or her prison in 4.1– from which actors would come out on to the main stage to play the majority of the scene. Stage space was remarkably fluid: the stage could morph into different locations during a single scene with little or no change in scenery. In 1.2, for example, the scene starts in the crowded court of the Duchess's audience chamber, then becomes a 'gallery' where Antonio is ordered to attend her, then a more private space for the secret wooing and wedding.

Theatrical historians and editors used to imagine that *Malfi* at the Blackfriars would have been markedly different from *Malfi* at the Globe in terms of the private theatre's greater potential for sophisticated theatrical effects. We have, for example, tended to assume that the Blackfriars would have had music while the Globe did not. But by 1613–14, when *Malfi* was first staged, the Globe had adopted the Blackfriars custom of dividing plays into five acts with music before the performance and between acts. Music would also accompany the churchmen's hymn (or ditty) in Loreto (3.4), the dance of madmen and the madman's song in 4.1 (this eerily effective consort song has survived and is reproduced in Appendix 3), and perhaps at other points during the performance. We have also assumed that the Blackfriars, as an indoor theatre, could do much more than the outdoor Globe with lighting onstage. But research by R. B. Graves suggests that although the Globe was lit by daylight, and Blackfriars by a combination of daylight and candlelight – though the windows may have been blocked by black velvet hanging for tragedies (Graves, 154) – neither venue allowed for more than the most minimal control of ambient lighting onstage. When the Duchess waits in darkness for Ferdinand's visit, then calls for lights and discovers the horror of the severed hand (4.1), the entire scene takes place in the light; the audience's recognition that the scene moves from darkness to light is a matter of stage convention signalled by the bringing of a torch or lantern, not by significant changes in the level of lighting onstage.

As Graves notes, the back of the stage would usually have been darker than the front, so that the vision of the wax bodies in 4.1 might have been fairly hard for the audience to discern clearly; actors were likely to gravitate towards the front of the stage to play their scenes because that was where the lighting

was best. The lessened visibility at the rear of the stage may well
have been used to advantage in scenes like 5.4, where Bosola
fails to recognize Antonio and stabs him, as he later states, 'In a
mist' (5.5.92) – a mist of panic and moral confusion, no doubt,
but also perhaps of relative darkness if the killing takes place
towards the rear of the stage. Plays were usually performed
during the afternoon at the Globe and the Blackfriars. At the
Globe, but possibly also at the Blackfriars to a lesser degree and
depending on the season, the visceral effect of tragedy onstage
could have been enhanced by the gradual setting of the sun as
the play drew to a close (Graves, 196–7).

Malfi was a success in its first performances and was frequently
revived during the seventeenth century. It was performed
again around 1617–18, as we know from Busino's memoir (see
pp. 24–5); several of the names on the cast list, especially those
listed second as having played a given role, probably belong to
this production. The boy actor Richard Sharpe was doubtless
playing the Duchess by this period, but the other two boy
players on the Q1 cast list would still have been too young
(Gunby, 425). The powerful and renowned Richard Burbage,
who played Ferdinand in the first run of performances, died in
1619, so the revival witnessed by Busino was Burbage's swan
song in the role of Ferdinand. However, the Q1 cast list also
includes the name of Joseph Taylor as Ferdinand. Taylor joined
the company only in 1619 on the death of Burbage – strong
evidence, when combined with the ages of the boy actors, that
there was another revival with a partly altered cast after 1618 and
before 1623, when the play was first published.

The early revivals of *Malfi* may, as was customary for
the period, have altered the text of the play: in performance
it was cut at least some of the time, as we know from the
Q1 title-page. Webster's complaint about the 'ditty' in 3.4
strongly suggests that the verses accompanying the dumb-show
were a later addition supplied by another author. Moreover,
Antonio's reference to the self-purification of the French court

post-dates the first performances, since it appears to refer to reforms enacted in France in 1617 to purge the court of Spanish influence, as represented by Marie de' Medici and her followers, and bring back the old trusted councillors of Henry IV. The main event of this purge was the assassination of the enormously powerful Florentine Concino Concini, Maréchal d'Ancre, in April 1617 (Lucas, 1.1.8n.). The brutal killing of the most powerful man in France reverberated throughout Europe; in England, not to applaud the killing was, according to a member of the Venetian legation, to brand oneself as 'more than half Spanish' (cited from the *State Papers Venetian* in Lucas, 1.1.8n.). It would be entirely in character for the puritanical Antonio of the play to applaud this diminution of Spanish and Italian influence in France, but the date of the assassination indicates that the passage is likely to have been added for the 1617–18 revival. There was at least one later revival around 1630–2, when Heminges's poem (discussed on p. 22) made its graceful compliment to the elaborateness of the Duchess's obsequies as taking up all available London transport. This revival was probably staged in the public theatres but also at court, since the King's Men are recorded as performing the play in the Cockpit in Court on 26 December 1630.

Q2, published at the beginning of the political crisis that was to culminate in the English Civil War, was almost certainly printed in 1640 not to commemorate a revival of the play but to take advantage of the play's resonance with anti-Laudian and anti-absolutist sentiment (see pp. 85–6), but Q3 reflects renewed performance after the Restoration, when the theatres were reopened after an eighteen-year gap and *Malfi* was revived along with numerous other plays of the early seventeenth century as part of an almost convulsive attempt to undo the rupture of the Civil War and Interregnum and recapture elements of a lost pre-war theatrical culture (Maguire). In Restoration productions, for the first time, the Duchess of Malfi was played by a woman, Mary Betterton, according to the Q3 cast list, opposite her famous husband Thomas Betterton as Bosola – a configuration that gave new prominence to Bosola's role and created the potential for interesting sparks onstage between Bosola and the Duchess. The play was quite popular during the 1660s and 1670s. Samuel Pepys saw *Malfi* in 1662 and pronounced it 'well performed' but demoted it to 'sorry' when he saw it again six years later (Pepys, 3.209, 9.375).

The last of the play's early quartos, Q4 (1708), records the play in production around 1707 with new precision: it not only offers a new cast list but also updates outmoded language, makes heavy cuts and records a second set of even deeper cuts that were made for the performance (see pp. 88–9). Given the proverbial conservatism of the London stage, the tantalizing explicitness of Q4 in terms of marked cuts and added stage directions may offer hints as to how the play had appeared on the stage almost a century earlier (see p. 88). In particular, Q4 makes clear that some scenes, such as Ferdinand's encounter with the doctor in 5.2, were played for laughs even in the midst of horror (see 5.2.59 SDn.) – a feature of the play that was probably true of early productions as well. Audiences in the nineteenth and early twentieth centuries often laughed in the 'wrong places', at least according to reviewers – in act 5, for example, at Ferdinand's mock-heroic entry as though into battle at 5.5.45ff., or at his death, as in a 1919 Phoenix Society performance in which Ferdinand died absurdly 'standing on his head' (Moore, 152). The theatre in 1708 was arguably still attuned to Webster's ability to provoke savage laughter, even as critics schooled in neoclassical strictures about generic purity considered such mixed effects inappropriate for tragedy.

The last known performance of *Malfi* for over a hundred years was Lewis Theobald's adaptation titled *The Fatal Secret*, staged unsuccessfully in 1733 and published in 1735. It is one of the period's typical sentimentalizations of early modern tragic intensity: just as Lear survives to bless the marriage of Cordelia and Edgar at the end of Nahum Tate's *King Lear* (1681), so the Duchess and Antonio miraculously survive the carnage to reunite at the end of *The Fatal Secret*. But, while Webster's work was vanishing from the stage, his reputation was sustained by other means. His works turned up on lists of 'old plays' and in poems and miscellanies, such as one from 1655 that ranked him only slightly behind Shakespeare and Jonson in terms of the number of times it excerpted his work (Moore, 7–11; Greg, 2.536). Considering Webster's scant output as a playwright, his prominence there is remarkable.

In the early nineteenth century, Charles Lamb and William Hazlitt expressed strong enthusiasm for Webster's work. Lamb's canon-making *Specimens of English Dramatic Poets* (1808) included several long excerpts from *Malfi* and pronounced Webster unrivalled at depicting horror that touches the 'soul to the quick' and lays 'upon fear as much as it can bear' (Lamb, 2.34n.). Alexander Dyce's timely edition of Webster's *Works* (1830) helped popularize the play and made it more accessible for performance. As might be expected, given the Victorians' quasi-erotic attachment to rituals of death and mourning, the play returned to the stage in that era, first in a highly acclaimed 1850 adaptation by R. H. Horne produced by Samuel Phelps's company at Sadler's Wells. Phelps had a stellar record for reviving Elizabethan and Jacobean dramatic texts. At least two markedly different acting texts of his 1850 *Malfi* survive in multiple editions; one of these is anonymous and much closer to Webster than is Horne's adaptation in that it contains numerous cuts and some updating of language but largely follows the original and preserves the feel of a revival by offering its own list of actors opposite a parallel list drawn from the Second Quarto (see *Acting Copy*; and Wadsworth, 'Revivals', 80, n. 6). Horne's version performs more radical surgery, renaming a number of characters (the Duchess is now Marina and the Cardinal is Graziani), rewriting most of the speeches, streamlining the plot in significant ways, yet still claiming in its new Prologue to offer the 'inspiring themes / Of great, old Webster' clad in the 'strong beams' of his 'high-wrought poesy' (Horne, 6; see also Wadsworth, 'Shorn').

While early productions of *Malfi* had relied on stages nearly empty of mood-enhancing scenery and lighting, Phelps's stagings were extremely opulent, calling in 1.1 for '*A Bridge in Malfi, with Gardens beyond*' in Horne's version and for '*the Gardens of a Palace, overlooking the Port of Malfi, with the Sea in the Distance*' in the anonymous *Acting Copy*, and in the Echo scene for '*A Cypress Grove, part of the Gardens of the Palace – Night*' in Horne's version, with the addition of '*Ruins of an ancient Abbey in the background*' in the *Acting Copy*. Henry Keen's depiction (see Fig. 14), though a book illustration rather than a set design, gives a sense of the vast space and atmospheric poignancy the scene could evoke onstage. In Phelps's stagings, the scenes that seventeenth-century theatrical convention had identified as dark, such as Ferdinand's presentation of the dead hand to the Duchess (4.1) and Bosola's accidental murder of Antonio (5.4), were actually played on a dark stage, with the sudden appearance of lanterns and other ambient lighting creating highly melodramatic effects (Wadsworth, 'Revivals'; McLuskie and Uglow). Phelps also strove for period authenticity in his use of music, although he lost Webster's anti-Catholic satire by associating the Duchess with the music and ritual of pre-Reformation Italy, as in the supplying of sacred music or, more specifically in Horne's version, a sung '*Mass*' from a chapel within, for the baptism of the Duchess and Antonio's first child (*Acting Copy*, 22–4; Horne, 24). In the 1850 *Malfi* and in the many subsequent productions in Britain and America that it inspired over the next few decades, the uncontested star of the show was always the actress who played the Duchess: in Britain, the 'powerfully expressive' Isabella Glyn followed by Alice Marriott, in America Emma Waller (McLuskie and Uglow, 30; Wadsworth, 'American'). In the United States, the play in production appears to have picked up on Webster's theme of political tyranny and its transcendence: there, but never in

THE CARDINAL'S WINDOW

14 Antonio and Delio outside the Cardinal's window, from *The Duchess of Malfi* (1930), illustrated by Henry Keen

Britain, performances ended with a final apocalyptic vision of the Duchess and Antonio united in death and ascending to heaven – a vision that echoed a similarly spectacular ascent of the protagonists at the end of the stage version of *Uncle Tom's Cabin* (Wadsworth, 'American').

By the final decades of the nineteenth century, *Malfi* in performance was caught up in a lively, proliferating critical debate about the merits and demerits of Webster as a dramatist. Few denied his poetic power; what was most in question was his ability to construct a play. His biggest champion was the poet Algernon Charles Swinburne, who placed him at the right hand of Shakespeare and second only to the Bard in the pantheon of literary deities. Proponents of realist drama such as George Bernard Shaw were less enthusiastic: referring to Madame Tussaud's waxworks, which had opened in London in the 1830s, Shaw derided Webster as the ridiculous 'Tussaud laureate' (see the detailed survey in Moore, 46–69). A new production of *Malfi* by the Independent Theatre Society at the Opera Comique in London in 1892, as adapted by the seasoned revivalist William Poel, was poorly received by critics but attracted the avant-garde literary set in London. Edith Cooper, one of two women poets who published as 'Michael Field', described the reactions of the audience members at one performance

> 'The Duchess of Malfi' at the Opera Comique! Fitz-Gerald gloats over executions behind us; Le Gallienne wanders about like a young Dante in the shades; Oscar sits as if blowing bubbles of enjoyment, so pervasive are his smiles – they float through the milieu. Arthur Symons comes up an instant & speaks . . . hollowly – does not arrest my attention & goes off. I catch his face in a mirror.
>
> (Dever)

In this account 'Fitz-Gerald' is painter John Anster Fitzgerald, who specialized in bizarre images of fairies, bats and monsters;

'Le Gallienne' is the man of letters Richard Le Gallienne, a poet and proponent of the French Symbolists; 'Oscar' is Oscar Wilde. Cooper's enigmatic final remark, 'I catch his face in a mirror', tells us something about how the play was staged by echoing the action in 3.2, where the Duchess in Poel's version no doubt first realized Ferdinand's unwelcome intrusion into her closet by seeing his face in her mirror.

Poel's version of the play was more faithful to Webster's original than previous stagings had been, though even Poel made numerous cuts and alterations. He eliminated the 'Madame Tussaud' effect by cutting the wax figures in 4.1. In an attempt to recapture elements of the bare stage of the Jacobean era, he used much less elaborate sets than Phelps had, and was not afraid of proto-Symbolist theatrical spectacle that picked up on the emblematic quality of Webster's play – the very feature that had made *Malfi* offensive to realists of the G. B. Shaw school. The most striking of Poel's emblematic spectacles was his mad scene, in which properly dressed Jacobean court ladies danced about the Duchess with the madmen to the sound of muffled drumbeats: when they turned their backs on the darkened stage, they were revealed as luminous skeletons (see Gunby, 433; Moore, 55–8; McLuskie and Uglow, 32–5).

Webster's reputation was solidified at the end of the nineteenth century when he received his own entry in the *Dictionary of National Biography* (1885–1900), but *Malfi* came into its own – both on the stage and among critics – during the twentieth century. The emerging aesthetic of modernism and the massive, cumulative cultural rupture of two world wars and the Holocaust resonated with Webster's dramatic emphasis on horror, disjunction and extreme suffering. T. S. Eliot famously described him as a 'very great literary and dramatic genius directed toward chaos' (Eliot, *Elizabethan Essays*, 19) and included him among the 'heap of broken images' in 'The Waste Land' (1922; see Eliot's notes to lines 74, 118 and 407; and Potter, 188–9). The poet Rupert Brooke, though writing before the First World War, was similarly attuned to Webster's potential to evoke nihilism. His full-length study of Webster, published after his 1915 death in the war, praised the dramatist as a great writer and noted the 'foul and indestructible vitality' of his characters: 'they kill, love, torture one another blindly and without ceasing. A play of Webster's is full of the feverish and ghastly turmoil of a nest of maggots', the sight of which is 'only alleviated by the permanent calm, unfriendly summits and darknesses of the background of death and doom' (Brooke, 162). Brooke considered it 'scandalous' that there was no more recent edition than Dyce available to him; that situation was remedied in 1927 with the much more historically sophisticated edition of F. L. Lucas, who was no doubt also inspired by the experimental Phoenix Society revival of *Malfi* on the stage in 1919, right after the end of the First World War, ending a dearth of professional productions in Britain that had lasted more than twenty years. This was the notorious production in which Ferdinand died, preposterously at least in the eyes of the uncomprehending critics, upside-down (see p. 96). Following Lucas, there was also a crop of beautifully illustrated editions. See, for example, Henry Keen's dynamic image of Ferdinand's final mad entrance (5.5) from 1930 (Fig. 15).

It is beyond the scope of this introduction to discuss the multitude of twentieth- and twenty-first-century productions of *Malfi* in any but the most cursory way. David Carnegie lists forty commercial productions in the period 1934–89 (Gunby, 409–10; see also McLuskie and Uglow, xi–xii; Potter; Forker; and the theatrical reviews in Holdsworth). There was even a radio version of the play in the US sponsored by President Franklin Delano Roosevelt's Works Progress Administration during the Great Depression.[1] During that period the longest gap between commercial productions in either Britain or the US was the eight years between 1937 and 1945, coinciding with the Second World

---

1 Library of Congress MS, Radio Scripts box, FTP Box 872, folder 3: 'Episode: *The Duchess of Malfi*, R22-2 (2) Elizabethan Theatre'.

15   The entrance of mad Ferdinand from *The Duchess of Malfi* (1930), illustrated by Henry Keen

War (although there was a BBC television version in 1938 and a noteworthy 'amateur' production at Oxford in 1939[1]). Given the frequent correlation between a public taste for Webster and broader social trauma, it was perhaps predictable that *Malfi* would receive what is generally agreed to have been its capstone twentieth-century performance in the immediate aftermath of the Second World War. The highly acclaimed production at the Theatre Royal, Haymarket, directed by George Rylands, opened on 18 April 1945 in London – three weeks before Hitler's formal surrender on 7–8 May.

The same page of the London *Times* that praised Rylands's *Malfi* also showed, directly above the review, five photographs of twisted bodies and other newly revealed atrocities from the German concentration camps[2] (see also Hogg, 147–9nn.). This time, when audiences saw the 'heap of corpses on which the final curtain falls' they did not laugh as pre-war audiences frequently had: art had imitated life with horrifying visual clarity. Michael Ayrton's illustration of Webster's madmen (Fig. 16) for Rylands's 1945 edition of *Malfi*, which was created as a complement to the stage revival, shows the influence of pre-war Expressionist art – and perhaps also of harrowing images like the *Times* photographs of Hitler's death camps – in its use of bodily distortion to communicate psychic pain. In the 1945 production, Peggy Ashcroft as the Duchess received high praise for her 'sparkle' in early scenes and her 'resistant spirit' during the torments of act 4. The production is also noteworthy as the first to offer a recognizably Freudian Ferdinand on the stage. John Gielgud later claimed to have taken little pleasure in the role, but his petulantly neurotic Ferdinand was convincing to many viewers and was picked up in other stagings and adaptations, especially Bertolt Brecht's version in collaboration with W. H. Auden, which gave Ferdinand a prologue confessing his incestuous passion for his sister. Brecht's *Duchess of Malfi*

1   See the *Times* review of 14 February 1939, 12.
2   *Times*, 19 April 1945, 6.

16 Group of madmen in 4.2, from *The Duchess of Malfi* (1945), illustrated by Michael Ayrton

rewrote the play in a materialist mode to emphasize the Cardinal and Duke Ferdinand's representation of the oppressive power of church and state respectively. He also offered yet another attempt at a first name for the Duchess – Angela Teresa (Brecht; Moore, 155; McLuskie and Uglow, 42–7).

Although Brecht's adaptation of *Malfi* was not successful, it was a bellwether for post-war performances, which often combined realistic acting with striking emblematic and Symbolist theatrical effects that were characteristic of experimental theatre in the post-war era and its assimilation of Antonin Artaud's dictum about the 'Theatre of Cruelty', by which extreme theatrical violence 'releases conflicts, disengages powers, liberates possibilities' (Artaud, 31). Post-war productions were often also influenced by existentialism and the encounter with 'nothingness'. John Bury's 1956 production was played on a giant chessboard draped in black; Peter Gill's 1971 production at the Royal Court picked up on the Duchess's speech about death's 'ten thousand several doors' in its set design, with rows of doors down either side of the stage and a drab overall effect that one reviewer compared to a 'London bomb site'. By the 1970s, 'second wave' feminism and the 'new historicism' were beginning to gain a foothold in British and American universities. Literary critics were beginning to devote new attention to questions like patriarchal domination in the play and its connection with early seventeenth-century history and cultural artefacts (see, in particular, Callaghan, Dollimore, Goldberg, Shepherd, Sinfield). A second 1971 production, directed by Clifford Williams for the Royal Shakespeare Company, was self-consciously based on emerging Webster criticism from the universities. It created an updated version of the Jacobean discovery space at the back of the stage and used it to enhance the emblematic quality of the play. For example, when the Duchess retired into it light-heartedly to undress in 3.2 it was covered with a grille that ominously suggested a prison. Judi Dench played the Duchess in this version. Critics were particularly struck by the apparent family resemblance of the Duchess and her two brothers, as in Antonio's description of them as 'three fair medals / Cast in one figure' (1.2.106–7; see Fig. 17). This resemblance was manipulated strategically in the production to play up issues of family honour and patriarchy. In this production, Bosola, in choric fashion, addressed his proto-existentialist musings directly to the audience. A striking production of 1975 directed by Philip Prowse at the Citizens' Theatre, Glasgow, achieved something of the same 'alienation effect' by featuring skeletons as part of its set design and keeping the figure of Death onstage throughout the action.[1]

Adrian Noble's 1980 production at the Manchester Royal Exchange Theatre was more naturalistic, but still used a highly emblematic set: an opulent white carpet leading to a throne in early scenes, later replaced by a 'long blood-stained rag bleeding to a prison chair'.[2] In this production, Helen Mirren was a riggish and openly sensual Duchess (Fig. 18). The Cardinal appeared onstage in bed with his mistress amidst a fog of incense, and a schizophrenic Ferdinand descended into hideously realistic lycanthropy: he murdered Bosola by jumping him and savaging his throat in a convincingly wolf-like manner. The waxworks of 4.1 were replaced by apparently real dead bodies wheeled in on mortuary carts, and the madmen, brought onstage in a giant cage, resembled the terrifying lunatics of Peter Brook's 1966 film *Marat/Sade* (McLuskie and Uglow, 55–8). One of the great triumphs of this production was that it recognized the tragic potential of laughter, especially in the roles of Ferdinand and Bosola. The overall effect was of a *Malfi* that was true to Webster's text and yet convincingly modern – 'seeing the play afresh', in the words of the *Times* reviewer.

Other twentieth-century productions tried for a similar modernity by setting the play in twentieth-century Italy, such

1 Irving Wardle, *Times*, 17 September 1980, 9.
2 For more detailed discussion of these and other examples, see McLuskie and Uglow, 47–55.

17 The Duchess (Judi Dench) and her brothers, the Cardinal (Emrys James), and Ferdinand (Michael Williams), directed by Clifford Williams, Royal Shakespeare Company (1971)

as a *film noir* version of 1950s Italy in the touring company Red Shift's 'Mafia Don' version (1982–4), which went through several directors over its two-year evolution and which tied the play's corruption to the Roberto Calvi affair, a breaking news story in early 1982 that linked Vatican notables with the collapse of Calvi's

18   Helen Mirren as the Duchess, directed by Adrian Noble, Royal Exchange
Theatre, Manchester (1980)

Banco Ambrosiano and a raft of unsavoury underworld types. This 'Mafia' *Malfi* was ingeniously staged by a cast of only six actors who doubled all the parts (see Fig. 19). A decade later the 1995 Cheek by Jowl production directed by Declan Donnellan, which toured widely before opening in London at Wyndham's Theatre, set the play in Mussolini's Italy with Bosola as a malcontent blackshirt and the three Aragonese siblings as overweening aristocrats, studies 'in ruling-class pathology', according to the *New York Times* reviewer. The concept worked well on the stage. The Cardinal, played by Paul Brennan, was a sado-masochist who, dressed in his very proper ecclesiastical robes, used the poisoned holy book as a fetishistic object in a seduction that climaxed in Julia's death (see Fig. 20). The Duchess, played by Anastasia Hille, coolly wielded a cigarette and started out as 'the very image of tyrannical aristocratic charm'; through her ordeal in act 4, she was stripped down to final recognition of the meaninglessness of her identity and of the human condition. Once again, the result was a *Malfi* that was charged with 'chilling immediacy', rethinking a 'well-known classic in a manner that will never let you look at it in the same way again'.[1] At the end of the twentieth century, Webster's play was assumed to be a 'well-known classic' (Webster would have liked that) but was also inexhaustibly modern.

Malfi has been appropriated over the years for a number of other media: as an *a cappella* song for male voices based on Bosola's dirge in 4.2 (1926; see Warlock); a recording by poet Dylan Thomas (Caedmon Records, 1952); a novel that retells the Duchess's story, David Stacton's *A Dancer in Darkness* (1960), and another by P. D. James about a planned performance of the play, *The Skull beneath the Skin* (1982); a deeply cut but highly credible television version of *Malfi* produced by Cedric Messina (1972); an adaptation for television titled *A Question about Hell* by Kingsley Amis (1964); an opera by Stephen Oliver staged at Oxford (1971), even a soft-porn film adaptation, Mike

---

1 Ben Brantley, *New York Times*, 11 December 1995, C11.

19   Bosola offering apricots to the Duchess, played by members of the Red
Shift Theatre Company, *film noir* version of the play set in 1950s Italy,
directed by Jonathan Holloway (1982–4)

20 The Cardinal (Paul Brennan) tempts Julia (Nicola Redmond) with the poisoned book, directed by Declan Donnellan, Cheek by Jowl, Wyndham's Theatre (1995)

Figgis's experimental *Hotel* (2001), shot in Venice, in which snippets of revised dialogue from the play – 'fast food McMalfi' – are interspersed with rambling improvised conversations, cannibalistic banquets, lesbian sexual encounters, catfights and the howling of werewolves in the Piazza San Marco.

But, given the influence that poets since Swinburne have had in sustaining Webster's reputation, it seems only fair to grant poets the last word: Allen Tate, whose 'Horatian Epode to the Duchess of Malfi' considers the void left by her death, which 'Split the straight line of pessimism / Into two infinities', and pretends not to care (A. Tate, 181–2); Gary Snyder, who is stimulated into contemplation 'Walking home from "The Duchess of Malfi"'; Anne Ridler, whose 'Dead and gone' uses the Duchess to probe the schizophrenic in us all: 'For, what the imagination dares, the heart / Refuses, what the eye perceives, the heart / Knows to be falsehood' (Ridler, 70–1); or Derek Mahon, whose 'Dirge' describes the poet climbing the hills above bustling, tourist-infested Amalfi to seek out the tower where, according to local tradition, the Duchess was imprisoned until her death, and addresses her as he thinks of Webster:

> Exposing gleefully your strange disdain
> to the weird violence of vengeful men,
> a morbid cleric and a choleric duke,
> your poet comes with his demented book –
> and I too who climb to your hill-top
> not, like the wolf, to find and dig you up
> but to do homage in our own violent time
> to one who lights time past and time to come.
>   (Mahon, 269)

THE
TRAGEDY

OF THE DVTCHESSE
Of Malfy.

*As it was Presented priuatly, at the Black-Friers; and publiquely at the Globe, By the
Kings Maiesties Seruants.*

The perfect and exact Coppy, with diuerse
things Printed, that the length of the Play would
not beare in the Presentment.

VVritten by *John Webster.*

Hora. —— *Si quid* ——
—— *Candidus impertis si non his vtere mecum.*

LONDON:

Printed by NICHOLAS OKES, for IOHN
WATERSON, and are to be sold at the
signe of the Crowne, in *Paules*
Church-yard, 1 6 2 3.

21   Q1 title-page, BL 644 f. 72

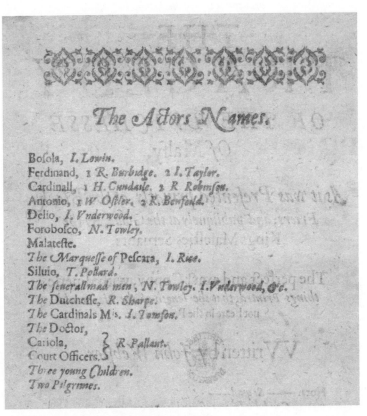

22   Q1 list of 'Actors' Names', BL 644 f. 72

The Tragedy of the Duchess of Malfi.

*As it was presented privately at the Blackfriars
and publicly at the Globe by the*

King's Majesty's Servants.

The perfect and exact copy, with diverse things
printed that the length of the play
would not bear in the presentment.

Written by John Webster.

Horace: *Si quid . . . candidus imperti si non his utere mecum.*

LONDON

Printed by NICHOLAS OKES for JOHN WATERSON

and are to be sold at the sign of the Crown

in Paul's Churchyard, 1623.

Blackfriars the King's Men's usual venue during cold months from 1610 onwards. It was considered a 'private' theatre because of its exclusiveness: it was an enclosed, covered space permitting audiences of approximately 600, and with higher ticket prices than 'public' theatres like the Globe.

Globe Rebuilt in 1614 after a fire in 1613, the Globe theatre was the King's Men's usual summer venue. It was considered 'public' because it was open-air and allowed for as many as 3,000 spectators per performance.

King's Majesty's Servants the King's Men, the leading dramatic company in Jacobean England, whose shareholders at the time of *The Duchess of Malfi*'s first performance included Shakespeare, Richard Burbage, John Heminges and Henry Condell, among others

presentment performance

Horace . . . mecum from Horace, *Epistles*, 1.6.67: 'If you know anything better than this, candidly pass it along; if not, use this with me' or, if '*candidus*' is a form of address, 'my good fellow, pass it along'. It was possibly supplied by the printer rather than the author, but appropriate to the text of the play.

NICHOLAS OKES active printer of playbooks and many other materials during the period; see p. 62.

JOHN WATERSON London stationer whose shop was, like many other bookshops, located in the churchyard of St Paul's cathedral, a favourite gathering place for London wits. Waterson published a number of plays, including Shakespeare and John Fletcher's *TNK* and plays by Philip Massinger and William Davenant.

The Actors' Names

Bosola	J. Lowin	
Ferdinand	1. R. Burbage; 2. J. Taylor	
Cardinal	1. H. Condell; 2. R. Robinson	
Antonio	1. W. Ostler; 2. R. Benfield	5
Delio	J. Underwood	
Forobosco	N. Towley	
Malateste		
The Marquess of Pescara	J. Rice	
Silvio	T. Pollard	10
The several madmen	N. Towley, J. Underwood, etc.	
The Duchess	R. Sharpe	
The Cardinal's Mistress	J. Tomson	
The Doctor ⎫		
Cariola ⎬	R. Pallant	15
Court Officers ⎭		
Three young Children		
Two Pilgrims		

1 *The Actors' Names* the first time such a list appears in a published playtext; players listed as '1.' evidently were part of the cast for the play's first performances (*c.* 1613–14) and those listed as '2.' their later replacements (*c.* 1618–23). All information is from Gurr, *Company*, 217–46; Gunby, 423–7; Bentley; and Kathman, 'Boy actors' and 'Freemen'.

2 **J. Lowin** John Lowin (1576–1653), a well-known, long-time member of the company who played Falstaff, Volpone, Mammon in Jonson's *Alchemist*, King Henry in *Henry VIII*, and many other important roles. He participated in clandestine performances of plays after the closing of the theatres (1642) and reportedly served as a source of information about Jacobean stage practices for William Davenant and others who revived London's theatres after the Restoration. Webster brings Lowin onstage to play himself as 'Lewin' in Webster's Induction to John Marston's *Malcontent* (1604; see Webster, 3.295–356).

3 **R. Burbage** Richard Burbage (1569–1619) was the leading actor and best known of the company, extolled by contemporaries for the power and naturalness of his performances; he played Richard III, Hamlet, Othello, Lear, Philaster, Malevole in Marston's *Malcontent*, and many other important roles, both comic and tragic. His enormous range would have been useful for the role of Ferdinand, which he played until his death. He plays himself as 'Dick Burbidge' in Webster's Induction to *Malcontent* (see 2n.).

J. Taylor Joseph Taylor (1586?–1652) joined the King's Men in 1619, evidently as a replacement for Burbage, and became one of its leading members during the reign of Charles I. He played Hamlet, Iago, Mosca in Jonson's *Volpone*, and many other important roles.

4 **H. Condell** Henry Condell (d. 1627) was a shareholder in the company and portrayed himself onstage as 'Harry Cundale' in Webster's Induction to *Malcontent*. He acted Mosca in *Volpone* and Surly in Jonson's *Alchemist*, and appears on cast lists for many other plays. He retired from acting around 1618 but remained active with the company, serving as one of the editors of the Shakespeare First Folio (1623).

R. Robinson Richard Robinson (d. 1648) played boy's parts including the Lady in Middleton's *Lady's Tragedy* and the title character in Fletcher's *Bonduca*, and was praised by Ben Jonson for his talents as a female impersonator. He was playing adult roles by 1618, when he probably took over the role of the Cardinal from Henry Condell, and became one of the King's Men's most prominent actors.

5 **W. Ostler** William Ostler (d. 1614) was a promising leading actor who started his career as a Blackfriars boy and died young, possibly while *Malfi* was still in its first run of performances.

R. Benfield Robert Benfield (d. 1649) joined the King's Men as replacement for Ostler in 1614. He played Lovewit in Jonson's *Alchemist*, Junius Rusticus in Massinger's *Roman Actor* and many other roles.

6 **J. Underwood** John Underwood (d. 1624) was a Blackfriars boy who joined the King's Men in 1608. He appears in cast lists for Jonson's *Alchemist*, Fletcher, Field and Massinger's *Knight of Malta*, Fletcher and Massinger's *Custom*, Fletcher's *Island Princess*, and many other plays.

7 **N. Towley** Nicholas Towley (1583–1623) was a boy actor attached to Richard Burbage from 1600 who went on to play men's parts, including Ananias in Jonson's *Alchemist* and Corvino in *Volpone*.

9 **J. Rice** John Rice (still alive in 1630) was a boy player in 1607–10 who received favourable notice as a nymph in a City pageant for the Prince of Wales in 1610. He had joined Lady Elizabeth's company by 1611 but rejoined the King's Men in 1614 and is on cast lists for Fletcher and

Massinger's *Barnavelt* and *Spanish Viceroy.*

10 **T. Pollard** Thomas Pollard was associated with the King's Men from 1613 to 1642, first as a hired man and later as a shareholder. He specialized in comedy, playing the title role in Fletcher's *Humorous Lieutenant* in addition to many more minor roles.

11 **The several madmen** Like Towley and Underwood, who are also listed as Forobosco and Delio respectively, all of the madmen would probably have doubled other roles.

12 **R. Sharpe** Richard Sharpe (1601–32) was a boy player apprenticed to John Heminges in 1616 who went on to be a shareholder and one of the leading actors in the company. Since he did not join the company until 1616, he could not have played the Duchess in the first run of performances. He

would have been between 17 and 21 when he played the Duchess in later performances (Kathman, 'Boy actors', 233).

13 **J. Tomson** John Thompson (d. 1634) was a leading boy player from 1619 until at least 1631, after which he probably played male roles. He is listed as Domitia in *Roman Actor*, Honoria the Queen in Massinger's *Picture* and in other female roles.

15 **R. Pallant** Robert Pallant (b. 1605 and still alive 1624) was a boy player apprenticed to Heminges in 1620 and so not available for the first staging of *Malfi*; he doubtless played the multiple roles (both male and female) of the Doctor, Cariola and a Court Officer all in the same later production(s), when he would have been 14–18 (Kathman, 'Boy actors', 234). See p. 132 on doubling in the play.

To the Right Honourable George Harding,
Baron Berkeley of Berkeley Castle and Knight of the Order of
the Bath, to the illustrious Prince Charles

My noble Lord,

That I may present my excuse why, being a stranger   5
to your lordship, I offer this poem to your patronage,
I plead this warrant: men who never saw the sea,
yet desire to behold that regiment of waters, choose
some eminent river to guide them thither and make
that, as it were, their conduct or postilion. By the   10
like ingenious means has your fame arrived at my
knowledge, receiving it from some of worth, who both
in contemplation and practice owe to your honour their
clearest service. I do not altogether look up at your
title, the ancientest nobility being but a relic of time   15
past and the truest honour indeed being for a man to
confer honour on himself, which your learning strives
to propagate and shall make you arrive at the dignity of
a great example.

---

1   *George Harding* Harding (1601–58) was a fitting recipient of Webster's bid for patronage, since he was the son and grandson on his mother's side of the Lords Hunsdon, who had served as patrons of the King's Men before 1604, when the company was still known as the Lord Chamberlain's Men. In 5 Webster calls himself a *stranger* to Harding. It was fairly common in the period for writers to dedicate their work to would-be patrons whom they did not know personally, in the hope of recognition or monetary reward.

3   *Prince Charles* later Charles I (1600–49)

8   **regiment** royal or magisterial authority (*OED* 1)

10 **conduct or postilion** conductor or carriage-driver

11 **ingenious** clever, inventive

12 **some of worth** some people of substance, or whose opinions I respect

14 **clearest** most esteemed (as in French *clair*, luminous); most honest

15–17 **ancientest . . . himself** That true nobility derives from action is an idea frequently expressed within the play.

I am confident this work is not unworthy your honour's   20
perusal, for, by such poems as this, poets have kissed
the hands of great princes and drawn their gentle eyes
to look down upon their sheets of paper when the poets
themselves were bound up in their winding-sheets.
The like courtesy from your lordship shall make you   25
live in your grave and laurel spring out of it when the
ignorant scorners of the Muses (that, like worms in
libraries, seem to live only to destroy learning) shall
wither, neglected and forgotten. This work and myself
I humbly present to your approved censure, it being   30
the utmost of my wishes to have your honourable self
my weighty and perspicuous comment, which grace so
done me shall ever be acknowledged

> By your lordship's in all duty and observance,
> John Webster   35

---

21 **poems** standard designation for plays in the period; poetry was thought to have higher status than dramatic composition.

23 **their sheets** the poets', but also the patrons' to whom the papers are dedicated and therefore given

27 **Muses** classical inspirers of the arts and therefore parallel to earthly patrons

30 **approved censure** seasoned judgement (Gibbons)

31 **utmost . . . wishes** Webster implicitly denies that he is seeking a monetary reward from Harding in return for his dedication. This claim gains credibility from the fact that Webster appears to have been fairly affluent in his own right (see pp. 4–5).

32 **perspicuous** clearly explained, or (in reference to people) clear in statement or expression (*OED* 2b)

32 **comment** commentator; embodiment of my words

35 **John Webster** Following convention in handwritten letters of the period, the name in Q1 is located several spaces below the closing salutation to indicate the writer's low status by comparison with the addressee's.

In the just worth of that well deserver, Mr John Webster,
and upon this masterpiece of tragedy

In this thou imitatest one rich and wise
That sees his good deeds done before he dies.
As he by works, thou by this work of fame   5
Hast well provided for thy living name.
To trust to others' honourings is worth's crime;
Thy monument is raised in thy lifetime.
And 'tis most just, for every worthy man
Is his own marble; and his merit can   10
Cut him to any figure and express
More art than death's cathedral palaces,
Where royal ashes keep their court. Thy note
Be ever plainness – 'tis the richest coat.
Thy epitaph only the title be: 15
Write 'Duchess'; that will fetch a tear for thee.
For who e'er saw this Duchess live and die
That could get off under a bleeding eye?

3   **imitatest** pronounced as three syllables
7   i.e. it is a characteristic error (*crime*) of worthy people to expect that others will provide their remembrance.
8   **monument** tomb or funerary memorial
10 **his own marble** i.e. his own best memorial; funerary 'monuments' (8) were frequently carved out of marble and bore carved testimonials to the worth of the person being memorialized.
11 **Cut . . . figure** continuing the metaphor from 10, sculpt him in any shape (implying that it is the *worthy man*'s deeds, not his epitaph carved on his tomb, that define him)

12–13 **death's . . . court** e.g. Westminster Abbey, where Elizabeth I and Mary, Queen of Scots were buried; it is a 'palace' for the dead as the royal *court* was the expected abode of monarchs while they were living.
13–14 **note . . . plainness** evidence that Webster's rough verse was seen by contemporaries as deliberately (and effectively) unpolished
14 **coat** Comparison of language to clothing was commonplace, particularly among iconoclastic Protestants for whom the most admired stylistic 'richness' was plainness of speech.
16 **fetch** bring forth
18 **under** with less than
    bleeding bloodshot from weeping

In Tragaediam

Ut lux ex tenebris ictu percussa Tomantis,   20
Illa, ruina malis, claris fit vita poetis.

Thomas Middletonus
Poeta & Chron: Londiniensis

---

19 ***In Tragaediam*** Latin = on the tragedy (*Malfi*). '*In*' could also connote
'to' but is used here as in the English
poem's title, '*In . . John Webster*'.

20–1 'As light springs from darkness
at the Thunderer's stroke [Jupiter's
thunder and lightning], so may she
[Tragedy], the ruin of the wicked, be
life for illustrious poets.' The 'wicked'
could be either bad poets or bad people.

22–3 ***Thomas Middletonus . . .***
Londiniensis Thomas Middleton
(1580–1627), poet and Chronologer
of London from 1620 but best known
as a playwright. He collaborated with
Webster on *Caesar's Fall* and *Quiet
Life* (Webster, 3.xl–xli).

To his friend Mr John Webster upon his Duchess of Malfi

I never saw thy Duchess till the day
That she was lively bodied in thy play.
Howe'er she answered her low-rated love,
Her brothers' anger did so fatal prove!   5
Yet my opinion is, she might speak more
But never in her life so well before.

William Rowley

2–3 **Duchess . . . bodied** imagining the Duchess as a living person
4 **Howe'er she answered** no matter how eloquently she accounted for (or argued for)
6–7 **she . . . before** She could have spoken even more, yet never so well in life

as in the play.
8 **William Rowley** actor and dramatist (*c*. 1585–1626) who collaborated with Webster and Thomas Heywood on *Cuckold* and with Webster, Dekker and John Ford on the lost play *Widow Waking* (Webster, 3.xl–xli).

To the reader of the author and his Duchess of Malfi

Crown him a poet whom nor Rome nor Greece
Transcend in all theirs for a masterpiece;
In which, whiles words and matter change, and men
Act one another, he, from whose clear pen   5
They all took life, to memory hath lent
A lasting fame to raise his monument.

John Ford

To the reader . . .
2 **nor . . . nor** neither . . . nor
3 **theirs** their writings
4 **which** Webster's masterpiece
   whiles while
5 **Act** perform on stage
   clear Cf. 'clearest' in *To the Right Honourable George Harding . . .*, 14n.

8 **John Ford** well-known poet and playwright (1586–?1640) who collaborated with Webster, Dekker and Rowley on the lost play *Widow Waking* and with Webster and Massinger on the completion of Fletcher's *Fair Maid* (Webster, 3. xl–xli).

THE DUCHESS
OF MALFI

LIST OF ROLES

DUCHESS of Malfi	*of the House of Aragon, ruler of Amalfi, later married to Antonio*	
ANTONIO	*the Duchess's household steward, later her husband*	
FERDINAND	*Duke of Calabria and twin brother of the Duchess*	
CARDINAL	*brother of the Duchess and Ferdinand*	
BOSOLA	*disaffected scholar-adventurer, later Master of Horse to the Duchess and retained as a spy by Ferdinand*	5
CARIOLA	*the Duchess's lady-in-waiting*	
DELIO	*Antonio's friend*	
PESCARA	*noble marquess and soldier*	
MALATESTE	*ignoble count and soldier*	
JULIA	*the Cardinal's mistress*	10
CASTRUCCIO	*Julia's husband*	
SILVIO } RODERIGO } GRISOLAN }	*courtiers*	
OLD LADY		15
DOCTOR		
ECHO	*from the Duchess's grave*	
MADMEN		
Two PILGRIMS	*to the Shrine of Our Lady of Loreto*	
SERVANTS	*to the Duchess, Ferdinand and Cardinal*	20
OFFICERS		
EXECUTIONERS		

Attendants, Guard of Soldiers, Ladies-in-Waiting, Musicians, Three Children

LIST OF ROLES Cf. the Q1 'Actors' Names' (see pp. 115, 118), which excludes the speaking roles of Castruccio, Roderigo, Grisolan, Old Lady, Servants and Executioners, all of whom no doubt doubled other parts in early stagings of the play. The Q1 list provides unprecedented information about the players of most of the major roles; brief biographies of each of the actors named in Q1 are to be found in the notes, pp. 119–20. The Q1 cast list does not conform to the later practice of listing male characters first, then female, since 'The Doctor' is listed after 'The Duchess' and 'The Cardinal's Mistress', and 'Court Officers' after those roles and 'Cariola'. Instead, the ordering principle of the list, as in the lists of roles published in the Shakespeare First Folio the same year, appears to be the status of actors in the company, with John Lowin as lead actor and Richard Burbage, long the principal actor of the King's Men, listed only second, no doubt because he had died in 1619, before the list was compiled for the 1623 edition of the play. Robert Pallant, listed as 'The Doctor', 'Cariola' and one of the 'Court Officers', was a boy player whose apprenticeship in the King's Men began only in 1620; he and the other boy players – Richard Sharpe, who played the Duchess, and John Thompson, who played Julia – are listed last as the lowest-ranking players attached to the company. Pallant and Thompson may well have doubled as the 'Two Pilgrims'. The notes that follow offer basic identification of the historical persons on whom the roles are based. For more information, see pp. 16–40.

1 DUCHESS The heroine, identified as 'Duchess' or 'Duchess of Malfi' throughout the play, is never referred to by a given name in any of the early quartos; in R. H. Horne's 1850 adaptation she is oddly christened 'Marina'. The historical figure on whom the Duchess was based was Giovanna d'Aragona (1478–1511?), Duchess of Amalfi from 1493 until her death, and about 26 years old in 1504, the only date specified in the play (2.3.57). Although the historical Duchess of Malfi (an old name for Amalfi) carried that title first as the wife of Alfonso Piccolomini, Duke of Amalfi, then after his death as regent for his underage son, also named Alfonso, she is portrayed throughout the play as ruler of Amalfi in her own right. She may appear onstage in 5.3 as Echo, or her voice may be heard from offstage; see also 17n.

2 ANTONIO also called Antonio Bologna and twice termed 'Antonia' by other characters (see pp. 70–1). He is described in the play as 'One of no birth' (3.5.117), meaning of no family distinction. The historical Antonio was from a decaying gentry family whose palazzo is still partially visible in the old section of Naples (Amendola, 98). He was the grandson of Antonio Beccadelli da Bologna, an illustrious 15th-century man of letters known as 'Il Panormita' who was crowned poet laureate by the Holy Roman Emperor. See also Painter's description of Antonio (Appendix 1).

3 FERDINAND of Aragon, Duke of Calabria; a fictitious character invented by Webster and loosely based on members of the Duchess's extended family. The actual Ferdinand, Duke of Calabria, was the Duchess's cousin, not her brother. Her (probably twin) brother was named Carlo of Aragon, Marquess of Gerace. For early audiences, the name Ferdinand doubtless evoked the monarchs Ferdinand and Isabella of Spain, well known for their part in the discovery of the New World in 1492 as sponsors of Christopher Columbus, and for their expulsion of Moors and Jews from Spain. That Ferdinand, known as 'the Catholic', was also a member of the House of Aragon – cousin of the Duchess's grandfather Ferrante I, King of Naples (Amendola, xiv).

4 CARDINAL the Duchess's older brother, not otherwise named in the play.

His historical prototype was Luigi of Aragon, Marquess of Gerace, who became a cardinal in the hope of eventually ascending to the papacy and gaining enough influence to restore his family's rule over the Kingdom of Naples. The Cardinal in the play retains his ecclesiastical title throughout, even after he formally relinquishes it to become a soldier (3.4). Cardinals were unusual in English drama before Webster; Cardinal Wolsey appears in *H8* (performed 1613) along with Queen Katherine, another member of the Spanish House of Aragon, and Cardinal Monticelso appears in Webster's *White Devil* (performed 1612). The stage interest in cardinals may have been fuelled by James I's celebrated controversy, waged through an exchange of Latin treatises beginning in 1608, with Cardinal Robert Bellarmine over royal absolutism and the condition of Catholics in England.

5 BOSOLA Daniel de Bosola, variously identified as a 'gentleman', a scholar at the University of Padua and a former galley slave. The historical Daniele da Bozzolo was a Lombard captain who was hired to assassinate Antonio (Amendola, 175). Webster greatly expands his presence in the Duchess's story. In the Q1 list of 'Actors' Names', Bosola appears first, and he appears in more scenes (all but five short scenes: 2.4–5, 3.4, 5.1, 5.3) than any other character in the play. The prominent billing could signal that by 1623, when the cast list was likely compiled for printing along with the text of the play, his role had come to be seen as the most significant in the play, despite his low social status by comparison with the Aragonese aristocrats. However, Q3 and Q4 both place Ferdinand first – the part played by Richard Burbage until his death in 1619 (see note on 'Actors' Names', p. 119).

6 CARIOLA not named in Webster's sources, but identified by Painter as a 'Gentlewoman who had been brought up with the Duchesse from hir cradle' (see Painter, in Appendix 1). Painter also states that she witnessed the consummation of the Duchess's marriage with Antonio – an idea Webster may suggest by naming her Cariola, which Florio glosses as 'trundle bed'. Her name in Q1 is usually spelled 'Cariola' but with the variant spelling 'Carolia' at 1.2.266 SP.

7 DELIO In the Duchess of Malfi's story as told by Bandello, Delio is Antonio's friend in Milan and almost certainly the alias of the author Bandello himself, who befriended the historical Antonio in Milan after 1512 but was not personally involved in Antonio's earlier history with the Duchess.

8 PESCARA consistently described in the play as an elderly, loyal old nobleman; however, the historical Marquess of Pescara contemporary with the Duchess was a much younger man. Webster conflates two figures: Alfonso d'Avalos, Marquess of Pescara, who died fighting for the Aragonese in 1495, and his son, Francesco Ferrante d'Avalos, born in 1490.

9 MALATESTE called the 'great Count Malateste' by Ferdinand (3.1.41) and evidently one of Ferdinand's followers with military ambitions. He is shown little respect by other characters and is frequently wrong-headed, as signalled by his name, which suggests 'bad head' or 'headache'.

10 JULIA identified only as 'The Cardinal's Mistress' in the Q1 cast list. The name Julia suggests a generic romantic figure, but it is also historically accurate, since the Duchess's brother Cardinal Luigi actually had a mistress named Giulia Campana, categorized according to Roman legal definitions as an 'honest courtesan' – the highest type of courtesan, one who could have some pretensions to gentility and mix in the highest social circles (Amendola, 114–15).

11 CASTRUCCIO the Italian spelling; pronounced Cas-truch-yo and often spelled 'Castruchio' in modern editions, as in Q1. At some points in the play, the metre requires the name to be pronounced as four clearly separated

syllables Cas-tru-chy-o, as at 2.3.72: 'Time will discover. Old Castruccio'. The name suggests 'castrated', like Italian *castrato*. As befits his status as a stereotypical cuckold, Castruccio is sexually impotent. He is, by profession, a serjeant-at-law, which in England is a barrister entitled to speak in the high courts. He may appear onstage in his official garb as barrister (see 2.1.5–6n).

12 SILVIO called 'lord Silvio' by Ferdinand at 1.2.56 and elsewhere. He appears as a courtier in Amalfi in 1.2, says he is bound for Milan at 1.2.138–9 and appears among the soldiers in Rome (or possibly Milan) in 3.3, after which his name disappears from the text. But he may return to the stage as an unnamed 'Officer' or 'Servant' in later scenes. Like the roles bracketed with his in the List of Roles, he is a free-form, all-purpose hanger-on: at various times a courtier and a soldier, by his title a member of the minor nobility, but nevertheless capable of being attached as a servant in a royal house. It was still standard in the period for the most important household officers in a royal or ducal court to come from the ranks of the aristocracy.

13 RODERIGO His name is, uncharacteristically for Q1, quite variable, spelled Rodecico, Rodorico and Rodorigo in opening SDs to 1.2, 2.1 and 2.2 respectively, before settling into the spelling to which it is normalized here. The variations could suggest that the name was unfamiliar – it was Spanish rather than Italian, and therefore in keeping with the Aragonese milieu of Webster's play. The name recalls Roderigo in *Othello*, where the two characters with Spanish names – Iago and Roderigo – use racially charged language to describe the 'miscegenation' of Othello and Desdemona, a language that parallels the Aragonese emphasis on 'purity of blood' in *Malfi* (see p. 26).

14 GRISOLAN Like Roderigo, he is not named in the Q1 cast list and, since he has very few lines, he can easily be assimilated into the mass of unnamed 'Servants' and courtiers that populate the play. At 5.5.18 Grisolan is omitted from the SD signalling the entrance of the courtiers, but he must enter with them because he is given a line of dialogue, which can, however, easily be reassigned to another courtier.

15 OLD LADY not otherwise identified, and important chiefly as an emblem of the sad inroads on female beauty over time. The Old Lady may be one of the Duchess's attendants, perhaps the one scolded for her inept mending and lemon breath at 2.1.122. Brown suggests that she is a midwife called in to assist at the delivery of the Duchess's first child, since her first entry as 'Old Lady' occurs at 2.2.0 SD, right after the Duchess has gone into labour in 2.1 and Antonio has assured Delio that he has arranged 'politic safe conveyance for the midwife' (2.1.168). The Old Lady's 'haste' at 2.2.4 suggests urgency, and Bosola's jokes about pregnancy suggest he is trying to discover if she has indeed been called in for some obstetric purpose. If so, the prearranged plan has misfired badly: for the midwife to encounter Bosola is neither politic nor safe.

16 DOCTOR probably slight of build, since he was played by one of the boy actors. This physical trait would make his planned buffeting of the seasoned soldier Ferdinand in 5.2 particularly comic. He may appear on stage in a professional gown of some sort, since the dialogue at 5.2.59–60 suggests that he removes it so that he can get down to the athletic business of curing Ferdinand.

17 ECHO Q1 lists Echo among the characters in the massed entrance for the scene as '*Eccho, (from the Dutchesse Graue.)*', suggesting that the Duchess may play the part of Echo. See 5.3.0 SDn.

18 MADMEN probably dressed in ragged garments, groaning or howling and dragging chains, since their 'noise' is evident before they enter. Madmen

onstage were a regular feature of Jacobean drama; cf. Tom o'Bedlam in *KL*; and Dekker and Webster's *Northward Ho!* (performed 1605), where the main characters stop off at Bedlam hospital to visit the madmen and the poet Bellamont is mistaken for one of them. The text of *Malfi* calls for '*eight Madmen*' to dance (4.2.113 SD), and one of them needs to have a good singing voice in order to perform the song called for at 4.2.60–71. Any of the actors other than those playing the Duchess, Cariola, the servant and Bosola could have doubled as madmen. The servant identifies the madmen by profession as a lawyer, priest, doctor, astrologer, tailor, gentleman usher (doorkeeper), farmer and broker (go-between, particularly for business), and they may have been costumed accordingly.

19 Two PILGRIMS possibly played by boys, since Robert Pallant, who also played Cariola, is listed in Q1 as one of them (see headnote on p. 129). They may have been dressed in traditional pilgrim's garb of staff, sandals and 'cockle hat', as in Ophelia's song (*Ham* 4.5.25–6), though hats decorated with cockle shells were associated with the Shrine of St James of Compostela, not Loreto. Although pilgrims had been a regular feature of English drama since medieval times, they may have struck an antiquated note onstage in Webster's play, since the type was not regularly to be found in aggressively Protestant England. In Ben Jonson's *Masque of Augurs*, performed at court in 1622, the second antimasque was '*a perplexed dance of straying and deformed pilgrims*' (Orgel and Strong, 1.337). Webster's pilgrims, by contrast, turn out to be trustworthy commentators on the scene at Loreto.

20 SERVANTS appear in many different scenes, usually attached to one of the noble characters, and probably interchangeable onstage. One exception is the solicitous unnamed servant who tries to help Antonio in 5.4 and is rewarded for his loyalty by being stabbed in 5.5. This could be Antonio's own servant or the servant to one of the Aragonese brethren who had defected to Antonio out of friendship.

21 OFFICERS used as a speech prefix only in 3.2, where the 'Officers' are probably interchangeable with the 'Servants' of earlier scenes; used elsewhere in the play also to designate military officers. Both terms refer to men who either explicitly are courtiers or can double as courtiers; see 12n. above.

22 EXECUTIONERS appear only in 4.2, where they are probably masked (like the '*guard of* Soldiers' in 3.5.93 SD) or wearing black hoods, like hangmen. There must be at least two, since the Q1 entry at 4.2.161 SD specifies '*Executioners*'. They could be doubled by any adult actor except Bosola and the madmen. Since the text calls for eight madmen, however, it might have been necessary for two madmen to double as executioners; they would have had time for a quick costume change, which could have been as simple as throwing on a robe and hood, if they exited at 4.2.114 or earlier and re-entered at 4.2.161.

23 **Guard of Soldiers** At least two are required to enter masked with Bosola in 3.5; they could double as executioners in 4.2.

23 **Three Children** Some modern editors specify two children and a doll, on the grounds that the Duchess's youngest child would be a mere babe in arms. But her younger son and daughter may be twins and old enough to be toddlers; even if they are not, by calling for three children, either Webster or whoever compiled the Q1 cast list appears to have aimed for maximum pathos onstage. The call for 'three young children' may have reflected actual performances: actors in the King's Men were not ordinarily apprenticed until the age of 12 or 14, but younger children may have been brought onstage in non-speaking roles as 'props'.

23 **Musicians** required to accompany the 'ditty' in 3.4 and the madmen's song and dance in 4.2. At Blackfriars, the 'act' or music by a highly skilled consort of musicians also played before the play and during intervals after every act. By 1623 this may have been the practice at the Globe theatre as well (Taylor and Jowett, 3–50). The musicians could also have provided some form of accompaniment for other highly formal speeches, such as Bosola's 'dirge' at 4.2.171–88.

THE DUCHESS
OF MALFI

1.1   *[Enter]* ANTONIO *[and]* DELIO.

DELIO

    You are welcome to your country, dear Antonio.
    You have been long in France, and you return
    A very formal Frenchman in your habit.
    How do you like the French court?

ANTONIO   I admire it.

    In seeking to reduce both state and people   5
    To a fixed order, their judicious king
    Begins at home: quits first his royal palace
    Of flattering sycophants, of dissolute
    And infamous persons – which he sweetly terms
    His master's masterpiece, the work of heaven –   10
    Considering duly that a prince's court
    Is like a common fountain, whence should flow
    Pure silver drops in general. But if't chance

like biblical water of lise

1.1 Location: outside the Duchess's audience chamber in Amalfi

1 **country** native land or district

3 **very . . . habit** Cf. frequent English complaints about the foreign affectations of returned travellers, as in Jonson's satiric portrait of 'Monsieur Fastidius Briske, otherwise cal'd the fresh Frenchefied courtier' (*Every Man Out*, 1.3.194–5).
very true (cognate with French *vrai*)
habit manners or clothing

5 **reduce** restore

7 **quits** rids. In Jacobean England, the references to court degeneracy that follow would have resonated with criticisms of the corrupt court of James I. There may also be a reference to contemporary French reforms (see p. 95).

9–10 – which . . . heaven – This appositive phrase was not set off by punctuation in Q1; it should refer to the entire process of cleansing the *palace* (7) but could easily be understood ironically as modifying *infamous persons* (9).

13 **in general** everywhere

1.1] *(Actus Primus. Scena Prima.)* 0 SD] *Q4; Antonio, and Delio, Bosola, Cardinall.* | *Q1* 4] *Q1 lines* Court? / it, / 8 flattering] *(flattring)* 9–10 which . . . heaven] *om. Q4* 13–22 But . . . foresee] *om. Q4*

Some cursed example poison't near the head,
'Death and diseases through the whole land spread.'   15
And what is't makes this blessed government
But a most provident council, who dare freely
Inform him the corruption of the times?
Though some o'th' court hold it presumption
To instruct princes what they ought to do,   20
It is a noble duty to inform them
What they ought to foresee.

[*Enter*] BOSOLA.

                    Here comes Bosola,
The only court-gall. Yet, I observe his railing
Is not for simple love of piety;
Indeed, he rails at those things which he wants –   25
Would be as lecherous, covetous or proud,

---

14 **head** source (as in the *head* of a stream); the prince, as *head* of the state

15 The quotation mark introducing this phrase in Q1 indicates it is a commonplace. Cf. Elyot, ch. 8, sig. D4ᵛ: 'the princis palaice is lyke a common fountayne or sprynge to his citie or countrey, wherby the people by the cleannes therof longe preserved in honestie, or by the impurenes therof, are with sundry vyces corrupted' (Dent, *Webster*).

16 **blessed** blessèd

17 **council** governing body like the Privy Council in England

18 **Inform him** inform him of

19 **presumption** pronounced as four syllables

21–2 **duty . . . foresee** a humanist commonplace; cf. the Roman Senate's comment to Trajan in Painter, fol. 87: 'sith you wrote unto us the maner and order what we ought to do: reason it is that we write to you againe what you ought to foresee . . . . Princes often-times be negligent of many things, not for that they will not foresee the same, but rather for want of one that dare tel them what they ought to doe' (Dent, *Webster*).

22 SD The mass entry at 0 SD of all the scene's characters in Q1 (see pp. 74–5) does not specify when Bosola enters. Q4 and Dyce have him enter with Cardinal at 28, in which case he will appear closely tied to the Cardinal from the first moment we see him onstage. Having him enter separately suggests that he is a free agent at the point of his first appearance.

23 **court-gall** satirist or irritant at court. A *gall* can also be a bitter plant or a pustule, hence the source of the infection rather than its corrective.

25 **wants** lacks; desires, needs

---

15 'Death . . . spread'] ("Death . . . spread)   22 SD] *Brown; Bosola,* | *0 SD Q1; opp. 22 Lucas*

Bloody or envious as any man
If he had means to be so.

[*Enter*] CARDINAL.

Here's the Cardinal.

BOSOLA
I do haunt you still. — *Indication of his character*
CARDINAL   So.
BOSOLA   I have done you
Better service than to be slighted thus.   30
Miserable age, where only the reward
Of doing well is the doing of it! — *murdered someone for the Cardinal*
CARDINAL
You enforce your merit too much.
BOSOLA   *, enforced slavery*
I fell into the galleys in your service,
where for two years together I wore two towels instead   35
of a shirt, with a knot on the shoulder after the fashion
of a Roman mantle. Slighted thus? I will thrive some *Speaking*
way. Blackbirds fatten best in hard weather: why not I, *in prose*
in these dog-days?
CARDINAL
Would you could become honest.   40

---

31 **only the** the only. Cf. the proverb 'Virtue is its own reward' (Dent, V81*).
34 **fell . . . galleys** was sentenced to row in the galleys, ships powered largely by the work of oarsmen; Delio states (71) that this was punishment for a murder.
35–7 **I . . . mantle** Bosola's sarcastic mockery indicates his perception of social distance from those who wore the noble Roman toga; cf. *1H4*

4.2.42–3, where Falstaff describes his ragged troops as possessing only a 'half-shirt' among them, 'two napkins tacked together and thrown over the shoulders'.
39 **dog-days** the hottest part of summer (under the sign of Sirius, the dog star), and associated with misfortune. Cf. Webster, *White Devil*, 3.3.63, where Lodovico wishes Flamineo 'dog-daies all yeare long'.

28 SD] *Brown; Cardinall.* | *0 SD Q1*; Enter Bosola, Cardinal. | *after 28 Q4*   29] *Q1 lines* still. / So. / you /   do] *om. Q4*   34] *prose Dyce*   36 the shoulder] my Shoulder *Q4*   40] *this edn; prose Q1*

BOSOLA

With all your divinity, do but direct me the way to it.
I have known many travel far for it and yet return as
arrant knaves as they went forth because they carried
themselves always along with them.   [*Exit Cardinal.*]
Are you gone? Some fellows, they say, are possessed   45
with the devil, but this great fellow were able to possess
the greatest devil and make him worse.

ANTONIO   He hath denied thee some suit?

BOSOLA   He and his brother are like plum trees that grow
crooked over standing pools: they are rich and o'erladen   50
with fruit, but none but crows, pies and caterpillars feed
on them. Could I be one of their flattering panders, I
would hang on their ears like a horse leech till I were
full, and then drop off. I pray, leave me. Who would
rely upon these miserable dependencies in expectation   55
to be advanced tomorrow? What creature ever fed

41 **With . . . it** printed here as verse because it is regular anapaestic pentameter. As in his previous speech (34 ff.), Bosola begins with a metrically regular line, then lurches into prose (see p. 83).

42–4 **travel . . . them** a commonplace; cf. Montaigne, 1.119: 'It was told *Socrates*, that one was no whit amended by his travell. *I beleeve it well* (saide he) *for he carried himselfe with him*' (Lucas).

44 SD The Cardinal may exit as early as 41 (see t.n.), but he may also remain onstage long enough to absorb more of Bosola's insults. He is certainly gone by the time Bosola notices his absence (45).

46–7 **this . . . worse** possibly suggested by *Ignatius*, 15, where Donne calls Ignatius Loyola, founder of the Jesuit order, 'so indued with the Divell that he was able . . . to possess the Divell'

48 **suit** request or petition

49–52 **plum . . . them** a commonplace, sometimes said of fig trees, as in Thomas Adams's sermon *Gallant's*, sig. E4ʳ, where figs are 'growing over deepe Waters, full of Fruit, but the Jayes eat them: Ruffians, Harlots, vicious Companions enjoy those Graces, that might honour God' (Dent, *Webster*)

50 **standing** stagnant; cf. proverbial 'Standing pools gather filth' (Dent, P465*).

51 **pies** magpies

52 **panders** panderers, pimps, who in Bosola's view are indistinguishable from courtiers

54 **full** full of blood

55 **dependencies** feelings of dependence; positions of dependence upon a greater man; matters awaiting legal settlement (D&S)

44 SD] *Q4 after 45* gone; *after 41 Brown*   50 o'erladen] *(ore-laden);* over-laden *Q4*   54 and] *Q2;* an *Q1*   I . . . me] *om. Q4*   55 dependencies] *(dependances)*

worse than hoping Tantalus? Nor ever died any man
more fearfully than he that hoped for a pardon. There
are rewards for hawks and dogs, and when they have
done us service; but, for a soldier that hazards his limbs   60
in a battle, nothing but a kind of geometry is his last
supportation.

DELIO   Geometry?

BOSOLA

Ay, to hang in a fair pair of slings,
take his latter swing in the world upon an honourable   65
pair of crutches, from hospital to hospital – fare ye well,
sir. And yet do not you scorn us, for places in the court
are but like beds in the hospital, where this man's head
lies at that man's foot, and so lower and lower.   *[Exit.]*

---

57 Tantalus mythological son of Zeus
tortured in Hades with alternat-
ing hope and disappointment. Food
and water appeared before his eyes,
but magically receded whenever he
reached out to taste them.
died Given the Q1a spelling 'did', the
meaning could alternatively be 'Nor
did any man more fearfully', meaning
'Nor acted any man more fearfully'.
Q1b's correction of 'did' to 'died' suggests that in the printing-house Q1a's
spelling was viewed as a typographic
error.

59 and when There is a blank space at
the end of the Q1 line after *and*, where
a word may have been omitted during printing. Dent, *Webster*, suggests
'horses', citing Montaigne's 'Apology
for Raymond Sebond', which refers to
the treatment of horses and then says,
'We share the fruites of our prey with
our dogges and hawkes, as a meede of
their paine and reward for their indus-
try' (Montaigne, 2.266). Alternatively,
Bosola may be veering off to a new
thought before the previous one is

fully expressed. Q2's omission of 'and'
before 'when' suggests that its editors
viewed its inclusion in Q1 as an error.

62 supportation means of relief or
maintenance; physical support

64–6 Ay . . . hospital Mathematics was
an important skill for military tacti-
cians: cf. *Oth* 1.1.18, where Cassio was
chosen as lieutenant because he was
a 'great arithmetician'. Bosola adopts
the *Geometry* of the military engineer
to the situation of a crippled veteran:
he swings on two crutches from one
hospital to the next as a geometrician
would swing his twin compasses from
point to point in drawing up plans for
military fortifications.

65 latter final (before he dies from his
war wounds); *latter swing* could also
refer to execution by hanging.

68–9 beds . . . lower Bosola uses the
crowding of early modern hospitals,
where beds were jammed closely
together, to suggest the sycophancy
of court politics, where each courtier
bowed his head at the feet of his immediate superior.

---

57 died] *Q1b;* did *Q1a*   58 pardon] *Q1b;* pleadon *Q1a*   59 and when] when *Q2*   64] *this edn; prose*
Q1   64+ Ay] *(1)*   65 latter swing] *(latter-swinge)*   66 crutches] *(Crowtches)*   68 like] *Q2;* likes
Q1   69 SD] *Q4*

139

DELIO

    I knew this fellow seven years in the galleys   70
    For a notorious murder, and 'twas thought
    The Cardinal suborned it. He was released
    By the French general Gaston de Foux
    When he recovered Naples.

ANTONIO   'Tis great pity
    He should be thus neglected. I have heard
    He's very valiant. This foul melancholy   75
    Will poison all his goodness; for I'll tell you,
    If too immoderate sleep be truly said
    To be an inward rust unto the soul,
    It then doth follow want of action   80
    Breeds all black malcontents; and their close rearing,
    Like moths in cloth, do hurt for want of wearing.   *[Exeunt.]*

1.2   *[Enter]* CASTRUCCIO, SILVIO, RODERIGO *and*
        GRISOLAN *[at one door,]* ANTONIO *[and]*
              DELIO *[at another]*.

DELIO

    The presence 'gins to fill. You promised me

---

70 **seven . . . galleys** Delio's comment contradicts Bosola's implication (34–5) that he spent two years' servitude there.

73 **Gaston de Foux** usually modernized to *Gaston de Foix*. But Webster may have intended a play on French *foux* (plural of *fou*), mad or foolish (Jellerson). The historical French military commander de Foix (1489–1512) arrived in Italy only in 1511, at least seven years after 1504, the date of the play's action as specified at 2.3.57.

74 **recovered Naples** won Naples back from papal, Spanish and/or Aragonese forces.

80 **action** pronounced as three syllables

81 **black** suffering from black bile or melancholy

   close rearing being trained in confined circumstances; out of action

82 As woollen cloth becomes vulnerable to moths by being kept closed up instead of worn, so men become malcontents by being given too little action. Paradoxically, the malcontents, like the moths, are also the source of the damage.

1.2 Location: the Duchess's audience chamber. Most modern editors do not follow Q1 in breaking for a new scene here, on the grounds that Antonio

---

71 murder] *(murther)*; murtherer *Q3* 73 Foux] *Foyx | Q2; Fox | Q3; Foix | Q4* 74] *Q1 lines Naples. / pitty /* 77–82 for . . . wearing] *om. in performance Q4* 81 malcontents] *(malcontents)* 82 SD] *Q4* 1.2] *(SCENA II.)* 0 SD] *this edn; Antonio, Delio, Ferdinand, Cardinall, Dutchesse, Castruchio, Siluio, Rodecico, Grisolan, Bosola, Iulia, Cariola. | Q1*

To make me the partaker of the natures
Of some of your great courtiers –

ANTONIO   The lord cardinals

And other strangers that are now in court.
I shall.

[*Enter*] FERDINAND.

Here comes the great Calabrian duke.   5

FERDINAND

Who took the ring oftenest?

SILVIO   Antonia Bologna, my lord.

FERDINAND

Our sister Duchess's great master of her household?
Give him the jewel.   [*Antonio receives the jewel.*]
When shall we leave

---

and Delio could well remain onstage;
productions since 1850 have typically
also ignored the break. But Q1's scene
break indicates a subtle shift in time
and place that may have been indicated
in early performances through the exit
of Antonio and Delio at the end of
1.1 and their re-entry along with a
larger group of courtiers in 1.2. See
pp. 171–4 and *WT* 1.1 and 1.2, which
have a similar structure (Brown).

1   **presence** the Duchess's official audience chamber
2   **make . . . partaker of** share with me
3   **cardinals** emended by some editors to
'Cardinal's', but there is no reason to
suppose that there is only one cardinal
who frequents the court. See 3.3.35.
Both readings would have sounded the
same onstage.
4   **strangers** foreigners (from states
other than Amalfi)

6   **took the ring** won the ring in ring-
jousting, a courtly sport in which players galloping on horseback tried to
carry off a ring on the tip of their
lance. Here, the sport carries bawdy
implications: cf. *Northward Ho!*,
1.3.91, where illicit sex is described as
'old running at the ring'.
Antonia The feminine form of the
name could be a misprint in Q1, but it
is preserved here because it could also
be a subtle form of deprecation; cf.
1.2.123, where the same form recurs
in a jibe by Delio.
7   **master . . . household** chief steward,
whose duties would include overseeing
the servants and managing the finances
8   **jewel** reward for winning at the tilting. Cf. 215–16, where the Duchess
compares herself to a jewel. The image
in connection with the Duchess reverberates through the play.

3] *Q1 lines* Courtiers. / Cardinalls /   your] our *Q3*   5 SD] *Lucas after* Duke; *Ferdinand,* | *0 SD*
Q1   6] *Q1 lines* oftnest? / Lord) /   oftenest] *(*oftnest*)*   Antonia] Antonio *Q3*   8–11] *this edn; Q1*
lines sportiue-action, / indeed? / Lord) / person. / Lord?) /   8 SD] *Weis*

This sportive action, and fall to action indeed?

CASTRUCCIO

Methinks, my lord, you should not desire to go   10
To war in person.

FERDINAND   Now for some gravity – why, my lord?

CASTRUCCIO   It is fitting a soldier arise to be a prince, but
not necessary a prince descend to be a captain.

FERDINAND   No?

CASTRUCCIO   No, my lord. He were far better do it by a   15
deputy.

FERDINAND   Why should he not as well sleep or eat by a
deputy? This might take idle, offensive and base office
from him, whereas the other deprives him of honour.

CASTRUCCIO   Believe my experience: that realm is never   20
long in quiet where the ruler is a soldier.

FERDINAND   Thou toldst me thy wife could not endure
fighting.

CASTRUCCIO   True, my lord.

FERDINAND   And of a jest she broke of a captain she met   25
full of wounds – I have forgot it.

CASTRUCCIO   She told him, my lord, he was a pitiful
fellow to lie, like the Children of Ishmael, all in tents.

10–11 **Methinks ... person** Q2 reverses
this sentiment by omitting *not* in 10
(see t.n.). Stereotypically, the image
of a ruler at the head of his troops
was strongly associated with heroism,
as in Shakespeare's *H5*. See also
p. 86 for speculation about the political
significance of the change in the 1640
quarto.

11 **gravity** pompous remarks

18–19 **This ... honour** If he gives up
fighting he might as well also give up
the other, less honourable, functions

(implying that soldiering is as natural
to the prince as eating or drinking).

22 **toldst** For this form of the verb as
opposed to the more usual 'toldest',
cf. Milton, 'Then toldst her doubting
how these things could be' (*Paradise
Regained*, 1.138).

25 **broke** made

28 **lie ... tents** The captain lies in *tents*
(bandages) because bandages cover his
wounds. But there is a pun on *tents*
in the sense of temporary sleeping
quarters: the implication is that the

10–61] *om. in performance Q4*   10 not] *om. Q2*   12 arise] rise *Q4*   15 do] to doe *Q2*   19 deprives]
reprives *Q2*   21 in] *om. Q4*   where the] Whose *Q4*   22–35] *Q1 lines* me / fighting. / Lord.) /
Captaine, / it. / lie, / Tents. / vndoe / although / weapons, / would / vp. / Lord) / Gennit? /; *prose
Dyce*   28 Ishmael] *Brown; Ismael | Q1*

FERDINAND   Why, there's a wit were able to undo all
 the surgeons o'the city, for although gallants should   30
 quarrel, and had drawn their weapons, and were ready
 to go to it, yet her persuasions would make them put
 up.

CASTRUCCIO   That she would, my lord. How do you like
 my Spanish jennet? — *quick horse*   35

RODERIGO   He is all fire.

FERDINAND   I am of Pliny's opinion: I think he was
 begot by the wind. He runs as if he were ballast with
 quicksilver.

SILVIO

True, my lord, he reels from the tilt often.   40

RODERIGO, GRISOLAN   Ha, ha, ha!

FERDINAND

Why do you laugh? Methinks you that are courtiers
Should be my touchwood: take fire when I give fire –

captain's wounds have lowered his status, since Ishmael was Abraham's rejected bastard by his slave Hagar (Genesis, 21.1–21) and Ishmael and his children were nomadic tent dwellers. Brennan's suggested emendation 'Israel' is also a possible reading.

32–3 **put up** sheathe their weapons, but with the bawdy implication that her solicitations might make them ready for a sexual 'duel'

34–5 **How . . . jennet** This line is indented in Q1 as though to indicate a change in speaker, but no new SP appears. Some editors give the line to Ferdinand, but if the horse is the Duke's it seems unlikely that the courtiers would criticize it to his face (40–1).

35 **jennet** small Spanish horse prized for speed

37 **Pliny's opinion** the authoritative opinion of the classical Roman naturalist and encyclopedist Pliny the Elder,

who says: 'In Portugall . . . when the West wind bloweth, the mares set up their tailes, and turne them full against it . . . and bring foorth foles as swift as the wind' (Pliny, 42.222; Lucas).

38 **ballast** ballasted, a form to which it is emended by some editors But the briefer form is common in the period and sorts better with Ferdinand's image of speed.

39 **quicksilver** mercury, which moves quickly and erratically; ballast should slow the horse down, but mercury makes him faster (Brown).

40 **reels . . . tilt** shies away from an oncoming lance. 'Tilting' could also be used of sexual intercourse, in which case 'reeling from the tilt' would be a sly reference to Castruccio's impotence. Mercury (*quicksilver*) was used as a remedy for syphilis.

43 **touchwood** easily flammable wood used as tinder

30 surgeons] *Q4;* Chyrurgeons *Q1* gallants] Sparks *Q4* 34 How] *Ferd.* How *Brown* 38 ballast]
*(*ballass'd*)* 40 reels] *Q2;* roeles *Q1*

That is, laugh when I laugh, were the subject never
    so witty.

CASTRUCCIO   True, my lord. I myself have heard a very   45
good jest and have scorned to seem to have so silly a wit
as to understand it.

FERDINAND   But I can laugh at your fool, my lord.

CASTRUCCIO

He cannot speak, you know, but he makes faces.

My lady cannot abide him.

FERDINAND   No?   50

CASTRUCCIO

Nor endure to be in merry company;

For she says too much laughing and too much company

Fills her too full of the wrinkle.

FERDINAND

I would then have a mathematical instrument

Made for her face, that she might not laugh out
    of compass.   55

– I shall shortly visit you at Milan, lord Silvio.

SILVIO

Your grace shall arrive most welcome.

FERDINAND

You are a good horseman, Antonio.

You have excellent riders in France; what do you think
of good horsemanship?   60

---

48 **fool** Castruccio's household is elaborate enough to have its own resident fool as entertainer; the implication is that the real *fool* is Castruccio himself.

49 Either the *fool* has defined himself professionally as a mime or, like many household fools of the period, he suffers from some mental or physical disability.

54–5 **instrument . . . compass** instrument, like the geometrician's compass, that will keep her face within wrinkle-free range

59–60 The French were reputedly the best horsemen in Europe (Lucas). Cf. the discussion of the 'wondrous' French horseman Lamond in *Ham* 4.7.81–92.

59 **You have** there are

---

44 laugh when] Not laugh but when *Q4* 50] *Q1 lines* him. / Noe? / 52–3] *this edn; Q1 lines* saies / her / wrinckle. / 53 the wrinkle] wrinkles *Q4* 54–6] *this edn; prose Q1* 56+ Milan] *(Millaine)* 58] *this edn; prose Q1*

ANTONIO   Nobly, my lord. As out of the Grecian
    horse issued many famous princes, so out of brave
    horsemanship arise the first sparks of growing
    resolution that raise the mind to noble action.
FERDINAND   You have bespoke it worthily.   65

[*Enter*] CARDINAL, DUCHESS, CARIOLA, JULIA
[*and* Attendants].

SILVIO
    Your brother, the lord Cardinal, and sister Duchess.
CARDINAL
    Are the galleys come about?
GRISOLAN   They are, my lord.
FERDINAND
    Here's the lord Silvio – is come to take his leave.
DELIO
    Now, sir, your promise: what's that Cardinal?
    I mean his temper. They say he's a brave fellow –   70
    Will play his five thousand crowns at tennis, dance,
    Court ladies – and one that hath fought single combats.

61–2 **Grecian horse** the Trojan horse,
    built by Greeks in Homer's *Iliad* and
    filled with soldiers as a trick to pen-
    etrate the walls of Troy; the Greek
    soldiers who bravely exited the horse
    once it was within the city and went on
    to defeat the Trojans were frequently
    cited in the early modern period as
    examples of heroism.
65 SD Upon entering, the Duchess may
    seat herself on her throne of state; her
    presence there would counterbalance
    Ferdinand's verbal dominance in the
    lines that follow (Gunby).
67 **come about** turned (to take advantage
    of the wind)
69 **Now . . . promise**   addressed   to

Antonio, who had promised to acquaint
Delio with the natures of the courtiers
(1–2); although Antonio and Delio are
resuming the conversation between
themselves that was interrupted by the
entrance of Ferdinand at 6, it is possible that at least snatches of Antonio's
satiric portraits that follow are overheard by those being described, all of
whom are now onstage.
70 **temper** temperament
    brave flamboyant, finely dressed
71 **play . . . tennis** make huge bets on
    tennis games
72 **single combats** duels (illegal in
    Jacobean England but reputedly com-
    mon in Italy)

65 SD] *Dyce (subst.) after 66; Cardinall . . . Iulia,* | *0 SD Q1*   67] *Q1 lines* about? / Lord.) /   68] *om.*
Q4   70 temper.] *(Temper?)*   72 and] *om. Q4*

145

ANTONIO   Some such flashes superficially hang on him,
for form. But observe his inward character: he is a
— melancholy churchman. The spring in his face is   75
nothing but the engendering of toads. Where he
is jealous of any man, he lays worse plots for them
than ever was imposed on Hercules, for he strews
in his way flatterers, panders, intelligencers, atheists
and a thousand such political monsters. He should   80
have been Pope, but, instead of coming to it by the
primitive decency of the church, he did bestow bribes
so largely and so impudently as if he would have
carried it away without heaven's knowledge. Some
good he hath done –   85

DELIO

You have given too much of him. What's his brother?

73–85 the first of three formal 'Characters' Antonio offers of the two brothers and the Duchess. Character sketches were popular in the period: cf. Hall, *Characters*; Overbury's *Characters*, augmented in its sixth edition in 1615 by 32 'New Characters' by Webster himself (Webster, 3.437–533); and the 'Character' of a whore in *White Devil*, 3.2.79–102.

73 **flashes** transient displays

75 **spring** youthfulness; appearance of freshness as in the season of spring or water from a spring

76 **engendering of toads** Cf. Bosola's pool image, 1.1.49–50: the appealing quality of the Cardinal's face is used only for revolting, immoral purposes. George Chapman has 'That toad-pool that stands in thy complexion' (*Bussy*, 3.2.452; Lucas).

77–8 **worse plots . . . Hercules** The mythical Greek hero was forced to atone for having killed his family by being given twelve seemingly impossible labours, such as wrestling the Nemean lion and cleaning the Augean stables in a single day.

79 *****flatterers** Q1's 'Flatters' (t.n.), meaning flattery, is also a possible reading (*OED*), since flattery can be as treacherous as any other monster.
intelligencers spies, who were much despised in the period
atheists people with unorthodox beliefs

80–1 **He . . . Pope** another anachronistic reference: the historical Cardinal, Luigi of Aragon, was an influential figure in the Vatican hierarchy and a serious candidate for the papacy after the death of Julius II in 1513.

82 **primitive . . . church** pristine early morality of the church, before it was polluted with corrupt institutions and practices. In seventeenth-century England, the phrase carried strong Protestant connotations, referring to the characteristics of the early church before it took on the rituals and hierarchy of Catholicism.

84 **carried it away** brought it off successfully; but also suggests 'carried away' in the sense of 'ran off with' or stole

86 **given** shared, expressed

78–80 for . . . monsters] *om. in performance Q4*   79 flatterers] *Q3;* Flatters *Q1*

ANTONIO

  The duke there? A most perverse and turbulent nature.
  What appears in him mirth is merely outside;
  If he laugh heartily it is to laugh   *harsh description,*
  All honesty out of fashion.   *he is not what he*
                                              seems

DELIO   Twins?

ANTONIO   In quality.   90

  He speaks with others' tongues and hears men's suits
  With others' ears, will seem to sleep o'th' bench
  Only to entrap offenders in their answers,
  Dooms men to death by information,
  Rewards by hearsay.

DELIO   Then the law to him   95

  Is like a foul black cobweb to a spider:
  He makes it his dwelling and a prison
  To entangle those shall feed him.

ANTONIO   Most true.

  He ne'er pays debts unless they be shrewd turns –
  And those he will confess that he doth owe.   100

---

88 **merely outside** only external; Antonio goes on in the rest of his 'character' to describe Ferdinand's thorough corruption on the inside.

90 **Twins** We learn later that all three siblings are similar in appearance (106–7 and n.) and that the Duchess and Ferdinand are twins (4.2.256).
  quality personal attributes

91–3 Cf. Alexander, *Alexandrian Tragedy*, sig. D1ᵛ: a ruler 'spake but with others tongues, heard with their eares . . . doomes by information men to death' (Dent, *Webster*).

91–2 **speaks . . . ears** He's a devious hypocrite.

92 **seem . . . bench** pretends to sleep during trials (in which he serves as judge)

94 **information** 'facts' gleaned through informers, and hence unreliable; pronounced as five syllables

95 **Rewards by hearsay** uses hearsay as a basis for judgement; the *Rewards* in question could be bribes.

95–8 **Then . . . him** proverbial (Dent, L116); cf. Dekker and Webster, *Sir Thomas Wyatt* (1607), 5.1.99–100: 'Great men like great Flies, through lawes Cobwebs breake, / But the thin'st frame, the prison of the weake.'

99–100 The only debts he is willing to acknowledge are evil deeds that he has received and therefore *owes* in payment out of a thirst for revenge. Cf. *Penitential Psalms*: a great and politic man 'paies never debt, but what he should not ow' (see Dent, *Webster*).

---

87 A] Of a *Q4*   90] *Q1 lines* fashion. / Twins? / qualitie: /   92–3 will . . . answers] *om. Q4*   95] *Q1 lines* heare-say. / him /   95–101 Then . . . Last] *om. Q4*   98] *Q1 lines* him. / true: /   99 shrewd] *Q2;* shewed *Q1*

147

Last, for his brother there, the Cardinal,
They that do flatter him most say oracles
Hang at his lips, and verily I believe them,
For the devil speaks in them.
But for their sister, the right noble Duchess, 105
You never fixed your eye on three fair medals — *eponymous*
Cast in one figure of so different temper.
For her discourse, it is so full of rapture,
You only will begin then to be sorry
When she doth end her speech, and wish in wonder 110
She held it less vainglory to talk much
Than your penance to hear her. Whilst she speaks
She throws upon a man so sweet a look
That it were able raise one to a galliard — *to a lively dance*
That lay in a dead palsy, and to dote 115
On that sweet countenance. But in that look
There speaketh so divine a continence
As cuts off all lascivious and vain hope.
Her days are practised in such noble virtue
That, sure, her nights – nay more, her very sleeps – 120
Are more in heaven than other ladies' shrifts.
Let all sweet ladies break their flattering glasses

102–4 In classical times oracles were believed to be divinely inspired; Antonio holds that they are inspired by the devil. Cf. 1.1.45–7, where the Cardinal is said to have possessed the devil, and Milton's 'Nativity Ode', which similarly describes the various classical oracles as demonic.

106–7 Cast bronze medallions of aristocrats were popular keepsakes during the early modern period; those of the three siblings would look deceptively similar because they share a family resemblance.

109–12 You . . . her based on Guazzo, book 2, fol. 69v: her 'discourses are so delightfull, that you wyll only then beginne to bee sory, when shee endeth to speake: and to wish that she would be no more weary to speake, then you are to heare' (Dent, *Webster*).

111 vainglory excessive pride

114 galliard lively, highly athletic dance

115 in . . . palsy paralysed by a stroke

121 shrifts acts of confession

122–3 break . . . her break their mirrors and use her as their reflection; clothe themselves in her attributes. As frequently during the period, the mirror reflects not external reality but an ideal for emulation.

105 right] most *Q4* 106 your] *Q2;* you *Q1* 107 temper] a Temper *Q4* 109 begin then] then begin *Q4* 110–12 and . . . her] *om. Q4* 117 speaketh] speaks *Q4* 122 flattering] (flattring *)*

And dress themselves in her.

DELIO   Fie, Antonia!

You play the wire-drawer with her commendations.

ANTONIO

I'll case the picture up. Only thus much –   125

All her particular worth grows to this sum:

She stains the time past, lights the time to come.

CARIOLA

You must attend my lady in the gallery

Some half an hour hence.

ANTONIO   I shall. [*Exeunt Antonio and Delio.*]

FERDINAND

Sister, I have a suit to you.

DUCHESS   To me, sir?   130

FERDINAND

A gentleman here, Daniel de Bosola,

One that was in the galleys –

DUCHESS   Yes, I know him.

FERDINAND

– A worthy fellow h'is – pray let me entreat

---

123 **Antonia** Delio's Q1 slip of femi-
   nizing Antonio's name suggests that
   Antonio has compromised his masculinity through his adulation of the
   Duchess. See also 6n. and t.n., where
   the same Q1 spelling occurs.
124 **play the wire-drawer** draw out to
   great lengths, like a craftsman forming
   metal into wire; cf. Queen Elizabeth's
   widely publicized speech of 24 November
   1586: 'or that I meant to make the Lords
   wire-drawers to draw the matter still into
   length' (Elizabeth I, 199).
125 **case . . . up** cease to give the
   Duchess's verbal portrait (that he has
   just drawn), as if putting a miniature
   in its case

126 **sum** epitome
127 **stains** makes look dark by comparison with herself; leaves an indel-
   ible mark. Cf. Alexander, *Alexandrian
   Tragedy*, sig. F4ᵛ: 'Staine of times
   past, and light of times to come'
   (Dent, *Webster*). Webster used very
   similar language to praise James I's
   eldest son Prince Henry, who died
   in 1612, in *Column*, 278 (Webster,
   3.383).
128 **gallery** long, narrow room for walking and access to other parts of the
   palace; when Antonio re-enters at 276,
   the stage space invisibly alters from the
   public audience chamber to the more
   private *gallery*.

123] *Q1 lines* her. / *Antonia,* / Antonia] *Antonio* | *Q2* 129–30] *Q1 lines* hence. / shall. / you: /
Sir? / 129 SD] *Q4 (subst.)* 132] *Q1 lines* Gallies. / him: / 133–4] *this edn; Q1 lines* for / horse.
/ him, /

Wants a spy

Trying to spy Bosola

is worthful

For the provisorship of your horse.

DUCHESS   Your knowledge of him   134

Commends him and prefers him.

FERDINAND   Call him hither.   [*Exit Attendant.*]

We now, upon parting, good lord Silvio,

Do us commend to all our noble friends

At the leaguer.

SILVIO   Sir, I shall.

FERDINAND   You are for Milan?

SILVIO

I am.

DUCHESS

Bring the caroches. We'll bring you down to the haven.   140

         [*Exeunt all but Cardinal and Ferdinand.*]

CARDINAL

Be sure you entertain that Bosola

For your intelligence. I would not be seen in't,

And therefore many times I have slighted him

When he did court our furtherance, as this morning.

FERDINAND

Antonio, the great master of her household,   145

Had been far fitter.

Contrast

134 **provisorship . . . horse** Master of the Horse, a prestigious position at court. Robert Dudley, Earl of Leicester, held an equivalent post under Elizabeth I.

136 **We . . . parting** The word 'are' may have been dropped out, or Ferdinand may be issuing a disjointed command.

138 **leaguer** military camp
You . . . Milan Following Sampson, some editors give this line to the Duchess on the grounds that Ferdinand should already know the

answer (56), but he may have forgotten or seek confirmation.

140 **caroches** large coaches
haven safe harbour for seagoing vessels

141–2 **entertain . . . intelligence** take into service as your spy

142 **I . . . in't** The Cardinal wants his role in Bosola's hiring to be invisible in order to preserve the public fiction that he wishes to have nothing to do with Bosola (cf. 1.1.29–44).

144 **furtherance** sponsorship

135] *Q1 lines* him. / heither, /   SD] *Dyce*   136 We] We are *Q4*   137 Do us commend] Commend us *Q4*   138] *Q1 lines* Leagues. / shall. / *Millaine?* /   leaguer] *Q2*; Leagues *Q1*; Camp *Q4*   140 caroches] Coaches *Q4*   SD] *Dyce (subst.)*   141 SP] *Car. to Ferd.* | *Q4*   143 I] *om. Q4*   146] *Q1 lines* fitter: / him, /

CARDINAL   You are deceived in him.
His nature is too honest for such business.
He comes – I'll leave you.   [*Exit.*]

why Antonio is not good

[*Enter*] BOSOLA.

BOSOLA   I was lured to you.
FERDINAND
My brother here, the Cardinal, could never
Abide you.
BOSOLA   Never since he was in my debt.   150
FERDINAND
Maybe some oblique character in your face
Made him suspect you.
BOSOLA   Doth he study physiognomy?
There's no more credit to be given to th' face
Than to a sick man's urine, which some call
The physician's whore, because she cozens him.   155
He did suspect me wrongfully.
FERDINAND   For that
You must give great men leave to take their times.
Distrust doth cause us seldom be deceived.

148 **lured** led, enticed; the word choice suggests that Bosola perceives himself to be entering into a trap.
149 **here** a verbal gesture towards the Cardinal, who had just left as Bosola was entering
150 **debt** for services rendered; cf. 1.1.34–7.
151 **oblique character** shady element
152 **physiognomy** science of determining character from facial and bodily features. During the Renaissance, new empirical study of the human body led some thinkers to postulate a codifiable relationship between physical and moral characteristics.

153 **credit** credibility, trustworthiness; belief
154–5 **sick . . . him** commonplace: 'Urine is the physician's whore' (Gunby). Physicians of the period examined a sick person's urine to try to determine the ailment. Bosola argues that, just as diagnosing from urine is a chancy business, so the face is an inexact indicator of character, seducing the observer into making a judgement, then betraying it.
156 **For that** in that matter
158 proverbial: 'He who trusts not is not deceived' (Dent, T559)

148] *Q1 lines* leave you: / to you. /   SD1] *Dyce*   SD2] *Dyce; Bosola,* | *0 SD Q1*   150–2] *this edn; prose Q1*   151+ Maybe] *(May be)*   152 you.] *(you?)*   155 she] it *Q4*   156] *Q1 lines* wrongfully: / that /

You see the oft shaking of the cedar tree
Fastens it more at root.

BOSOLA   Yet take heed: 160
For to suspect a friend unworthily
Instructs him the next way to suspect you,
And prompts him to deceive you.

FERDINAND   There's gold.

BOSOLA   So.
What follows? Never rained such showers as these
Without thunderbolts i'th' tail of them.   165
Whose throat must I cut?

FERDINAND
Your inclination to shed blood rides post
Before my occasion to use you. I give you that
To live i'th' court here and observe the Duchess,
To note all the particulars of her 'haviour,   170
What suitors do solicit her for marriage
And whom she best affects. She's a young widow;
I would not have her marry again.

BOSOLA   No, sir?

FERDINAND
Do not you ask the reason, but be satisfied

159–60 **oft . . . root** commonplace. Cf. Hall, *Epistles*, 2.171, where Hall uses the image for religious doubts that serve to reconfirm faith: 'The oft-shaking of the tree, fastens it more at the roote' (Dent, *Webster*). The opposite sentiment was also current. The cedar was often used as an emblem of greatness, and 'High cedars fall when low shrubs remain' (Dent, C208*).

161–2 **For . . . you** If you distrust your friend you will cause him to distrust you.

164–5 **showers . . . tail** seemingly an observation about weather, but refers also to Jupiter the Thunderer's rape of Danae in a shower of gold (Brown)

167 **rides post** is getting ahead of (because riding on a fast *post*-horse)

168 **occasion** need; opportunity

172 **affects** shows partiality for

174–5 **Do . . . would not** Be satisfied [that] I say I would not. Alternatively, this could be two clauses: 'Do not ask for reasons; I repeat that I don't want the Duchess to marry.'

160] *Q1 lines* roote. / heed: / 163] *Q1 lines* you. / gold. / So: / SP FERDINAND] *Q2; Berd.*|*Q1* 165–6] *Brennan; one line Q1* 170 'haviour] behaviour *Q2* 173] *Q1 lines* againe. / Sir? / 174 reason, . . . satisfied.] *(reason: . . . satisfied,)*

I say I would not.

BOSOLA   It seems you would create me   175
One of your familiars.

FERDINAND   Familiar? What's that?

BOSOLA

Why, a very quaint invisible devil, in flesh –
An intelligencer. *— absurd and warped sense of morality*

FERDINAND   Such a kind of thriving thing
I would wish thee; and ere long thou mayst arrive
At a higher place by't.

BOSOLA   Take your devils,   180
Which hell calls angels: these cursed gifts would make
You a corrupter, me an impudent traitor;
And, should I take these, they'd take me hell.

FERDINAND

Sir, I'll take nothing from you that I have given.
There is a place that I procured for you   185
This morning: the provisorship o'th' horse.
Have you heard on't?

BOSOLA   No.

FERDINAND   'Tis yours. Is't not worth thanks?

BOSOLA

I would have you curse yourself now, that your bounty,

---

176 **familiars** household intimates;
devils (like the demonic animals who
reportedly lived with witches). The
term was also applied by English
Protestants to agents of the Catholic
Church, especially of the Inquisition
(Lucas).

177 **quaint** cunning

180–1 **devils . . . angels** gold coins called
angels because they bore the image
of an angel on them; they are *devils*
because they have helped Ferdinand

to bribe Bosola and therefore compromised his honesty. Cf. Middleton,
Revenger, 2.1.88: 'forty angels can
make fourscore devils.'

183 **take me hell** In taking possession of
the coins he will also take possession
of hell. Most editors follow Q4 and
emend to 'take me to hell', which is
less forcefully abrupt.

187 ***on't** about it (the appointment)

188–9 **bounty . . . noble** Magnanimous
generosity is essential to nobility.

175–6] *Q1 lines* not. / me / familiars. / that? / 178] *Q1 lines* Intelligencer. / thing / intelligencer]
Informer *Q4*   179 thee] three *Q2*   180] *Q1 lines* by't. / Diuels. /   183 they'd] *(they'll'd)*   me] me
to *Q4*   186 provisorship] Mastership *Q4*   187] *Q1 lines* out? / Noe. / thankes? /   on't] *Q2 (ont);*
out *Q1*

Which makes men truly noble, e'er should make
Me a villain. Oh, that to avoid ingratitude   190
For the good deed you have done me, I must do
All the ill man can invent! Thus the devil
Candies all sins o'er, and what heaven terms vile,
That names he complemental.

FERDINAND   Be yourself.

Keep your old garb of melancholy. 'Twill express   195
You envy those that stand above your reach,
Yet strive not to come near 'em. This will gain
Access to private lodgings, where yourself
May, like a politic dormouse –

BOSOLA   As I have seen some
Feed in a lord's dish, half asleep, not seeming   200
To listen to any talk; and yet these rogues
Have cut his throat in a dream. What's my place?
The provisorship o'th' horse? Say then my corruption
Grew out of horse dung. I am your creature.

FERDINAND   Away!

BOSOLA

Let good men for good deeds covet good fame,   205

---

193 **Candies** sugar-coats; cf. *White Devil*, 5.6.57–9: 'O the cursed Devill, / Which doth present us with all other sinnes / Thrice candied ore.'
194 **complemental** an accomplishment, something to be proud of
195 **garb** clothing; Ferdinand implies Bosola's melancholy is nothing but a pose.
199 **politic dormouse** According to Pliny, the dormouse stays young by sleeping snug and close but unseen all winter long, then emerges revived and regenerated in spring (Pliny, 8.233); similarly the spy will *sleep* and conserve his energies until he can be useful to his masters.

200 **Feed . . . dish** occupy a place of great favour, where they share the same food. Cf. Jonson, 'To Penshurst', lines 61–4, where the poet boasts that in dining at the Sidney estate he eats of the 'Lord's own meat'.
202 **in a dream** while he was sleeping; or (if the dream in question belongs to the rogues) with such ease that it seemed no more than a dream
203–4 **corruption . . . dung** According to the theory of spontaneous generation, flies and vermin could develop out of dung.
205 **fame** reputation

189 e'er] *(ere)* 193 o'er] *Q2 (ore)*; are *Q1* vile] *Q3*; vild *Q1* 194] *Q1 lines* complementall. / selfe: / 195–204 'Twill . . . Away] *om. Q4* 199] *Q1 lines* dormouse, / some, / 204] *Q1 lines* creature. / Away. /

Since place and riches oft are bribes of shame.
Sometimes the devil doth preach.   *Exit.*

[*Enter* CARDINAL, DUCHESS *and* CARIOLA.]

CARDINAL
We are to part from you, and your own discretion
Must now be your director.
FERDINAND   You are a widow.
You know already what man is, and therefore   210
Let not youth, high promotion, eloquence –
CARDINAL
No, nor anything without the addition 'honour'
Sway your high blood.
FERDINAND   Marry? They are most luxurious
Will wed twice.
CARDINAL   Oh, fie!
FERDINAND   Their livers are more spotted
Than Laban's sheep.
DUCHESS   Diamonds are of most value,   215
They say, that have passed through most jewellers'
     hands.
FERDINAND
Whores by that rule are precious.

207 proverbial: 'The Devil can cite scrip-
     ture for his purpose' (Dent, D230*)
210 **You . . . is** You already have sexual
     experience; you know what to expect
     of men.
213 **high blood** noble lineage; passionate
     nature (Gibbons)
     luxurious lecherous
214–15 **livers . . . sheep** The liver was
     believed to be the seat of the passions,
     particularly lust; cf. *AYL* 3.2.404–6,

where Rosalind tells Orlando she will
'wash your liver . . . that there shall
not be one spot of love in't'. Laban's
spotted sheep come from Genesis,
30.25–43; Jacob caused Laban's sheep
to be born spotted to increase his payment for services rendered. Shylock
uses the same passage to justify usury
(*MV* 1.3.73ff.).
215–16 **Diamonds . . . hands** i.e. because
     each jeweller adds further polish

207 doth preach] preaches *Q4*   SD1] *(Exit Bosola.)*   SD2] *Dyce² (subst.)*   209] *Q1 lines* director. /
Widowe: /   213–15] *Q1 lines* blood. / luxurious, / twice, / fie: / spotted / sheepe. / value /   214–15
Their . . . sheep] *om. Q4*

[handwritten: precious/ cuts off her brother]

DUCHESS   Will you hear me?
    I'll never marry.

CARDINAL   So most widows say,
    But commonly that motion lasts no longer
    Than the turning of an hourglass; the funeral sermon   220
    And it end both together.

FERDINAND   Now hear me –
    You live in a rank pasture here i'th' court.
    There is a kind of honeydew that's deadly;
    'Twill poison your fame. Look to't. Be not cunning,
    For they whose faces do belie their hearts   225
    Are witches ere they arrive at twenty years –
    Ay, and give the devil suck.

DUCHESS
    This is terrible good counsel.

FERDINAND
    Hypocrisy is woven of a fine, small thread,
    Subtler than Vulcan's engine; yet, believe't,   230

---

218 **I'll never marry** Q1 indicates a colon here. Alternatively, editors wishing to save the Duchess's reputation from the blot of a lie have suggested that the line could be a statement interrupted by the Cardinal before its completion (see t.n.).

219 **motion** inclination, emotion; spectacle or show, e.g. the *motion* of 'Hero and Leander', the puppet-show in Jonson's *Bartholomew Fair*, 5.3

220–1 **hourglass . . . together** Sermons were often timed with an hourglass, in this case for the funeral of the new widow's husband.

222 **rank pasture** grazing land that has rotted

223 **honeydew** sticky substance found on leaves, often as the residue of aphids,

but then believed to be a form of dew

226 **twenty years** If Ferdinand is right about young women, then the Duchess is already a witch: her historical age in 1504 was about 26 (see List of Roles, 1n.).

227 **give . . . suck** Witches were commonly believed to have special teats used to nurse their familiars, or devils; so, unknowingly, the Duchess is giving sustenance to Ferdinand's 'familiar', Bosola.

228 **terrible good** terribly good (said with trenchant irony); very bad

229 proverbial (Dent, H844.11)

230 **Vulcan's engine** the fine nets by which the god Vulcan trapped his wife Venus in an adulterous tryst with Mars

217–18] *Q1 lines* precious: / me? / marry: / say: / DINAL] *Ferd.* | *Q2*   221] *Q1 lines* together. / me: /   218 marry.] *(marry:); marry – Gunby*   SP CAR-   229 of] in *Q4*

Your darkest actions – nay, your privatest thoughts,
Will come to light.

CARDINAL   You may flatter yourself
And take your own choice – privately be married
Under the eaves of night –

FERDINAND   Think't the best voyage
That e'er you made, like the irregular crab,   235
Which, though't goes backward, thinks that it goes
    right
Because it goes its own way. But observe:
Such weddings may more properly be said
To be executed than celebrated.

CARDINAL   The marriage night
Is the entrance into some prison.

FERDINAND   And those joys,   240
Those lustful pleasures, are like heavy sleeps,
Which do forerun man's mischief.

CARDINAL   Fare you well.
Wisdom begins at the end. Remember it.   [*Exit.*]

DUCHESS
I think this speech between you both was studied,
It came so roundly off.

FERDINAND   You are my sister.   245

---

231 **darkest** most secret; worst

234 **eaves of night** imagining night as an eave-like shelter for nefarious activities, since eaves are frequented by bats and owls. Cf. Dekker on the secrecy of Catholic agents infiltrating England, in *Whore*, 3.1.158: they 'Flie with the Batt under the eeves of night'.

235–7 **crab . . . way** Cf. Sidney, 'Crab-fish, which . . . lookes one way and goes another' (*Arcadia*, book 2, ch. 3, 164; Lucas).

239 **executed** performed; put to death

241 **heavy sleeps** like those of a drunkard: when a person is 'drunk' with sensuality, reason lies asleep.

242 **forerun** precede

243 **Wisdom . . . end** proverbial: 'Think on the end before you begin' (Dent, E124). There is a sexual innuendo on 'end'; cf. *tail*, 165.

244–5 **I . . . off** Your joint speech must have been planned in advance because it was so polished.

232] *Q1 lines* light. / your selfe, /   234] *Q1 lines* night. / voyage /   eaves] *Brown;* Eues *Q1;* Eves *Q2*   239–40] *Q1 lines* celibrated. / night / prison. / ioyes, /   242] *Q1 lines* mischiefe / well. /   243 SD] *Q4*   245] *Q1 lines* off. / sister, /

This was my father's poniard. Do you see?

[*Shows her a poniard.*]

I'd be loath to see't look rusty, 'cause 'twas his.
I would have you to give o'er these chargeable revels;
A visor and a masque are whispering rooms
That were ne'er built for goodness. Fare ye well.   250
And women like that part which, like the lamprey,
Hath ne'er a bone in't.

DUCHESS   Fie, sir!

FERDINAND   Nay,
I mean the tongue. Variety of courtship –
What cannot a neat knave with a smooth tale   254
Make a woman believe? Farewell, lusty widow!   [*Exit.*]

DUCHESS

Shall this move me? If all my royal kindred
Lay in my way unto this marriage,
I'd make them my low footsteps. And even now,
Even in this hate, as men in some great battles
By apprehending danger have achieved   260
Almost impossible actions – I have heard soldiers
    say so –

246 **poniard** dagger (with phallic impli-
    cations)
247 As his dagger will rust if left out in
    the air, so the Duchess will become
    contaminated and lose her reputation
    if she shows herself too much in pub-
    lic.
248 **chargeable revels** expensive cel-
    ebrations (presumably to mark the
    visit of her brothers to Amalfi)
249 **visor** mask, as worn in court revels
    masque elaborate theatrical perform-
    ance with magnificent spectacles and
    dancing
    whispering rooms echo chambers in
    which things whispered almost inaudi-
    bly can be heard at great distance

251 **lamprey** type of eel, with a bawdy
    suggestion of 'penis'
253 **Variety of courtship** fickleness or
    changeability of seduction
254 **tale** story; 'tail', penis
255 **lusty widow** a stereotyped figure in
    the Italian *commedia dell'arte*, but also
    in English drama. Cf. Hamlet's hor-
    ror at his widowed mother's sexuality
    (*Ham* 1.2.129–59).
258 **make . . . footsteps** walk over them
    to achieve my end
259 **this hate** the deep disapproval her
    brothers would feel for her proposed
    marriage, were they to know of it
260 **apprehending** perceiving the pres-
    ence of

246 SD] *this edn*   247 I'd] *(*I'll'd*)*   251–5 And . . . widow] *om. in performance Q4*   251 women like]
beware of *Q4*   252] *Q1 lines* in't. / Sir: / Nay, /   255 SD] *Q4*   258 I'd] *(*I'll'd*)*   259 hate] heat *Q4*

So I, through frights and threatenings, will assay
This dangerous venture. Let old wives report
I winked and chose a husband. Cariola,
To thy known secrecy I have given up   265
More than my life – my fame.

CARIOLA   Both shall be safe;
For I'll conceal this secret from the world
As warily as those that trade in poison
Keep poison from their children.

DUCHESS   Thy protestation
Is ingenious and hearty. I believe it.   270
Is Antonio come?

CARIOLA   He attends you.

DUCHESS   Good! Dear soul,
Leave me, but place thyself behind the arras,
Where thou mayst overhear us. Wish me good speed,
For I am going into a wilderness
Where I shall find nor path nor friendly clue   275

262–3 **assay . . . venture** undertake this
dangerous enterprise (her secret marriage)
263–4 **Let . . . husband** i.e. I don't care
what people think: gossips (*old wives*) can
imagine that I chose with my eyes shut.
264 **Cariola** Some editors, following
Brown and R. H. Horne's influential
1850 stage adaptation of *Malfi*, have
Cariola enter only here, which solves
the later problem of how she knows
that Antonio is waiting (271). But she
could look out quickly for Antonio at
271. Having her hear the conversation with the Duchess's brothers helps
motivate her reaction at the end of the
scene (410–12).
269 **Keep . . . children** Cariola's likening
of the Duchess's proposed match to

poison reveals her covert disapproval
of it and her fear for the status of its
offspring (whose lineage may be 'poisoned', tainted).
270 **ingenious** cleverly invented
271 **Good . . . soul** Alternatively, *Good*
could modify *dear soul*, and, given Q1's
punctuation (t.n.), *Dear soul* could
refer either to Cariola or to Antonio.
272 **arras** curtain, probably hung across
the back of the stage; cf. Polonius' hiding place in *Ham* 3.4.
273 **overhear us** so she can serve as a
witness
275 **nor . . . nor** neither . . . nor
clue The Q1 spelling 'clewe' could also
mean a ball of thread, suggesting the
thread by which Theseus escaped the
labyrinth of the Minotaur (Gibbons).

---

262 threatenings] *(threatnings)* assay] affray *Q2* 264 Cariola,] Cariola, [*Enter* CARIOLA.]
Brown 266] *Q1 lines* fame: / safe: / SP] *Q2*; *Carolia*|*Q1* 269] *Q1 lines* children. / protestation
/ 271] *Q1 lines* come? / you: / soule, / Good! Dear] *this edn;* Good deare *Q1* 275 nor path] no
path *Q2* clue] *(clewe)*

To be my guide.   [*Cariola goes behind the arras.*]

[*Enter* ANTONIO.]

I sent for you. Sit down.
Take pen and ink and write. Are you ready?

ANTONIO   Yes.

DUCHESS

What did I say?

ANTONIO   That I should write somewhat.

DUCHESS

Oh, I remember.
After this triumphs and this large expense   280
It's fit like thrifty husbands we enquire
What's laid up for tomorrow.

ANTONIO

So please your beauteous Excellence.

DUCHESS   Beauteous?
Indeed I thank you. I look young for your sake.
You have ta'en my cares upon you.

ANTONIO   I'll fetch your grace   285

---

276 At this point the stage becomes a more private space than the bustling audience chamber where the scene began.

277 The Duchess asks Antonio to write, not because she is incapable of doing so herself, but because as her servant he is expected to act as her scribe, as courtiers often did, for example, in the court of Elizabeth I. The House of Aragon was noted for giving its women a good humanist education (Amendola).

278 **somewhat** something

280 **this triumphs** these celebrations of her brothers' visit; cf. Ferdinand's complaints (248). The historical Duchess's brothers made a similar visit to Amalfi in 1509. Some editors emend *this* to 'these', but 'this' with a plural noun was common usage in the period.

281 **husbands** good managers, savers, with a hint of 'marriage partner'; cf. 297, 302.

282 **laid up** put aside, conserved

284–5 **I look . . . upon you** It's easy for me to look young because you manage all my problems; *for your sake* also suggests that she takes care of her appearance to please Antonio.

276 SD1] *Dyce; Exit. Car.* | *opp. 272 Q4; Cariola withdraws behind the arras. The Duchess draws the traverse revealing Antonio.* | *Lucas* SD2] *opp. 273 Q4* 277–8] *Q1 lines* ready? / Yes: / say? / some-what. /   280 this triumphs] this triumph *Q3;* these triumphs *Dyce* 283–6] *Sampson; Q1 lines* Excellence. / sake. / you. / the / expence. /

The particulars of your revenue and expense.

DUCHESS

    Oh, you are an upright treasurer, but you mistook.

    For when I said I meant to make enquiry

    What's laid up for tomorrow, I did mean

    What's laid up yonder for me.

ANTONIO   Where?

DUCHESS   In heaven.   290

    I am making my will, as 'tis fit princes should,

    In perfect memory, and I pray, sir, tell me:

    Were not one better make it smiling thus

    Than in deep groans and terrible ghastly looks –

    As if the gifts we parted with procured   295

    That violent destruction?

ANTONIO   Oh, much better.

DUCHESS

    If I had a husband now, this care were quit;

    But I intend to make you overseer.

    What good deed shall we first remember? Say!

ANTONIO

    Begin with that first good deed began i'th' world   300

    After man's creation – the sacrament of marriage.

    I'd have you first provide for a good husband:

---

286 **particulars** specifics
292 **In perfect memory** while of sound mind (legal terminology)
295–6 **As . . . destruction** as if we were driven to our deathbed by horror at being forced to give up our worldly possessions
297 **quit** moot. Under English law of the time, her husband would be owner of all her assets. Italian law was more variable: in Venice and some other states, women kept control of their property after marriage.
298 **overseer** executor (of the will and her estate)
299 **good deed** She apparently plans to reward her virtuous survivors with shares of her estate.
300–1 **that first . . . marriage** the marriage of Adam and Eve, when God bid them to be fruitful and multiply (Genesis, 1.28)

290] *Q1 lines* me. / Where? / Heauen, /   293 better] better to *Q2*   296] *Q1 lines* distruction? / better. / destruction] distraction *Q3*   298 you overseer] *Q2;* yon Ouer-seer *Q1*   300 first good deed] good deed that first *Q2*   302 I'd] *(*I'ld*)*

Give him all.

DUCHESS   All?

ANTONIO   Yes, your excellent self.

DUCHESS   In a winding sheet?

ANTONIO

In a couple.

DUCHESS   St Winfred! That were a strange will!

ANTONIO

'Twere strange if there were no will in you   305
To marry again.

DUCHESS   What do you think of marriage?

ANTONIO

I take't as those that deny purgatory:
It locally contains or heaven or hell;
There's no third place in't.

DUCHESS   How do you affect it?

ANTONIO

My banishment, feeding my melancholy,   310
Would often reason thus –

---

303 Antonio says that she should give her *self* to a husband in marriage. She pretends to misunderstand Antonio as still referring to her will; when it is executed she will be dead – in her *winding sheet* or shroud – and hence unavailable for marriage. Q3's reading, which substitutes 'me' for *him*, though not authoritative, is interesting for its portrayal of pre-existing ambition in Antonio.

304 **In a couple** as part of a married pair
St Winfred or Winifred, a seventh-century Welsh saint who was beheaded for refusing to marry Caradoc ap Alauc, then restored to life (Brown)

307 **those . . . purgatory** a reference to contemporary Protestants, for whom there was no *third place* (309) after death. This was a major ideological divergence from Catholicism after the Reformation. It is a variation of the proverb 'Marriage is a heaven or a hell' (Dent, M680.11).

309 **affect** feel about

310 **banishment** According to Painter and other sources, the historical Antonio de Bologna was banished to France along with King Federico after he lost the Kingdom of Naples in 1501 (see Appendix 1). At the beginning of the play (1.1.1–3) Delio describes Antonio as recently returned from France.

303–4] *Q1 lines* all. / All? / selfe. / sheete? / cople. / will. /   303 him] me *Q3; om. Q4*   304 Winfred] Winifred *Dyce*   306] *Q1 lines* againe. / marriage? /   309] *Q1 lines* in't. / it? /   311] *Q1 lines* thus. / it. /

DUCHESS   Pray, let's hear it.

ANTONIO

Say a man never marry nor have children –
What takes that from him? Only the bare name
Of being a father, or the weak delight
To see the little wanton ride a-cock-horse   315
Upon a painted stick, or hear him chatter
Like a taught starling.

DUCHESS   Fie, fie, what's all this?

One of your eyes is bloodshot; use my ring to't.
    [*Gives him her ring.*]
They say 'tis very sovereign: 'twas my wedding ring,
And I did vow never to part with it   320
But to my second husband.

ANTONIO   You have parted with it now.

DUCHESS

Yes, to help your eyesight.

ANTONIO   You have made me stark blind.

DUCHESS   How?

ANTONIO

There is a saucy and ambitious devil

312–17 **Say . . . starling** Cf. Elyot, cap. 26, sig. P1ᵛ: Alexander Severus tells his mother, 'I am sure, that sterilitie can no more hurte me, but onely take frome me the name of a father, or the dotynge pleasure to se my lytell sonne ryde on a cokhorse, or to here hym chatter and speake lyke a wanton' (Dent, *Webster*).

315 **wanton** fool, rogue (but not particularly pejorative; commonly used of children in the period)

317 **taught starling** In this period starlings were taught to speak but not, Antonio implies, to understand the meaning of the words. Cf. *1H4* 1.3.222–3, where Hotspur, forbidden to speak the name of Mortimer, vows to 'have a starling shall be taught to speak / Nothing but "Mortimer"'.

318 **use my ring** Gold was believed efficacious against eye ailments (Gunby).

319 **sovereign** efficacious (a *sovereign* remedy); also suggests sovereignty in the sense of rule, but leaves ambiguous which of the couple is to be the ruler

322 **stark blind** blinded (by ambition)

323–4 **devil . . . circle** Antonio imagines the circumference of the ring as a

315 wanton] Wantons *Q4* 316 him] 'em *Q4* 317] *Q1 lines* Starling. / this? / 318 SD] *Gunby (subst.)* 321–4] *Q1 lines* husband. / now. / eye-sight. / blind. / How? / diuell / circle. / him. / How? /

163

Is dancing in this circle.

DUCHESS   Remove him.

ANTONIO   How?

DUCHESS

There needs small conjuration when your finger   325
May do it thus.   [*Puts the ring on his finger.*]
                    Is it fit?

ANTONIO   What said you?   (*He kneels.*)

DUCHESS   Sir,

This goodly roof of yours is too low built.
I cannot stand upright in't, nor discourse,
Without I raise it higher. Raise yourself;
Or, if you please, my hand to help you.
        [*Gives her hand. Antonio rises.*]   So.   330

ANTONIO

Ambition, madam, is a great man's madness
That is not kept in chains and close-pent rooms
But in fair lightsome lodgings and is girt
With the wild noise of prattling visitants,
Which makes it lunatic beyond all cure.   335

---

magic circle into which the devil has been conjured, as happens repeatedly in Marlowe's *Faustus*. Reginald Scot, however, discusses how magic circles can be used to protect against evil spirits (Scot, book 15, ch. 13, 416). To 'put the devil in the ring' also suggests sexual intercourse, since *devil* was a colloquial term for 'penis' (Rebhorn, 55).

325 **conjuration** exorcism (of the devil, ambition)

326 **Is it fit** is it fitting; does it fit

327 **roof ... built** You are being too humble (comparing Antonio to a simple house). Cf. Hall's character of a 'Humble Man': 'a true Temple of God built with a low roofe' (Lucas).

329 **Without** unless

330 SD Some editors specify 'She raises him.' Antonio stands at this point, but the degree of his agency is left open in the text.

331 Cf. proverbial 'Ambition is blind' (Dent, A233.11).

332 **kept ... rooms** standard treatment for madness in the period; cf. 4.2, where madmen appear in chains onstage.

333 **lightsome** well-lit, elegant

333–4 **girt ... visitants** encircled not with chains and *prattling* madmen, but with respectful courtiers plying him with various suits. Antonio suggests that the madness is the same, despite the contrasting setting.

326] *Q1 lines* fit? / you? / Sir, /   SD1] *Dyce (subst.)*   330 SD] *this edn; Raises him* | *Dyce²*   334 visitants] (*visitans*)

Conceive not I am so stupid but I aim
Whereto your favours tend. But he's a fool
That, being a-cold, would thrust his hands i'th' fire
To warm them.

DUCHESS   So – now the ground's broke,
You may discover what a wealthy mine   340
I make you lord of.

ANTONIO   Oh, my unworthiness –

DUCHESS

You were ill to sell yourself.
This darkening of your worth is not like that
Which tradesmen use i'th' city: their false lights
Are to rid bad wares off. And I must tell you,   345
If you will know where breathes a complete man
(I speak it without flattery) turn your eyes,
And progress through yourself.

ANTONIO   Were there nor heaven, nor hell,
I should be honest: I have long served virtue,
And ne'er ta'en wages of her.

DUCHESS   Now she pays it.   350
The misery of us that are born great!

---

336 **aim** guess; share the same goal
338 **a-cold** cold; cf. 'Poor Tom's a-cold'
    in *KL* 3.4.57.
340 **mine** not her estate, but herself
    (with sexual implications). Cf. *MV*
    3.2.166, where Portia similarly con-
    flates 'Myself and what is mine' in
    giving herself to Bassanio.
342 You would do a bad job selling your-
    self.
343 **darkening . . . worth** self-deprecation
344–5 **tradesmen . . . off** Tradesmen
    display shoddy goods in a low light so
    customers will buy them without see-

ing their defects – a trick referred to so
frequently by dramatists that it probably reflected contemporary London
practice. Cf. *Philaster*, 5.3.141–3.
346 **complete man** well-rounded, per-
    fect man, as in the popular book of
    comportment, *The Compleat Gentleman*
    (Peacham)
348 **progress** journey, suggesting a royal
    progress through a kingdom
349–50 **I have . . . her** variant of the
    proverb 'Virtue is its own reward'
    (Dent, V81*); cf. 1.1.31–2.
350 **it** his wages

---

336 but I aim] as not perceive *Q4*   339] *Q1 lines* them. / broake, /   342 were] do *Q4*   343 darkening]
(darkning)   344 city] *(City)*   345 must] *om. Q4*   346 will] would *Q2*   348] *Q1 lines* selfe. / hell,
/   350] *Q1 lines* her. / it, /

We are forced to woo because none dare woo us.
And as a tyrant doubles with his words
And fearfully equivocates, so we
Are forced to express our violent passions   355
In riddles and in dreams, and leave the path
Of simple virtue, which was never made
To seem the thing it is not. Go – go brag
You have left me heartless: mine is in your bosom;
I hope 'twill multiply love there. You do tremble.   360
Make not your heart so dead a piece of flesh
To fear more than to love me. Sir, be confident –
What is't distracts you? This is flesh and blood, sir:
'Tis not the figure cut in alabaster
Kneels at my husband's tomb. Awake, awake, man!   365
I do here put off all vain ceremony
And only do appear to you a young widow
That claims you for her husband; and, like a widow,
I use but half a blush in't.

ANTONIO   Truth speak for me:
I will remain the constant sanctuary   370

---

352 **woo** appears twice in the line. The Q1
spelling 'woe' for both suggests that it is
'woe' to be the wooer, but also hints at
the danger of the situation: their wooing may turn to 'woe' (Jellerson).

353 **doubles** says them in one sense but
means them in another

355 **passions** pronounced as three
syllables

358–60 **Go . . . there** The exchang-
ing of hearts was a frequent trope in
Petrarchan poetry of the period.

363 **This . . . blood** a variation of the
proverb 'To be flesh and blood as
others are' (Dent, F367*)

364–5 **figure . . . tomb** Cf. *MV* 1.1.83–4:
'Why should a man whose blood is warm
within, / Sit like his grandsire, cut in

alablaster?' Frequently, at the time, a
sculptural image of the kneeling wife
would be carved on the tomb of her dead
husband, as is evidently the case with the
Duchess's first husband's tomb.

365 **man** The Duchess here employs
a brusque form of address that at
the time implied condescension, in
marked contrast with the *sir* of 363
and the *gentle love* of 371. Perhaps she
hopes that her change in tone will jolt
him out of his fear and hesitation.

366 **ceremony** rituals associated with her
high social status

370 **constant sanctuary** reliable place
of safety, perhaps with a hint of the
sanctuary offered by churches for fugi-
tives from justice

352+ woo] *(woe)* 360–9 You . . . in't] *om. in performance Q4* 360 do] *om. Q4* 364 alabaster]
(Allablaster) 369] *Q1 lines* in't. / me, /

Of your good name.

DUCHESS   I thank you, gentle love.

And 'cause you shall not come to me in debt,

Being now my steward, here upon your lips

I sign your *Quietus est.* [*Kisses him.*]

                         This you should have begged now.

I have seen children oft eat sweetmeats thus,   375

As fearful to devour them too soon.

ANTONIO

But for your brothers?

DUCHESS   Do not think of them.

All discord without this circumference

Is only to be pitied and not feared.

Yet, should they know it, time will easily   380

Scatter the tempest.

ANTONIO   These words should be mine,

And all the parts you have spoke, if some part of it

Would not have savoured flattery.

DUCHESS [*Brings out Cariola.*]   Kneel.

ANTONIO   Ha?

---

374 ***Quietus est*** proverbial: to 'Get one's
quietus' (Dent, Q16*) is to receive
release from a debt. The phrase is
also used for the release of death, as
in *Ham* 3.1.74–5: 'might his quietus
make / With a bare bodkin'.
This her kiss

375–6 Evidently Antonio's kiss has been
too hesitant.

375 **sweetmeats** sweets

378 **without this circumference** outside our embrace, or outside the walls
of this room. Cf. Donne, 'The Good

Morrow', 10–11: 'love, all love of other
sights controls, / And makes one little
room, an everywhere.'

380–1 **time . . . tempest** proverbial:
'Time heals all wounds' or 'Time
cures all disease' (Dent, T325). The
Duchess's choice of the word *tempest*
turns out to be apt: when Ferdinand
eventually hears that his sister has
been sexually active, he is like one
carried 'On violent whirlwinds'
(2.5.51).

383 **savoured** tasted like, smacked of

371] *Q1 lines* name. / loue) /   374 SD] *Brown*   376 them] 'em *Q4*   377] *Q1 lines* Brothers? / them,
/   378–86 All . . . marriage] *om. in performance Q4*   381] *Q1 lines* tempest. / mine, /   383] *Q1 lines*
flattery. / Kneele. / Hah? /   savoured] favour'd *Q2;* savour'd of *Q4*   SD] *this edn;* Enter *Cariola.*
| *Q4*

DUCHESS

Be not amazed – this woman's of my counsel.

I have heard lawyers say a contract in a chamber   385

Per verba presenti is absolute marriage.   [*They kneel.*]

Bless, heaven, this sacred Gordian, which let violence

Never untwine.

ANTONIO

And may our sweet affections, like the spheres,

Be still in motion –

DUCHESS   Quickening, and make   390

The like soft music –

ANTONIO

That we may imitate the loving palms,

Best emblem of a peaceful marriage,

That ne'er bore fruit divided.

---

384 **of my counsel** my confidante; also, legal language

385 **a contract . . . chamber** a private contract of marriage; see 386n.

386 *Per verba presenti* by words said in the present – the legal formula *per verba de presenti* defining valid clandestine marriage, which comprised mutual promises to wed in the present followed by consummation of the marriage. In Jacobean England (earlier in continental Europe), marriage in church had become the preferred form, but marriage *per verba de presenti* was still considered binding.
absolute perfectly valid

386 SD At 383 the Duchess has asked Antonio to kneel, and some editors call for him to kneel then. Having the couple kneel together emphasizes the mutuality of their contract.

387–8 **Bless . . . untwine** The Duchess prays for blessings on her marriage, imagined, as frequently in the period,

as the mythic Gordian knot that no one could untie until Alexander the Great violently sliced through it with his sword. Cf. *Insatiate Countess*, 2.1.6–8: 'O may . . . this individual Gordian grasp of hands / . . . Never be severed.'

389 **spheres** crystalline orbits of the planets, according to Ptolemaic astronomy

390 **still** always

390–1 **Quickening . . . music** stimulating each other with a touch that creates harmonious music like the planetary sound, the 'music of the spheres', created by the heavenly bodies in motion

392 **That** Antonio's responses here and at 395 begin with *That*, like litanies of the Church of England (Brown).
palms common emblem of marriage; according to Pliny, 13.386, a single palm standing alone never bore fruit.

393 **marriage** pronounced as three syllables

394 a hexameter line

386 SD] *Dyce²* (*subst.*)   *verba*] verba de | *Brown*   390] *Q1 lines* motion, / make / Quickening] (Quickning)   394] *Q1 lines* deuided. / more? /

DUCHESS   What can the church force more?

ANTONIO

    That fortune may not know an accident,   395

    Either of joy or sorrow, to divide

    Our fixed wishes.

DUCHESS   How can the church build faster?

    We now are man and wife, and 'tis the church

    That must but echo this.   [*They rise.*]

                         – Maid, stand apart.

    I now am blind.

ANTONIO   What's your conceit in this?   400

DUCHESS

    I would have you lead your Fortune by the hand

    Unto your marriage bed.

    You speak in me this, for we now are one.

    We'll only lie and talk together, and plot

    T'appease my humorous kindred; and if you please,   405

    Like the old tale in *Alexander and Ludowick*,

    Lay a naked sword between us, keep us chaste.

    Oh, let me shroud my blushes in your bosom,

What . . . more? How can the church force us to marry there, when the marriage we have just contracted is perfectly valid? According to some accounts, however, the historical Duchess and Antonio did eventually validate their union in church.

397 **fixed** fixèd

    faster more firmly

400–1 **blind . . . Fortune** The Duchess enacts a common proverb: 'Fortune is blind' (Dent, F604*).

400 **conceit** metaphorical meaning

403 **we . . . one** a frequent conceit in love poetry of the period. Cf. Donne, 'The Ecstasy', 74: the lovers, their souls united, speak a 'dialogue of one'.

405 **humorous** ill-humoured, unbalanced

406 *Alexander and Ludowick* A play by this title was performed in 1597; a contemporary ballad probably based on it tells of two 'faithful friends' who resembled each other so closely that Ludowick married the Princess of Hungary in Alexander's name, then laid a sword between himself and the princess every night so he would not wrong his friend (Gunby).

408 **shroud** hide, but with possible ominous implications, since a shroud could also be a covering for the dead; cf. *winding sheet* (303).

397] *Q1 lines* wishes. / faster? /   build] bind *Brown*   399 SD] *Gunby*   399–403 Maid . . . together] Let us retire *Q4*   400] *Q1 lines* blinde. / this? /   405–7 and . . . chaste] *om. Q4*

Since 'tis the treasury of all my secrets.

CARIOLA

Whether the spirit of greatness or of woman   410
Reign most in her, I know not; but it shows
A fearful madness. I owe her much of pity.   *Exeunt.*

2.1   [*Enter*] BOSOLA [*and*] CASTRUCCIO.

BOSOLA   You say you would fain be taken for an eminent
courtier?

CASTRUCCIO   'Tis the very main of my ambition.

BOSOLA   Let me see – you have a reasonable good face
for't already, and your nightcap expresses your ears   5
sufficient largely. I would have you learn to twirl the
strings of your band with a good grace, and in a set
speech at th'end of every sentence to hum three or four
times, or blow your nose till it smart again, to recover
your memory. When you come to be a president in   10

---

409 Beginning with Dyce, many editors
   have the Duchess and Antonio exit
   here, but the Q1 SD calls for an *exeunt*
   at the end of the scene, and it is truer
   to the 'whispering room' atmosphere
   of the play (see pp. 75–6) to have the
   couple onstage when Cariola utters
   her fears.
410 **spirit . . . woman** heroism, associated with *greatness*, or waywardness,
   traditionally associated with women
412 **fearful madness** madness that is
   frightening, much to be feared
2.1   Location: the Duchess's palace
1   **would fain** desire to
3   **main** most important element; purpose

5–6 **nightcap . . . largely** Castruccio
   evidently wears the close-fitting white
   cap of a serjeant-at-law, which causes
   his ears to have comical prominence.
7   **band** pointed white collar worn by lawyers with a string attached; ruff worn
   by courtiers. Cf. Jonson, *Cynthia's
   Revels*, 5.4.158, where a satirical portrait of a courtier includes the fact that
   he plays officiously with his 'band-
   string' (Brown).
7–8 **set speech** speech that has been
   composed in advance and is delivered
   from memory
9   **again** in response
10   **president** presiding magistrate

412 of] *om. Q4*   SD] *Exeunt* Duchess *and* Antonio *after 410 Dyce*   **2.1**] *(ACTVS II. SCENA
I.)*   0 SD] *Q4 (subst.); Bosola, Castruchio, an Old Lady, Antonio, Delio, Duchesse, Rodorico, Grisolan.
| Q1*   5–49 and . . . yourselves] *om. Q4*

criminal causes, if you smile upon a prisoner, hang him;
but, if you frown upon him and threaten him, let him
be sure to 'scape the gallows.

CASTRUCCIO   I would be a very merry president.

BOSOLA   Do not sup a' nights – 'twill beget you an   15
admirable wit.

CASTRUCCIO   Rather it would make me have a good
stomach to quarrel, for they say your roaring boys eat
meat seldom, and that makes them so valiant. But how
shall I know whether the people take me for an eminent   20
fellow?

BOSOLA   I will teach a trick to know it: give out you lie a-
dying, and, if you hear the common people curse you,
be sure you are taken for one of the prime nightcaps.

[*Enter*] OLD LADY.

You come from painting now?   25

OLD LADY   From what?

BOSOLA   Why, from your scurvy face-physic; to behold
thee not painted inclines somewhat near a miracle.
These in thy face here were deep ruts and foul sloughs

15 **a' nights** at night (colloquial)
18 **stomach** courage, spirit
  roaring boys slang term for London
  rowdies – gangs of foppish, unruly
  youths who are often represented
  in plays of the time. Cf. *Roaring
  Girl*, based on the life of the female
  'roarer' Moll Frith, who dressed as a
  man, drank in public, attended plays
  and comported herself as one of
  the *roaring boys*; cf. also the 'roarer'
  Val Cutting and his companions in
  Jonson's *Bartholomew Fair*, 4.4, and
  the denizens of the 'Roaring School'
  in *Quarrel*, 4.1. Webster was suf-

ficiently fascinated by the type that
one of his *Characters* offers an elaborate description of 'A Roaring Boy'
(Webster, 3.469–70).
22 **give out** make it known that; spread
  the word that
24 **prime nightcaps** chief lawyers
24 SD OLD LADY probably a midwife
  for the Duchess (see List of Roles,
  15n.)
25 **painting** using cosmetics
27 **scurvy face-physic** contemptible
  face treatment
29 **These** wrinkles
  foul sloughs muddy ditches

20–38 for . . . *plastic*] *prose Dyce; Q1 lines* fellow. / it, / if you, / curse you, / night-caps, / now? /
what? / face-physicke, / neere / rutes, / progresse: / pockes, / leuell; / Nutmeg-grater, / hedge-hog.
/ painting? / old / againe, / plastique. /   24 SD] *Dyce (subst.); an* Old Lady, | *0 SD Q1*

the last progress. There was a lady in France that,   30
having had the smallpox, flayed the skin off her face
to make it more level; and, whereas before she looked
like a nutmeg grater, after she resembled an abortive
hedgehog.

OLD LADY   Do you call this painting?   35

BOSOLA   No, no, but you call careening of an old
    morphewed lady to make her disembogue again –
    there's roughcast phrase to your plastic.

OLD LADY

  It seems you are well acquainted with my closet?

BOSOLA

  One would suspect it for a shop of witchcraft: 40
  to find in it the fat of serpents, spawn of snakes, Jews'

---

30 **progress** ceremonial royal journey,
which courtiers would have accompanied

30–2 **There ... level** The lady used a
precursor of the modern chemical
peel, in this case to erase the deep
scars left by *smallpox*. Cf. Montaigne,
1.132, who describes a Parisian lady
who 'to get a fresher hew of a new
skinne, endured to have hir face fleand
all over' (Lucas).

33 **abortive** useless, defective; born
prematurely

35 **this painting** evidently referring to
the makeup on her own face

36–8 **careening ... plastic** Bosola is
being deliberately obscure – hiding
his meaning with complicated language, the linguistic equivalent of
using makeup, or *painting*, which he
accuses the Old Lady of doing to hide
her wrinkles. But his description of his
own language as *roughcast*, or gravelly
and rough-hewn, simultaneously suggests that he is playing the satirist
– attempting a brutal frankness to
counteract, perhaps even correct, her
plastic, the artificial reshaping of her

face through makeup. He describes
her as if she were an old ship whose
rotting or *morphewed* hull must be
turned on its side or 'careened' and
scraped before it will be fit to leave
port or *disembogue*, implying that her
makeup must be scraped off before she
will be fit to be seen in public.

39 **closet** bedroom, or the most private of
the Old Lady's rooms. Her tone could
be either seductive or outraged.

41–50 mostly prose, but gradually modulates towards verse in Q1, where 41–4
are printed as extremely long lines and
45–50 as lines that become progressively shorter, but without being iden-
tifiable as verse until, perhaps, 49, 'I do
wonder you doe not loath your selves.'
Keeping the whole speech prose up
to 50 highlights the contrast between
Bosola's satiric prose invective and his
verse meditation that follows.

41 **serpents** creeping reptiles

41–2 **Jews' spittle** in an anti-Semitic
age, considered particularly virulent;
cf. *Mac* 4.1.26, where the witches add
the 'Liver of blaspheming Jew' to their
cauldron.

41–50] *Q1 lines prose to 47* his*; thereafter* change his / leafe: / selues, / now: /

spittle, and their young children ordures – and all these
for the face. I would sooner eat a dead pigeon taken
from the soles of the feet of one sick of the plague than
kiss one of you fasting. Here are two of you whose sin   45
of your youth is the very patrimony of the physician,
makes him renew his foot-cloth with the spring, and
change his high-prized courtesan with the fall of the
leaf. I do wonder you do not loathe yourselves. Observe
my meditation now: 50

What thing is in this outward form of man
To be beloved? We account it ominous
If nature do produce a colt or lamb,
A fawn or goat, in any limb resembling
A man, and fly from't as a prodigy.   55
Man stands amazed to see his deformity
In any other creature but himself.
But in our own flesh, though we bear diseases
Which have their true names only ta'en from beasts –
As the most ulcerous wolf and swinish measle –   60

42 **children ordures** children's faeces;
children as faeces, in which case a
better punctuation would be 'children
– ordures!' Most editors emend to
'children's ordures', which is slightly
less anti-Semitic in that it effaces the
second of the two possible meanings.

43–4 **dead . . . plague** Pigeons were
placed at the feet of plague victims to
draw out the infection; to eat such a
bird would presumably be fatal.

45 **fasting** believed to cause bad breath,
like what is now called 'morning breath';
cf. *TGV* 3.1.315–16: 'She is not to be
kissed fasting in respect of her breath.'
  two the Old Lady and Castruccio

45–6 **sin . . . physician** youthful lapses,
such as fornication (leading to venereal
disease) or alcoholism, that would provide continuing income for the doctor

who treats them

47 **foot-cloth** long ceremonial garment
worn by the extra-privileged horse

48 **high-prized** highly valued, but also
suggests high-priced

50 **meditation** formal spiritual exercise
(one of several contemplations of death
Bosola delivers in the course of the play)

55 **prodigy** freak

56 **deformity** suggesting that normal
human physical traits are revealed as
deformed if seen out of their usual
context

58 **bear** suffer; carry

60 **ulcerous wolf** cancerous growth,
such as can be caused by lupus (Latin
for 'wolf')
  swinish measle swine-pox, animal
virus with symptoms similar to human
measles

42 children] childrens *Q2*   48 high-prized] high-priced *Dyce*   48+ courtesan] *(curtezan)*   51 form
of] *om. Q4*   58–61] *om. in performance Q4*   60 measle] *(Meazeall)*

Though we are eaten up of <u>lice and worms</u>,
And though continually we <u>bear</u> about us
A rotten and <u>dead body</u>, we delight
To hide it in rich tissue. All our fear,
Nay all our terror, is lest our physician   65
Should put us in the ground to be made sweet.
Your wife's gone to Rome: you two couple, and get you
to the wells at Lucca to recover your aches.

             [*Exeunt Castruccio and Old Lady.*]

I have other work on foot. I observe our Duchess
Is sick a–days: she pukes, her stomach <u>seethes</u>,   70
The fins of her eyelids look most teeming blue;
She wanes i'th' cheek and waxes fat i'th' flank,
And, contrary to our Italian fashion,
Wears a loose–bodied gown. There's somewhat in't.

62–3 **we bear . . . body** alluding to the Christian doctrine of the 'corruption of the flesh' – a corruption of the physical body that, in Protestant doctrine, is based on original sin and cannot be relieved except through death. Cf. Fig. 10, p. 47, where the soul, depicted as a child, is trapped within the dead skeleton of the body.

64 **tissue** fabric

65–6 **lest . . . sweet** We fear death and burial, but the process of decomposition, or possibly the process of embalming, is the only way our body will finally be relieved of its corruption, *made sweet*. Cf. *Column*, 16, where embalming is used as part of an argument that princes need to take heed to their posthumous reputation: 'Princes think that Ceremony meet / To have their corps imbalm'd to keepe them sweet' (Webster, 3.375).

68 **Lucca** an Italian town famous for its warm springs

69 **on foot** afoot

70 **a–days** in the daytime

seethes is upset, agitated

71 The Duchess has bluish-black circles around the corners of the eyes ('fins of her eyelids'); Sadler lists 'a blue circle about the eyes' among the signs of pregnancy. Bosola's pairing of *fins* and *teeming* also suggests, at least fleetingly, that he is thinking of her as a fish, which were believed at the time to reproduce very rapidly. Cf. Herrick, 'Nuptial Song or Epithalamie on Sir Clipsby Crew and His Lady', where 'thousands gladly wish / You multiply, as doth a Fish' (lines 49–50; in Herrick).

72 **waxes** grows

74 **loose–bodied** flowing rather than tightly fitted around the waist (with a suggestion of morally 'loose'); Bosola suggests that Italian fashion of the period was for tight-fitting bodices, while English gowns often had higher waists, and thus more room to hide a pregnancy.

in't to it, *it* being the Duchess's unusual mode of dress

64 tissue. All] *Q3;* tissew all *Q1*   65 lest] *Q4;* least *Q1*   67–8] *Dyce; Q1 lines* you / aches. /   67 you . . . and] *om. Q4*   68+ Lucca] *(Leuca)*   68 SD] *Dyce after 69* foot   70–1 she . . . blue] *om. Q4*

I have a trick may chance discover it –   75
A pretty one. I have bought some apricocks,
The first our spring yields.

[*Enter*] ANTONIO [*and*] DELIO.

DELIO   And so long since married?
You amaze me!

ANTONIO   Let me seal your lips for ever.
For did I think that anything but th'air
Could carry these words from you, I should wish   80
You had no breath at all. – Now, sir, in your
    contemplation?
You are studying to become a great, wise fellow?

BOSOLA   Oh, sir, the opinion of wisdom is a foul tetter
that runs all over a man's body. If simplicity direct us
to have no evil, it directs us to a happy being, for the   85
subtlest folly proceeds from the subtlest wisdom. Let
me be simply honest.

ANTONIO

I do understand your inside.

76 **apricocks** apricots; the older form of the word carries a bawdy suggestion of 'cocks': cf. the jests on 'Apricocks' in Webster's 'Induction' to Marston's *Malcontent*, 22–6 (see Webster, 3.318). Bosola hopes that his *trick* (75) will reveal the Duchess's pregnancy. In Guevara, book 2, ch. 9, sig. t2, eating unripe apricots puts a pregnant woman into labour and causes her child to be stillborn.

77 **long since married** Delio's comment suggests that several months – perhaps nine or more, as the Duchess is advanced in pregnancy – have passed since Antonio and Delio have exchanged confidences.

79–81 **anything . . . all** I would rather have you dead than sharing my secret with anyone.

81 **contemplation** suggests Bosola may have overheard some of the preceding conversation

83 **tetter** skin rash

84–6 **If . . . wisdom** Cf. 'Apology for Raymond Sebond': 'Whence proceedes the subtilest follie, but from the subtilest wisdome? . . . if simplicitie directeth us to have no evil, it also addresseth us . . . to a most happy estate' (Montaigne, 2.284–5; Lucas).

88 **inside** i.e. what you really mean as opposed to what you say

76 apricocks] apricots *Gibbons*   77–8] *Q1 lines* yeelds. / married? / me. / euer, /   77 SD] *Q4 (subst.)*; *Antonio, Delio,* | *0 SD Q1*   83–7] *Dyce*; *Q1 lines* tettor, / simplicity / happy / from the / honest. /   83 tetter] terror *Q2*   88] *Q1 lines* in-side. / so? / *; prose Gunby*

175

BOSOLA   Do you so?

ANTONIO

Because you would not seem to appear to th'world
Puffed up with your preferment, you continue   90
This out-of-fashion melancholy. Leave it, leave it!

BOSOLA

Give me leave to be honest in any phrase,
in any compliment whatsoever. Shall I confess myself
to you? I look no higher than I can reach. They are
the gods that must ride on winged horses; a lawyer's   95
mule of a slow pace will both suit my disposition and
business. For, mark me, when a man's mind rides faster
than his horse can gallop, they quickly both tire.

ANTONIO

You would look up to heaven, but I think
The devil that rules i'th' air stands in your light.   100

BOSOLA   Oh, sir, you are lord of the ascendant, chief man
with the Duchess: a duke was your cousin-german

---

90 **Puffed up** swollen with pride

91 **out-of-fashion melancholy** Bosola's melancholy is out of place, either because the fashion for it is past, having reached its zenith around the turn of the seventeenth century, or because his attainment of a high place at court means he should no longer feel it. But see Ferdinand's advice that Bosola retain his melancholy as a pose for strategic purposes (1.2.195–200).

94 **look . . . reach** a variation on the proverb 'One may look at a star but not reach at it' (Dent, S825*)

95 **gods . . . horses** Mythology states the opposite: the human horse master Bellerophon succeeded (with divine help) in taming the *winged horse* Pegasus – a telling counter-example for Bosola,

since he is Master of the Horse.

95–7 **lawyer's . . . business** Lawyers at the period frequently rode mules. Given Bosola's baiting of the lawyer Castruccio early in the scene, this protestation that he desires no more than a lawyer's mount rings hollow.

100 **devil . . . air** Cf. Ephesians, 2.2, in the Geneva Bible, where Paul calls the devil 'the prince that ruleth in the aire'. *Devil's Law-Case*, 5.5.22, has the same phrase (Webster, 2.163).

101 **lord . . . ascendant** the rising star; from astrology, where the planet in the ascendant governs the other heavenly (and earthly) bodies

102–3 **cousin-german removed** first cousin, once removed (ironically parodying aristocratic genealogies of the period)

---

91 out-of-fashion] *Q2;* out off shashion *Q1*   92] *this èdn; prose Q1*   93–8] *Dyce; Q1 lines* any / you? / reach. / horses, / suit / me) / gallop, / tyre. /   93 compliment] *(*Complement*)*   whatsoever] whatever *Q4*   94 to you] t'ye *Q4*   101–13] *Dyce; Q1 lines* ascendant, / your / lineally / himselfe, / in / water: / brought / persons, / them: / makes / tithe-pig, / spoile / goodly / Cannon. /

removed. Say you were lineally descended from King
Pepin, or he, himself – what of this? Search the heads
of the greatest rivers in the world, you shall find them   105
but bubbles of water. Some would think the souls of
princes were brought forth by some more weighty
cause than those of meaner persons; they are deceived.
There's the same hand to them, the like passions sway
them; the same reason that makes a vicar go to law for   110
a tithe-pig and undo his neighbours, makes them spoil
a whole province and batter down goodly cities with
the cannon.

[*Enter*] DUCHESS [*and* Ladies], RODERIGO
[*and*] GRISOLAN.

DUCHESS

Your arm, Antonio. Do I not grow fat?
I am exceeding short-winded. Bosola,   115
I would have you, sir, provide for me a litter –
Such a one as the Duchess of Florence rode in.

103–4 **lineally . . . Pepin** in a direct line
from Pepin, the name carried by several Carolingian kings of the eighth
and ninth centuries
104–6 **Search . . . water** Renaissance
commonplace based on Seneca, 3.29.4
104 **heads** sources
108 **cause** means
meaner lower in the social hierarchy
110–11 **vicar . . . neighbours** In
England, Anglican priests were entitled to a 'tithe' – one-tenth of their
parishioners' incomes, in this case
imagined as a pig. It was a contemporary grievance that priests were often
willing to go to law to secure their
tithe, even to the point of bringing

members of the parish to financial
ruin (Hill).
111 **spoil** destroy through war
112 **goodly** prosperous
113 SD Brown suggests that the Duchess
could enter on Bosola's words 'the like
passions sway them' (109–10), which
would give his comment ironic bite as
referring to her. Roderigo and Grisolan
are mentioned in Q1's massed entry at
the beginning of the scene but do not
speak; the most logical place for them
to enter is here, as part of the Duchess's
entourage. Alternatively, some editors
eliminate them from the scene.
116 **litter** bed or curtained couch that
could be carried on servants' shoulders

104 Pepin] *Q4; Pippin*|*Q1*   112 goodly] fair *Q4*   113 the] their *Q4*   113.1 *Enter . . . Ladies*] *Q4;
Duchesse* | *0 SD Q1*   113.1–2] RODERIGO [*and*] GRISOLAN | *0 SD Q1; with* Attendants *Brown*   116
for] *om. Q4*

BOSOLA

The duchess used one when she was great with child.

DUCHESS

I think she did.

[*to one of her Ladies*] Come hither; mend my ruff.

Here, when? Thou art such a tedious lady! 120

And thy breath smells of lemon peels. Would thou
    hadst done.

Shall I sound under thy fingers? I am so

Troubled with the mother.

BOSOLA   I fear, too much.

DUCHESS

I have heard you say that the French courtiers

Wear their hats on 'fore the king. 125

ANTONIO

I have seen it.

DUCHESS

                In the presence?

ANTONIO   Yes.

---

118 **great with child** pregnant
119 SD Weis specifies that this 'lady' is the Old Lady from earlier in the scene, but she could be any of the Duchess's ladies-in-waiting.
120 **when?** When will you get on with it?
121 **lemon peels** taken to sweeten the breath; the Duchess is presumably troubled by the scent because of her pregnancy, which was understood at the time to cause unusual food aversions and attractions. Q1's spelling 'pils' also suggests 'lemon pills', or pills containing lemon-balm, a herb known as a tranquillizer and soporific.
hadst done were finished

122 an irregular line, best scanned with major stresses on *sound*, *un-*, *fin-*, *I* and *so*
sound swoon, faint
123 **mother** hysteria, also called 'wandering womb', and often implying sexual promiscuity; also ironically revealing her true condition
124–5 Montaigne refers to this custom as a 'particular libertie of our *French* nobilitie' that had already fallen into disuse in his time (Montaigne, 1.146). By publicly keeping his hat on in her presence, Antonio would symbolically acknowledge his equality with the Duchess.

---

119 SD] *Gunby (subst.)*   119 my ruff] this *Q4*   120–3] *this edn; Q1 lines* and / done, / am / mother. / much. /; *prose Gunby*   121 lemon peels] *Thorndike;* Lymmon pils *Q1;* Limon-peel *Q4*   122 sound] swound *Q2;* swoon *Dyce*   124 courtiers] *Q2;* Courries *Q1*   125–6] *Q1 lines* King. / it. / Presence? / Yes: /   125 'fore] before *Q4*   126 Yes] Yes, Madam *Q4*

DUCHESS

> Why should not we bring up that fashion?
> 'Tis ceremony more than duty that consists
> In the removing of a piece of felt.
> Be you the example to the rest o'th' court: 130
> Put on your hat first.

ANTONIO   You must pardon me. *leave stadas*

> I have seen, in colder countries than in France,
> Nobles stand bare to th'prince, and the distinction,
> Methought, showed reverently.

BOSOLA

> I have a present for your grace.

DUCHESS   For me, sir?   135

BOSOLA

> Apricocks, madam.

DUCHESS   Oh, sir, where are they?

> I have heard of none to year.

BOSOLA   Good, her colour rises.

DUCHESS

> Indeed, I thank you. They are wondrous fair ones.
> What an unskilful fellow is our gardener!
> We shall have none this month.

BOSOLA   Will not your grace pare them?   140

---

127 SP *In Q1 there is no separate SP for 127–31, so that Antonio speaks from 126, *Yes*, to 131, *first*. This makes him sound more radical on the subject of *ceremony* than his following remarks suggest. It also makes little sense for him to speak 130–1, as it is unclear whom he would order to put on a hat. Since the next speech is also his, it is likely that the SP 'Duchess' was inadvertently omitted, either in MS or in the printing-house. Several early readers wrote 'Duchess' into their copies to rectify the omission.

129 **felt** usual material for hats
130 **you** addressed to Antonio
133 **bare** bare-headed
       distinction between prince and people
134 **showed reverently** displayed proper respect for office
137 **to year** this year
       colour rises She is reddening from excitement, which Bosola takes as another sign of pregnancy.

127 SP] *Q4* 128–9] *om. Q4* 131] *Q1 lines* first. / me: / 134 Methought] *Q4;* My thought *Q1* 135–7] *Q1 lines* Grace. / sir? / (Madam.) / they? / yeare. / rises. / 137 to] this *Q4* 140] *Q1 lines* moneth. / them? / them] 'em *Q4*

DUCHESS

No, they taste of musk, methinks – indeed they do.

BOSOLA

I know not, yet I wish your grace had pared 'em.

DUCHESS

Why?

BOSOLA   I forgot to tell you the knave gardener,

Only to raise his profit by them the sooner,

Did ripen them in horse dung.

DUCHESS   Oh, you jest!   145

– You shall judge: pray taste one.

ANTONIO   Indeed, madam,

I do not love the fruit.

DUCHESS   Sir, you are loath   *Babys*

To rob us of our dainties. 'Tis a delicate fruit.   *causes*

They say they are restorative.   *problems*

BOSOLA   'Tis a pretty art,

This grafting.

DUCHESS   'Tis so – a bettering of nature.   150

BOSOLA

To make a pippin grow upon a crab,

---

141 **musk** glandular secretion of the musk-deer used as the base for perfumes

145 **ripen ... dung** Dung could be either manure or other decayed matter used as fertilizer. Cf. Bacon's experiments with apples, which he successfully ripened using fertilizers and a compost made from crabs and onions (Bacon, *Sylva*; Clement).

149 **restorative** possessed of healing properties

150 **grafting** referring, by innuendo, to the cross-breeding that has produced the Duchess's child as well as the fruit: as gardeners can produce a new type of fruit by grafting one species on to another, so the Duchess and her unknown sexual partner have produced a new type of human by grafting one human 'species' or social class on to another. Bosola's examples that follow (151–2) parallel the Duchess's case, since they cross-breed higher and lower forms.

151 **pippin** type of apple

crab crab-apple tree, whose fruit is inedible and therefore inferior to the *pippin*

143] *Q1 lines* Why? / Gardner, /   gardener] *(Gardner)*   145–7] *Q1 lines* horse-doung, / iest: / one.
/ Madam, / fruit. / loath /   149–50] *Brennan; Q1 lines* restoratiue? / pretty / grafting. / nature.
/   150 a] *om. Q2*   bettering] *(bettring)*   of] the *Q4*   151 a pippin] pippin *Q2;* Pippins *Q4*

A damson on a blackthorn. – How greedily she eats
   them!
A whirlwind strike off these bawd farthingales,
For, but for that and the loose-bodied gown,
I should have discovered apparently   155
The young springal cutting a caper in her belly.

DUCHESS

I thank you, Bosola; they were right good ones,
If they do not make me sick.

ANTONIO   How now, madam?

DUCHESS

This green fruit and my stomach are not friends.
How they swell me!

BOSOLA   Nay, you are too much swelled already.   160

DUCHESS

Oh, I am in an extreme cold sweat.

BOSOLA   I am very sorry.

DUCHESS

Lights to my chamber! O good Antonio,
I fear I am undone.

                     Exeunt Duchess [and Ladies].

DELIO   Lights there, lights!
           [Exeunt Bosola, Roderigo and Grisolan.]

---

152 **damson** prized variety of plum
   blackthorn thorny shrub bearing
   sloes, very small plums that are inferior to the *damson*
153 **bawd farthingales** hooped petti-
   coats, which Bosola calls *bawd* because
   they conceal sexual activity and its
   results
155 **apparently** visibly
156 **springal** youth, stripling

159 **green** unripe
161 **cold sweat** possible sign of poisoning, but also of the onset of labour,
   which often presents initially as if it
   were a stomach ailment
   I . . . sorry Some editors follow Q4
   and have Bosola exit at the end of this
   line, in which case 'I am very sorry'
   could be an apology for his leaving
   rather than regret over her illness.

152] *aside* | *opp.* them *Q4*   153–6] *om. Q4*   158] *Q1 lines* sicke. / Madame? /   160–1] *Q1 lines* me? /
already. / sweat. / sorry: /   160] *aside* | *opp.* already *Q4*   161] *Exit.* | *after* sorry *Q4*   163] *Q1 lines*
vndone. / lights. /   SD1] *Dyce after* lights; *Exit Duchesse.* | *Q1; / Exit. Dutchess, Lady,* | *Q4*   SD2]
this edn; / Exit, on the other side, Bosola. *Dyce²*

ANTONIO

O my most trusty Delio, we are lost!
I fear she's fallen in labour, and there's left   165
No time for her remove.

DELIO   Have you prepared
Those ladies to attend her, and procured
That politic safe conveyance for the midwife
Your Duchess plotted?

ANTONIO   I have.

DELIO

Make use then of this forced occasion: 170
Give out that Bosola hath poisoned her
With these apricocks. That will give some colour
For her keeping close.

ANTONIO   Fie, fie – the physicians
Will then flock to her.

DELIO   For that you may pretend
She'll use some prepared antidote of her own,   175
Lest the physicians should re-poison her.

ANTONIO

I am lost in amazement; I know not what to think on't.

                                              Exeunt.

167 **ladies . . . her** At this period, child-birth was an activity presided over solely by women.
168 **politic** prudent, strategically appropriate
   conveyance coach or carriage; private or secret passage
170 **occasion** pronounced as four syllables
171 **Give out** make it known
172 **colour** pretext
173 **keeping close** remaining secluded

176 These seemingly far-fetched pretexts would have carried credence in the Renaissance, when poisoning of political enemies was widely feared and practised, as in the case of the Duchess's own father, poisoned by his brother (see p. 16), or the notorious case of the Duchess's contemporary Lucrezia Borgia, who was rumoured to have poisoned rivals and political enemies.
177 **on't** about it

164 most trusty Delio] Dear Friend *Q4*   166] *Q1 lines* remoue. / prepar'd /   169] *Q1 lines* plotted. / haue: /   173–4] *Q1 lines* close. / Physitians / her. / pretend /   176 Lest] *(*Least*)*   177 SD] *(Ex.)*

2.2   [*Enter*] BOSOLA [*and*] OLD LADY.

BOSOLA   ·

So, so: there's no question but her tetchiness
And most vulturous eating of the apricocks
Are apparent signs of breeding, now?

OLD LADY   I am in haste, sir.

BOSOLA   There was a young waiting woman had a   5
monstrous desire to see the glass house –

OLD LADY   Nay, pray let me go.

BOSOLA   – And it was only to know what strange
instrument it was should swell up a glass to the fashion
of a woman's belly.   10

OLD LADY   I will hear no more of the glass house. You are
still abusing women!

BOSOLA   Who, I? No, only by the way, now and then,
mention your frailties. The orange tree bear ripe and
green fruit and blossoms all together, and some of   15
you give entertainment for pure love, but more for

2.2 Location: the Duchess's palace

0 SD Q1 has only a massed entrance at
the beginning of the scene, so it is
uncertain when the Old Lady enters.
Bosola's question in 1–3 appears to
be addressed to her. Some editors
have her enter only at 4, in which case
Bosola is talking to himself.

1 **tetchiness** irritability (as in the
Duchess's reproof of her lady at
2.1.119–23)

2 **vulturous** ravenous

3 **signs of breeding** indications of
pregnancy, at a time when modern
medical tests were not yet available

4 **in haste** presumably, to attend at the
Duchess's delivery; cf. 'ladies to attend
her' (2.1.167).

6 **glass house** glass factory. Bosola
implies a connection between the
blowing of glass into round shapes and
pregnancy.

9 **instrument** with sexual innuendo

12 **still** always

14–15 **The orange ... together** commonplace; cf. *Column*, 45–6, where
Webster uses the idea in a more positive context to praise Prince Henry:
'But, like the *Orange* tree, his fruits
he bore; / Some gather'd, he had
greene, and blossomes store' (Webster,
3.376).

15–17 **some ... reward** Sexually available women give different types of
entertainment just as the orange tree
produces different types of products.

2.2] *(SCENA II.)*   0 SD] *Q4 (subst.); Bosola, old Lady, Antonio, Rodorigo, Grisolan: seruants,*
Delio, Cariola. | *Q1* 1–3] *this edn; Q1 lines* teatchiues / apparant / now? /; *prose Dyce* 1 tetchi-
ness] *(teatchiues);* teatchiues *Q2;* eager *Q4* 5–28] *om. in performance Q4* 12 women!] *(woemen?)*
14 bear] bears *Q4* 15 all together] *Dyce²;* altogether *Q1*

more precious reward. The lusty spring smells well, but drooping autumn tastes well. If we have the same golden showers that rained in the time of Jupiter the Thunderer, you have the same Danaes still, to hold up   20
their laps to receive them. Didst thou never study the mathematics?

OLD LADY   What's that, sir?

BOSOLA   Why, to know the trick how to make a many lines meet in one centre. Go, go – give your foster daughters   25
good counsel. Tell them that the devil takes delight to hang at a woman's girdle like a false rusty watch, that she cannot discern how the time passes.   [*Exit Old Lady*.]

[*Enter*] ANTONIO, DELIO, RODERIGO [*and*] GRISOLAN.

ANTONIO
Shut up the court gates.

17 **lusty spring** youth, when women have sex for love. It *smells well* because it is associated with spring flowers and external beauty.

18 **autumn** later years, when women have sex for money or other benefits. This harvest time *tastes well* in that the promises of spring have been rewarded with edible foodstuffs, implying that sex with older women is more rewarding for men, perhaps because of mature women's greater sexual responsiveness.

18–21 **If . . . them** implies a link between the shower of gold through which Jupiter impregnated Danae, according to legend, and the gold that women expect as a reward for sexual favours. While Danae was raped, Bosola suggests that modern women are more than willing.

21–3 **Didst . . . that** The Old Lady's ignorance of even the existence of mathematics may indicate her lack of education; however, mathematics

at the period was a university subject to which women, who were barred from universities, had only limited access. Alternatively, she may be feigning ignorance to play along with an anticipated joke from Bosola.

24–5 **Why . . . centre** Bosola suggests that mathematics is a pimp because it brings lines together in a point whose *centre* is sexual intercourse. Cf. Mercutio's joke in *RJ* about telling time, which also sexualizes the meeting of two lines: 'the bawdy hand of the dial is now upon the prick [penis] of noon' (*RJ* 2.4.111–12).

25 **foster daughters** pregnant women who need her services as midwife; prostitutes for whom she, according to Bosola, served as madam. They are her *foster* daughters because she provides for their maintenance (in return for the income they generate).

27 **girdle** belt, waistband

17 more] *om. Q4*   20 Danaes] *Q4; Danes | Q1; Danies | Q3*   26 them] 'em *Q4*   28 SD1] *Dyce   SD2; Sampson; Antonio, Roderigo, Grisolan: ...Delio, | 0 SD Q1*   29] *Q1 lines* gates: / danger? /   Shut] *Q2;* Shht *Q1*

RODERIGO   Why, sir? What's the danger?

ANTONIO

Shut up the posterns presently, and call   30
All the officers o'th' court.

GRISOLAN   I shall, instantly.   [*Exit.*]

ANTONIO

Who keeps the key o'th' park gate?

RODERIGO   Forobosco.

ANTONIO

Let him bring't presently.

[*Enter* GRISOLAN *and*] SERVANTS.

1 SERVANT

Oh, gentlemen o'th' court, the foulest treason!

BOSOLA

– If that these apricocks should be poisoned now   35
Without my knowledge!

1 SERVANT   There was taken even now
A Switzer in the Duchess's bedchamber.

---

30 **posterns** back doors or gates
   presently at once
32 **Forobosco** evidently one of the courtiers. Forobosco appears in the Q1 list of 'Actors' Names' (see p. 118), although he is given no entrances or speeches in the play. Forobosco is presumably one of the servants who enter at 33 SD; he may carry a large key and speak one of the servants' lines. Alternatively, inclusion of the name 'Forobosco' on the cast list could be a sly joke on someone's part: Florio defines the Italian '*Forabosco*' as, among other meanings, '*a sneaking or prying busie fellow*' – an appropriate name for a courtier in a play full of spies and whispering, and for a character who

sneaks out of the playtext except for a single mention. Possibly the name was suggested by Marston's *Antonio and Mellida*, where there is a courtier named Forobosco who is called a 'parasite' (see Brown, lxvii–lxviii).
33 SD **GRISOLAN** Grisolan exited to summon the 'officers o'th' court'; he does not have any further speaking lines in the scene, but it makes sense for him to re-enter with the Duchess's servants, who are the 'officers' he was ordered to bring before Antonio at 31. On the various titles given to the Duchess's servants, see List of Roles, 21n.
37 **Switzer** member of the Swiss Guard, mercenary soldiers frequently hired in feuds between Italian noblemen

31–3] *Q1 lines* Court. / instantly: / Parke-gate? / *Forobosco.* / presently. /   31 SD] *Dyce*   33 SD] *Dyce; seruants,* | *0 SD Q1*   34] *om. Q4*   36–9] *Brennan; Q1 lines* knowledge. / Switzer / Bed-chamber. / Switzer? / cod-piece. / ha. / for't. /   36–46 1 SERVANT . . . do] *om. in performance Q4*   36] *aside* | *opp.* knowledge *Q4*   even] just *Q4*   37 bedchamber] chamber *Q4*

2 SERVANT

    A Switzer?

1 SERVANT   With a pistol in his great codpiece.

BOSOLA

    Ha, ha, ha!

1 SERVANT   The codpiece was the case for't.

2 SERVANT   There was a cunning traitor! Who would have   40
searched his codpiece?

1 SERVANT   True. If he had kept out of the ladies' chambers.
And all the moulds of his buttons were leaden bullets.

2 SERVANT   Oh, wicked cannibal! A firelock in's codpiece?

1 SERVANT   'Twas a French plot, upon my life!   45

2 SERVANT   To see what the devil can do.

ANTONIO

    All the offices here?

SERVANTS   We are.

ANTONIO   Gentlemen,
We have lost much plate, you know; and but this evening

---

38 **pistol . . . codpiece** with a bawdy pun on 'pizzle', 'penis'; the codpiece was a fashionable ornamental covering for the male genitals.

40–2 **Who . . . chambers** more bawdy humour; if he had gone into ladies' chambers they would have *searched his codpiece* as part of their sexual advances.

43 A button *mould* was usually a disc of wood or other material to be covered with cloth to form a button. The First Servant alleges that the (imagined) Switzer's buttons were instead made out of covered bullets; cf. the Switzer in Thomas Nashe, *Unfortunate Traveller* (1594): 'the molds of his buttons they turnd out, to see if they were not bullets covered over with thred; the codpeece . . . was a case for a pistol.'

44 **cannibal** (with play on 'cannon-ball') violent savage; devourer of his own kind in that he carried a pistol, instru-ment of death, instead of a penis, instrument of generation

firelock musket furnished with a device in which sparks were ignited by friction or percussion to ignite the charge, with sexual implications

45 **French plot** scheme by the French, presumably related to their campaign to conquer Italy (see p. 17); reference to syphilis, called in England the 'French disease'

plot, . . . life Alternatively, given the absence of Q1 punctuation (see t.n.), the servant may be expressing the (comically excessive) fear that the plot was against him personally.

47 **offices** courtiers denoted by their positions. Some editors emend to 'officers', the Q2 reading.

48 **plate** silver or gold serving pieces, which in noble households were often heavy, ornate and valuable

---

39 Ha] *(Hh)* 45 plot, upon] *Q3;* plot vpon *Q1* 47] *Q1 lines here?* / are: / Gentlemen, / All] Are all *Q4* offices] Officers *Q2*

Jewels to the value of four thousand ducats
Are missing in the Duchess's cabinet.   50
Are the gates shut?

1 SERVANT   Yes.

ANTONIO   'Tis the Duchess's pleasure
Each officer be locked into his chamber
Till the sun rising, and to send the keys
Of all their chests, and of their outward doors
Into her bedchamber. She is very sick.   55

RODERIGO
At her pleasure.

ANTONIO   She entreats you take't not ill.
The innocent shall be the more approved by it.

BOSOLA
Gentleman o'th' wood yard, where's your Switzer now?

1 SERVANT
By this hand, 'twas credibly reported by one o'th'
blackguard.   [*Exeunt all but Antonio and Delio.*]

DELIO
How fares it with the Duchess?

ANTONIO   She's exposed   60
Unto the worst of torture, pain and fear.

DELIO
Speak to her all happy comfort.

---

50 **cabinet** private bedchamber
54 **outward** outer
57 **be . . . approved** be more favoured (as
a result of their obedience)
58 **Gentleman . . . yard** i.e. servant, one
who frequents menial places. Bosola
mocks the First Servant's reference to
him and his comrades as 'gentlemen
o'th' court', 34 (Brown).

59 **blackguard** kitchen servants (*OED n.*
I.1)
59 SD Delio may enter here, rather than
with Antonio and courtiers at 28.
His name is listed next to last in the
massed entry at the beginning of 2.2.
Usually, but not infallibly, characters
enter in the order that they are listed
there.

51] *Q1 lines* shut? / Yes. / pleasure / the Duchess's] her Graces *Q4*   56–7] *Q1 lines* pleasure. /
Innocent / it. /   58–9] *om. in performance Q4*   59 SD] *Dyce; Exeunt* Gentlemen. *opp. 57 Q4*   60] *Q1
lines* Dutchesse? / expos'd /

ANTONIO

    How I do play the fool with mine own danger!

    You are this night, dear friend, to post to Rome.

    My life lies in your service.

DELIO   Do not doubt me.   65

ANTONIO

    Oh, 'tis far from me; and yet fear presents me

    Somewhat that looks like danger.

DELIO   Believe it.

    'Tis but the shadow of your fear, no more.

    How superstitiously we mind our evils!

    The throwing down salt or crossing of a hare,   70

    Bleeding at nose, the stumbling of a horse

    Or singing of a cricket, are of power

    To daunt whole man in us. Sir, fare you well.

    I wish you all the joys of a blest father;

    And, for my faith, lay this unto your breast: 75

    Old friends, like old swords, still are trusted best.

[Enter] CARIOLA.

Sententiae Heroes use of them (handwritten annotation)

64 We learn in 2.4 that Delio is being sent to find out what the Cardinal knows about the Duchess's sexual activity; there he pretends to seduce the Cardinal's mistress, Julia, apparently as a way of gaining information.
    post ride post-horses (the fastest means of travel)

67 **Somewhat** something
    Believe it Believe that I am trustworthy (reaffirming his statement at 65).

68 **shadow . . . fear** in modern psychoanalytic language, the projection of Antonio's fear

69 **mind** attend to

70–2 It was considered bad luck to waste salt. Delio's list consists of everyday events mistakenly taken, he argues, for ominous portents.

73 **daunt . . . man** compromise our manhood with fear

75 **lay . . . breast** take this to heart

76 **still** always. Most editors have Delio exit here, after he has pronounced his sententious couplet. But it is also possible that he remains onstage to hear the good news that follows.

76 SD Following Q4, some editors have Cariola enter carrying Antonio's newborn child.

65] *Q1 lines* seruice. / me, /   66 presents me] presents *Q4*   67] *Q1 lines* danger. / it, /   looks] *Q2*; looke *Q1*   74] *Exit.* | *opp.* father *Q4*   75–6] *om. Q4*   76 SD] *Dyce; Cariola.* | *0 SD Q1*; Enter *Cariola with a Child.* | *Q4*

CARIOLA

Sir, you are the happy father of a son.
Your wife commends him to you.

ANTONIO   Blessed comfort!
For heaven sake tend her well. I'll presently   79
Go set a figure for's nativity.   *Exeunt.*

2.3   [*Enter*] BOSOLA [*with a dark lantern*].

BOSOLA

Sure I did hear a woman shriek. List – ha?
And the sound came, if I received it right,
From the Duchess's lodgings. There's some stratagem
In the confining all our courtiers
To their several wards. I must have part of it;   5
My intelligence will freeze else. List again –
It may be 'twas the melancholy bird,
Best friend of silence and of solitariness,
The owl, that screamed so.

[*Enter*] ANTONIO.

Ha? Antonio?

78 **Blessed** blessèd
79–80 **I'll . . . nativity** To be considered
valid, horoscopes had to reflect the
precise moment of birth. Antonio will
set a figure – draw an astrological chart
– in order to calculate the precise position of key planets at the moment of
his child's birth.
2.3 **Location**: the Duchess's palace
0 SD *dark lantern* light with opaque
covering so that it is concealed unless a
door on the side is opened
1 **List** listen

4 **confining** confining of; also suggesting the Duchess's 'confinement' or
childbirth
5 **several wards** various apartments
have . . . it have it shared with me
6 **intelligence** information gleaned as a
spy
9 SD Following Q4, some editors have
Antonio enter melodramatically
'with a candle, his sword drawn'.
Alternatively, Antonio may be visibly
carrying the horoscope, as Gibbons
suggests.

78] *Q1 lines* you. / comfort: /   80 set . . . for's] Calculate his *Q4*   **2.3**] *(SCENA III.)*   0 SD] *Q4;*
Bosola, Antonio. | *Q1*   1 List – ha] *om. Q4*   6 List] hist *Q4*   9 screamed] *(*schream'd*)*   SD] *Dyce;*
Antonio. | *0 SD Q1;* Enter *Antonio*, with a Candle his Sword drawn. *Q4*

ANTONIO

    I heard some noise. Who's there? What art thou? Speak!   10

BOSOLA

    Antonio? Put not your face nor body

    To such a forced expression of fear.

    I am Bosola, your friend.

ANTONIO   Bosola?

    – This mole does undermine me. – Heard you not

    A noise even now?

BOSOLA   From whence?

ANTONIO   From the Duchess's lodging.   15

BOSOLA

    Not I. Did you?

ANTONIO   I did, or else I dreamed.

BOSOLA

    Let's walk towards it.

ANTONIO   No, it may be 'twas

    But the rising of the wind.

BOSOLA   Very likely.

    Methinks 'tis very cold, and yet you sweat.

    You look wildly.

ANTONIO   I have been setting a figure   20

    For the Duchess's jewels.

BOSOLA   Ah! And how falls your question?

    Do you find it radical?

---

10 **What** what type of creature
12 **expression** pronounced as four syllables
14 **This . . . me** enclosed in parentheses in Q1 and possibly that text's only clear indication of an aside (see t.n. and pp. 76–7). As moles tunnel beneath the earth and destabilize the solid ground, so the *mole* Bosola is 'undermining' Antonio.
20 **look wildly** appear disturbed; are

looking about in an excited manner
    setting a figure estimating a value for the 'lost' jewels (2.2.49–50); setting the *figure*, or astrological chart, of the child's nativity (see 2.2.79–80 and n.)
21 **how . . . question** what conclusions can you draw
22 **radical** a great loss (of money); capable of being decided (technical term from astrology)

13] *Q1 lines* friend. / *Bosola?* /   14 – This . . . me. –] *((This . . . me))*   15–18] *Q1 lines* now? / whence? / lodging. / you? / dream'd. / it. / 'twas / winde: / likely. /   20–2] *Q1 lines* wildly. / figure / Iewells; / question? / radicall? / you? /   21 Ah] Ay *Q4*

ANTONIO   What's that to you?

'Tis rather to be questioned what design,

When all men were commanded to their lodgings,

Makes you a night-walker.

BOSOLA   In sooth I'll tell you: 25

Now all the court's asleep, I thought the devil

Had least to do here. I came to say my prayers.

And, if it do offend you I do so,

You are a fine courtier.

ANTONIO   – This fellow will undo me. –

You gave the Duchess apricocks today.   30

Pray heaven they were not poisoned.

BOSOLA   Poisoned? A Spanish fig

For the imputation.

ANTONIO   Traitors are ever confident,

Till they are discovered. There were jewels stolen too.

In my conceit, none are to be suspected

More than yourself.

BOSOLA   You are a false steward.   35

ANTONIO

Saucy slave, I'll pull thee up by the roots!

BOSOLA

Maybe the ruin will crush you to pieces.

ANTONIO

You are an impudent snake indeed, sir.

---

25 **sooth** truth

26 **Now** now that

26–7 **devil . . . do** implying that the devil would be busy tempting the courtiers during their waking hours

28–9 **And . . . courtier** Bosola implies that courtiers are by nature impious.

31 **Spanish fig** expression of insult, similar to giving the finger

34 **conceit** thinking

35 **You . . . steward** Bosola implies that, by allowing the jewels to be stolen, Antonio has been derelict in his duty to protect the Duchess's estate.

37 **ruin . . . pieces** implying that not only Antonio, but all his estate, would be uprooted

25] *Q1 lines* night-walker. / you: / In sooth] Faith *Q4*   29] *Q1 lines* Courtier. / me; /   29] *aside* | *opp.* me *Q4*   31–2] *Q1 lines* poysond? / figge / imputation. / confident, /   35] *Q1 lines* selfe. / steward. /

BOSOLA

Are you scarce warm, and do you show your sting?

ANTONIO

You libel well, sir.

BOSOLA   No, sir. Copy it out,   40

And I will set my hand to't.

ANTONIO   – My nose bleeds.

One that were superstitious would count

This ominous when it merely comes by chance.

Two letters that are wrought here for my name

Are drowned in blood.   45

Mere accident. – For you, sir, I'll take order

I'th' morn you shall be safe. – 'Tis that must colour

Her lying in. – Sir, this door you pass not.

I do not hold it fit that you come near

The Duchess's lodgings till you have quit yourself.   50

'The great are like the base; nay, they are the same

When they seek shameful ways to avoid shame.'   *Exit.*

39 SP *In Q1 this line has no SP and
appears to continue Antonio's speech
from 38. However, Q1 also labels the
following speech as his. Beginning
with Q2, early editions of the play
consolidated 38–40 (to *well, sir*) into
a single speech by Antonio. More
recently, following Lucas, most editors have suggested that an insult by
Bosola, to which Antonio responds
at 40, 'You libel well, sir', has simply
dropped out of the text, and leave
an empty line. However, it is equally
likely that 39 is Bosola's returning
of Antonio's *snake* insult back upon
him by suggesting that, like a snake
in hibernation, Antonio is too cold
and sluggish to be capable of a potent
sting or insult. It is more likely that a
compositor omitted a SP than that he

omitted a line, though either is possible.
40–1 **Copy . . . to't** Put it in writing and
I will sign it.
41–3 **My nose . . . ominous** Cf. Delio's
comment on nosebleeds as portents,
2.2.71.
44 **letters . . . here** Presumably Antonio's
handkerchief has his name embroi-
dered, *wrought*, on it.
47 **I'th' . . . safe** Either Antonio will
take order in the morning for Bosola's
safety, or he will take order now to
assure Bosola's safety in the morning;
in the latter case, *safe* may mean safely
locked up.
50 **quit** exonerated
51–2 The fact that these lines are italicized in Q1 suggests that they were
understood as a commonplace.

39 SP] *this edn* 40–2] *Sampson; Q1 lines* (sir.) / (sir,) / to't. / count / 40 SP] *om. Q2* 44 wrought]
wrote *Q3* 45–6] *Dyce; one line Q1* 50 quit] (quite) 51–2] *ital. Q1;* "The . . . "When | *Q4* 52
SD] (Ex.)

BOSOLA

Antonio hereabout did drop a paper.
Some of your help, false friend! Oh, here it is.
What's here? A child's nativity calculated?   55
[*Reads.*] '*The Duchess was delivered of a son 'tween the
hours twelve and one in the night,* Anno domini *1504*' –
that's this year – '*decimo nono Decembris*' – that's this
night – '*taken according to the meridian of Malfi*' – that's
our Duchess, happy discovery! – '*The lord of the first*   60
house being combust in the ascendant signifies short life;
and Mars being in a human sign joined to the tail of the
Dragon in the eight house doth threaten a violent death.'
Caetera non scrutantur.'
Why now 'tis most apparent. This precise fellow   65
Is the Duchess's bawd. I have it to my wish.
This is a parcel of intelligency

[handwritten marginalia: v. dense / never theology / plays gabrie / another sententia]

54 **false friend** probably the dark lantern, which is *false* because it hides itself from others, but a *friend* because it will help Bosola find the horoscope. Dollimore and Sinfield suggest the moon, which is known for inconstancy (D&S).

55 **nativity** astrological interpretation based on the time of a person's birth

57 **Anno domini** in the year of our Lord (Latin)

58 **decimo nono Decembris** the nineteenth of December (Latin)

59 *meridian* circle of longitude passing through the North and South Poles and indicating the midpoint of the heavens; at any given place, the sun crosses the *meridian* at noon.

60–3 Brown notes that the configuration of planets described here did not occur at the time of the play's historical setting in the early sixteenth century, but was 'probably invented by Webster (or a professional astrologer) to prog-

nosticate a violent death as clearly as possible'.

60–1 *lord . . . ascendant* The rising planet is burned up, being too close to the sun, and therefore able to exert little influence.

62 *human sign* astrological sign based on the human form; these are Gemini, Aquarius, Virgo and Sagittarius.

62–3 *tail . . . Dragon* the point in the heavens at which the descending moon crosses the path of the sun. This configuration was thought to generate bad luck.

64 **Caetera non scrutantur** The rest is not examined (Latin); presumably the horoscope is so alarming that Antonio has not worked it out completely.

65 **precise** strict; term often applied to Puritans in Webster's time

66 **bawd** pimp
   to my wish as I wish

67 **parcel of intelligency** piece of covert information

53 did drop] dropt *Q4*   56 SD] *Dyce²*   64 Caetera] *Q2;* Caeteta *Q1*   67 intelligency] Intelligence *Q4*

Our courtiers were cased up for. It needs must follow
That I must be committed on pretence
Of poisoning her, which I'll endure and laugh at.   70
If one could find the father now! But that,
Time will discover. Old Castruccio
I'th' morning posts to Rome; by him I'll send
A letter that shall make her brothers' galls
O'erflow their livers. This was a thrifty way.   75
'Though Lust do mask in ne'er so strange disguise,
She's oft found witty but is never wise.'   [*Exit.*]

2.4   [*Enter*] CARDINAL *and* JULIA.

CARDINAL

Sit. Thou art my best of wishes. Prithee tell me
What trick didst thou invent to come to Rome
Without thy husband?

JULIA   Why, my lord, I told him
I came to visit an old anchorite

---

68 **cased** locked
69 **committed** jailed
74–5 **galls . . . livers** cause their black
  bile, associated with melancholy, to
  increase to the point that it over-
  flows its usual container in the liver
  and causes bodily functions to become
  imbalanced. Cf. 3.2.152n.
75 **This . . . way** could refer either to the
  letter Bosola plans to send, in which
  case *was* means 'will be', or to the
  horoscope which he was lucky enough
  to find. Both documents were *thrifty* in
  the sense of expeditious, efficient.
76 no matter how much Lust (personified
  as one of the seven deadly sins) tries to
  disguise herself
77 The contrast of wit and wisdom is
  proverbial (Dent, W564.11).

2.4 Location: the Cardinal's palace in
  Rome
0 SD On Julia, mistress of the historical
  Cardinal of Aragon, see List of Roles,
  10n.). The sight of a Cardinal and his
  mistress flirting onstage would have
  fuelled anti-Catholic sentiment in early
  audiences. Horatio Busino, chaplain of
  the Venetian ambassador, reported after
  seeing a performance of *Malfi* in 1618
  that such scandalous things were staged
  'in derision of ecclesiastical pomp
  which in this kingdom is scorned and
  hated mortally' (Busino, 145–6).
1 **best of wishes** just what I was wishing for
4 **anchorite** hermit closed up for life in
  a small cell: a jesting reference to the
  Cardinal's supposed celibacy

---

68 cased up] *(caside-vp)*   76–7] *ital. Q1*   76 ne'er] *(nea'r)*   77 SD] *Q4*   2.4] *(SCENA. IIII.)*
0 SD] *Q4; Cardinall, and Iulia, Seruant, and Delio. | Q1*   1+ Prithee] *(pre-thee)*   3] *Q1 lines*
husband. / him /

Here, for devotion.

CARDINAL   Thou art a witty false one!   5

– I mean to him.

JULIA   You have prevailed with me

Beyond my strongest thoughts. I would not now

Find you inconstant.

CARDINAL   Do not put thyself

To such a voluntary torture, which proceeds

Out of your own guilt.

JULIA   How, my lord?

CARDINAL   You fear   10

My constancy because you have approved

Those giddy and wild turnings in yourself.

JULIA

Did you e'er find them?

CARDINAL   Sooth, generally for women!

A man might strive to make glass malleable

Ere he should make them fixed.

JULIA   So, my lord.   15

CARDINAL

We had need go borrow that fantastic glass

---

5 **false** Is Julia *false* only to her husband, or also to the Cardinal?

6–7 **prevailed . . . thoughts** influenced
me more than I would ever have
thought possible; persuaded me (to be
false to my husband)

9 **voluntary** self-willed, self-inflicted

10–12 **You . . . yourself** The Cardinal
describes a phenomenon that psychoanalysts now call projection: Julia
projects her own unacknowledged
promiscuity on to the Cardinal.

12 ***turnings** changes of affection

13 **Did . . . them** i.e. did you ever find
me to be unfaithful
generally for women i.e. all women are
changeable; proverbial (Dent, W674).

14–15 **A . . . fixed** It would be easier to
make glass pliable than to make women
constant.

16 **glass** the telescope, invented (or at
least improved and refined) by Galileo
in 1609–11, a full century after the
period represented in the play but
topical in England at the time it was
written and staged

5–6] *Q1 lines* deuotion / one: / him. / me / 8] *Q1 lines* inconstant. / selfe / 10–11] *Sampson; Q1 lines* guilt. / Lord?) / approou'd / 12 turnings] *Q3;* turning *Q1* 13] *Q1 lines* them? / woemen: / e'er] *(ere)* Sooth] Why *Q4* 14 malleable] *(male-able)* 15] *Q1 lines* fixed. / Lord) /

Invented by Galileo the Florentine
To view another spacious world i'th' moon,
And look to find a constant woman there.

JULIA

This is very well, my lord!

CARDINAL   Why do you weep?   20
Are tears your justification? The selfsame tears
Will fall into your husband's bosom, lady,
With a loud protestation that you love him
Above the world. Come, I'll love you wisely –
That's jealously – since I am very certain   25
You cannot me make cuckold.

JULIA   I'll go home
To my husband.

CARDINAL   You may thank me, lady.
I have taken you off your melancholy perch,
Bore you upon my fist, and showed you game,
And let you fly at it. I pray thee, kiss me.   30
When thou wast with thy husband, thou wast watched
Like a tame elephant. Still you are to thank me:
Thou hadst only kisses from him and high feeding,
But what delight was that? 'Twas just like one

---

18 Cf. *Ignatius*, 81, in which Donne describes Galileo's investigation of 'hills, woods, and Cities in the new world, the *Moone*' (Dent, *Webster*).

19 The Cardinal presents a constant woman as an impossibility; the moon, like woman, was notoriously inconstant (cf. 13n.).

20 **very well** uttered in sarcasm, since she is weeping

26 **You . . . cuckold** Only married men can be cuckolded, so the Cardinal is immune.

28–30 **taken . . . it** imagery from falconry. Falcons were kept hooded on perches until carried outside on the trainer's wrist or arm (*fist*) and then let loose to catch their prey (*game*). Similarly, the Cardinal has taken Julia away from her impotent husband and introduced her to sexual 'games'.

31–2 **watched . . . elephant** Even tame elephants could not entirely be trusted and consequently were kept under guard.

33 The limitations imply Castruccio's impotence.
high feeding gourmet dining

20] *Q1 lines* Lord.) / weepe? /   25 That's] That *Q2*   26–7] *Q1 lines* cuckould. / home / husband. / (Lady) /   26 me make] make me *Q2*   30+ pray thee] prithee *Q4*   30 thee, kiss] *(the kisse)*

That hath a little fingering on the lute,   35
Yet cannot tune it. Still you are to thank me.

JULIA

You told me of a piteous wound i'th' heart
And a sick liver when you wooed me first,
And spake like one in physic.   [*Knocking*]

CARDINAL   Who's that?

Rest firm, for my affection to thee –   40
Lightning moves slow to't.

[*Enter*] SERVANT.

SERVANT   Madam, a gentleman
That's come post from Malfi desires to see you.

CARDINAL

Let him enter; I'll withdraw.   *Exit.*

SERVANT   He says your husband,
Old Castruccio, is come to Rome,
Most pitifully tired with riding post.   [*Exit.*]

[*Enter*] DELIO.

JULIA

Signior Delio? – 'Tis one of my old suitors.   46

35–6 **fingering . . . it** Since Castruccio
is impotent, Julia's sexual relationship
with him has been as unfulfilling as
music by one who knows lute fingering, but not how to keep it in tune (or
make it play actual music).

37 **wound i'th' heart** typical Petrarchan
image of the lover's heart, bleeding
because hit by Cupid's arrow. By
Webster's time, the image was so over-
used in love poetry that it had become
trite or even a signal of insincerity.

38 **sick liver** as a result of love melancholy, believed to be seated in the liver
(cf. 1.2.214–15).

39 **in physic** undergoing medical treatment

41 **to't** compared with it

46 **old suitors** Julia assumes Delio's visit
will be a continuation of a former
attempt at seduction. Delio may be
using this excuse to follow Antonio's
wishes (2.2.64–5) and seek information.

35 fingering] *(*fingring*)*   38 wooed] *(*woed*)*   39] *Q1 lines* physicke. / that? /   SD] *Gunby*   41] *Q1*
lines to't. / Gentleman /   SD] *Dyce after 39; Seruant,* | 0 SD *Q1*   41–2 Madam . . . you] *om. in*
performance Q4   43–4] *this edn; Q1 lines* with-draw. / sayes, / Rome, /   43 He says] *om. in performance*
Q4   45 SD1] *Dyce*   SD2] *Q4; Delio.* | 0 SD *Q1*

DELIO

    I was bold to come and see you.

JULIA   Sir, you are welcome.

DELIO

    Do you lie here?

JULIA   Sure, your own experience

    Will satisfy you no. Our Roman prelates

    Do not keep lodging for ladies.

DELIO   Very well.   50

    I have brought you no commendations from your
        husband,

    For I know none by him.

JULIA   I hear he's come to Rome.

DELIO

    I never knew man and beast, of a horse and a knight,

    So weary of each other. If he had had a good back

    He would have undertook to have borne his horse,   55

    His breech was so pitifully sore.

JULIA   Your laughter

    Is my pity.

DELIO   Lady, I know not whether

    You want money, but I have brought you some.

JULIA

    From my husband?

DELIO   No, from mine own allowance.

JULIA

    I must hear the condition ere I be bound to take it.   60

---

48 **lie** sleep; tell falsehoods
49–50 **Our . . . ladies** We find out at 5.2.202 that Julia does indeed have a room in the Cardinal's palace.
51–2 **I . . . him** a backhanded way of saying that her husband disapproves of her behaviour
53 **of** specifically
55 **borne** carried
56 **breech** thighs and buttocks
59 **allowance** private funds
60 'What's the catch?'

47–8] *Q1 lines* you. / wel-come. / here? / experience /   47 I . . . are] Servant Lady, I am glad to see you at *Rome. / Jul.* I thank you Sir, you're *Q4*   to come and] and come to *Q2*   49 no] now *Q2* 50] *Q1 lines* Ladies. / well: /   52] *Q1 lines* him. / *Rome?* /   54–6 If . . . sore] *om. Q4*   56–7] *Q1 lines* sore. / laughter. / pitty. / whether /   57 Lady] Madam *Q4*   59] *Q1 lines* husband? / allowance. /

DELIO

Look on't. 'Tis gold. Hath it not a fine colour?

JULIA

I have a bird more beautiful.

DELIO

Try the sound on't.

JULIA   A lute-string far exceeds it.

It hath no smell, like cassia or civet;

Nor is it physical, though some fond doctors   65

Persuade us seeth't in cullisses. I'll tell you,

This is a creature bred by –

[*Enter* SERVANT.]

SERVANT   Your husband's come –

Hath delivered a letter to the Duke of Calabria

That, to my thinking, hath put him out of his wits.   [*Exit.*]

JULIA

Sir, you hear.   70

Pray let me know your business and your suit

As briefly as can be.

DELIO   With good speed. I would wish you,

At such time as you are non-resident

63 **Try . . . on't** Test its sound to make sure it is genuine.

64 **cassia** fragrant shrub sometimes identified with the cinnamon tree
civet musky secretion of the civet cat, used as a base for perfume

65 **physical** useful as a medicine
fond foolish

66 *****seeth't in cullisses** [to] boil it in broths for medicinal purposes. Cf. Chaucer's avaricious Doctor of Physic, for whom gold was a particularly valuable 'cordial' (*Canterbury Tales*,

General Prologue, 443).

67 **This** i.e. gold. Julia appears poised to utter traditional platitudes about the desire for gold as being bred by avarice. 'Breeding gold' could also mean 'making money'.

69 **him** Duke Ferdinand

72 **With . . . you** The Q1 punctuation is ambiguous (see t.n.). Delio means either 'I'll say this quickly' or 'I want you to become my mistress as quickly as possible'.

63] *Q1 lines* on't / it, / lute-string] Fiddle *Q4*   64 civet] *(Cyuit)*   66 seeth't] *Dyce;* seeth's *Q1;* seeth'd *Q3;* 'tis a Cordial *Q4*   67–9] *Sampson; Q1 lines* by— / come, / that, / wits. /   67 SD] *Q4*   67 come] come to Rome and *Q4*   69 of his] of's *Q4*   69 SD] *Q4 opp.* 70   71+ Pray] *(*'Pray*)*   72] *Q1 lines* be. / you / speed.] *(*speed,*)*

199

With your husband, my mistress.

JULIA

Sir, I'll go ask my husband if I shall,   75
And straight return your answer.   *Exit.*

DELIO   Very fine.

Is this her wit or honesty that speaks thus?
I heard one say the duke was highly moved
With a letter sent from Malfi. I do fear
Antonio is betrayed. How fearfully   80
Shows his ambition now! Unfortunate fortune!
'They pass through whirlpools and deep woes do shun
Who the event weigh ere the action's done.'   *Exit.*

2.5   [*Enter*] CARDINAL *and* FERDINAND *with a letter.*

FERDINAND

I have this night digged up a mandrake.

CARDINAL   Say you?

---

77 Is she just being sarcastic (using her *wit*), or does she really want her husband's permission (which he will presumably fail to give, with the result that she will maintain her chastity or *honesty*)?

79 **letter . . . Malfi** Bosola's letter informing Ferdinand of the birth of the Duchess's son (2.3.74)

80–1 **fearfully / Shows** dreadful appears

81 **Unfortunate fortune** commonplace oxymoron; cf. *TN*'s '*Fortunate Unhappy*' (*TN* 2.5.155).

82–3 As with other concluding rhymed couplets in the play, the Q1 punctuation indicates commonplace or proverbial status; cf. 'Look before you leap' (Dent, L429*).

2.5 Location: the Cardinal's palace in Rome

1 **mandrake** mysterious forked root shaped like a human torso; it was widely believed to grow under gallows, to feed on blood and to utter a shriek that could madden or cause death to the hearer if it was pulled from the ground. Cf. *White Devil*, 5.6.67 and 3.3.104–5, where Lodovico calls for blood to 'water a mandrake'. Mandrake, or mandragora, was variously used as an aphrodisiac, anaesthetic and sleep aid, as in Cleopatra's request for 'mandragora, that I may sleep' (*AC* 1.5.4).
Say you? Really?; Is that so?

76] *Q1 lines* answere. / fine. /   79 do] *om. Q4*   82–3 'They . . . done.'] ("They . . . done.*)*; They . . . done. *Q3; ital. Q4*   83 SD] *om. Q2*   **2.5**] *(SCENA V.)*   0 SD] *Q1 (subst.); Enter Cardinal, and Ferdinand, Furious, with a Letter.* | *Q4*   1–2] *Q1 lines* man-drake. / you? / with't. / progedy? /   1 digged] dig'd *Q1b;* dig *Q1a*   mandrake] *(*man-drake*);* man-darke *Q2*

200

FERDINAND

And I am grown mad with't.

CARDINAL   What's the prodigy?

FERDINAND

Read there – a sister damned. She's loose i'th' hilts –
Grown a notorious strumpet. ~ *degrading her*

CARDINAL   Speak lower.

FERDINAND   Lower?

Rogues do not whisper't now, but seek to publish't,   5
As servants do the bounty of their lords,
Aloud; and with a covetous, searching eye
To mark who note them. Oh, confusion seize her!
She hath had most cunning bawds to serve her turn,
And more secure conveyances for lust   10
Than towns of garrison for service.   ↙ *Concered*

CARDINAL   Is't possible? *about*
                                                     reputation
Can this be certain?   *of family*

---

2 **grown mad** According to some classical authorities, mandrake ingested
in large quantities could cause madness, as could its shriek (see 1n.);
other authorities claimed it could cure
melancholy.
   prodigy something extraordinary or
monstrous; 'progeny' is also a possible
emendation of Q1's 'progedy' (see
t.n.), in which case the Cardinal could
be suggesting that Ferdinand's madness is the 'progeny' of the mandrake.
3 **loose i'th' hilts** promiscuous; cf.
Cotgrave, the second edition of which
(1632) defines French *cocu* (cuckold)
as 'one whose wife is loose in the hilts'
(Brown).
4 **lower** more softly
5 **publish't** broadcast it; make it generally known

6–8 **As . . . them** Like servants who
seek to gain stature by bragging
about their master's generosity (and
perhaps also to gain income, if they
notice, or *mark*, potential suitors
they can bribe to help the suitors gain access to their master), so
rogues feel that they stand to gain
by gossiping about the Duchess's
promiscuity.
8 **confusion seize her** may she be put
to shame
9 **bawds . . . turn** pimps to get her
sexual partners
10–11 **And . . . service** The Duchess has
had more successful strategies for hiding her sexual practices than fortified
towns have for concealing their military installations (with sexual innuendo on *service*).

---

2 prodigy] *Q3;* progedy *Q1* 3 damned] *(*dampn'd*)* 4] *Q1 lines* Strumpet. / lower. / Lower? /
8 them] 'em *Q4* 9 hath] has *Q4* 11–12] *Q1 lines* Seruice. / possible? / certaine? / rubarbe /
11 towns of garrison] Garrison Towns *Q4*

FERDINAND   Rhubarb! Oh, for rhubarb
　To purge this choler! Here's the cursed day
　To prompt my memory, and here't shall stick
　Till of her bleeding heart I make a sponge   15
　To wipe it out.
CARDINAL   Why do you make yourself
　So wild a tempest?
FERDINAND   Would I could be one,
　That I might toss her palace 'bout her ears,
　Root up her goodly forests, blast her meads,
　And lay her general territory as waste   20
　As she hath done her honours!
CARDINAL   Shall our blood,
　The royal blood of Aragon and Castile,
　Be thus attainted?
FERDINAND   Apply desperate physic.
　We must not now use balsamum, but fire –

12–13 **rhubarb . . . choler** Cf. *White Devil*, 5.1.189–90 where Flamineo proposes rhubarb, a well-known purgative, to relieve choler.

13–14 **Here's . . . stick** Ferdinand may first indicate the letter, which includes the *day* of the Duchess's childbirth, then indicate his heart or head, where the date will remain indelibly fixed.

13 **cursed** cursèd

16 **make yourself** turn yourself into; make for yourself

18–21 Continuing the military figure of speech from 10–11, Ferdinand imagines the Duchess's territories as extensions of her body that can be raped and destroyed.

21 **honours** Brennan, Dollimore and Sinfield read 'honour's', which places the emphasis on the Duchess's destruction of her sexual reputation rather than 'honours' in the sense of achievements,

distinctions, aristocratic status (D&S).

21–3 **our . . . attainted** As Webster may have known, the Spaniards at this period were particularly insistent on purity of blood (*limpieza de sangre*); candidates for high office were required to prove their freedom from Moorish or Jewish ancestry. The Spanish monarchs Ferdinand and Isabella, who had instigated the expulsion of Moors and Jews from Spain in 1492, united the 'royal blood of Aragon and Castile', since Ferdinand was Aragonese and Isabella was Castilian. The Spanish King Ferdinand was a cousin of the grandfather of the Duchess and her brothers (Amendola).

23 **desperate physic** extreme forms of medical intervention

24 **balsamum** one of a group of herbs, such as lemon balm, used to soothe anxiety and promote sleep

---

14 here't] *(*here'it*)*   16–17] *Q1 lines* out. / selfe / Tempest? / one, /   20 general territory] whole Territories *Q4*   21] *Q1 lines* honors. / blood? /   honours] honour's *Brennan*   23] *Q1 lines* attaincted? / physicke, /

The smarting cupping-glass, for that's the mean   25
To purge infected blood, such blood as hers.
There is a kind of pity in mine eye;
I'll give it to my handkercher.   [*Wipes his eyes.*]
                              And now 'tis here,
I'll bequeath this to her bastard.

CARDINAL   What to do?

FERDINAND

Why, to make soft lint for his mother wounds,   30
When I have hewed her to pieces.

CARDINAL   Cursed creature!

Unequal nature, to place women's hearts
So far upon the left side.

FERDINAND   Foolish men,

That e'er will trust their honour in a bark
Made of so slight, weak bulrush as is woman,   35
Apt every minute to sink it.

CARDINAL

Thus ignorance, when it hath purchased honour,

---

25 **cupping-glass** a glass, used along with painful small knives, to extract blood through vacuum pressure. Controlled blood-letting was believed to be beneficial.
27 Ferdinand evidently has tears in his eyes, most likely out of self-pity, but perhaps at the thought of injuring his sister's body.
28 **handkercher** common seventeenth-century form of the word 'handkerchief'
   here i.e. in his handkerchief
29 **What to do** for what purpose
30 **lint** soft material used for bandages
   mother usually emended to 'mother's', the Q2 reading ('mothers'), but 'mother' is more evocative, suggesting wounds that are the child's and the

mother's simultaneously
31 **hewed** hacked
   Cursed creature The Cardinal could refer to Ferdinand, to the Duchess or to her child.
33 **left side** associated with deviance and unreliability, as in the 'bar sinister' or left-leaning bar that in heraldry signified bastardy
34–5 **bark. . . bulrush** A boat (*bark*) made of rushes (*bulrush*) would be easy to sink. Cf. the story of the infant Moses, who was floating in a boat made of bulrush when he was found by the Pharaoh's daughter (Exodus, 2.3–5).
37–8 **ignorance . . . it** The ignorant may be able to buy an honour or title, but that doesn't make them able to behave

---

28 handkercher] *(*hand-kercher*)*; handkerchief *Q3* SD] *Gibbons (subst.)* 29] *Q1 lines* Bastard. /
do? /   30 mother] mothers *Q2*   31] *Q1 lines* peeces. / creature, /   33] *Q1 lines* left-side. / men,
/   34 e'er] *(*ere*)*   35 is] this *Q2*   36–8] *Sampson; Q1 lines* it? / Thus / honour, / it. / laughing, /

It cannot wield it.

FERDINAND   Methinks I see her laughing.
Excellent hyena! Talk to me somewhat – quickly,
Or my imagination will carry me   40
To see her in the shameful act of sin.

CARDINAL
With whom?

FERDINAND   Happily with some strong-thighed bargeman,
Or one o'th' wood yard that can quoit the sledge
Or toss the bar, or else some lovely squire
That carries coals up to her privy lodgings.   45

CARDINAL
You fly beyond your reason.

FERDINAND   Go to, mistress!
'Tis not your whore's milk that shall quench my wild
    fire,
But your whore's blood.

CARDINAL
How idly shows this rage, which carries you,

---

as would be expected of the honourable (adapted from Hall, *Characters*, 'The Truly Noble', 53; Dent, *Webster*).

39 **hyena** then as now, known for a cry like maniacal laughter; Ferdinand may also imply that his sister's behaviour is too manly for a woman: according to Pliny, 8.30, the hyena was naturally bisexual and changed its sex every year (Enterline).

somewhat about something

42 **Happily** possibly 'haply', which was sometimes spelled 'happily' in the period; but 'happily' suggests ambiguity in Ferdinand's reaction to his pornographic fantasies about his sister. Cf. 3.2.82.

43 **wood yard** place frequented by the most menial servants; cf. 2.2.58.

quoit the sledge wield or throw a

sledge-hammer, perhaps as a sport requiring considerable brute force

44 **toss the bar** another sport (with sexual implications)

44–5 **squire . . . lodgings** higher class of servant who might carry warm coals to heat her private bedroom (with sexual suggestion)

46 **You . . . reason** You are becoming irrational. (As if to prove the Cardinal's point, Ferdinand addresses the rest of the line to the absent Duchess.)

47 **wild fire** highly flammable substance used in warfare (D&S); Ferdinand's rage; sexual desire: cf. his reference to *coals* (45), which will, in his imagination, fuel the fire of his sister's lust. The sexual *fire* at 47 is his own but incestuously indistinguishable from hers.

42] *Q1 lines* whom? / Bargeman; / Happily] Happly *Q4*   43–5] *om. Q4*   45 privy] private *Q2*
46] *Q1 lines* reason. / (Mistris.) /   47 shall] can *Q2*   48–50] *Dyce; Q1 lines* blood. / rage? / ayre, /

As men conveyed by witches, through the air   50
On violent whirlwinds! This intemperate noise
Fitly resembles deaf men's shrill discourse –
Who talk aloud, thinking all other men
To have their imperfection.

FERDINAND   Have not you
My palsy?

CARDINAL   Yes. I can be angry   55
Without this rupture. There is not in nature
A thing that makes man so deformed, so beastly,
As doth intemperate anger. Chide yourself:
You have diverse men who never yet expressed
Their strong desire of rest but by unrest,   60
By vexing of themselves. Come, put yourself
In tune.

FERDINAND   So. I will only study to seem
The thing I am not. I could kill her now
In you or in myself, for I do think
It is some sin in us heaven doth revenge   65
By her.

---

50 **men . . . air** Particularly on the Continent, there were many stories of abduction by witches flying on broomsticks.

53 **aloud** loudly

55 **palsy** infirmity; condition of utter powerlessness

56 **rupture** departure from reason (such as Ferdinand has just displayed)

59 **You have** there are (implying Ferdinand is one of them)

59–61 **never . . . themselves** claim to want peace and quiet, but seek for it in an agitated manner that defeats the purpose

61–2 **put . . . tune** get back into balance; i.e. curb the excess of choler that has caused your irrational outbursts

62 **So** an expression of agreement, Ferdinand's putting himself *in tune*; or, if Q1's comma (see t.n.) is followed, the first word of the following sentence, meaning 'in that case'

62–3 **study . . . not** try to appear sane

63–6 **I could . . . her** By killing himself or his brother, Ferdinand would extinguish the sin that exists both in them and in their sister – a sin for which God uses her behaviour to punish them. His inability to separate himself from his siblings, particularly from his twin, causes him to see in the Duchess an incestuous lust that is actually in himself (cf. 47 and n.).

54–5] *Q1 lines* imperfection. / you, / palsey? / angry /   62] *Q1 lines* tune. / seeme /   So.] *(So,)*
66] *Q1 lines* her. / mad? / bodies /

205

CARDINAL   Are you stark mad?

FERDINAND   I would have their bodies
Burnt in a coal pit, with the ventage stopped,
That their cursed smoke might not ascend to heaven;
Or dip the sheets they lie in, in pitch or sulphur,
Wrap them in't and then light them like a match;   70
Or else to boil their bastard to a cullis
And give't his lecherous father to renew
The sin of his back.

CARDINAL   I'll leave you.

FERDINAND   Nay, I have done.
I am confident, had I been damned in hell,
And should have heard of this, it would have put me   75
Into a cold sweat. In, in – I'll go sleep.
Till I know who leaps my sister I'll not stir;
That known, I'll find scorpions to string my whips,
And fix her in a general eclipse.   *Exeunt.*

---

66 **bodies** of the Duchess and her (imagined) lovers

67 **ventage stopped** vents plugged up

69–70 punishment like that of Otho, Earl of Montferrato, whom Painter, fol. 192, specifically compares to the Duchess's brothers for cruelty: Otho burned one of his servants to death in a sulphur-laced sheet simply for sleeping late (Lucas).

69 **pitch** viscous, highly flammable substance derived from tar

71 **cullis** rich broth (from French *coulis*); cf. 2.4.66.

72–3 Cf. the classical myth of Tereus and Philomela: as revenge for his rape of Philomela, Tereus was served a meal of his own son's flesh.

renew . . . back Rich broths were

thought to have an aphrodisiac effect. For copulation as the *sin* of one's *back*, cf. Iago's gibe in *Oth* 1.1.114–15 that Othello and Desdemona are 'making the beast with two backs'.

73 **have done** am finished

76–7 **I'll . . . stir** Ferdinand evidently expects his dreams to reveal the man who is sleeping with his sister.

78–9 I will string scorpions on a whip so that when I punish my sister she will be stung by them and die. 'Scorpions' could also be barbed whips: cf. *White Devil*, 2.1.244, and 1 Kings, 12.11, in the King James version, 'my father hath chastised you with whips, but I will chastise you with scorpions.'

79 **fix** affix, settle immovably
general total

73] *Q1 lines* backe. / you. / done, /   78 string] sting *Q2*

3.1   [*Enter*] ANTONIO *and* DELIO.

ANTONIO
　　Our noble friend, my most beloved Delio!
　　Oh, you have been a stranger long at court.
　　Came you along with the lord Ferdinand?
DELIO
　　I did, sir. And how fares your noble Duchess?
ANTONIO
　　Right fortunately well. She's an excellent   5
　　Feeder of pedigrees: since you last saw her,
　　She hath had two children more, a son and daughter.
DELIO
　　Methinks 'twas yesterday. Let me but wink
　　And not behold your face, which to mine eye
　　Is somewhat leaner, verily I should dream   10
　　It were within this half-hour.
ANTONIO
　　You have not been in law, friend Delio,
　　Nor in prison, nor a suitor at the court,
　　Nor begged the reversion of some great man's place,
　　Nor troubled with an old wife, which doth make   15
　　Your time so insensibly hasten.
DELIO   Pray, sir, tell me:

3.1 Location: the Duchess's palace
1　**Our** Antonio's and the Duchess's
　　beloved belovèd
3　**along with** as part of Ferdinand's
　　entourage
5–11 At least two years must have
　　passed since 2.5, unless the Duchess's
　　younger son and daughter are twins.
　　Webster makes a clever jest on the
　　awkward passage of time between 2.5
　　and 3.1.

8　**Let . . . wink** if I were only to blink
12　**in law** pursuing a law case. The courts,
　　whether in Italy or in England, were
　　notoriously slow.
13　**suitor** petitioner
14　**reversion . . . place** the right to
　　assume an office at court when the
　　present holder dies or resigns
15　**which** i.e. your freedom from which
16　**insensibly** imperceptibly
　　Pray I pray

3.1] *(ACTVS III. SCENA I.)* 0 SD] *Q4; Antonio, and Delio, Duchesse, Ferdinand, Bosola.* | *Q1* 5
Right] Most *Q4*　7 and] and a *Q4*　8–16 Methinks . . . hasten] *om. Q4*　16] *Q1 lines* hasten. / me, /

Hath not this news arrived yet to the ear
Of the lord Cardinal?

ANTONIO   I fear it hath.
The lord Ferdinand, that's newly come to court,
Doth bear himself right dangerously.

DELIO   Pray why?   20

ANTONIO

He is so quiet that he seems to sleep
The tempest out, as dormice do in winter.
Those houses that are haunted are most still,
Till the devil be up.

DELIO   What say the common people?

ANTONIO

The common rabble do directly say   25
She is a strumpet.

DELIO   And your graver heads,
Which would be politic, what censure they?

ANTONIO

They do observe I grow to infinite purchase
The left-hand way, and all suppose the Duchess
Would amend it if she could. For, say they,   30

---

17 **news** of the supposedly unmarried
Duchess's having borne children.
Since Delio suspected at 2.4.79–80
that Ferdinand had been informed
of the first birth or of the marriage,
his question here may be designed
to find out the extent of Antonio's
knowledge (and also to orient the
audience).

20 **bear ... dangerously** carry himself
with a reserve that suggests suppressed
rage (with a pun on 'dangerous' in the
usual sense of the word)

22 **dormice** 'To sleep like a dormouse'
was proverbial (Dent, D568); cf.
1.2.199, where Ferdinand compares

Bosola's duties as household spy to
those of a *politic dormouse*.

23 **still** silent

24 **devil be up** devil becomes active
(implying that the ghosts haunting the
house are demonic in origin)

25 **directly** unambiguously; openly

27 **politic** circumspect; sophisticated in
dealing with public matters (implying
a higher class of critic than the *common
people* referred to at 24)
censure judge

28 **purchase** wealth, with a possible
sexual pun on *purchase* as prostitution

29 **left-hand** sinister, illegal; cf. 2.5.33n.

18] *Q1 lines Cardinall?* / hath, /   20] *Q1 lines* dangerously. / why? /   right] most *Q4*   23 haunted]
most haunted *Q4*   24] *Q1 lines* vp. / people. /   26] *Q1 lines* Strumpet. / heades, /   27 be] *Q2;* he
Q1   28 purchase] Wealth *Q4*   29 left-hand] *Q2;* leaft-hand *Q1*   30–5 For . . . people] *om. Q4*

Great princes, though they grudge their officers
Should have such large and unconfined means
To get wealth under them, will not complain,
Lest thereby they should make them odious
Unto the people. For other obligation   35
Of love or marriage between her and me,
They never dream of.

[*Enter*] FERDINAND, DUCHESS [*and*] BOSOLA.

DELIO   The lord Ferdinand
Is going to bed.
FERDINAND   I'll instantly to bed,
For I am weary. I am to be – bespeak
A husband for you.
DUCHESS   For me, sir? Pray, who is't?   40
FERDINAND
The great Count Malateste.
DUCHESS   Fie upon him!
A count? He's a mere stick of sugar candy –

31–5 **Great . . . people** Princes may resent the fact that their administrators have the means to become wealthy at their expense, but they will not publicly object because they do not want the administrators to become hated by the people or, alternatively, make themselves, the princes, hated by the people; borrowed almost verbatim from *Ignatius*, 65 (Dent, *Webster*).

31 **grudge** be resentful that

32 **unconfined** unconfinèd

35 **For other obligation** that there may be another connection

37–8 **Ferdinand . . . bed** When last seen onstage at 2.5.76, Ferdinand had similarly been on his way to bed and vowed not to stir until he knew the identity of the Duchess's lover. However, in terms of the action within the play, two years have passed (see 5–11n.) – rather a long time for Ferdinand to remain in bed.

39 **be – bespeak** usually assumed to be a printing error and emended to 'bespeak', but Ferdinand's misstatement can also be taken as a revelation of his secret incestuous wishes.

42–3 **stick . . . him** implying he is trivial as well as too transparent; cf. *Devil's Law-Case*, 2.1.147–8, which repeats the metaphor almost verbatim (Webster, 2.98).

34 Lest] *(Least)* 37–8] *Q1 lines* off. / *Ferdinand* / going to bed. / instantly to bed, / 37 of] *(off)* SD] *Q4 after 37; Duchesse, Ferdinand, Bosola.* | *0 SD Q1; Enter* Duchess, Ferdinand, *and* Attendants. *Dyce²* 38 Is going to bed] *om. Q4* 39 be] *om. Q2* 40–1] *Q1 lines* you. / is't? / *Malateste.* / him, /

You may look quite through him. When I choose
A husband I will marry for your honour.

FERDINAND

You shall do well in't. How is't, worthy Antonio?   45

DUCHESS

But, sir, I am to have private conference with you
About a scandalous report is spread
Touching mine honour.

FERDINAND   Let me be ever deaf to't:
One of Pasquil's paper bullets, court calumny,
A pestilent air, which princes' palaces   50
Are seldom purged of. Yet, say that it were true:
I pour it in your bosom, my fixed love— *strange language*
Would strongly excuse, extenuate, nay deny
Faults, were they apparent in you. Go –
Be safe in your own innocency.

DUCHESS   Oh, blest comfort!   55
This deadly air is purged.

Exeunt [all but Ferdinand and Bosola].

---

44 **for your honour** in a way that will add lustre to your name and reputation

45 **How . . . Antonio** At 2.3.65–6 Bosola concluded that Antonio was the Duchess's pimp, and presumably he informed Ferdinand. Ferdinand's sudden acknowledgement of Antonio may carry a leering suggestiveness or implied threat, which the Duchess's following line attempts to deflect.

46 **I . . . conference** I need to speak privately

48 **Touching** concerning; tainting

49 **Pasquil's paper bullets** Pasquil, in Rome, was a famous statue where wits would post pages of satire or slander – *bullets* because of their power to damage the target of the satire. Cf. *MA*

2.3.232, where Benedick expects to endure 'paper bullets of the brain' for marrying Beatrice against his former principles.

50 **pestilent air** i.e. the poisoned environment brought about by constant malicious gossip

52 **pour . . . bosom** insist (in peculiarly intimate and possibly sexualized language). In *White Devil*, 1.2.188–9, the same phrase is used by Brachiano in love with Vittoria.

52–4 **love . . . you** echoes Alexander, *Alexandrian Tragedy*, sig. I3ʳ: 'Love . . . doth excuse, extenuate, or denie / Faults where it likes.'

56 **deadly . . . purged** Cf. Ferdinand's reference to 'pestilent air' at court (50).

43 through] *Q4*; thorough *Q1*   48] *Q1 lines* honour. / to't: /   49–54 One . . . you] *om. Q4*   51 of] (off)   54 were] *Q3*; where *Q1*   55–6] *Sampson*; *Q1 lines* safe / innocency. / comfort, / purg'd. / on /   56 SD] *Q4 (subst.); Exeunt. | Q1*

FERDINAND   Her guilt treads on
  Hot burning coulters. Now, Bosola,
  How thrives our intelligence?
BOSOLA   Sir, uncertainly.
  'Tis rumoured she hath had three bastards, but
  By whom we may go read i'th' stars.
FERDINAND   Why some   60
  Hold opinion all things are written there.
BOSOLA
  Yes, if we could find spectacles to read them.
  I do suspect there hath been some sorcery
  Used on the Duchess.
FERDINAND   Sorcery? To what purpose?
BOSOLA
  To make her dote on some desertless fellow   65
  She shames to acknowledge.
FERDINAND   Can your faith give way
  To think there's power in potions or in charms
  To make us love, whether we will or no?
BOSOLA
  Most certainly.

[Handwritten marginal notes: "means could only happen if someone poisoned her"]

56–7 ***Her . . . coulters** i.e. her guilt
  is obvious. According to Camden,
  Britannia, 211, suspects in medieval England could be made to walk
  barefoot on red-hot plough-blades or
  coulters; if they were burned, their
  guilt was established (Dent, *Webster*).
  Brown has Bosola enter only after
  coulters, in which case he does not
  witness Ferdinand's feigned reconciliation with the Duchess.
58 **How . . . intelligence?** How are we
  doing in our attempt to gain information?
60 **we . . . stars** an expression of futil-

ity, which assumes that the stars do
not offer valid astrological information
61 **all . . . there** Cf. Camden, *Remains*,
  sigs V3ᵛ–V4ʳ: 'as Astrologians say, all
  things are written in heaven, if a man
  could reade them.'
62 **spectacles . . . them** Cf. 2.4.16–18,
  where the Cardinal refers to Galileo's
  glass – a device Bosola would presumably find inadequate for reading human
  secrets.
65 **desertless fellow** undeserving lout
  (*fellow* implies low status)
66 **give way** weaken

56–7 Her . . . coulters] *om. Q4* 57 coulters] *Dyce²*; cultures *Q1* coulters. Now] coulters. *Enter*
Bosola. Now *Dyce²* 58] *Q1 lines* intelligence? / vncertainly. / 59 but] *om. Q4* 60] *Q1 lines* Starres.
/ some / 62 them] 'em *Q4* 63–78 I . . . blood] *om. in performance Q4* 64] *Q1 lines* Duchesse. /
purpose? / 66] *Q1 lines* acknowledge. / way /

FERDINAND

Away! These are mere gulleries, horrid things   70
Invented by some cheating mountebanks
To abuse us. Do you think that herbs or charms
Can force the will? Some trials have been made
In this foolish practice, but the ingredients
Were lenitive poisons, such as are of force   75
To make the patient mad – and straight the witch
Swears by equivocation they are in love.
The witchcraft lies in her rank blood. This night
I will force confession from her. You told me
You had got within these two days a false key   80
Into her bedchamber.

BOSOLA   I have.   [*Gives him the key.*]

FERDINAND   As I would wish.

70 **gulleries** tricks
71 **mountebanks** travelling salesmen, like Volpone disguised in Jonson, *Volpone*, 2.2; he 'mounts a bank', stands on a raised platform, to peddle patent medicine to gullible customers.
72–3 **Do . . . will** Do you think that herbs or charms can cause people to do what they would not otherwise; *will* can also be sexual appetite. Ferdinand's scepticism about pharmacology is interesting given that he himself had earlier asked for rhubarb to purge his anger (2.5.12).
75–6 **lenitive . . . mad** drugs that appear sweet and soothing (*lenitive*) but have the power (*are of force*) to induce madness. Through this phrase Ferdinand appears to be conceding that drugs can cause madness, but implying that it is madness rather than the drug that renders moot the concept of free will.
76 **witch** the hypothetical sorcerer or sorceress who administers the love potion

77 **Swears by equivocation** gives an oath that appears to affirm something, but that can also be understood through the trickiness of its wording to state the opposite. The word *equivocation* was used in England of the Jesuits, especially Father Garnet, who was executed for treason in 1605 for participating in the Gunpowder Plot to execute James I. Garnet had claimed the right to make ambiguous answers during his interrogation to avoid incriminating himself. Cf. *Mac* 2.3.9–11, where the Porter claims that an equivocator resembling Garnet will go to hell because he could not 'equivocate to heaven'. The Duchess, by contrast, associates *equivocation* with a *tyrant* (1.2.353–4).
78 ***The . . . blood** At this point the *witch* (76) becomes the Duchess, whose *rank* (foul, polluted) *blood* Ferdinand believes to have bewitched him into madness.
80 **false** duplicate, but *false* in that it will betray the Duchess

78 blood] *Q2;* bood *Q1*   78–9 This . . . her] *om. Q4*   81–2] *Q1 lines* Bed-chamber. / haue. / wish. / doe? / ghesse? / No: /   81 SD] *this edn*

BOSOLA

    What do you intend to do?

FERDINAND   Can you guess?

BOSOLA   No.

FERDINAND

    Do not ask then.

    He that can compass me and know my drifts

    May say he hath put a girdle 'bout the world   85

    And sounded all her quicksands.

BOSOLA   I do not

    Think so.

FERDINAND   What do you think, then, pray?

BOSOLA   That you

    Are your own chronicle too much, and grossly

    Flatter yourself.

FERDINAND   Give me thy hand; I thank thee.

    I never gave pension but to flatterers,   90

    Till I entertained thee. Farewell.

    'That friend a great man's ruin strongly checks

    Who rails into his belief all his defects.'   *Exeunt.*

                                  sententia

---

84 **compass** encircle; hem in; grasp with the mind

   drifts aims; plots; procrastinations

85 **put . . . world** commonplace, echoing, among other texts, Puck's less malevolent vow to 'put a girdle round about the earth' (*MND* 2.1.175), but Ferdinand seems to regard the earth and himself as coterminous. Repeated, with the inclusion of a parallel to Ferdinand's next line (86), in Webster's *Characters*, where '*A noble and retir'd House-keeper*' is said to have 'put a gird about the whole world, and sounded all her

quicksandes' (Webster, 3.465–6).

88 **chronicle** history; that is, he spends too much time extolling his own deeds and purposes. Cf. *White Devil*, 5.1.97: ''Tis a ridiculous thing for a man to bee his owne Chronicle.'

90 I only had flatterers in my pay

92–3 The friend who *rails* the great man's faults *into his belief* – that is, articulates the great man's faults so vehemently that he is finally forced to acknowledge them – thereby *checks* (halts or curbs) the faults (that might otherwise undo him). Cf. Antonio's first speech 1.1.13–22.

86–9] *Sampson; Q1 lines* quick-sands. / not / so. / pray? / are / grosly / selfe. / thee: / 92–3] *ital. Q1* 93 belief] *Faith* | *Q4*

3.2   [*Enter*] DUCHESS, ANTONIO [*and*] CARIOLA.

DUCHESS

>Bring me the casket hither and the glass.
>
>You get no lodging here tonight, my lord!

ANTONIO

>Indeed, I must persuade one.

DUCHESS   Very good.

>I hope in time 'twill grow into a custom
>
>That noble men shall come with cap and knee   5
>
>To purchase a night's lodging of their wives.

ANTONIO

>I must lie here.

DUCHESS   Must? You are a Lord of Misrule.

ANTONIO

>Indeed, my rule is only in the night.

DUCHESS

>To what use will you put me?   *— Duchess being flirtatious*

ANTONIO   We'll sleep together.

3.2 Location: the Duchess's bedchamber

1   **casket** small box for jewellery or other
       valuables
       glass mirror. The request is addressed
       either to Cariola, who as her maid
       would ordinarily do the fetching, or to
       Antonio, who describes himself at 6 as
       purchasing his lodging and may offer
       the casket as a jesting 'payment'.

3   **persuade one** convince you to give
       me one

5   **noble men** emended in most editions
       to 'noblemen', which adds an element
       of class exclusion. Antonio can be seen
       as *noble* whether or not he has a title.
       with . . . knee on bended knee and
       with cap in hand as a sign of supplica-

tion

7   **Lord of Misrule** during Carnival
       or as part of Christmas festivities, a
       temporary ruler, often of lower sta-
       tus than those he governs; since his
       role is to preside over the disorderly
       festivities, his 'rule' is actually 'mis-
       rule'. The Q1 spelling 'Misse-rule'
       also suggests a pun on 'Mistress':
       Antonio is a *Lord* ruled by his mis-
       tress.

8   **my . . . night** As 'master' of the clan-
       destine household, he 'rules' only dur-
       ing the night-time hours when he and
       the Duchess are together as husband
       and wife. The festivities over which
       Lords of Misrule would preside were

3.2] *(SCENA. II.)*   0 SD] *Q4 (subst.); Dutchesse, Antonio, Cariola, Ferdinand, Bosola, Officers.* |
Q1 3] *Q1 lines* one: / good: /   5 noble men] noblemen *Dyce*   7–21] *om. in performance Q4*   7] *Q1*
lines here. / Misse-rule. /   Misrule] *(Misse-rule)*   9] *Q1 lines* me, / together: /

DUCHESS

Alas, what pleasure can two lovers find in sleep?   10

CARIOLA

My lord, I lie with her often and I know

She'll much disquiet you –

ANTONIO   See, you are complained of!

CARIOLA

– For she's the sprawlingest bedfellow!

ANTONIO

I shall like her the better for that.

CARIOLA

Sir, shall I ask you a question?

ANTONIO   I pray thee, Cariola.   15

CARIOLA

Wherefore still when you lie with my lady

Do you rise so early?

ANTONIO   Labouring men

Count the clock oftenest, Cariola –

Are glad when their task's ended.

DUCHESS   I'll stop your mouth.

    [*Kisses him.*]

ANTONIO

Nay that's but one. Venus had two soft doves   20

---

often nocturnal.

11 **lie . . . often** It was commonplace even for aristocrats to share beds, often as a sign of special friendship. See *MA* 4.1.149, where Beatrice testifies that she has for a 'twelvemonth' been Hero's 'bedfellow'.

16–17 **Wherefore . . . early** asked in jest, since Cariola already knows he leaves the Duchess's bed early to avoid detection by the rest of the household

16 **still** always

18 **Count** watch

19 **stop your mouth** shut you up (by kissing you)

20–1 **Venus . . . chariot** Doves were sacred to Venus, goddess of love. Cf. *Fountain*, sig. Cc3^r: '*Pausanius* saith, that Venus is drawne in a coach through the airie passages, with two white Doves . . . called the birds of Venus.' Doves were also associated with fidelity, since they were believed to mate for life and, if parted, for ever

---

12] *Q1 lines* you: / of. /   13 sprawlingest] (sprawlingst)   15] *Q1 lines* question? / *Cariola*. /   I pray]
Ay, pray *Dyce*   pray thee] prithee do *Q4*   17] *Q1 lines* early? / men, /   18 oftenest] (oftnest)   19]
Q1 lines ended. / mouth. /   SD] *Lucas*

To draw her chariot. I must have another.   [*Kisses her.*]
When wilt thou marry, Cariola?

CARIOLA   Never, my lord.

ANTONIO

Oh, fie upon this single life! Forgo it.
We read how Daphne, for her peevish slight,
Became a fruitless bay tree; Syrinx turned   25
To the pale, empty reed; Anaxarete
Was frozen into marble; whereas those
Which married or proved kind unto their friends
Were by a gracious influence transshaped
Into the olive, pomegranate, mulberry –   30
Became flowers, precious stones or eminent stars.

(he's glad he's married)

mourn their lost mate.

21 SD Norton specifies instead '*She kiss-es him again*', but that takes away the reciprocity of the gesture.

22 **Never** an ironic intimation of death. Cf. *AC* 1.2.31ff., where a Soothsayer tells Charmian that she will outlive her mistress, but fails to specify that she will survive Cleopatra by only a few minutes.

24–31 Antonio's reinterpretations of Ovid exemplify a common pastime among early modern wits. Cf. Marvell's version in 'The Garden', 29–32, in which the gods are claimed to have desired plants rather than women all along.

24–5 **Daphne . . . tree** Daphne, refusing Apollo's embraces, fled from him and was transformed into a laurel (*bay*) tree (Ovid, 1.452–567). Many editions read 'flight' instead of *slight* (see t.n.). Brown discounts 'slight' on *OED* evidence that the word was not used in the sense of 'display of indifference' until 1701. But that argument is circular, since the *OED* editors probably used texts of Webster in which the emendation to 'flight' had already been made.

25 **fruitless bay tree** The laurel does

bear small berries but is most val-ued for its aromatic leaves, in classical times used to make wreathes honour-ing poets and heroes.

25–6 **Syrinx . . . reed** Syrinx escaped from Pan's amorous passion and was transformed into the reeds that were used to make 'Pan' pipes (Ovid, 1.689–712). To call the reed *empty* is Antonio's witty distortion: though the reeds were hollow, when filled with breath they produced music.

26–7 **Anaxarete . . . marble** Unmoved by her lover's entreaties, Anaxarete watched him hang himself at her door, then watched his body on its jour-ney to the grave; Venus in retribution changed her into a statue of stone (Ovid, 14.698–764).

28 **kind** sexually yielding

29 **transshaped** transformed

30–1 **olive . . . stars** Cf. *Heptameron*, sig. C4[r], which parallels Antonio's exam-ples of the barren Daphne, Syrinx and Anaxarete, then adds: 'But in the behalf of Mariage, thousands have ben changed into Olyve, Pomegranate, Mulberie, and other fruitfull trees, sweete flowers, Starres, and precious Stones, by whom

21 SD] *Lucas*   22] *Q1 lines Cariola? / Lord.) /*   24 slight] flight *Dyce*   25 Syrinx] *Q4; Sirina | Q1a; Siriux | Q1b*   30 olive] *(Oliffe)*

CARIOLA

This is a vain poetry. But, I pray you, tell me:
If there were proposed me wisdom, riches and beauty
In three several young men, which should I choose?

ANTONIO

'Tis a hard question. This was Paris' case,   35
And he was blind in't; and there was great cause:
For how was't possible he could judge right,
Having three amorous goddesses in view,
And they stark naked? 'Twas a motion
Were able to benight the apprehension   40
Of the severest counsellor of Europe.
Now I look on both your faces, so well formed,
It puts me in mind of a question I would ask.

CARIOLA

What is't?

ANTONIO   I do wonder why hard-favoured ladies
For the most part keep worse-favoured waiting-women   45
To attend them, and cannot endure fair ones.

DUCHESS

Oh, that's soon answered.

the worlde is beautified, directed and
nourished' (Dent, *Webster*). No source
for the *pomegranate* reference is known.
The *mulberry*, according to Ovid, 4.55–
166, became red from the blood of the
dead lovers Pyramus and Thisbe.

32 vain poetry useless fiction

34 several separate; individual

35 Paris' case The 'Judgement of
Paris' ultimately caused the Trojan
War. Paris was asked to choose among
three goddesses – Juno (Hera) offering riches, Venus (Aphrodite) offering
beauty or Minerva (Athena) offering
wisdom – and fatefully chose Venus.
She rewarded him for his choice by

giving him the beautiful Helen, who
was inconveniently already married to
the Greek Menelaus, and Menelaus
went to war to secure her return.

36 was blind in't chose blindly

37–9 Cf. Alexander, *Julius Caesar*, sig.
R6ᵛ, where Juno complains of Paris's
choice, 'No wonder too though one all
judgement lost, / That had three naked
goddesses in sight' (Dent, *Webster*).

39 motion show (see 1.2.219n.). Brown
suggests 'incitement'.

40 benight the apprehension cloud the
perception

41 counsellor adviser, especially to a
ruler

32 vain] vein of *Q4* I pray you] pray *Q4* 33 and] *om. Q4* 36 cause] Reason *Q4* 37 could] should
Q2 39–41] *om. Q4* 40 apprehension] *Q1b* (apprehention); approbation *Q1a* 44] *Q1 lines* is't? /
Ladies /

Did you ever in your life know an ill painter
Desire to have his dwelling next door to the shop
Of an excellent picture maker? 'Twould disgrace   50
His face-making and undo him. I prithee,
When were we so merry? My hair tangles.

ANTONIO

Pray thee, Cariola, let's steal forth the room
And let her talk to herself. I have diverse times
Served her the like, when she hath chafed extremely.   55
I love to see her angry. Softly, Cariola.

Exeunt [Antonio and Cariola].

DUCHESS

Doth not the colour of my hair 'gin to change?
When I wax grey I shall have all the court
Powder their hair with arras to be like me.

[Enter] FERDINAND *[unseen].*

You have cause to love me. I entered you into my heart   60
Before you would vouchsafe to call for the keys.
We shall one day have my brothers take you napping.

---

44 **hard-favoured** unattractive
48 **ill** unskilled
51 **face-making** portrait painting; applying makeup
55 **Served . . . extremely** behaved towards her in the same manner, at which she has been extremely annoyed
59 **arras** orris root, a violet-scented iris root fashionably used to perfume and grey the hair
59 SD Since the early texts do not indicate Ferdinand's entrance, editors and players have timed it differently to achieve different theatrical effects. Q4, the first to include a SD, has Ferdinand enter after line 60. More commonly in

modern editions, he enters at line 62, either from behind or from a balcony or upper gallery, as Lucas suggests (2.165). The placement here at 59 emphasizes the theme of incest, since Ferdinand can understand the Duchess's loving words as applying to himself.
60–1 **I . . keys** Cf. *Arcadia*, book 1, ch. 11, 69: 'his fame had so framed the way to my mind, that his presence . . . had entred there before he vouchsafed to call for the keyes' (Lucas). When he enters, Ferdinand may be holding the key to the Duchess's bedchamber supplied by Bosola in the previous scene

---

49 his] *Q1b;* the *Q1a*   52 so] *om. Q2*   55 hath] had *Q2*   chafed] (chafde) *Q2*   56 SD] *Dyce; Exeunt. | Q1*   59 with arras] *om. Q4*   SD] *Q4 after 60; Ferdinand | 0 SD Q1; opp. 60–2 Lucas*   60 I entered you] (I entred you); I entred *Q2;* it enter'd *Q4*

Methinks his presence, being now in court,
Should make you keep your own bed. But you'll say   *key line,*
Love mixed with fear is sweetest. I'll assure you   *degree or*   65
You shall get no more children till my brothers   *truthint*
Consent to be your gossips. Have you lost your tongue?
   Ferdinand [shows himself and] gives her a poniard.
'Tis welcome.
For know, whether I am doomed to live or die,
I can do both like a prince. — *stunning acceptance*

FERDINAND   Die then quickly!   70

Virtue, where art thou hid? What hideous thing
Is it that doth eclipse thee?

DUCHESS   Pray, sir, hear me –

FERDINAND

Or is it true thou art but a bare name,
And no essential thing?

DUCHESS   Sir –

FERDINAND   Do not speak!

(3.1.80–1).

63 **his presence** that of Ferdinand, with a possible suggestion of royal *presence*

65 **Love . . . sweetest** a variation on the proverb 'Stolen fruit is sweet' (Tilley, F779)

66 **get . . . children** a jesting suggestion either that Antonio will be banned from her bed or that she will use some form of birth control. The most usual during the period was *coitus interruptus.*

67 **gossips** godparents; intimates, special friends

67 SD Beginning with Poel's 1892 production (see pp. 100–1), the Duchess sometimes first sees Ferdinand reflected in her mirror; or, as Norton proposes, 'She turns and sees Ferdinand'. Usually only the Duchess's awareness

of Ferdinand's presence is registered in a SD here, and his giving of the poniard occurs at 70 in Q1b (see t.n.), but the Duchess's line *'Tis welcome* (68) is more likely to refer to the poniard than to the sight of her brother. The SD in Q1b was a stop-press correction, and the closest available space for its insertion, since the preceding lines were already crowded, was opposite 70 (Gunby).

69–70 **whether . . . prince** Cf. *Arcadia*, book 1, ch. 4, 25: 'whether your time call you to live or die, doo both like a prince' (Lucas).

71–4 **Virtue . . . thing** Cf. *Arcadia*, book 2, ch. 1, 146: 'O Vertue, where doost thou hide thy self? or what hideous thing is this which doth eclips thee?' (Lucas).

67–8] *Dyce; one line Q1*   67 SD] *this edn; not in Q1a; Ferdinand giues her a ponyard.* | *opp. 70 Q1b*
69 doomed] *(doomb'd)*   70] *Q1 lines* Prince. / quickle: /   72] *Q1 lines* thee? / me: /   eclipse] *(ecclipze); clip Q2*   74–5] *this edn; Q1 lines* thing? / Sir: / speake. / sir: / you. /

DUCHESS

No, sir, I will plant my soul in mine ears to hear you. 75

FERDINAND

Oh, most imperfect light of human reason,

That makest so unhappy to foresee

What we can least prevent! Pursue thy wishes

And glory in them. There's in shame no comfort,

But to be past all bounds and sense of shame. 80

DUCHESS

I pray, sir, hear me: I am married.

FERDINAND   So.

DUCHESS

Happily not to your liking, but for that –

Alas, your shears do come untimely now

To clip the bird's wings that's already flown.

Will you see my husband?

FERDINAND   Yes, if I could change 85

Eyes with a basilisk.

DUCHESS   Sure, you came hither

76–80 Cf. *Arcadia*, book 2, ch. 1, 146: 'O imperfect proportion of reason, which can too much forsee, and too little prevent . . . In shame there is no comfort, but to be beyond all bounds of shame' (Lucas).

77 **makest** usually emended to 'mak'st us', but 'makest' without a direct object emphasizes the breadth of the claim, which applies to everyone

77–8 **Pursue . . . them** could be addressed either to flawed *reason* (76) or to the Duchess, in reference to her *wishes* (78)

81 **I am married** according to the contract *per verba de presenti* of 1.2.386ff.

82 **Happily** haply, perhaps; happily, since her marriage is indeed happy from her point of view, but her married happiness is in itself cause for Ferdinand's disapproval

83–4 **shears . . . flown** proverbial (Dent, B364). Cf. *Arcadia*, book 2, ch. 5, 177: 'your sheeres come too late to clip the birds wings that already is flowne away' (Lucas).

85 **Will you see** The Duchess means 'Would you be willing to meet'; Ferdinand takes the phrase literally (85–6).

85–6 **change . . . basilisk** trade his eyes for those of a mythological monster, king of serpents, whose gaze and breath were both fatal. Cf. *R3* 1.2.153–4: 'Rich. Thine eyes, sweet lady, have infected mine. / Anne. Would they were basilisks to strike thee dead.'

---

75 will] wou'd *Q4*   76–8 Oh . . . prevent] *om. in performance Q4*   77 makest] *(*mak'st*)*; mak'st us *Q4*   81] *Q1 lines* married, / So: /   82 Happily] Happly *Q4*   85–7] *Sampson; Q1 lines* Husband? / I / Basilisque: / hither / consideracy. / Wolfe /

By his confederacy.

FERDINAND   The howling of a wolf
Is music to thee, screech owl! Prithee, peace! –
Whate'er thou art that hast enjoyed my sister
(For I am sure thou hear'st me), for thine own sake   90
Let me not know thee. I came hither prepared
To work thy discovery, yet am now persuaded
It would beget such violent effects
As would damn us both. I would not for ten millions
I had beheld thee; therefore use all means   95
I never may have knowledge of thy name.
Enjoy thy lust still, and a wretched life
On that condition. – And for thee, vile woman,
If thou do wish thy lecher may grow old
In thy embracements, I would have thee build   100
Such a room for him as our anchorites
To holier use inhabit. Let not the sun
Shine on him till he's dead. Let dogs and monkeys
Only converse with him; and such dumb things

– she will be banished

87 **his** Antonio's; the basilisk's
howling . . . wolf a foreshadowing of
Ferdinand's later lycanthropy
88 **music to thee** 'music in comparison to thee' (Gunby). If the *wolf* in
question is Ferdinand (87n.), then he
may be expressing an unacknowledged
desire for her love and approval.
screech owl In calling the Duchess
a *screech owl* Ferdinand associates her
with madness, witchcraft and the
supernatural; the owl's *screech* was
often considered an omen of death:
cf. *3H6* 2.6.56–7, 'that fatal screech-
owl . . . that nothing sung but death'.
89 **Whate'er thou art** implying that the
Duchess's husband is less than human

or at least lacking in social status
92 **work** bring about
94 *__damn__ Given Ferdinand's predilection
in later lines for fire imagery to describe
both himself and the Duchess, Q1's
'dampe' could also mean 'extinguish'.
The two words might have been heard
the same way in the theatre.
98 *__vile__ The Q1 spelling 'vilde' also suggests 'wilde', the Q2 reading (see t.n.).
101 *__anchorites__ hermits who, as a sign of
religious renunciation of the world, had
themselves walled up for life in a small
cave or cell with no means of exit
104–5 **dumb . . . name** Let his name
cease to be spoken since it is uttered
only by those who cannot speak.

87 confederacy] *Q3;* consideracy *Q1*   88 thee] *Q4;* the *Q1*   90 hear'st] *(*hearst*);* heardst *Q2*   thine]
mine *Q2*   93 such] so *Q2*   94 damn] *Q2;* dampe *Q1*   94–8 I . . . condition] *om. in performance*
Q4   98 vile] *Q4;* vilde *Q1;* wilde *Q2*   99 lecher] *(*Leacher*);* Lover *Q4*   100 embracements] Embrace
Q4   thee] you *Q4*

To whom nature denies use, to sound his name. 105
Do not keep a paraquito lest she learn it.
If thou do love him, cut out thine own tongue
Lest it bewray him.

DUCHESS   Why might not I marry?
I have not gone about, in this, to create
Any new world or custom.

FERDINAND   Thou art undone. 110
And thou hast ta'en that massy sheet of lead
That hid thy husband's bones and folded it
About my heart.

DUCHESS   Mine bleeds for't.

FERDINAND   Thine? Thy heart?
What should I name't, unless a hollow bullet
Filled with unquenchable wildfire?

DUCHESS   You are in this 115
Too strict; and were you not my princely brother
I would say, too wilful. My reputation
Is safe.

FERDINAND   Dost thou know what reputation is?
I'll tell thee – to small purpose, since th'instruction
Comes now too late. 120

---

106 **paraquito** talking parakeet or parrot
(imagined as female)
108 **bewray** betray
109–10 **I . . . custom** a seemingly reasonable statement, yet showing
how far the Duchess differs from
Ferdinand in her perception of the
requirements of their class and status
(see p. 14)
111–12 **massy . . . bones** Her dead
husband, the former duke, like other
aristocrats, would have been placed
in a coffin lined with lead to delay
decomposition.

111 **massy** heavy, solid; cf. *White Devil*,
3.2.330: 'They wrapt her in a cruell
fould of lead.'
114–15 **hollow . . . wildfire** cannon-ball
filled with a chemical explosive whose
fire cannot be readily extinguished.
The explosive shell was introduced
in the mid-sixteenth century (Lucas).
Since cannon-balls, like coffin lin-
ings, were traditionally made of lead,
Ferdinand is establishing an identity
between her heart and his.
117 **reputation** pronounced as five
syllables

---

105 use] use of Speech *Q4*   108] *Q1 lines* him. / marry? /   bewray] betray *Q4*   110] *Q1 lines* custome. / vndone. /   113] *Q1 lines* heart. / for't. / heart?   115] *Q1 lines* wild-fire? / this /   117 too]
(to)   118] *Q1 lines* safe. / is /   119–20] *om. Q4*

Upon a time Reputation, Love and Death
Would travel o'er the world, and it was concluded
That they should part and take three several ways.
Death told them they should find him in great battles
Or cities plagued with plagues. Love gives them
    counsel   125
To enquire for him 'mongst unambitious shepherds,
Where dowries were not talked of, and sometimes
'Mongst quiet kindred that had nothing left
By their dead parents. 'Stay,' quoth Reputation,
'Do not forsake me, for it is my nature,   130
If once I part from any man I meet,
I am never found again.' And so for you:
You have shook hands with Reputation
And made him invisible. So fare you well.
I will never see you more.

DUCHESS   Why should only I,   135
Of all the other princes of the world,

121–35 **Upon . . . more** Cf. Matthieu,
sig. Ss1ᵛ: 'Reputation . . . the goddesse of great courages is so delicate,
as the least excesse doth blemish it, an
unjust enterprise dishonoreth it . . . It
is a spirit that goes and returnes no
more. They report that water, fire,
and reputation, undertooke to goe
throughout the world, and fearing
they should goe astray, they gave
signes one unto another; Water said
that they should finde her where as
they sawe reeds, and fire whereas the
smoke appeared, loose me not said
reputation, for if I get from you, you
will never finde mee againe' (Dent,
Webster).
122 **Would** desired to

126–7 **shepherds . . . of** Shepherds were
often too poor to offer or expect dowries, and were therefore free to marry
for love. In pastoral literature of the
period, shepherds were often stereotyped as lovers.
128–9 **quiet . . . parents** those too poor
or too unassertive to receive an inheritance from their dead relatives
133–4 **shook . . . invisible** exchanged
farewells and lost sight of Reputation
for ever
136 **princes** rulers. The Duchess's use of
the male form rather than 'princesses'
may have resonated for early audiences
with the habitual rhetoric of Queen
Elizabeth I, who frequently referred to
herself as 'prince' or even 'king'.

121–34 Upon . . . invisible] *om. in performance Q4*   124 them] 'em *Q4*   125 plagued] visited *Q4*   128
left] left 'em *Q4*   129 'Stay,' quoth] But, says *Q4*   133 shook] *Q1c;* shooked *Q1a, Q1b*   135] *Q1 lines*
more. / I, /

Be cased up like a holy relic? I have youth
And a little beauty.

FERDINAND   So you have some virgins
That are witches. I will never see thee more.   *Exit.*

Enter ANTONIO *with a pistol* [*and* CARIOLA].

DUCHESS
You saw this apparition?

ANTONIO   Yes. We are   140
Betrayed. How came he hither? I should turn
This to thee for that.   [*Aims the pistol at Cariola.*]

CARIOLA   Pray, sir, do. And when
That you have cleft my heart, you shall read there
Mine innocence.

DUCHESS   That gallery gave him entrance.

ANTONIO
I would this terrible thing would come again   145

---

137 **cased . . . relic** kept closed up in a special case like the *relic* of a saint in Catholic religious practice; relics were anathema to English Protestants. For the Duchess's sentiment, cf. Guazzo, sig. Ee5ᵛ: 'not to suffer a mayde to go abrode but once or twise in the yeere, and to keepe her inclosed like a holy relique, is the way to make her . . . more easie to bee caughte in an net' (Dent, *Webster*).

138–9 **virgins . . . witches** Some women accused of witchcraft in the period were virgins; there may also be a glancing reference to Elizabeth I, the Virgin Queen, who was widely suspected of witchcraft in Europe after England's seemingly uncanny defeat of the Spanish Armada in 1588.

139 **I . . . more** Ferdinand here repeats what he said at the close of the par-

able of Reputation (135). The implication is that the Duchess will part with her reputation in parting from Ferdinand; in his own mind, therefore, Ferdinand's identity is closely linked to the Duchess's reputation.

142 **This . . . that** the pistol to Cariola on account of her imagined betrayal (*that*)

143 **cleft** divided; broken not only by Antonio's bullet, but also by his distrust of her

144 **gallery** a long room adjoining her bedroom; an upper stage allowing Ferdinand to enter unseen (Lucas)

145–7 **I . . . love** Since Antonio admits to having seen Ferdinand, critics have asked why he did not immediately accost him. Lucas protests, 'One almost wishes that Webster had spared his Antonio at all events this

---

138] *Q1 lines* beautie. / Virgins, / you] we *Q4*   139 SD2] *Dyce*; *Enter Antonio with a Pistoll* | *after 140* apparition *Q1*   140] *Q1 lines* apparition. / are /   142] *Q1 lines* that. / when /   SD] *Lucas (subst.)*   144] *Q1 lines* innocence: / entrance. /

That, standing on my guard, I might relate
My warrantable love.   (*She shows the poniard.*)
                    Ha! What means this?

DUCHESS
    He left this with me.

ANTONIO   And, it seems, did wish
You would use it on yourself?

DUCHESS   His action seemed
    To intend so much.

ANTONIO   This hath a handle to't   150
As well as a point. Turn it towards him
And so fasten the keen edge in his rank gall!   [*Knocking*]
How now? Who knocks? More earthquakes?

DUCHESS   I stand
    As if a mine beneath my feet were ready
To be blown up.

CARIOLA [*Goes to the door.*] 'Tis Bosola.

DUCHESS   Away!   155
Oh, misery! Methinks unjust actions
Should wear these masks and curtains, and not we.
You must instantly part hence. I have fashioned it
    already.   *Exit Antonio.*

[*Enter*] BOSOLA.

bluster of courage after the event.'
But the scene can also be staged
so that Antonio, returning, catch-
es a mere glimpse of the fleeing
Ferdinand.
152 **rank gall** proud, excessive bitter-
ness; foul-smelling pustule. Both the
character trait and the physical flaw
derived, according to Galenic medi-

cine, from an excess of bile in the
liver. Cf. Bosola as 'court-gall' 1.1.23
and n.
154 **mine** in early modern warfare, an
underground trench filled with gunpowder to blow up a fortification
157 **masks and curtains** forms of
dissembling
158 best understood as a hexameter line

147 SD] *opp. 148 Q1* 148–50] *Sampson; Q1 lines* me: / wish / selfe? / Action / much. / to't, / 152
SD] *Lucas (subst.)* 153] *Q1 lines* Earthquakes? / stand / 155] *Q1 lines* vp. / *Bosola*: / Away, SD]
Gunby (subst.) 158 SD1] *(Ex. Ant.)* SD2] *Q4; Bosola, | 0 SD Q1*

225

BOSOLA

    The duke your brother is ta'en up in a whirlwind –
    Hath took horse and's rid post to Rome.

DUCHESS   So late?   160

BOSOLA

    He told me as he mounted into th' saddle
    You were undone.

DUCHESS   Indeed, I am very near it.

BOSOLA

    What's the matter?

DUCHESS

    Antonio, the master of our household,
    Hath dealt so falsely with me in's accounts –   165
    My brother stood engaged with me for money
    Ta'en up of certain Neapolitan Jews,
    And Antonio lets the bonds be forfeit.

BOSOLA

    Strange! – This is cunning.

DUCHESS

    And hereupon my brother's bills at Naples   170
    Are protested against. Call up our officers.

BOSOLA

    I shall.   *Exit.*

[*Enter* ANTONIO.]

---

159 **whirlwind** Cf. Hosea, 8.7: the idolators and sexual transgressors of Israel 'have sown the wind, and they shall reap the whirlwind'.

166–8 **My . . . forfeit** Ferdinand, she claims, had offered security for money borrowed by the Duchess from Jews in nearby Naples, the main Italian stronghold of the House of Aragon. When Antonio, as steward in charge of her finances, failed to repay the money or made Ferdinand liable for the debt, the security was forfeited.

170–1 **bills . . . against** The Jews of Naples have made a written declaration that Ferdinand's *bills* of exchange have not been met. This was a preliminary required before legal action could be taken to recover the debt (Gunby).

160] *Q1 lines* Rome. / late? /   162–3] *Q1 lines* vndone. / it. / matter? /   170–1] *this edn; Q1 lines* hereupon / protested / Officers. /   172 SD2] *Q4*

DUCHESS

The place that you must fly to is Ancona.
Hire a house there. I'll send after you
My treasure and my jewels. Our weak safety   175
Runs upon enginous wheels: short syllables
Must stand for periods. I must now accuse you
Of such a feigned crime as Tasso calls
Magnanima mensogna: a noble lie,
'Cause it must shield our honours. Hark! They are
    coming.   180

[*Enter* BOSOLA *and*] OFFICERS.

ANTONIO

Will your grace hear me?

DUCHESS

I have got well by you: you have yielded me
A million of loss. I am like to inherit
The people's curses for your stewardship.

---

173 **Ancona** an independent republic on the east coast of Italy that was outside the Kingdom of Naples and therefore, the Duchess assumes, outside the direct control of Ferdinand and the Cardinal

176 **enginous wheels** intricate wheels that control the motion of larger wheels; cf. *Whore*, 1.2.165–6, where Titania is speaking of the marriage of monarchs: 'For that one Acte gives like an enginous wheele / Motion to all.' Alternatively, *enginous* could be a variant spelling of 'ingenious' (Q2), in which case the two clauses in 175–7 should be separated with a semicolon, to indicate that they are parallel ideas, rather than as here, where the second clause is introduced with a colon to

indicate that it serves as an explanation of the first.

178 **feigned** feignèd

179 *Magnanima . . . lie* The English phrase translates the Italian. Cf. the Italian poet Torquato Tasso's epic about the Crusaders' liberation of Jerusalem, *Gerusalemme liberata* (trans. Edward Fairfax, 1600), 2.22: Sophronia tries to save her fellow Christians by uttering a 'noble lie' – falsely admitting that she has taken a statue of the Virgin Mary from a mosque.

182 **I . . . you** Like many of her comments in the following indictment, this is capable of a double interpretation: besides the ironic suggestion of monetary loss, she has *got well* by Antonio in that he has 'given' her three children.

---

176 enginous] *Dyce;* engenous *Q1;* ingenious *Q2*   180 SD] *Dyce; Officers | 0 SD Q1;* Enter *Bosola,* and *Gentlemen. | Q4*

You had the trick in audit time to be sick   185
Till I had signed your quietus, and that cured you
Without help of a doctor. Gentlemen,
I would have this man be an example to you all,
So shall you hold my favour. I pray, let him –
For he's done that, alas, you would not think of   190
And, because I intend to be rid of him,
I mean not to publish. – Use your fortune elsewhere.

ANTONIO   *– being banished for his own good*
I am strongly armed to brook my overthrow,
As commonly men bear with a hard year.
I will not blame the cause on't, but do think   195
The necessity of my malevolent star
Procures this, not her humour. Oh, the inconstant
And rotten ground of service you may see!
'Tis e'en like him that in a winter night
Takes a long slumber o'er a dying fire   200
A-loath to part from't, yet parts thence as cold
As when he first sat down.

DUCHESS   We do confiscate
Towards the satisfying of your accounts

185–7 **You . . . doctor** She accuses
Antonio of feigning illness during
audit time – the time formally set
aside for going over the household
accounts – so that his transactions
with the Duchess's money could not
be examined closely, then recovering
miraculously once she had approved
them.

186 **quietus** release from a debt or, ominously, release from life into death (cf.
1.2.374)

187–9 **Gentlemen . . . favour** ostensibly
ironic: Antonio is a negative example
to be avoided if the rest of her retain-
ers wish to keep the Duchess's favour.

189 **let him** let him go. The Duchess
pretends that she prefers not to con-
front Antonio with his crimes because
she wishes to keep them private.

190 **done . . . of** The Duchess implies
some crime but refers to their intimate
relations.

192 **publish** make public

193 **brook** endure

197–8 **Oh . . . see** ironically recalls
Bosola's objection to the Cardinal's
neglect of him (1.1.29–32).

190 he's] *(* h'as*)*   197–202 Oh . . . down] *om. Q4*   199 e'en] *(eu'n)*   201 A-loath] *Q1a, Q1b;* As loth
Q1c   202] *Q1 lines* downe. / confiscate /

All that you have.

ANTONIO   I am all yours, and 'tis very fit

All mine should be so.

DUCHESS   So, sir; you have your pass.   205

ANTONIO

You may see, gentlemen, what 'tis to serve

A prince with body and soul.   *Exit.*

BOSOLA

Here's an example for extortion:

what moisture is drawn out of the sea, when foul weather

comes, pours down and runs into the sea again.   210

DUCHESS

I would know what are your opinions

Of this Antonio.

2 OFFICER   He could not abide to see a pig's head gaping.

I thought your grace would find him a Jew.

3 OFFICER   I would you had been his officer, for your own   215

sake.

---

204 **all yours** entirely at your service, with a sexual double entendre (cf. 206–7)

205 **pass** written notification, in a time before uniform state-issued passports, allowing him passage from one Italian state to another

208–10 Bosola here gives a cynical adaptation of a commonplace about the origin of weather, typically used to illustrate benevolent reciprocity: the rain falls into the river, which flows into the sea, from which vapours ascend to the sky and fall again as rain. Cotgrave, however, glosses the French proverb 'the rivers return to the sea' as 'Said when princes doe squeeze out of their spungie Officers the moisture which they have purloyned from them' (Cotgrave, 'Mer', sig. Fff6ʳ).

213 **He . . . gaping** a disparaging comment about Jews who observed Levitical laws against eating pork. Brown sees a conflation of two proverbs: 'Some cannot abide to see a pig's head gaping', one of Shylock's examples of an irrational prejudice in *MV* 4.1.47; and 'Invite not a Jew either to pig or pork' (Tilley, P310 and J50).

214 **I . . . Jew** Some Jews did serve as high officers in noble households, but this remark may reflect the prejudice in Spanish circles against Jews after their expulsion from Spain in 1492 (see Ferdinand's remark on purity of blood at 2.5.21–3 and n.).

215–16 spoken to the Duchess: if she had been Antonio's officer rather than the reverse, she would have been better off. Cf. Bacon's *Apophthegms*, 1.352: 'Bishop Latimer said, in a sermon at court, that he heard great speech that the king was poor; and many ways

---

204–5] *Q1 lines* haue. / fit / so. / Passe. /   208] *this edn; prose Q1*   211–41 DUCHESS . . . justice] *om. in performance Q4*   215 his] *om. Q2*

4 OFFICER You would have had more money.

1 OFFICER He stopped his ears with black wool and, to those came to him for money, said he was thick of hearing.   220

2 OFFICER Some said he was an hermaphrodite, for he could not abide a woman.

4 OFFICER How scurvy proud he would look when the treasury was full! Well, let him go.

1 OFFICER Yes, and the chippings of the buttery fly after   225
him to scour his gold chain!

DUCHESS
Leave us.

Exeunt [Officers].

What do you think of these?

BOSOLA
That these are rogues that in's prosperity
But to have waited on his fortune could have wished
His dirty stirrup riveted through their noses   230
And followed after's mule like a bear in a ring;
Would have prostituted their daughters to his lust,

were propounded to make him rich: for his part he had thought of one way, which was that they should help the king to some good office, for all his officers were rich' (Lucas).

218 **stopped . . . wool** a folk remedy prescribed to *cure* deafness, not cause it. Cf. *Batman*, 7.21, 'Of Deafnesse': 'take the gall of an Hare, mixe it with the greace of a Foxe, and with blacke wooll, instill this into the eare' (Brown).

219 **thick** hard

221 **hermaphrodite** effeminate man, homosexual

223 **scurvy** despicably

225 **chippings . . . buttery** discarded bread crusts, kitchen trash

226 **scour . . . chain** polish his gold chain of office (which Antonio has

presumably relinquished before his exit), an insulting reminder that he is, after all, no more than a servant. Cf. *TN* 2.3.116–17, where Sir Toby suggests to another uppity steward, Malvolio: 'Go, sir, rub your chain with crumbs.'

228–42 Here and below, Bosola's verse is so rough that his speeches are sometimes printed as prose (see pp. 80–3).

228 **in's** in Antonio's (referring to the period during which he was a much-favoured servant of the Duchess)

231 **mule** beast of burden carrying Antonio or his household effects. On mules, see 2.1.95–7 and n.
    bear in a ring bear led by a ring in its nose, and therefore submissive

223 he would] would he *Q2* 226 gold] golden *Q2* 227 SD] *Dyce; Exeunt. | opp.* 226 Chain *Q1* 228–42] *prose Norton*

Made their firstborn intelligencers,
Thought none happy but such as were born
Under his blest planet and wore his livery.   235
And do these lice drop off now?
Well, never look to have the like again.
He hath left a sort of flattering rogues behind him;
Their doom must follow. Princes pay flatterers
In their own money: flatterers dissemble their vices   240
And they dissemble their lies. That's justice.
Alas, poor gentleman!

DUCHESS

Poor? He hath amply filled his coffers!

BOSOLA

Sure, he was too honest! Pluto, the god of riches,
When he's sent by Jupiter to any man,   245
He goes limping to signify that wealth
That comes on God's name comes slowly. But when
  he's sent

234–5 **born ... planet** with the same lucky astrological sign
235 **livery** uniform of a servant
236 **lice ... now** Lice abandon a dead body once there is no more blood to suck.
238 **sort** particular kind; company, group
239 **doom** judgement
240 **money** i.e. deceit
240–1 **flatterers ... lies** Flatterers lie to their prince by pretending that he does not have faults (*vices*), and the prince rewards them by pretending not to notice they are lying. Cf. Matthieu, sig. Cc3ʳ: 'Princes pay flattery with her owne money, Flatterers dissemble the vices of Princes, and Princes dissemble the lyes of flatterers' (Dent, *Webster*).
244 **Pluto** god of the underworld. More usually, the god of wealth is Plutus,

but see Bacon, 'Of Riches': 'The poets faigne that when *Plutus*, (which is *Riches*,) is sent from *Jupiter*, he limps and goes slowly; but when he is sent from *Pluto*, he runnes and is Swift of Foot: Meaning, that *Riches* gotten by Good Meanes and Just Labour, pace slowly ... it mought be applied likewise to Pluto taking him for the Devill. For when *Riches* come from the Devill, (as by Fraud, and Oppression, and unjust Meanes) they come upon Speed' (Bacon, *Essays*, 109–10; Dent, *Webster*).
247–8 These lines, with their numerous extra syllables, are the most metrically anomalous of Bosola's speech, which is sometimes set entirely as prose; see pp. 81–2.
247 **on** in

233–6] *this edn; Q1 lines* happy / Plannet: / now? /   233 firstborn] *Q1c;* first-borne *and Q1a, Q1b*   235 blest] *om. Q2*   238 flattering] *(flattring)*   244–60] *prose Norton*   244–8 Pluto ... scuttles] *om. in performance Q4*

On the devil's errand he rides post and comes in by
   scuttles.
Let me show you what a most unvalued jewel
You have in a wanton humour thrown away,   250
To bless the man shall find him:
He was an excellent courtier, and most faithful;
A soldier that thought it as beastly to know his own
   value
Too little as devilish to acknowledge it too much.
Both his virtue and form deserved a far better fortune;   255
His discourse rather delighted to judge itself
Than show itself.
His breast was filled with all perfection,
And yet it seemed a private whispering room,
It made so little noise of 't.   260

DUCHESS
   But he was basely descended. *– social class,*
   Bosola sticks up for
   Antonio

248 **rides post** uses post-horses (the
   fastest means of travel during the
   period)
   scuttles large baskets; short, hurried
   runs
249 **unvalued** unappreciated, under-val-
   ued
249–51 **jewel . . . him** Cf. *Othello*'s 'base
   Indian [or Judean]' who 'threw a pearl
   away, / Richer than all his tribe' (*Oth*
   5.2.345–6).
250 **wanton** careless, with an ironic
   undertone of sexual wantonness that
   suggests the Duchess's continuing
   attraction to Antonio rather than her
   ostensible rejection of him
255 Cf. Ben Jonson's dedication to
   Prince Henry in the *Masque of Queens*
   (1609), 'Both your vertue, and your
   forme did deserve your fortune';
   and Webster's *Column*, 28, where the

phrase is also used of Prince Henry
   (Webster, 3.375).
   form outward appearance, but perhaps
   also suggesting 'form' in the Platonic
   sense: Antonio was the embodiment
   of abstract, idealized qualities.
256–7 Cf. *Arcadia*, book 1, ch. 5, 32:
   Parthenia has 'a wit which delighted
   more to judge it selfe then to showe it
   selfe' (Lucas).
259 **whispering room** echo chamber in
   which things whispered almost inau-
   dibly can be heard at great distance.
   Antonio's inward virtues resound in
   the world outside despite his attempts
   to keep them private.
261 **he . . . descended** not true, according to the historical record, since
   Antonio belonged to the gentry and
   was the grandson of a celebrated
   humanist man of letters

251–4] *this edn; Q1 lines* excellent / it / little, / much, /   253–4] *om. Q4*   256–7] *this edn; one line
Q1*   259 whispering] *(whispring)*   260 of 't] on't *Q4*

BOSOLA *— wishes to do good but can't help himself*

Will you make yourself a mercenary herald,
Rather to examine men's pedigrees than virtues?
You shall want him.
For know, an honest statesman to a prince   265
Is like a cedar planted by a spring:
The spring bathes the tree's root; the grateful tree
Rewards it with his shadow. You have not done so.
I would sooner swim to the Bermoothes on two
politicians' rotten bladders tied together with an   270
intelligencer's heart-string than depend on so
changeable a prince's favour. – Fare thee well, Antonio!
Since the malice of the world would needs down with

---

262 **herald** court officer whose job was to establish and confirm aristocratic titles, which depended on lineage, not personal integrity. Cf. *Arcadia*, book 1, ch. 2, 15: 'I am no herald to enquire of mens pedigrees, it sufficeth me if I know their vertues' (Lucas). Bosola's herald is *mercenary* because, like his actual Jacobean counterparts in the Royal College of Heralds, he can be bribed to invent a title.

264 **want him** feel his loss (with sexual suggestion)

265–6 **honest . . . spring** In this simile the prince is the cedar, a common figure of speech. See the prophecy in *Cym* 5.4.140; and *Philaster*, 5.3.25, where princely Philaster and Arethusa are called 'two fair cedar branches'.

266–8 **cedar . . . shadow** Cf. *Arcadia*, book 1, ch. 15, 96: 'a little River neere hand, which for the moisture it bestowed upon rootes of some flourishing Trees, was rewarded with their shadowe' (Dent, *Webster*). Contrast Bosola's previous examples of reciprocity at 208–10 and 239–41.

269 **Bermoothes** Bermudas, known for stormy weather after Sir George Summers's widely publicized shipwreck there in 1609. The same form appears in the First Folio text of *The Tempest*, 1.2.229, where Ariel recalls that Prospero once sent him to fetch dew from the 'still-vex'd Bermoothes'.

270 **bladders** bags filled with (hot) air, a standard symbol for the vanity of rhetoric. In this case, the bags appear to be made of the politicians' actual diseased bladders.

271 **intelligencer's heart-string** an unreliable cable for securing Bosola's makeshift water wings, given his low opinion of 'intelligencers'

273–6 **Since . . . virtue** a commonplace of Roman stoicism, most readily available to Webster in *Arcadia*, book 1, ch. 4, 24: 'if the wickednes of the world should oppresse it [prosperity], it can never be said, that evil hapneth to him, who falles accompanied with vertue' (Lucas). Bosola's metrically rough lines are usually printed as verse, but

---

262–8] *prose Norton*   269–76] *this edn; Q1 lines* Politisians / hart-string: / fauour, / world / yet / fall, / vertue. /   269–72 I … favour] *om. Q4*   269 Bermoothes] *Q1a, Q1b;* Bermootha's *Q1c;* Bermudas *Brown*

thee, it cannot be said yet that any ill happened unto
thee, considering thy fall was accompanied with 275
virtue.

DUCHESS

Oh, you render me excellent music!

BOSOLA   Say you? STUPIDITY

DUCHESS

This good one that you speak of is my husband.

BOSOLA

Do I not dream? Can this ambitious age
Have so much goodness in't as to prefer 280
A man merely for worth, without these shadows
Of wealth and painted honours? Possible?

DUCHESS

I have had three children by him.

BOSOLA   Fortunate lady! powerless
                                                                            gold
For you have made your private nuptial bed   betray
The humble and fair seminary of peace. 285
No question but many an unbeneficed scholar
Shall pray for you for this deed and rejoice
That some preferment in the world can yet
Arise from merit. The virgins of your land
That have no dowries shall hope your example 290
Will raise them to rich husbands. Should you want

can usefully be understood as prose
because doing so creates unconscious
irony in the Duchess's following praise
of Bosola's *music*.

273–4 **down with thee** cast you down
274 **yet** nevertheless
277 **render** play, perform
281 **shadows** delusions. Cf. Ecclesiastes,
   7.2, in the Geneva Bible: 'For who
   knoweth what is good for man in the

life & in the nomber of the dayes of
the life of his vanitie, seing that he
maketh them as a shadow?' The corresponding passage in the King James
Bible is at 6.12.

282 **painted honours** signs of status that
   are merely external
285 **seminary** seed plot; school or college
286 **unbeneficed** lacking in financial
   support

277] *Q1 lines* Musicke. / you? / Say you] Madam *Q4*   280 prefer] prefer true Merit *Q4*   281] *om.*
Q2   282 Of] To *Q4*   283] *Q1 lines* him. / Lady,   289–301 The . . . men] *om. in performance Q4*

Soldiers, 'twould make the very Turks and Moors
Turn Christians and serve you for this act.   *Speaks in prose,*
Last, the neglected poets of your time,
In honour of this trophy of a man,   *intelligent*   295
Raised by that curious engine, your white hand,
Shall thank you in your grave for't, and make that
More reverend than all the cabinets
Of living princes. For Antonio,
His fame shall likewise flow from many a pen   300
When heralds shall want coats to sell to men.   *— Sententia*

DUCHESS

As I taste comfort in this friendly speech,
So would I find concealment.

BOSOLA

Oh, the secret of my prince,
Which I will wear on th'inside of my heart!   305

DUCHESS

You shall take charge of all my coin and jewels
And follow him, for he retires himself
To Ancona. —— *sells him out*

BOSOLA   So.

DUCHESS   Whither, within few days,
I mean to follow thee.

292 **very . . . Moors** i.e. your worst
enemies, since the Ottoman Turks
were at the time threatening to conquer Europe and occupying eastern
portions of it

295 **trophy** evidently intended as praise,
but with a suggestion that Antonio is
a mere hunting trophy or prize for the
Duchess

296 **curious engine** delicate, beautifully
crafted machine (cf. *enginous wheels*,
176)

297 **in your grave** after your death (by
celebrating the Duchess in verse)

298 **cabinets** curiosity cabinets, in which
wealthy collectors of the time kept
strange and rare objects; perhaps with
an ironic side reference to *cabinets* in
the sense of royal councils of advisers

301 **want coats** lack coats of arms; a
reference to the cheapening of aristocratic titles under James I, who
sold knighthoods and baronetcies as a
way of increasing his revenues

304–5 Cf. *Ham* 3.2.68–9, describing the
epitome of friendship, 'I will wear him
/ In my heart's core – ay, in my heart
of heart.'

308–9] *Q1 lines Ancona. / So. / dayes, / thee. / thinke: /   308 Whither] *Q4;* Whether *Q1*

235

BOSOLA   Let me think:
I would wish your grace to feign a pilgrimage   310
To our Lady of Loreto, scarce seven leagues
From fair Ancona; so may you depart
Your country with more honour, and your flight
Will seem a princely progress, retaining
Your usual train about you.

DUCHESS   Sir, your direction   315
Shall lead me by the hand.

CARIOLA   In my opinion,
She were better progress to the baths at Lucca
Or go visit the Spa in Germany;
For, if you will believe me, I do not like
This jesting with religion, this feigned pilgrimage.   320

DUCHESS
Thou art a superstitious fool.
Prepare us instantly for our departure.
Past sorrows, let us moderately lament them;
For those to come, seek wisely to prevent them.

Exeunt [Duchess and Cariola].

BOSOLA
A politician is the devil's quilted anvil: 325
He fashions all sins on him, and the blows

---

311 our ... Loreto a famous shrine 15 miles south-east of Ancona and symbolically appropriate for the Duchess's present migratory household, since it centres on a relocated dwelling, the House of Mary the Virgin, which was believed to have magically floated to Italy in 1291 when it was threatened by Turks in Nazareth

314 princely progress the formal tour made by a monarch to visit noble houses and towns of the kingdom

317 baths at Lucca famous warm springs frequented as a spa in Webster's time; cf. 2.1.68.

318 Spa in Germany Spa, near Liège, now in Belgium, was famous for its curative waters.

325 quilted anvil anvil on which something can be silently pounded into shape; cf. *Gallant's*, sig. B4r: 'an insensible Heart is the Devils Anvile, he fashioneth all sinnes on it, and the blowes are not felt' (Dent, *Webster*).

326 He the devil

315–16] *Q1 lines* you. / direction / hand. / opinion, /   317–20] *this edn; Q1 lines* bathes / *Spaw* / me) / religion, / Pilgrimage. /   323–4] *ital. Q4*   324 SD] *Q4; Exit. | Q1*

Are never heard. He may work in a lady's chamber,
As here for proof. What rests but I reveal
All to my lord? Oh, this base quality
Of intelligencer! Why, every quality i'th' world   330
Prefers but gain or commendation.
Now for this act I am certain to be raised –
'And men that paint weeds to the life are praised.'   *Exit.*

3.3   [*Enter*] CARDINAL, FERDINAND, MALATESTE,
                PESCARA, SILVIO [*and*] DELIO.

CARDINAL

Must we turn soldier then?

MALATESTE   The emperor,

Hearing your worth that way ere you attained
This reverend garment, joins you in commission
With the right fortunate soldier the Marquess of Pescara

328 **rests** remains
331 **Prefers but** advances only
333 This line is preceded by a double quotation mark in Q1, suggesting that it was understood as a rhetorical commonplace or adage. Bosola self-deprecatingly recognizes that his efficiency in spying against the Duchess, although it will be *praised* by her brothers, is like painting a highly realistic (*to the life*) portrait of *weeds* – a bad use of a human talent.
3.3 Location: Rome
1–33 Many of the lines in this bantering encounter hover uneasily between verse and prose.
1 **Must . . . soldier** must we all become soldiers (at a time when there were few standing armies)
emperor probably, anachronistically, Charles V (1500–58), who became

Holy Roman Emperor in 1519
2 **worth that way** talent in that profession
3 **garment** his cardinal's hat or robes. Presumably he was dressed in cardinal's red onstage.
joins . . . commission gives you authority along with other officers to raise forces for military operation (no doubt against the French)
4 **Pescara** Since Pescara is onstage, Malateste presumably indicates him in some way. According to Amendola, Webster conflates Alfonso d'Avalos, Marquess of Pescara, with his son, Francesco Ferrante d'Avalos, born in 1490. The father was the one who supported the Aragonese cause and died heroically fighting for it in 1495, well before the action of the play.

330 intelligencer] Inteligencers *Q2*   332–3] *ital. Q4*   333 'And . . . praised.'] ("And . . . prais'd.*); And . . . prais'd. *Q2*   **3.3**] (SCENA III.*)   0 SD] *Q4 (subst.); Cardinall, Ferdinand, Malateste, Pescara, Siluio, Delio, Bosola. | Q1*   1] *Q1 lines* then? / Emperour, /   3 garment] Habit *Q4*   4 right] most *Q4*

And the famous Lannoy.
CARDINAL   He that had the honour   5
Of taking the French king prisoner?
MALATESTE   The same.
Here's a plot drawn for a new fortification at Naples.
FERDINAND
This great Count Malateste, I perceive,
Hath got employment?
DELIO   No employment, my lord –
A marginal note in the muster book that he is   10
A voluntary lord.
FERDINAND   He's no soldier?
DELIO
He has worn gunpowder in's hollow tooth
For the toothache.
SILVIO
He comes to the leaguer with a full intent
To eat fresh beef and garlic, means to stay   15
Till the scent be gone, and straight return to court.
DELIO
He hath read all the late service

---

5 **Lannoy** Historically, Charles de Lannoy (*c.* 1487–1527) was a favourite of Charles V, who helped defeat France at the Battle of Pavia (1525).
6 **French king** François I (1494–1547) was defeated by Spanish forces at Pavia (see 5n.); this and the previous reference are anachronistic in that the action of the play takes place earlier than 1525.
7 **plot** plan, drawing to scale
9 **employment** as a soldier or commander of troops
10–11 **marginal . . . lord** i.e. he is so inconsequential as a soldier that, in the formal records kept of troops called into service, he only rates a note in the margin saying that he has volunteered.
12–13 **gunpowder . . . toothache** an ancient remedy, here implying cowardice, since it is the closest Malateste has actually been to battle; cf. Webster's *Characters*, 'A Roaring Boy', where the mock-heroic would-be gallant uses gunpowder in precisely the same way (Webster, 3.469).
14 **leaguer** military encampment
16 **scent** of garlic
17 **service** military action

5–6] *Q1 lines* Lanoy. / honour / Prisoner? / same, / 7] *this edn; Q1 lines* Fortification, / *Naples.* / 8 Malateste] *Q2; Malastete* | *Q1* 9–11] *Q1 lines* got employment? / Lord) / is / Lord. / Souldier? / 11 soldier?] Soldier. *Q4* 12–31] *om. Q4* 12–13] *Lucas; one line Q1* 14 comes] come *Q2* 16 scent be gone] *(*sent begon*)*

As the city chronicle relates it,
And keeps two pewterers going only to express
Battles in model.

SILVIO   Then he'll fight by the book.   20

DELIO

By the almanac, I think, to choose good days
And shun the critical. That's his mistress's scarf.

SILVIO

Yes, he protests he would do much for that taffeta.

DELIO   I think he would run away from a battle to save
it from taking prisoner.   25

SILVIO   He is horribly afraid gunpowder will spoil the
perfume on't.

DELIO   I saw a Dutchman break his pate once for calling

---

18 **city chronicle** ancestor of the modern newspaper; a more formal record, like those published by the antiquarian John Stow in his *Annals* (1592), which Anthony Munday was appointed to revise in 1611. From 1620, London had an official city chronologer, the playwright Thomas Middleton, whose duties included the keeping of a city chronicle. Middleton was working closely with Webster at the time of Q1's 1623 publication; see his commendatory poem (p. 123).

19 **pewterers** workers in pewter who made toy soldiers for Malateste's military re-enactments; *pewterers* is changed to 'painters' in Q1c (see t.n. and p. 68), and in most modern editions. In the act of making models, pewterers are also kept *going* in that they are constantly hammering away, and they *express* real battles in that their hammering sounds like the

clash of arms.

20 **model** miniature
   fight . . . book Instead of following the codified rules of warfare in actual combat, he will copy the battles as recorded in the *book* of the city chronicles by creating re-enactments with his toy soldiers.

21 **almanac** book of astrological forecasts arranged by date

22 **critical** days marked astrologically as uncertain or risky
   scarf At this point Malateste may be toying with the scarf; the implication is that he may wear it as a love token in his miniaturized 'toy' battles in the same way that dashing knights traditionally wore their mistresses' love tokens in actual battles.

24–5 **save . . . prisoner** save the scarf from being taken prisoner (an ironic suggestion that Malateste is too cowardly to fight)

---

19 keeps] *Q2;* keepe *Q1*   pewterers] *Q1a, Q1b;* Painters *Q1c*   20] *Q1 lines* modell. / booke. /   he'll] *Q2;* hel; *Q1*   21–3] *this edn; Q1 lines* thinke / Criticall. / skarfe. / protests / taffita. /   22 mistress's] *(mistris)*   24–31] *this edn; Q1 lines* battaile, / prisoner. / afraid, / on't, / once / head / musket. / to't. /

him potgun. He made his head have a bore in't like a
musket.   30

SILVIO   I would he had made a touch-hole to't.

DELIO

   He is indeed a guarded sumpter cloth
   Only for the remove of the court.

             [*Enter* BOSOLA.]

PESCARA

   Bosola arrived? What should be the business?
   Some falling out amongst the cardinals.   35
   These factions amongst great men, they are like foxes:
   When their heads are divided they carry fire in their
      tails,
   And all the country about them goes to wrack for't.

SILVIO

   What's that Bosola?

DELIO   I knew him in Padua

---

29 **potgun** mortar or cannon; presumably by calling the Dutchman
potgun Malateste was insulting him
by accusing him of drunkenness
– attending too much to his 'pot'
of ale. Dutchmen were frequently
satirized as drunkards in drama of
the period.
29–30 **bore . . . musket** hole shaped like
a gun cylinder
31 **touch-hole to't** hole for igniting the
charge in a firearm, which, in this case,
would blow Malateste's head to pieces;
obscene reference to anal sex (igniting
the touch-hole)
32 SP *Q1 gives 32–3 to Silvio, as part
of his previous speech. But these
lines occur at the top of a page (sig.

H1ʳ), and the catchword at the bottom of the previous page is the SP
'*Del.*' for 'Delio'. Most likely, the
SP was inadvertently omitted by the
printers.
32–3 This implies that Malateste is all
decoration on the surface, but less
than human beneath: *guarded* means
decorated; a *sumpter cloth* was used
to cover pack animals during court
progresses.
36–8 i.e. they create mayhem. See Judges,
15.4–5, the story of Samson, who tied
firebrands to the tails of foxes and
sent them out to burn the crops of the
Philistines.
39 **Padua** distinguished university called
'nursery of arts' in *TS* 1.1.2

---

32 SP] *Gibbons (conj. Brown); not in Q1*   33 SD] *Q4; Bosola.* | *0 SD Q1*   36–8] *this edn; Q1 lines* like
/ deuided / Country / for't. /   36 they are] *are Q4*   39] *this edn; Q1 lines* Bosola? / *followed by prose*

– a fantastical scholar like such who study to know   40
how many knots was in Hercules' club, of what
colour Achilles' beard was or whether Hector were not
troubled with the toothache. He hath studied himself
half blear-eyed to know the true symmetry of Caesar's
nose by a shoeing-horn, and this he did to gain the   45
name of a speculative man.

PESCARA

Mark Prince Ferdinand –
A very salamander lives in's eye,
To mock the eager violence of fire.

SILVIO   That Cardinal hath made more bad faces with his   50
oppression than ever Michelangelo made good ones.
He lifts up's nose, like a foul porpoise before a storm.

PESCARA

The lord Ferdinand laughs –

40–2 **such . . . beard was** Cf. Matthieu, sig. Qq3ᵛ, on those who study vain things: they 'spend whole nights to finde how many knots were in *Hercules* club, and of what colour *Achilles* beard was . . . and the end of their curiosity is always ignorance'.

40 **fantastical** pursuing illusions; odd and irrational. The 'character' that follows suggests that Bosola, like many young men in England of the period, started out as an unemployed university graduate.

41 **Hercules' club** in Greek myth, the club used by the strong-man Hercules to kill the Nemean lion

42 **Achilles** Greek hero in Homer's epic *The Iliad*
   Hector son of King Priam of Troy in *The Iliad*

44–5 **symmetry . . . shoeing-horn** i.e. he foolishly sees a shoehorn as a fit implement for discovering the shape of Caesar's nose.

46 **speculative** highly thoughtful

47 **Mark** look at; at some point during the previous conversation, Ferdinand and the Cardinal have evidently drawn aside to confer privately with Bosola.

48 **salamander** believed to have the ability to live in fire and therefore a frequent emblem for the lover. A popular madrigal of the period refers to the lover, 'salamander-like in fire'.

50 **bad** unhappy (and therefore unattractive). Cf. Dallington, sig. N2ʳ: 'when I was in Italy, ye should heare them say in derision, that the King of Spayne had made more ill faces upon the Exchange, in one day, then *Michael Angelo*, the famous Paynter and Carver, had ever made good faces in all his life' (Dent, *Webster*).

52 **foul** unwelcome and therefore bad
   porpoise . . . storm proverbial: 'The porpoise plays before the storm' (Dent, P483). When porpoises appeared in the Thames, according to *Eastward Ho*, 3.3.143–4, they were 'always the messenger of tempests'.

44 symmetry] *(semitry)*   52 porpoise] *(Por-pisse)*   53] *Q1 lines* laughes. / Cannon, /

DELIO   Like a deadly cannon
     That lightens ere it smokes.
PESCARA
     These are your true pangs of death –   55
     The pangs of life that struggle with great statesmen.
DELIO
     In such a deformed silence, witches whisper
     Their charms.
CARDINAL   Doth she make religion her riding hood
     To keep her from the sun and tempest?
FERDINAND   That!
     That damns her. Methinks her fault and beauty,   60
     Blended together, show like leprosy:
     The whiter, the fouler. I make it a question
     Whether her beggarly brats were ever christened.
CARDINAL
     I will instantly solicit the state of Ancona
     To have them banished.
FERDINAND   You are for Loreto?   65
     I shall not be at your ceremony. Fare you well.
     Write to the Duke of Malfi, my young nephew

---

54 **lightens . . . smokes** implying that his
   smile is the precursor of some great
   evil, like the flash of light that accompanies the firing of a deadly cannon
55 **your** the
56 Just as a dying person may suffer
   death pangs, politicians struggling to
   be 'born' suffer life pangs.
57 **deformed** unnatural
58–9 **Doth . . . tempest?** Does she use
   religion as a mere hypocritical protection against misfortune?
61 **leprosy** Cf. *Penitential Psalms*: the
   'great Man' lays ill upon the state
   'like a leprosie, / The whiter, still
   the fouler' (Lucas); and Milton's
   'whited sepulchre' in *Areopagitica*,

where whiteness is also a sign of
disease rather than purity (Milton).
The Q1 spelling 'leaprosie' suggests
a bawdy pun on 'leaping' or sexual
intercourse.
62 **make . . . question** consider it
   unknown
65 **for** going to
66 **ceremony** in which he renounces his
   Cardinal's hat to become a warrior (3.4)
67 **Duke of Malfi** the play's only reference to the Duchess's son by her first
   husband. Historically, the Duchess of
   Malfi reigned as regent for her son,
   who was still a minor. Except for these
   lines (omitted in Q4 and many modern
   performances), Webster makes her a

57–61] *this edn; Q1 lines* charmes. / hood / tempest? / and / leaprosie /   61 leprosy] *(*leaprosie*)*   63
christened] *(*christned*)*   65] *Q1 lines* banish'd. / *Loretto?* /   66–9] *om. Q4*

She had by her first husband, and acquaint him
With's mother's honesty.

BOSOLA   I will.

FERDINAND   Antonio?
A slave that only smelled of ink and counters   70
And ne'er in's life looked like a gentleman,
But in the audit time! Go – go presently.
Draw me out an hundred and fifty of our horse,
And meet me at the fort bridge.   *Exeunt.*

3.4   [*Enter*] two PILGRIMS *to the shrine of Our*
                        Lady of Loreto.

1 PILGRIM
I have not seen a goodlier shrine than this,
Yet I have visited many.

2 PILGRIM   The Cardinal of Aragon
Is this day to resign his cardinal's hat.
His sister Duchess likewise is arrived
To pay her vow of pilgrimage. I expect   5
A noble ceremony.

---

ruler in her own right and dispenses with the son. At the end of the play, it is the Duchess's son by Antonio rather than her son by the Duke of Amalfi who is poised to take over his mother's position and inheritance.

69 **honesty** spoken with deep irony

70 **counters** discs used in calculations such as a mere merchant might make, and hence beneath the honour of an aristocrat

72 **audit time** period of formal accounting for credits and debits, when Antonio would presumably dress more formally than usual; cf. 3.2.185–7.

73 **Draw me out** bring out of pasturage (so they can be used in battle)

74 **fort bridge** presumably at the entrance to the 'leaguer' where the troops are gathering

3.4 Location: Loreto

0.1–2 *shrine . . . Loreto* famous pilgrimage site that boasted one of the Mediterranean's awe-inspiring 'black Virgins'; see 3.2.311n. and p. 35.

1 **goodlier** better; more sumptuous

6 SD by far the most elaborate SD in the play, and showing signs of revision by Webster himself in the words '*in dumb-show*' (6.6; see t.n.), apparently added to clarify for readers of Q1 that the action is mimed during the singing of the hymn, 7–22 (see p. 66). The praise of the Cardinal in the hymn is

---

69] *Q1 lines* honesty. / will. / *Antonio?* /   70 counters] *(coumpters)*   71 life] *Q2;* like *Q1*
73 hundred] *Q2;* hundredth *Q1*   3.4] *(SCENA* IIII.*); entire scene om. Q4*   0.1 *Enter*] *Dyce*
1 shrine] Shrive *Q2*   2] *Q1 lines* many. / *Arragon* /   6] *Q1 lines* Ceremony. / come. /

1 PILGRIM   No question! – They come.

Here the ceremony of the CARDINAL'*s instalment in the habit
of a soldier performed in delivering up his cross, hat, robes and
ring at the shrine, and investing him with sword, helmet, shield
and spurs. Then* ANTONIO, *the* DUCHESS *and their Children,
having presented themselves at the shrine, are, by a form of
banishment in dumb-show expressed towards them by the
Cardinal and the state of Ancona, banished. During all which
ceremony, this ditty is sung to very solemn music by diverse
churchmen, and then*   Exeunt.

Arms and honours deck thy story,
To thy fame's eternal glory.
Adverse fortune ever fly thee,   9
No disastrous fate come nigh thee.   The author
                                                         disclaims
I alone will sing thy praises,   this ditty
                                                         to be his.

ironically juxtaposed against his act of repudiating the Duchess and her family. A second revision probably by Webster is the alteration of Q1a's '*Hymne*' to Q1b's *ditty* (6.8) in the course of printing the play (t.n.).

6.1–4 The Cardinal's divestiture as a churchman and installation as a soldier, performed in removing four ecclesiastical objects from his person and replacing them with four military ones, parodically echoes the formal ceremonies by which priests and higher officials of the Roman Church were invested with their robes of office and, if found unworthy, publicly divested of them. For staging, see pp. 24–5.

6.7 *state of Ancona* Representatives of the independent Italian state of Ancona would also have been onstage along with the Cardinal, the Duchess

and their entourages. There may therefore have been two official groups onstage: the churchmen and the secular officials of Ancona.

7 In Q1a, the title 'The Hymne' headed the verses that begin at 7, and there was no marginal note (10ff.) informing readers that the author disclaimed authorship. Webster probably visited the printing-house and demanded that the disclaimer be inserted to save his artistic reputation from the attribution of verses that he considered insufficiently serious for their occasion – a *ditty* rather than a 'hymn' (see pp. 63–7). Its authorship is unknown.

11 **I alone** an odd locution, given the statement at 6.8–9 that the ditty was sung by '*diverse churchmen*'. Perhaps individual choristers sang individual

6.1 *habit*] *Q1b; order* | *Q1a*   6.2 *of*] *Q2; not in Q1*   6.6 *in dumb-show*] *Q1b; not in Q1a*   6.8 *ditty*] *Q1b;*
Hymne | *Q1a*   7–22] *stanza breaks om. Q2*   7 Arms] *Q1b; The Hymne. / Armes* | *Q1a*   9 fly thee]
(flie-thee)   10–12 The . . . his.] *opp. 9–11 Q1b; not in Q1a; om. Q2*   10 nigh thee] *(nigh-thee)*

Whom to honour virtue raises;
And thy study, that divine is,
Bent to martial discipline is.
Lay aside all those robes lie by thee;   15
Crown thy arts with arms: they'll beautify thee.

O worthy of worthiest name, adorned in this manner,
Lead bravely thy forces on under war's warlike banner.
O mayst thou prove fortunate in all martial courses.
Guide thou still by skill in arts and forces.   20

Victory attend thee nigh whilst fame sings loud thy
    powers,
Triumphant conquest crown thy head, and blessings
    pour down showers.

1 PILGRIM

Here's a strange turn of state! Who would have thought
So great a lady would have matched herself
Unto so mean a person? Yet the Cardinal   25
Bears himself much too cruel.

2 PILGRIM   They are banished.

1 PILGRIM

But I would ask what power hath this state
Of Ancona to determine of a free prince?

---

stanzas antiphonally. Or else the words are syntactically awkward and mean 'I will sing thy praises alone'.

13–14 suggests that martial discipline is as *divine* as the Cardinal's earlier godly pursuits

15 **lie** that lie

19 **courses** passages at arms

20 This line is metrically shorter than the preceding three, and breaks the dominant pattern of the hymn by which the verses in each stanza grad-

ually add metrical feet, culminating in the heptameters of the final couplet (21–2).

23–5 **Who . . . person** The reason for the Duchess's banishment has in some manner been communicated to the pilgrims.

26 **Bears . . . cruel** behaves much too cruelly

28 **determine of** enact justice upon
free prince sovereign authority, not bound by local laws

13 divine is] *(diuine-is)* 14 discipline is] *(discipline-is)* 18 war's] war *Q2* 20–1] *no stanza break Q1* 26] *Q1 lines* cruell. / banish'd. / much] *om. Q2*

2 PILGRIM

They are a free state, sir, and her brother showed
How that the Pope, forehearing of her looseness,   30
Hath seized into th' protection of the church
The dukedom, which she held as dowager.

1 PILGRIM

But by what justice?

2 PILGRIM   Sure, I think by none –
Only her brother's instigation.

1 PILGRIM

What was it with such violence he took   35
Off from her finger?

2 PILGRIM   'Twas her wedding ring,
Which he vowed shortly he would sacrifice
To his revenge.

1 PILGRIM   Alas, Antonio!
If that a man be thrust into a well,
No matter who sets hand to't, his own weight   40
Will bring him sooner to th' bottom. Come, let's hence.

---

29 **free state** sovereign political unit, able to enforce its laws upon people within its jurisdiction. During the early 16th century Ancona was coming under papal influence, hence no longer really *free*.

30–2 Influenced by the Cardinal and fearing that the Duchess's alleged promiscuity would compromise the aristocratic bloodlines that secured the inheritance of the dukedom, the Pope has deprived her of her sovereign authority over it.

30 **forehearing** hearing in advance

32 **dowager** woman whose title or property has come to her through her husband's death; contradicts 3.3.67, where the Duchess is merely her son's regent

34 **brother's** Presumably the Cardinal informed the Pope, but, since both of

her brothers object to the Duchess's marriage, the instigation may be joint: the word 'brothers' in Q1 includes no clarifying apostrophe.

instigation pronounced as five syllables

36 possibly the same ring with which the Duchess wooed Antonio in 1.2. She had worn the ring publicly at Loreto to acknowledge her marriage to Antonio, and by taking the ring the Cardinal symbolically effects a divorce.

37–8 He would have the ring melted down as retribution against the Duchess's secret marriage.

40 **sets hand to't** does the throwing

his i.e. that of the person thrown in the well. The more *weight* he carries in the world, the sooner he will sink.

---

29 sir] *Q1b; not in Q1a*   31 Hath] *Q1b; Had Q1a*   33] *Q1 lines* iustice? / none, /   36] *Q1 lines* finger? / ring, /   Off] *Q2;* Of *Q1*   38] *Q1 lines* reuenge. / *Antonio,* /

Fortune makes this conclusion general:
'All things do help th'unhappy man to fall.'   *Exeunt.*

3.5   [*Enter*] ANTONIO, DUCHESS, Children,
                    CARIOLA, Servants.

DUCHESS
    Banished Ancona?
ANTONIO   Yes. You see what power
    Lightens in great men's breath.
DUCHESS   Is all our train
    Shrunk to this poor remainder?
ANTONIO   These poor men,
    Which have got little in your service, vow
    To take your fortune; but your wiser buntings,   5
    Now they are fledged, are gone.
DUCHESS   They have done wisely.
    This puts me in mind of death. Physicians thus,
    With their hands full of money, use to give o'er

43 Another scene-concluding proverb varying commonplace laments
   over the fickleness of fortune (Dent,
   F606*); the precise wording echoes
   Alexander, *Alexandrian Tragedy*, sig.
   I2ʳ: 'All things must help th'unhappy
   man to fall' (Dent, *Webster*).
3.5 Location: Loreto
1 **Banished Ancona** banished from
   the state of Ancona; cf. Lodovico's
   'Banisht' – the first word of *White
   Devil*.
2 **Lightens** flashes, perhaps implying
   combustibility; the same word was
   used earlier (3.3.54) of a cannon.
3 **remainder** remnant
4 **got** earned, profited; echoes the
   Duchess's ironic comment before
   Antonio's banishment from Amalfi, 'I

have got well by you' (3.2.182).
5 **take** share
   buntings group of birds of the family *Emberizidae*; in England there are
   residents such as the reed bunting and
   corn bunting, and migrants such as the
   snow bunting.
6 **fledged** sufficiently well feathered to
   fly; cf. the Duchess's earlier characterization of herself at 3.2.84.
7 **puts ... mind** reminds me
7–9 **Physicians ... patients** a common complaint. Cf. Painter, fol. 277ᵛ,
   where physicians, having failed to
   cure their patient, 'with handes full
   of money ... gave him over' (Dent,
   Webster).
8 **use ... o'er** make a practice of aban-
   doning

43 'All ... fall.'] ('All ... fall.*); All ... fall. *Q3*   do] to *Q2*   3.5] *(SCENA V.)*   0 SD] *Q4; Antonio,
Duchesse, Children, Cariola, Seruants, Bosola, Souldiers, with Vizards.* | *Q1*   1–3] *Q1 lines* Ancona /
powre / breath, / traine / remainder? / men, /   3 These] These are *Q2*   5 wiser] fatter *Q4*   6] *Q1
lines* gon. / wisely, /

Their patients.

ANTONIO   Right the fashion of the world –
From decayed fortunes every flatterer shrinks;   10
Men cease to build where the foundation sinks.

DUCHESS
I had a very strange dream tonight.

ANTONIO   What was't?

DUCHESS
Methought I wore my coronet of state,
And on a sudden all the diamonds
Were changed to pearls.

ANTONIO   My interpretation   15
Is, you'll weep shortly; for to me the pearls
Do signify your tears.

DUCHESS   The birds that live i'th' field,
On the wild benefit of nature, live
Happier than we; for they may choose their mates,
And carol their sweet pleasures to the spring.   20

[Enter] BOSOLA *[with a letter]*.

BOSOLA
You are happily o'erta'en.   *[Gives her the letter.]*
DUCHESS   From my brother?
BOSOLA
Yes, from the lord Ferdinand, your brother,

---

9 **Right** just
12–17 The Duchess's dream and its
  interpretation echo a similar dream by
  Henri IV of France's queen a few days
  before he was assassinated in 1610; see
  Matthieu, sig. H3ʳ.
14 **on a sudden** suddenly
17–20 **birds . . . spring** Cf. the care-

free scriptural 'lillies of the field'
  (Matthew, 6.28).
18 **benefit** generosity, gift
20 SD Editors differ as to whether Bosola's
  letter is conspicuous enough to be visible as he enters, but he may flourish
  it upon entering, since the Duchess's
  question at 21 most likely refers to it.

9] *Q1 lines* Patients. / world, /   12] *Q1 lines* tonight. / was't? /   was't] is't *Q2*   15] *Q1 lines* Pearles.
/ Interpretation /   17] *Q1 lines* teares: / field /   your] you *Q2*   20 SD] *Q4; Bosola,* | *0 SD Q1*   21]
Q1 lines ore-ta'ne. / brother? /   SD] *this edn*

All love and safety.

DUCHESS   Thou dost blanch mischief –

Wouldst make it white. See, see, like to calm weather

At sea before a tempest, false hearts speak fair   25

To those they intend most mischief.

> [*Reads the*] *letter. 'Send Antonio to me. I want his*
> *head in a business.'*

A politic equivocation!

He doth not want your counsel, but your head: 30

That is, he cannot sleep till you be dead.

And here's another pitfall that's strewed o'er

With roses. Mark it. 'Tis a cunning one:

> [*Reads.*] '*I stand engaged for your husband for several*
> *debts at Naples. Let not that trouble him. I had rather have*   35
> *his heart than his money.'*

And I believe so too.

BOSOLA   What do you believe?

DUCHESS

That he so much distrusts my husband's love,

---

23 **blanch** bleach; make pale with fear (implying that Bosola is more dangerous than mischief itself). Cf. the 'Envious' man in Hall, *Characters*, 172: 'hee saith, *Fame is partiall, and is wont to blanch mischiefs*' (Dent, *Webster*).

24–5 **calm . . . tempest** the proverbial calm before a storm (Dent, C24*)

25 **fair** agreeably

27 SD Q1's 'A Letter' could be a question by the Duchess, in which case she receives the letter only at this point, but more likely, as frequently in the period, this is a heading to indicate the special status of the text that follows.

27–8 *want his head* seek his advice; desire his execution, as in 'I'll have his head!' A similar double meaning is recorded in a frequently borrowed passage from

Bodin, 631, during a discussion of tricks used by princes for breaking faith (Dent, *Webster*).

29 **politic** carefully calculated **equivocation** pronounced as six syllables (for the word's implications, see 3.1.77n.)

34–5 *I . . . Naples* Ferdinand claims to have served as surety for Antonio's loans, perhaps taking advantage of the Duchess's earlier *noble lie* about Antonio's corrupt financial dealings (3.2.179ff.)

36 *heart* love, but with sinister double meaning. Camden, *Remains*, sig. Ee4ᵛ, records of the infamous Richard III that when his subjects offered him a subsidy he refused it, 'saying, I know not in what sence; *I had rather have your hearts, than your money.*'

23] *Q1 lines* safetie / mischiefe /   24 calm] the calme *Q2*   27 SD] *Dyce, after 28;* A Letter. *Q1;* Reads *Q4*   27–9] *Dyce; one line Q1*   34 SD] *Brown*   37] *Q1 lines* too. / beleeue? /   38 so much] *om. Q4*

He will by no means believe his heart is with him
Until he see it. The devil is not cunning enough   40
To circumvent us in riddles. ~~brother 2 devil~~

BOSOLA

Will you reject that noble and free league
Of amity and love which I present you?

DUCHESS

Their league is like that of some politic kings,
Only to make themselves of strength and power   45
To be our after-ruin. Tell them so.

BOSOLA

And what from you?

ANTONIO   Thus tell him: I will not come.

BOSOLA

And what of this?

ANTONIO   My brothers have dispersed
Bloodhounds abroad, which, till I hear are muzzled,
No truce, though hatched with ne'er such politic skill,   50
Is safe that hangs upon our enemies' will.
I'll not come at them.

---

39 **with him** loyal to Ferdinand
40 **see it** see it directly, outside Antonio's body, in which case the heart is *with* Ferdinand in a much more literal sense. Donne's Jesuit Ignatius speaks of treasonous princes, 'whose hearts wee do not believe to be with us, till we see them' at the time of their execution (*Ignatius*, 63).
41 **circumvent** outwit, cheat
42 **free** generous; uncoerced
   league presumably a formal political alliance spelled out in the letter
44 **politic** manipulative, savvy
45–6 **make . . . after-ruin** pretend friendship long enough to consolidate

their power to the point that they can destroy us
48 **this** Bosola may here indicate the letter, as suggested by Gunby, or he may be referring to the overall situation.
   brothers brothers-in-law. This is a standard early modern locution but nevertheless significant as the first time Antonio claims his place as one of the aristocratic family.
49 **Bloodhounds abroad** dogs, or more probably men, spread throughout the vicinity to track down the fugitive Duchess and her entourage
52 **come at them** come into their presence; attack them

47–8] *Q1 lines* you? / come. / this. / dispers'd / 48 And . . . this] *om. Q4* 52] *Q1 lines* them. / breeding, /

BOSOLA   This proclaims your breeding:
Every small thing draws a base mind to fear
As the adamant draws iron. Fare you well, sir.
You shall shortly hear from's.   *Exit.*

DUCHESS   I suspect some ambush.   55
Therefore, by all my love, I do conjure you
To take your eldest son and fly towards Milan.
Let us not venture all this poor remainder
In one unlucky bottom.

ANTONIO   You counsel safely.
Best of my life, farewell, since we must part.   60
Heaven hath a hand in't, but no otherwise
Than as some curious artist takes in sunder
A clock or watch, when it is out of frame,
To bring't in better order.

DUCHESS   I know not which is best,
To see you dead or part with you. – Farewell, boy.   65
Thou art happy that thou hast not understanding
To know thy misery, for all our wit
And reading brings us to a truer sense

---

breeding upbringing; said in deep sarcasm: Bosola goes on at 53 to refer to Antonio's *base mind*, echoing Ferdinand's earlier jibes about Antonio's baseness of origin.

54 **adamant** magnet, centre of attraction; adamant was sometimes associated with diamond, sometimes with the lodestone or magnet, as here (on the word's many conflicting meanings, see *OED*).

56 **conjure** entreat, call upon

57 **your eldest son** the firstborn of Antonio and the Duchess. She shows her continuing respect for Antonio by referring to their child as *yours*, according to the standard patriarchal

doctrine of the time by which the child 'belongs' to the father.

59 **unlucky bottom** ship that is likely to sink; cf. *MV* 1.1.42: 'My ventures are not in one bottom trusted.'

61 **no otherwise** in no other way

62 **curious** careful, ingenious, skilful
in sunder apart

63 **out of frame** malfunctioning

64–5 **I . . . you** most likely addressed to Antonio, but possibly also to the Duchess's and Antonio's elder son

67–9 **all . . . sorrow** echoes Ecclesiastes, 1.18: 'For in the multitude of wisdome is muche grief: & he that encreaseth knowledge, encreaseth sorrow.'

55] *Q1 lines* from's. / Ambush: /   59] *Q1 lines* bottome. / safely: /   60 farewell, . . . part.] *this edn;* farewell: . . . part *Q1*   61–4 Heaven . . . bring't] *om. in performance Q4*   64] *Q1 lines* order. / best, /   67–79 for . . . scourge-stick] *om. in performance Q4*

Of sorrow. – In the eternal church, sir,
I do hope we shall not part thus.

ANTONIO   Oh, be of comfort!   70

Make patience a noble fortitude,
And think not how unkindly we are used.
'Man, like to cassia, is proved best, being bruised.'

DUCHESS

Must I, like to a slave-born Russian,
Account it praise to suffer tyranny?   75
And yet, O Heaven, thy heavy hand is in't.
I have seen my little boy oft scourge his top
And compared myself to't: naught made me e'er
Go right, but Heaven's scourge-stick.

ANTONIO   Do not weep.

Heaven fashioned us of nothing and we strive   80
To bring ourselves to nothing. – Farewell, Cariola,
And thy sweet armful. – If I do never see thee more,

69 **eternal church** the community of
blessed spirits in heaven, where they
can be married for ever. Cf. *Arcadia*,
book 2, ch. 13, 233: Erona, thinking
Antiphilus dead, attempts suicide so
she will 'be maried in the eternall
church with him' (Dent, *Webster*).
71 **Make . . . fortitude** Patience and
fortitude were considered co-ordinate
virtues at the time: fortitude was the
active part that enabled one to take on
difficult tasks; patience was the more
passive part that allowed one to endure
hardships.
72 **unkindly** cruelly; unnaturally, against
one's own 'kind' in the sense of family
or humanity in general
73 **cassia** See 2.4.64n. As the quotation marks preceding this line in Q1
suggest (see t.n.), the idea that spices
are more aromatic when pounded is
proverbial: cf. Dent, S746, 'If you beat
spice it will smell the sweeter.'

74 **slave-born Russian** Russian serf.
Cf. *Astrophil and Stella*, Sonnet 2,
'and now like slave-borne Muscovite:
/ I call it praise to suffer tyrannie'
(Lucas).
75 **Account it** consider it
77 **scourge his top** whip a top to make it
spin faster
79 **scourge-stick** stick used to whip a
top
80–1 According to Genesis, Adam was
fashioned out of clay, but numerous
biblical passages support the idea that
God created the universe *ex nihilo*,
out of nothing. Cf. Donne, *First
Anniversary* (1611), 155–7: 'Wee seeme
ambitious, Gods whole worke t'undoe;
/ Of nothing hee made us, and we
strive too, / To bring our selves to
nothing backe' (Donne; Lucas).
82 **sweet armful** Cariola is presumably
holding one or both of the younger
children.

70] *Q1 lines* thus. / comfort, /   73 'Man . . . bruised.'] ("Man . . . bruiz'd.)   74 Russian] Ruffian
Q2   78–9] *Sampson; Q1 lines* right, / scourge-sticke. / weepe: /   81–2 Farewell . . . armful] *om. Q4*

Be a good mother to your little ones,
And save them from the tiger. Fare you well.

DUCHESS

Let me look upon you once more, for that speech   85
Came from a dying father. Your kiss is colder
Than that I have seen an holy anchorite   — *religious ritual*
Give to a dead man's skull.

ANTONIO
                                                    - clear expression
My heart is turned to a heavy lump of lead,   *of emotional*
With which I sound my danger. Fare you well.   90 *grief*

                                    Exit [*with his elder son*].

DUCHESS

My laurel is all withered.

CARIOLA

Look, madam, what a troop of armed men
Make toward us!

Enter BOSOLA *with a guard* [*of*] Soldiers, [*all wearing*] *vizards*.

DUCHESS   Oh, they are very welcome.

86–8 **Your . . . skull** Contemplating a skull, or kissing it, was an important element of the medieval and early modern *memento mori* (remembrance of death) tradition. Cf. the gravedigger scene (*Ham* 5.1), where Hamlet is reminded of human frailty by the skull of Yorick.

89–90 As sailors use a lead weight to *sound*, or measure, the depth of the sea and gauge their distance from dangerous rocks on the bottom, so Antonio describes his heart as a weight that 'sounds' the danger of his situation. Cf. 3.2.111–13, where Ferdinand describes his heart as enfolded in lead.

90 **my** Does his pronoun choice suggest

that Antonio has forgotten the peril to his family?

91 **laurel** or bay tree, associated since classical times with victory and poetic achievement; according to ancient Roman superstition, laurel trees would die upon the death of the emperor (Lucas). Cf. *R2* 2.4.7–8: ''Tis thought the king is dead . . . / The bay-trees in our country are all wither'd.'

92 **armed** armèd

93 SD The quarto SD does not specify that Bosola, too, is wearing a mask, or *vizard*, but very likely he is, since the Duchess goes on to address him in a way that suggests his identity is uncertain (98) and later refers to his *counterfeit face* (116).

90 SD] *Dyce² (subst.); Exit.* | *Q1* 92 what a] *Q1b;* what *Q1a* 93] *Q1 lines* vs. / welcome: / SD] *Weis; Enter Bosola with a Guard.* | *Q1b; not in Q1a; Souldiers, with Vizards.* | *0 SD Q1; Enter Bosola with Guard, disguis'd.* | *Q4*

253

When Fortune's wheel is overcharged with princes
The weight makes it move swift. I would have my ruin   95
Be sudden. I am your adventure, am I not?

BOSOLA

You are. You must see your husband no more.

DUCHESS

What devil art thou, that counterfeits heaven's thunder?

BOSOLA

Is that terrible? I would have you tell me whether
Is that note worse that frights the silly birds   100
Out of the corn, or that which doth allure them
To the nets. You have hearkened to the last too much.

DUCHESS

Oh, misery! Like to a rusty o'ercharged cannon,
Shall I never fly in pieces? Come – to what prison?

94–5 **Fortune's . . . swift** As in contemporary illustrations of the wheel of Fortune, the Duchess imagines it as actually carrying the princes that it plunges into ruin: the more they are weighted with worldly honours, the faster the wheel brings them down. Cf. Alexander, *Alexandrian Tragedy*, sig. M3ᵛ: 'The wheele of Fortune still must slippery prove, / And chiefly when it burdend is with kings, / Whose states as weightiest most must make it move' (Dent, *Webster*).

94 **overcharged** overloaded

96 **adventure** target, quarry; commercial enterprise (*OED* 7), suggesting the soldiers are mercenaries

98 **counterfeits . . . thunder** usurps God's power to judge humankind; sets off firearms, which Bosola's soldiers may have done at this point to intimidate the Duchess. Cf. *Oth* 3.3.359,

where Othello refers to cannons as counterfeiting 'th'immortal Jove's dread clamours'.

99–102 Comparing the Duchess to a bird, Bosola implies that he is there to help her, not hurt her. He asks her which is worse, a sound (*note*) designed to frighten the birds out of the fields and thereby protect the crops, or a more sinister sound designed to force birds into entrapping nets so that they can be killed, and he suggests that she has mistaken the former for the latter.

100 **silly** lowly, senseless, defenceless. Brown sees ironic pity in Bosola's word choice.

103 *****o'ercharged** overloaded, fired too often. The same image of death occurs in Donne's *Second Anniversary* (1612), 181–2 (Donne). The Q1 reading 'ore-char'd' – burned all over – is also possible (see t.n.).

95 move] *Q1b;* more *Q1a*   would] *Q2;* wonld *Q1*   99–100] *Dyce; Q1 lines* me / birds /   99 SP] *Q1b; not in Q1a*   103 SP] *Q1b; Ant.* | *Q1a*   103–4 Like . . . pieces] *om. Q4*   103 o'ercharged] *Q2;* ore-char'd *Q1*

BOSOLA

  To none.

DUCHESS   Whither, then?

BOSOLA   To your palace.

DUCHESS   I have heard   105

  That Charon's boat serves to convey all o'er

  The dismal lake, but brings none back again.

BOSOLA

  Your brothers mean you safety and pity.

DUCHESS   Pity?

  With such a pity men preserve alive

  Pheasants and quails, when they are not fat enough   110

  To be eaten.

BOSOLA

  These are your children?

DUCHESS   Yes.

BOSOLA   Can they prattle?

DUCHESS   No.

  But I intend, since they were born accursed,

  Curses shall be their first language.

BOSOLA   Fie, madam!

  Forget this base, low fellow –

DUCHESS   Were I a man   115

  I'd beat that counterfeit face into thy other.

106–7 **Charon's . . . lake** In Greek mythology Charon, the ferryman of the dead, rows departed souls across the River Acheron into Hades – a more pessimistic view of the afterlife than the Duchess's earlier evocation of the 'eternal church' (69). Cf. Alexander, *Julius Caesar*, sig. bb4ʳ: 'th'unrelenting *Charons* restlesse barge / Stands to transport all over, but brings none backe' (Dent, *Webster*).

113–14 **But . . . language** Cf. Caliban in *Tem* 1.2.364–5: 'You taught me language, and my profit on't / Is I know how to curse.'

115 **fellow** a term usually used only of members of the lower social orders; hence, an insulting reference to Antonio. Contrast Bosola's earlier egalitarianism (3.2.262ff.).

116 **counterfeit face** Bosola's mask; see 93 SDn.

other actual face

105–9] *Sampson; Q1 lines* none: / then? / Pallace. / conuay / againe. / pitie. / aliue /   105+ Whither] *(Whether)*   109–11] *om. Q4*   112] *Q1 lines* children? / Yes: / prattle? / No: /   114–15] *Q1 lines* language. / (Madam) / low-fellow. / man: /

BOSOLA

  – One of no birth.

DUCHESS   Say that he was born mean –

  Man is most happy when's own actions

  Be arguments and examples of his virtue.

BOSOLA

  A barren beggarly virtue!   120

DUCHESS

  I prithee, who is greatest, can you tell?

  Sad tales befit my woe. I'll tell you one:

  A salmon, as she swam unto the sea,

  Met with a dogfish, who encounters her

  With this rough language: 'Why art thou so bold   125

  To mix thyself with our high state of floods,

  Being no eminent courtier, but one

  That for the calmest and fresh time o'th' year

  Dost live in shallow rivers; rank'st thyself

  With silly smelts and shrimps? And darest thou   130

  Pass by Our Dogship without reverence?'

  'Oh,' quoth the salmon, 'sister, be at peace.

  Thank Jupiter we both have passed the net.

  Our value never can be truly known

  Till in the fisher's basket we be shown.   135

---

119 **arguments** proof, evidence

124 **dogfish** type of small shark, and therefore higher in the hierarchy of fish than the salmon. The term was, however, derogatory when applied to people.

125 **thou** The dogfish addresses the salmon with a demeaning familiar instead of the more respectful 'you'.

126 **high . . . floods** the ocean, ranked higher than mere rivers where salmon go to spawn. Cf. *2H4* 5.2.129–33, where Prince Hal says his blood, when he is king, will flow to the sea, 'mingle

with the state of floods, / And flow henceforth in formal majesty'.

130 **smelts and shrimps** The dogfish implies that the salmon ranks lower even than these other inconsequential water creatures.

133 **passed** escaped

135 **fisher's basket** basket of the fisherman who displays the fish at market, but with a hint of the Last Judgement Day, when Christ will judge the value of all the souls 'caught' by his disciples, the 'fishers of men'.

117] *Q1 lines* Birth. / meane. /   123–38] *om. in performance Q4*   123 unto] into *Q4*   128 fresh] freshest *Q4*   129 Dost] *(Do'st)*   130 smelts] *(Smylts)*

I'th' market, then, my price may be the higher,
Even when I am nearest to the cook and fire.'
So to great men the moral may be stretched:
'Men oft are valued high, when they're most wretched.'
But come, whither you please, I am armed 'gainst
    misery –   140
Bent to all sways of the oppressor's will.
'There's no deep valley but near some great hill.'   *Exeunt.*

4.1   *[Enter]* FERDINAND *[and]* BOSOLA.

FERDINAND
    How doth our sister Duchess bear herself
    In her imprisonment?
BOSOLA   Nobly. I'll describe her.
    She's sad, as one long used to't, and she seems
    Rather to welcome the end of misery
    Than shun it – a behaviour so noble   5
    As gives a majesty to adversity.
    You may discern the shape of loveliness
    More perfect in her tears than in her smiles.

137 **Even** just
140 **whither you please** wherever you
    like
141 **all sways** every alteration
142 proverbial (Dent, H467): 'There's no
    hill without its valley.'
4.1 Location: Amalfi
1 **bear** carry, comport
2 **imprisonment** i.e. house arrest,
    assuming that Bosola has kept his
    word and returned the Duchess

To your palace (3.5.105)
3–6 Like several ensuing passages, this
    echoes *Arcadia*, book 2, ch. 29, 332,
    '*Erona* sadde indeede, yet like one
    rather used, then new fallen to sad-
    nesse . . . seemed rather to welcome
    then to shunne that end of miserie';
    and book 1, ch. 2, 16, 'a behaviour
    so noble, as gave a majestie to adver-
    sitie'.
4 **end of misery** i.e. death

139 'Men . . . wretched.'] (,,Men . . . wretch'd.) 141–2] *ital. Q4* 142] *ital. Q1* SD] *(Ex.)*
4.1] *(ACTVS IIII. SCENA. I.)* 0 SD] *Q4 (subst); Ferdinand, Bosola, Dutchesse, Cariola, Seruants.*
| *Q1* 2] *Q1 lines* imprisonment? / her: / 3 long] *om. Q2*

> She will muse four hours together, and her silence,
> Methinks, expresseth more than if she spake. 10

FERDINAND

> Her melancholy seems to be fortified
> With a strange disdain.

BOSOLA   'Tis so; and this restraint,

> Like English mastiffs that grow fierce with tying,
> Makes her too passionately apprehend
> Those pleasures she's kept from.

FERDINAND   Curse upon her! 15

> I will no longer study in the book
> Of another's heart. Inform her what I told you.   *Exit.*

[*Enter*] DUCHESS.

BOSOLA

> All comfort to your grace.

DUCHESS   I will have none.

> Pray thee, why dost thou wrap thy poisoned pills
> In gold and sugar? 20

9 **four** sometimes used generally to mean 'several'; Q1's 'foure' could alternatively mean 'for'.

12 **strange** unlike her usual demeanour; rare, unaccountable
restraint the Duchess's imprisonment

13 **with tying** from being tied up

14 **apprehend** feel the force of

16–17 **I . . . heart** Reading of hearts was a commonplace idea in love poetry of the period.

17 SD2 The group entry at 4.1.0 SD (see t.n.) calls for Cariola to enter at some point during the scene. I follow most editors in having the Duchess enter on her own here so that she will

be alone with Ferdinand at 30ff., as in her earlier encounter with him at 3.2.60ff. Alternatively, Cariola could enter with the Duchess here and exit with Bosola at 29 when he removes the lights. Brennan suggests, with high theatricality, 'Bosola draws the traverse to reveal the Duchess, Cariola, and Servants', who would have been concealed in the alcove or 'discovery area' at the rear of the stage. On the use of the traverse, which is probably identical with the *arras* in 1.2.272, see p. 92.

19–20 **wrap . . . sugar** The Duchess compares Bosola's hypocritical words of comfort to poison wrapped in sugar to disguise its bitter taste and in gold

10 expresseth] expresses *Q4*   12] *Q1 lines* disdaine. / restraint /   13] *om. in performance Q4*   15] *Q1 lines* from. / her: /   Curse upon her] *om. Q4*   17 SD2] *Q4; Dutchesse,* | *0 SD Q1; Enter Duchess and Attendants.* | *Sampson*   18] *Q1 lines* Grace; / none: /

BOSOLA

> Your elder brother, the lord Ferdinand,
> Is come to visit you, and sends you word,
> 'Cause once he rashly made a solemn vow
> Never to see you more, he comes i'th' night;
> And prays you gently neither torch nor taper   25
> Shine in your chamber. He will kiss your hand
> And reconcile himself; but, for his vow,
> He dares not see you.

DUCHESS

> At his pleasure. Take hence the lights.
>
> > *[Bosola exits with the lights.]*
> > He's come.

[Enter FERDINAND.*]*

FERDINAND

> Where are you?

DUCHESS   Here, sir.

FERDINAND   This darkness suits you well.   30

DUCHESS

> I would ask you pardon.

---

leaf to make it more attractive: gold was believed to have healing properties in addition to high value. Proverbial (Dent, P325); cf. *White Devil*, 3.2.190–1, 'I decerne poison, / Under your guilded pils.'

21 **elder** This is historically incorrect, and in the play Ferdinand later implies that the Duchess is his slightly older twin (4.2.256–8). Bosola may assume Ferdinand to be the elder because he is so fixated on controlling his sister. On the relative ages of all three siblings, see pp. 16–17.

23 **vow** Cf. 3.2.135, 'I will never see you more.'

27 **reconcile himself** make peace; reconcile himself to you

29 SD1 Most editors keep Bosola onstage here, having servants remove the lights, but his presence could detract from the ensuing scene with Ferdinand. In some productions he remains onstage, visible to the audience but concealed from the Duchess, so that although she is unaware of his agency the audience is not allowed to forget it.

28–9] *this edn; Q1 lines* you: / pleaure: / come. /   29 SD1] *Brown (subst.); Bosola removes the lights and walks apart.* | *Weis* SD2] *Q4 (subst.); Ferdinand,* | *0 SD Q1* 30–1] *Q1 lines* sir: / well. / pardon: / it; /

FERDINAND   You have it.

For I account it the honourablest revenge,

Where I may kill, to pardon. Where are your cubs?

DUCHESS

Whom?

FERDINAND   Call them your children;

For, though our national law distinguish bastards   35

From true legitimate issue, compassionate nature

Makes them all equal.

DUCHESS   Do you visit me for this?

You violate a sacrament o'th' church

Shall make you howl in hell for't.

FERDINAND   It had been well,

Could you have lived thus always, for indeed   40

You were too much i'th' light. But no more.

I come to seal my peace with you. Here's a hand,

32–3 revenge . . . pardon Ferdinand assumes that he would be justified in killing the Duchess because of her alleged sexual promiscuity. Cf. the proverb 'To pardon is a divine revenge' (Dent, R92*).

33 cubs For Ferdinand, the children of Antonio are too low to be considered human. This possibly foreshadows Ferdinand's later lycanthropy, in which case the children could, symbolically at least, be his own wolf *cubs*, a product of incest.

34 Whom? The Duchess's question could mean 'Whom are you speaking of?', 'Whom would you kill?' or 'Who are the cubs?'

35–7 national . . . equal Ferdinand is distinguishing between *national* and 'natural' law (*nature*): bastards would ordinarily be denied inheritance by law, whether Italian or English, but they are *equal* to legitimate children in that it is natural for parents to love all

their children, whatever their circumstances of birth. Cf. an almost identical passage in *Devil's Law-Case*, 4.2.261, which adds, 'nay, shee [Nature] many times preferres them' (Webster, 2.141); and *KL* 1.1.18–19, where Gloucester says that his son Edgar, born 'by order of law', 'yet is no dearer in my account' than his bastard son Edmund.

38 sacrament o'th' church i.e. her marriage, which the Duchess considers holy despite its irregular status under ecclesiastical law; see 1.2.386n.

40 thus in the dark

41 You . . . light too visible, too public, and too promiscuous (another meaning of *light*); cf. Hamlet's multiple pun about his mother's adulterous remarriage; in her presence he is 'too much in the sun' and 'in the son' (*Ham* 1.2.67).

42 seal conclude; mark with an official seal (like those made in wax by signet rings)

---

32 honourablest] *(honorabl'st)*   37] *Q1 lines* equall. / this? /   39] *Q1 lines* for't. / well, /

To which you have vowed much love. The ring upon't
You gave.   (*Gives her a dead man's hand.*)

DUCHESS   I affectionately kiss it.

FERDINAND

Pray do, and bury the print of it in your heart.
I will leave this ring with you for a love-token,   45
And the hand as sure as the ring; and do not doubt
But you shall have the heart too. When you need a
    friend,
Send it to him that owed it. You shall see
Whether he can aid you.

DUCHESS   You are very cold.   50
I fear you are not well after your travel.
Ha? – Lights! Oh, horrible!

FERDINAND   Let her have lights enough. *Exit.*

[*Enter* BOSOLA *with a light.*]

43–4 **ring . . . gave** presumably the same
ring pledging marital fidelity that the
Duchess had originally given Antonio
(1.2.318); he had returned it to her
in marriage, and the Cardinal had
forcibly taken it from her at Loreto
(3.4.35–6)

44 SD *dead man's hand* probably a
hand made of wax in early stagings,
but designed to resemble a dead man's
hand. Early audiences might have
associated this prop with the magical
severed dead hands called the 'hand
of glory' or '*maindegloire*' and used in
England and elsewhere as a key element of witchcraft rituals (Rowe).

45 **print** the imprint made by the ring,
as upon wax; Ferdinand evidently
expects the Duchess to assume that
the hand is his, and in performance he
frequently extends it as if it is his own.
He appears to be calling upon her to
use the ring to 'imprint' his love in

her heart in the same way that she earlier had *entered* Antonio into her heart
(3.2.60–1). Cf. 16–17 above, where
Ferdinand claims to have had enough
of reading his sister's heart.

48 **you . . . heart** Cf. 3.5.35–6, where
Ferdinand's letter threatened, '*I had
rather have [Antonio's] heart than his
money.*'

49 **him . . . it** Antonio; *owed* here means
'owned' (*OED* 1).

50–1 **You . . . travel** At this point the
Duchess still believes the extended
hand to be Ferdinand's. The dead
hand was cut from most productions
before the 20th century. In Phelps's
1850 staging, the Duchess kissed her
brother's *cold* hand.

52 SD2 If Bosola has remained
onstage, either visibly or 'apart' as in
Weis, he will not need to re-enter here;
some editors have 'Servants' bring in
the lights.

44] *Q1 lines* gaue. / it: SD] *opp. 42–4 Q1*   50] *Q1 lines* you. / cold. /   52] *Q1 lines* horrible: / enough
/   SD2] *Q4 (subst.)* (Enter Bosola); Bosola, | 0 SD Q1; Re-enter Servants with lights. | Lucas

DUCHESS

What witchcraft doth he practise that he hath left
A dead man's hand here?

*Here is discovered, behind a traverse, the artificial figures of
Antonio and his Children, appearing as if they were dead.*

BOSOLA

Look you, here's the piece from which 'twas ta'en.   55
He doth present you this sad spectacle
That, now you know directly they are dead,
Hereafter you may wisely cease to grieve
For that which cannot be recovered.   *– starting up*
                                             Other

DUCHESS

There is not between heaven and earth one wish   60
I stay for after this. It wastes me more
Than were't my picture, fashioned out of wax,

54 SD By whose hand is this grisly tableau discovered? Some editors have
Bosola draw the *traverse*, but it is arguably more effective to leave unseen the
method by which Ferdinand reveals
the figures, as was done in 1850, when
the traverse was replaced by a wall that
magically opened by itself.

54.1 *discovered* revealed. The word was
often used in the period for sudden
theatrical displays, such as those characteristic of the court masque.
traverse curtain or screen concealing the
alcove or 'discovery space' at the back
of the Jacobean stage. It is here drawn
or slid open to reveal the figures hidden
behind it. Some modern productions
instead make use of a separate cage,
diorama or even cabinet.
artificial figures images created by art.
The language suggests wax images,
which were frequently made at the time
as funerary effigies. At the Globe and
Blackfriars, however, the actors playing
Antonio and the children could easily
have stood in the discovery space to be
revealed when the traverse was drawn. In

1850, only Antonio's figure was revealed;
when the Duchess tried to approach it,
the wall closed. More recent productions have sometimes substituted hospital stretchers or shrouds. (See McLuskie
and Uglow, 151.)

55 **piece** Antonio's effigy, which is presumably missing a hand

57 **directly** plainly, immediately

59 **recovered** recoverèd

61 **stay** linger (on earth)

61–4 **wastes . . . dunghill** Some contemporaries accused of witchcraft claimed to
make pictures or effigies of their victims
out of wax or clay, then pierce the figures
with thorns or pins to magically produce
pain or sickness in the corresponding
parts of the victim. Cf. the sensational tes-
timony by the Lancashire witch Elizabeth
Sowtherns (Potts, sig. B3ᵛ). Jonson's
Masque of Queens (1609), 84–6, features
an anti-masque of witches who make a
doll of wax and wool and stick it with
pins to injure their victim; similarly, in
Dekker's *Whore* a wax image of Elizabeth
I is pierced in the heart with pins and
buried in a dunghill (*Whore*, 2.2.168–72).

54.1 *behind a traverse*] *om. Q4*   57–8 know . . . you] *om. Q4*   60 and] and the *Q2*

Stuck with a magical needle and then buried
In some foul dunghill. And yond's an excellent property
For a tyrant, which I would account mercy –

BOSOLA   What's that?   65

DUCHESS

If they would bind me to that lifeless trunk,
And let me freeze to death.

BOSOLA   Come, you must live.

DUCHESS

That's the greatest torture souls feel in hell –
In hell! – that they must live and cannot die.
Portia, I'll new kindle thy coals again
And revive the rare and almost dead example
Of a loving wife.

BOSOLA   Oh, fie! Despair? Remember
You are a Christian.

DUCHESS   The church enjoins fasting;
I'll starve myself to death.

64 **property** the wax figure of Antonio's body, which the Duchess imagines as a prop for a theatrical or state spectacle (Bevington)

66–7 **If . . . death** Binding a living person to a dead body was usually imagined as a punishment, as in Virgil's *Aeneid*, 8.485–8, where the tyrant Mezentius used it as a form of torture. Contemporaries also saw it as an emblem of loveless marriage, as in the explanatory poem accompanying Geoffrey Whitney's emblem (Fig. 11, p. 49).

66 **trunk** torso

69 **In hell** There is heavy punctuation after this phrase in Q1, which suggests that it is an emphatic repetition of the previous phrase (68) rather than the beginning of a new clause that would read 'In hell that they must live'. Either reading is possible.

70–2 **Portia . . . wife** Portia, wife of the Brutus who helped to assassinate Julius Caesar, choked herself to death with hot coals after her husband's defeat and death, or shortly before, as in Shakespeare's version; cf. *JC* 4.3.153–5.

72–3 **Despair . . . Christian** The temptation to despair was considered particularly dangerous to those facing death because it could lead to eternal damnation. Bosola implies that, as a Christian, the Duchess should not despair because to do so would be to deny the saving power of divine grace.

73 **church enjoins fasting** The Roman Catholic Church required ('enjoined') abstinence from meat on designated days, and even in Protestant England meat was officially banned on Wednesdays and Fridays, though the ban was widely flouted.

65] *Q1 lines* mercy, / that? /   66 lifeless] *Q4;* liueles *Q1;* livelesse *Q2*   67] *Q1 lines* death. / liue. / 72–4] *Q1 lines* wife. / remember / Christian. / fasting: / death. / sorrow; /

263

BOSOLA   Leave this vain sorrow.
Things being at the worst begin to mend.   75
The bee when he hath shot his sting into your hand
May then play with your eyelid.
DUCHESS   Good comfortable fellow,
Persuade a wretch that's broke upon the wheel
To have all his bones new set. Entreat him live,
To be executed again. Who must dispatch me?   80
I account this world a tedious theatre,
For I do play a part in't 'gainst my will.
BOSOLA
Come, be of comfort. I will save your life.
DUCHESS
Indeed, I have not leisure to tend so small a business.
BOSOLA
Now, by my life I pity you.
DUCHESS   Thou art a fool then,   85
To waste thy pity on a thing so wretched
As cannot pity it. I am full of daggers.
Puff! Let me blow these vipers from me.

[*Enter*] SERVANT.

76–7 two hexameter lines; for the thought, cf. *Heptameron*, 196, where almost identical language appears as prose rather than verse: 'The Bee, when he hath lefte his stinge in your hand without dainger may playe with your eye lidde.'

78 that's . . . wheel who has multiple fractures as a result of being tortured upon a wheel that stretches and disjoins the limbs

80 To be only so that he can be dispatch kill, finish off

87 it itself. The Duchess imagines herself as depersonalized to the point of being a mere object.

full of daggers expressing either her internal pain or her suppressed hostility towards her persecutors

88 vipers presumably equivalent to the daggers from the previous line: the Duchess seeks to relieve her inner torment by blowing it away.

88 SD Q1 does not indicate when the servant enters. Some editors have the Duchess turn suddenly in the following line to address a servant already onstage. But if the Duchess is alone onstage, alternately with Bosola (18ff.), Ferdinand (30ff.) and Bosola (53ff.), the servant should enter only at 88, specifically to offer her assistance.

77] *Q1 lines* eye-lyd. / fellow /   81–2] *om. Q4*   85] *Q1 lines* you. / then, /   87 it] it self *Q4*
88 SD] *Q4; Seruants.* | *0 SD Q1*

What are you?

SERVANT　　　　　　One that wishes you long life.

DUCHESS

I would thou wert hanged for the horrible curse　　　90
Thou hast given me. I shall shortly grow one
Of the miracles of pity. I'll go pray –
No, I'll go curse.

BOSOLA　　　　　　Oh, fie!

DUCHESS　　　　　　　　　　I could curse the stars –

BOSOLA

Oh, fearful!

DUCHESS

– And those three smiling seasons of the year　　　95
Into a Russian winter; nay, the world
To its first chaos.

BOSOLA

Look you – the stars shine still.

DUCHESS　　　　　　　　　　Oh, but you must
Remember my curse hath a great way to go.
Plagues that make lanes through largest families　　100
Consume them!

91 Brown has the servant exit after *me*, presumably in fright at the Duchess's threatening language.
92 **miracles of pity** objects for extreme compassion on the part of the viewer
95 **three smiling seasons** spring, summer and autumn, which were frequently depicted allegorically as charming women
97 **chaos** Cf. *Oth* 3.3.92: 'Chaos is come again.'
98 **Look . . . still** Bosola's assertion may be an example of his habitual cynicism about the indifference of the universe to human suffering, or a demonstration that the Duchess's curse at 93 is impotent. Alternatively, it could be an uncharacteristic attempt to inspire hope in the Duchess – the stars that seem so malevolent to her now may yet shine benevolently upon her.
98–9 **Oh . . . go** i.e. the stars are still visible because her lethal curse has not reached them yet. (The Duchess reaffirms the power of the curse she uttered at 93.)
100–1 **Plagues . . . them** The Duchess may be continuing her invective against the stars, or specifically cursing her brothers.
100 **make lanes** create a wide path of destruction; cf. *Bussy*, 3.2.469: 'a murthering piece, making lanes in armies'.

89] *Q1 lines* you? / life. /　90 I] *om. Q4*　91 me.] me. *Exit Servant.* | *Brown* 92–3] *this edn; Q1 lines* No, / curse: / fye ; / Starres. /　98–104 Look … them.] *om. in performance Q4*　98–9 Oh … go] *Dyce; one line Q1*　101] *Q1 lines* them: / Lady: / tyrants /

BOSOLA   Fie, lady!

DUCHESS   Let them, like tyrants,
Never be remembered but for the ill they have done.
Let all the zealous prayers of mortified churchmen
Forget them.

BOSOLA   Oh, uncharitable!

DUCHESS

Let heaven, a little while, cease crowning martyrs   105
To punish them.
Go – howl them this, and say I long to bleed. *sententia*
'It is some mercy when men kill with speed.'

                         Exit [followed by Servant].

[*Enter* FERDINAND.]

FERDINAND

Excellent! As I would wish: she's plagued in art.
These presentations are but framed in wax   110
By the curious master in that quality,
Vincentio Lauriola, and she takes them

---

103 **mortified** pious, otherworldly
105 Let heaven stop making new saints
(with the suggestion that new saints
appear in the firmament as new stars)
(Weis).
108 commonplace echoing Seneca, 2.5.3.
Cf. *White Devil*, 1.1.56–7: 'And would
account them nobly mercifull / Would
they dispatch me quicklie'.
108 SD1 *Exit . . . Servant* The Duchess
may exit alone; adding the servant
here continues his role as would-be
protector of her, and leaves Bosola
and Ferdinand alone to resume their
clandestine conversation at 109.
109–10 Although the printed text's SD
at 54 has earlier apprised readers that
Ferdinand's horrific tableau is merely

sculpture, this is the first moment that
the theatrical audience is given the
same information. During the 'discovery' of the tableau at 54 SD, Ferdinand
was evidently watching voyeuristically,
perhaps from the place where Bosola
had hidden himself earlier if he did
not exit the stage completely at 29 (see
29 SD1n.).
110 **framed in wax** Wax effigies of notables were borne on their coffins during
funeral processions, as in the death of
Prince Henry (1612).
111 **curious** careful, ingenious
     quality skill
112 **Vincentio Lauriola** possibly a fic-
tional name, since no such Italian
master has been identified

103–4] *this edn; Q1 lines* mortefied / them, / vncharitable: / 105–7] *om. in performance Q4* 106–7]
one line Q1 108 'It . . . speed.'] (It . . . speed.) SD1] *Lucas (subst.)* SD2] *Q4* 109 in] *by
Q4* 111–12 By . . . Lauriola] *om. Q4*

For true substantial bodies.

BOSOLA   Why do you do this?

FERDINAND

To bring her to despair.

BOSOLA   Faith, end here

And go no farther in your cruelty.   115
Send her a penitential garment to put on
Next to her delicate skin, and furnish her
With beads and prayer books.

FERDINAND   Damn her! That body of hers,
While that my blood ran pure in't, was more worth
Than that which thou wouldst comfort, called a soul.   120
I will send her masques of common courtesans,
Have her meat served up by bawds and ruffians,
And, 'cause she'll needs be mad, I am resolved
To remove forth the common hospital
All the mad folk, and place them near her lodging.   125
There let them practise together, sing and dance,
And act their gambols to the full o'th' moon.

114 **Faith** in faith
116 **penitential garment** such as a hair
    shirt, worn next to the skin by some
    Christians to 'mortify the flesh'
118 **beads** rosary
118–19 **body . . . in't** Ferdinand conflates
    his and the Duchess's body and blood.
120 **called a soul** Ferdinand's language
    suggest that he fails to credit the exist-
    ence of the human soul. At the time,
    this would have been considered a
    form of atheism: to deny the soul was
    to deny God.
121 **masques . . . courtesans** The usual
    performers in court masques were
    titled aristocrats, not common prosti-
    tutes. Cf. 4.2, where Ferdinand sends
    the Duchess a masque of madmen.
123 **needs be mad** must be insane; must

be made insane. Ferdinand continues
to conflate himself with his sister (see
118–19): if he is going insane, then he
must also drive her insane.
124 **remove forth** take from
    common hospital community shel-
    ter. In London, the insane were housed
    at Bethlehem hospital, popularly
    known as 'Bedlam'.
126 **practise together** with sexual impli-
    cations; cf. *White Devil*, 2.1.109, where
    Giovanni is jokingly accused of 'prac-
    tising your pike'.
127 **full o'th' moon** The mad were
    believed to be particularly unruly during
    a full moon, and hence were called 'luna-
    tic' from Latin *luna*, moon. In *Northward
    Ho!*, 4.3, the keeper of the Bedlam mad-
    men is named 'Full-moone'.

113–14] *Q1 lines* Bodies. / this? / despaire. / here: /   114 Faith] (*Faith*)   118] *Q1 lines* bookes. /
hers, /   121 common] *om. Q4*

If she can sleep the better for it, let her.
Your work is almost ended.

BOSOLA   Must I see her again?

FERDINAND
    Yes.

BOSOLA   Never.

FERDINAND   You must.

BOSOLA   Never in mine own shape.   130
    That's forfeited by my intelligence
    And this last cruel lie. When you send me next,
    The business shall be comfort.

FERDINAND   Very likely!
    Thy pity is nothing of kin to thee. Antonio
    Lurks about Milan. Thou shalt shortly thither   135
    To feed a fire as great as my revenge,
    Which ne'er will slack till it have spent his fuel.
    'Intemperate agues make physicians cruel.'   *Exeunt.*

4.2   [*Enter*] DUCHESS [*and*] CARIOLA.

DUCHESS
    What hideous noise was that?

130–2 **Never . . . lie** Bosola can't appear as himself before the Duchess because she is now aware of his complicity with her brothers.

131 **intelligence** spying

132 **this . . . lie** Productions of the play sometimes clarify these words by making use of the severed hand, as in a 1976 Los Angeles staging where Bosola picked up the hand to underscore *this* (Gunby).

134 **of kin to** like

137 **spent his fuel** i.e. brought Antonio to ashes

138 proverbial: 'A desperate disease must have a desperate cure' (Dent, D357*); Ferdinand apparently sees himself as a physician 'curing' Antonio's and the Duchess's deceit by persecuting them. But in Webster's wording the disease could also be the physician's: Ferdinand is *cruel* to them because he suffers from an 'intemperate ague'.

4.2 Location: Amalfi

1 **noise** Gunby specifies 'Discordant singing within' but the noise could be banging, weird cries or the dragging of chains. In some productions, the

---

129–30] *Q1 lines* ended. / againe? / Neuer. / must. / shape, /   132 cruel lie] Cruelty *Q4*   133] *Q1 lines* comfort. / likely, /   137–8] *ital. Q4*   138 'Intemperate . . . cruel.'] ("Intemperate . . . cruell.*); Intemperate . . . cruel. *Q3*   **4.2**] *(SCENA II.)*   0 SD] *Q4 (subst.); Duchesse, Cariola, Seruant, Madmen, Bosola, Executioners, Ferdinand. | Q1*   1] *Q1 lines* that? / consort /

CARIOLA   'Tis the wild consort
Of madmen, lady, which your tyrant brother
Hath placed about your lodging. This tyranny,
I think, was never practised till this hour.

DUCHESS
Indeed, I thank him: nothing but noise and folly   5
Can keep me in my right wits, whereas reason
And silence make me stark mad. Sit down.
Discourse to me some dismal tragedy.

CARIOLA
Oh, 'twill increase your melancholy.

DUCHESS   Thou art deceived.
To hear of greater grief would lessen mine.   10
This is a prison.

CARIOLA   Yes, but you shall live
To shake this durance off.

DUCHESS   Thou art a fool.
The robin redbreast and the nightingale
Never live long in cages.

CARIOLA   Pray, dry your eyes.
What think you of, madam?

DUCHESS   Of nothing. When I muse thus,   15

---

offstage noise of madmen is heard at intervals throughout the scene.
consort musical group; gathering
2–3 **tyrant . . . tyranny** Cariola characterizes Ferdinand's abuse in political terms: a *tyrant* was a ruler who was dangerous because of weakness – an inability to master his passions (in Ferdinand's case, choler and 'black bile' or melancholy).
8 **Discourse** tell
11 **This . . . prison** either a comment or a question, as in Q1 (see t.n.). It seems unlikely that the Duchess would fail to recognize that she was in her own palace: she can be seen as comment-

ing on the discrepancy between the luxurious setting and her actual state of confinement.
12 **durance** imprisonment; punishment
13 **robin . . . nightingale** the first of several bird images in this scene, all of them relating to imprisonment – of the Duchess in her palace, of the soul in the body or of the soul imprisoned on earth – as in Bosola's 'lark in a cage' (125); cf. also Bosola's earlier comment about birds in a 'net' (3.5.101–2).
15 **think . . . of** think about
15–16 **When . . . sleep** Evidently the Duchess is daydreaming.

9] *Q1 lines* mellancholly. / deceiu'd, /   11 prison.] prison? *Q1*   15–16] *this edn; Q1 lines* nothing: / sleepe. / open? /

I sleep.

CARIOLA   Like a madman, with your eyes open?

DUCHESS

Dost thou think we shall know one another

In th'other world?

CARIOLA   Yes, out of question.

DUCHESS

Oh, that it were possible we might

But hold some two days' conference with the dead!   20

From them I should learn somewhat, I am sure,

I never shall know here. I'll tell thee a miracle:

I am not mad yet, to my cause of sorrow.

Th' heaven o'er my head seems made of molten brass;

The earth of flaming sulphur, yet I am not mad.   25

I am acquainted with sad misery,

As the tanned galley slave is with his oar:

Necessity makes me suffer constantly,

And custom makes it easy. Who do I look like now?

CARIOLA

Like to your picture in the gallery: 30

A deal of life in show, but none in practice;

Or rather like some reverend monument

Whose ruins are even pitied.

18 **other world** afterlife
  out of without
20 **conference** conversation
21 **somewhat** something
23 **to my cause of** which causes me
24–5 **heaven . . . sulphur**   Cf.
  Deuteronomy, 28.23, part of a list of
  divine punishments: 'And thine heaven
  that is over thine head, shall be brass,
  and the earth that is under thee, yron.'
27 **galley slave** Cf. Bosola's past in that
  role (1.1.70) and Serres, 817, where an
  imprisoned noblewoman uses almost
  exactly the Duchess's wording. It was

not uncommon in the period for civil-
ians captured by Ottoman Turks or
pirates to end up rowing in the galleys, where they would be *tanned* by
constant exposure to the sun. Cf. *Fair
Maid*, 5.3.202–3, where Prospero says
he 'tugd at the oare' for twelve years as
'a prisoner to the *Turkish* gallies'.
30 **gallery** long hallway where family
  portraits were often hung
31 **deal** portion; quantity
32–3 **reverend . . . pitied** anticipates the
  setting of 5.3, a ruined abbey
33 **even** regularly; properly

16 Like a madman] Mad man like *Q4*   17–35 Dost . . . tragedy] *om. Q4*   17 another] *(*an other*)*
24 o'er] *(*ore*)*

DUCHESS   Very proper;
And Fortune seems only to have her eyesight
To behold my tragedy. How now –   35
What noise is that?

[*Enter*] SERVANT.

SERVANT   I am come to tell you
Your brother hath intended you some sport.
A great physician, when the Pope was sick
Of a deep melancholy, presented him
With several sorts of madmen, which wild object,   40
Being full of change and sport, forced him to laugh,
And so th'impostume broke. The selfsame cure
The duke intends on you.
DUCHESS   Let them come in.

[*Enter*] MADMEN.

34–5 **Fortune . . . tragedy** Cf. the wed-
    ding scene (1.2.400–1 and n.), where
    the Duchess impersonated blind
    Fortune. Now the roles are reversed
    and Fortune becomes a spectator for
    the Duchess's fall, implied by the omi-
    nous word *tragedy*.
37 **intended you** decided to offer you
38–42 **physician . . . broke** A doctor
    cured the Pope's madness as one would
    drain a boil (imagining melancholy to be
    like a physical infection – an *impostume*,
    pustule or abscess). Ferdinand's pro-
    posed cure resonates with a number of
    imagined stage cures for insanity in plays
    of the period. In *Nice Valour*, friends
    and family attempt to cure the madman
    by enacting in reality what he sees in his
    delusions; at the other end of the spec-
    trum from benignity to cruelty, Lollio
    in *Changeling* uses a whip to control the
    counterfeit madman Franciscus.

43 SD Some editors have the madmen
    enter at 59, after the servant's brief
    introduction of each, but Q4 calls
    for them to enter here, evidently one
    '*Mad-Man*' at a time (see t.n.), so that
    each can be described as he enters, no
    doubt to comic effect. In more recent
    productions, by contrast, the madmen
    often enter together and crowd about
    the Duchess in a threatening manner.
    Having them enter at 43 in obedience
    to the Duchess's command suggests
    that she preserves a vestige of her
    agency. The Q2 reading 'Let me come
    in' (43 t.n.) suggests, instead, that the
    Duchess goes to them. The dance at
    113 SD calls for eight madmen, all of
    whom presumably enter at 43, but the
    precise number could well depend on
    the number of actors available. All of
    the madmen probably doubled other
    roles (see List of Roles, 18n.).

36] *Q1 lines* that? / you, /   SD] *Q4; Seruant,* | *0 SD Q1*   43] *Q1 lines* you. / in. /   them] me *Q2;*
'em *Q4*   SD] *Dyce; Mad-men* | *0 SD Q1; Enter Mad-Man.* | *Q4*

271

SERVANT

    There's a mad lawyer and a secular priest,
    A doctor that hath forfeited his wits   45
    By jealousy; an astrologian
    That in his works said such a day o'th' month
    Should be the day of doom and, failing of't,
    Ran mad; an English tailor crazed i'th' brain
    With the study of new fashion; a gentleman usher   50
    Quite beside himself with care to keep in mind
    The number of his lady's salutations,
    Or 'how do you' she employed him in each morning;
    A farmer, too, an excellent knave in grain,
    Mad 'cause he was hindered transportation.   55

---

44 **mad lawyer** a common figure onstage at the time, as though the enormous lies allegedly required in the normal conduct of the profession regularly led to a disconnection from reality. Cf. Penitent Brothel in *Mad World* and Tangle in Middleton's *Phoenix*.
  secular priest a priest living in the world and under the jurisdiction of a bishop, as opposed to a 'regular' priest, a member of an order like the Jesuits; *secular* could also suggest 'irreligious'.
45 **forfeited his wits** been driven mad
46 **astrologian** astrologer
48 **day of doom** Judgement Day; the end of the world
  failing of't being mistaken
49–50 **English . . . fashion** The *tailor* was a common butt of jokes; this one lost his wits as a result of trying to keep up with the English craze for up-to-the-minute styles in clothing, also much satirized onstage. Cf. *Fair Maid*, 4.2.155–8, where the Man in the Moon is presented as a lunatic, an English tailor 'that stands there starke naked . . . cutting out of new fashions'. According to Cordatus in *Every*

Man Out, 1.2.33ff., a young man cannot claim to be a gentleman of the time unless he has sold his ancestral lands to buy 'two or three trunks of apparel' and mix with London gallants who 'flourish in the spring of the fashion'.
50 **usher** doorkeeper
51–3 The usher, charged with introducing guests, is driven mad by the *number* of guests or the confusing number of particularized forms of address or '*how do you*'s he must remember when correctly introducing each of his mistress's visitors (a witty reference to overblown rituals of politeness among courtiers and those who emulated them).
54 **knave in grain** scoundrel who deals in grain; deep-dyed villain (Brown)
55 **hindered transportation** prevented from exporting grain and therefore dealt a financial blow; topical reference to a 1613 proclamation forbidding export in time of scarcity (Larkin and Hughes, 285). Cf. Webster, *Characters*, 'An Ingrosser of Corne' (Webster, 3.474–5).

46 an astrologian] A *French* Prophet *Q4*   47 in . . . said] *om. Q4*   50 fashion] fashions *Q2*   52 lady's] (Ladies)   53 do you] *d'ye's* | *Q4*   55 hindered] (hindred)

And let one broker that's mad loose to these,
You'd think the devil were among them.

DUCHESS

Sit, Cariola. – Let them loose when you please,
For I am chained to endure all your tyranny.

Here by a Madman this song is sung, to a dismal kind of
music.

> Oh, let us howl some heavy note,   60
>   Some deadly, dogged howl,
> Sounding as from the threatening throat
>   Of beasts and fatal fowl –
> As ravens, screech owls, bulls and bears
>   We'll bill and bawl our parts   65
> Till yerksome noise have cloyed your ears
>   And corrosived your hearts.
> At last, whenas our choir wants breath,
>   Our bodies being blest,
> We'll sing like swans to welcome death,   70
>   And die in love and rest.

56 **broker** one who acts as a middleman in bargaining (and is therefore well situated to wreak havoc among the madmen)

59 **chained** like the chained madmen who, unlike the Duchess, are about to be unshackled (*Let them loose*, 58). Cf. 1.2.332, where Antonio described the proper housing for the mad as 'chains and close-pent rooms'.

59 SD Some editors specify '1 Madman' as the singer of the song but any of the madmen could perform it. A contemporary setting for this song has survived. Cf. the discussion in Gunby, 706–13, and Appendix 3 below, where the setting, which includes weird chromatics appropri-ate to madness, is reproduced.

63 **fatal fowl** birds of prey

65 **bill** utter a bird cry; bellow (frequent-ly emended to Q2–4's 'bell', bark or roar); chop, hack, mutilate

66 **yerksome** may simply be 'irksome', but the 'yerk' spelling ominously recalls Iago, 'yerked [i.e. stabbed] him here, under the ribs' (*Oth* 1.2.5)

67 **corrosived** corroded

68 **whenas** when
wants is out of

69 **blest** by the imagined priest presiding over the services at which the mad 'choir' is singing

70 **swans** proverbially believed to sing just before their death; cf. Dent, S1028*.

60–71] *ital. Q1*   61 deadly, dogged] *(deadly-dogged)*   62 threatening] *(threatning)*   64 screech owls]
(Schrich-owles)   65 bill] *bell | Q2*   66 yerksome] *Irksome | Q4*   67 corrosived] *(corasiu'd)*

1 MADMAN   Doomsday not come yet? I'll draw it nearer by a perspective, or make a glass that shall set all the world on fire upon an instant. I cannot sleep; my pillow is stuffed with a litter of porcupines.   75

2 MADMAN   Hell is a mere glass house, where the devils are continually blowing up women's souls on hollow irons, and the fire never goes out.

3 MADMAN   I will lie with every woman in my parish the tenth night. I will tithe them over like haycocks.   80

4 MADMAN   Shall my 'pothecary outgo me because I am a cuckold? I have found out his roguery: he makes alum

---

72 SP evidently the astrologer, since he is still obsessed with doomsday (46–9). Beginning with Q4, some editors specify '*Astrologer*' in the SP; this edition follows Q1 in leaving the madmen unidentified by profession in the speech prefixes.

73 **perspective** telescope; see 2.4.16n.

73–4 **glass . . . fire** evidently a giant magnifying glass

74–5 **pillow . . . porcupines** suggesting extreme disquiet; cf. *White Devil*, 1.2.71–2, where the cuckolded Camillo's pillow is stuffed with 'horne-shavings'.

76 SP identified by Q4 as '*Taylor*' and by Lucas as '*Lawyer*'; Lucas's conjecture makes more sense in the light of 93–4.

76 **glass house** factory for glass-blowing; for audiences at Blackfriars this would have been a local reference, since a glassworks, frequently likened to hell in plays of the period, was nearby. Cf. 2.2.6, where the glass house is associated with pregnancy. In *White Devil*, 1.2.125–7, glass-blowers' fires are associated with lust.

77 **irons** glass-blowers' pipes

79 SP identified by Q4 as '*Priest*', which

is appropriate in view of his plan to *tithe* the parish – collect the 10 per cent set aside for the church – by sleeping with each woman parishioner one night out of ten. Tithing was controversial in the England of the period; many dissenters objected to being required to tithe in support of the established church.

80 **haycocks** haystacks, a more traditional farm product for tithing. Here and below at *cuckold* (82) and *woodcock's* (87) the Q1 spellings highlight a series of bawdy puns on 'cock' or penis (see t.n.).

81 SP identified by Q4 and some recent editors as '*Doctor*'; he is routinely outsmarted by an apothecary and is called *mad doctor* at 98.

82–3 **alum . . . urine** Ammonia from urine was regularly used to crystallize *alum*, a compound that because of its astringent qualities was used to cure sore throats and other minor inflammations. The implication may be that the apothecary is bypassing the usual elaborate chemical process by which alum was manufactured and creating a counterfeit version by crystallizing the urea from urine.

---

72 SP] *Astro.* | *Q4*   74 upon] in *Q4*   75 litter] (littour)   76+ SP MADMAN] (*Mad.*)   76 SP] *Taylor* | *Q4*   77 women's] mens *Q2*   79 SP] *Priest* | *Q4*   80 haycocks] (hay-cockes)   81 SP] *Doct.* | *Q4*   82 cuckold] (Cuck-old)   alum] (allom)

of his wife's urine and sells it to Puritans that have sore
throats with over-straining.

1 MADMAN   I have skill in heraldry.   85

2 MADMAN   Hast?

1 MADMAN   You do give for your crest a woodcock's head
with the brains picked out on't; you are a very ancient
gentleman.

3 MADMAN   Greek is turned Turk – we are only to be   90
saved by the Helvetian translation.

1 MADMAN   Come on, sir – I will lay the law to you.

2 MADMAN   Oh, rather lay a corrosive; the law will eat to
the bone.

3 MADMAN   He that drinks but to satisfy nature is   95
damned.

4 MADMAN   If I had my glass here, I would show a sight
should make all the women here call me mad doctor.

1 MADMAN   What's he, a ropemaker?

83–4 **Puritans . . . over-straining** a
stock joke during the period: Puritans
were imagined to strain their voices
from too much singing of psalms.

84 **with** from

87–8 **woodcock's . . . on't** a mock coat-
of-arms implying lunacy because of
the *picked brains* and folly because
the woodcock was a bird very easily
caught

88 **very ancient** implies lunacy and folly
are hereditary in the family

90 **Greek . . . Turk** True religion (*Greek*)
has turned to apostasy (*Turk*, with reference to the 1453 fall of Constantinople
to the Ottoman Turks).

91 **Helvetian translation** the Calvinist
Geneva Bible, preferred by leftward-
leaning Protestants because of its
strongly Reformist interpretations of
scripture

92 **lay** lay down; expound

93–4 implying that the law is more
destructive than the abuses it purports
to correct

95–6 suggests that the Puritan is an
alcoholic, since he invents doctrinal
support for drinking in excess

97–8 **If . . . doctor** He may use a perspective glass, as at 73, but there its
user was the First Madman; this *glass*
may be a device that shows a pornographic image, hence the women's
anticipated reaction.

99 **he** most likely the priest, since the
Second Madman goes on to specify
that he takes visitors on tours of
the churchyard and has the lascivious interest in women indicated at
79–80
ropemaker stigmatized because
closely linked to the hangman

---

83 wife's urine] *(wiues vrin)*   85 heraldry] *(Harroldry)*   86+ SP 2 MADMAN] *(2.)*   87+ SP 1
MADMAN] *(1.)*   87 woodcock's] *(wood-cockes)*   90+ SP 3 MADMAN] *(3.)*   93 corrosive] *(corazi-
ue)*   97+ SP 4 MADMAN] *(4.)*   99–102] *om. Q4*

2 MADMAN No, no, no – a snuffling knave that while   100
he shows the tombs will have his hand in a wench's
placket.

3 MADMAN Woe to the caroche that brought home my
wife from the masque at three o'clock in the morning!
It had a large feather bed in it.   105

4 MADMAN I have pared the devil's nails forty times,
roasted them in raven's eggs, and cured agues with
them.

3 MADMAN Get me three hundred milch bats to make
possets to procure sleep.   110

4 MADMAN All the college may throw their caps at
me. I have made a soap-boiler costive. It was my
masterpiece.

---

100 **snuffling** breathing heavily through the nose; speaking nasally, which may imply hypocrisy: contemporary Puritans were sometimes characterized as singing their hymns in a disagreeably nasal voice.

102 **placket** slit at the top of a skirt; bawdy reference to vagina

103–5 Evidently the priest's wife had used her attendance at a court masque as an occasion for sexual dalliance. Jokes about courtiers seducing citizens' wives were popular during the period, as was the charge that the privacy afforded by coaches allowed sexual activity: cf. *Match Me*, 2.4.109–10, where a coach is called a 'Bawdy house . . . / That runs on foure wheeles'. The priest here, if married, is clearly English, not Italian; his cuckolding is appropriate given his own philandering. The lines could also be transferred to any of the other madmen.

106–8 Nail pairings were a frequent ingredient in magic rituals; here the mad doctor admits to practising

medicine with demonic assistance. 'To pare the Devil's nails' was also proverbial, meaning to curb his power (Dent, N12*).

109 **milch bats** bats kept for milking (like cows)

110 **possets** warm drinks made from milk, sherry and spices, possibly intended by the priest as an aid to his seduction of parish women. Newly married couples traditionally drank *possets* to kindle their spirits for the sexual initiation that followed; cf. *Maid's Tragedy*, 4.2.51–69, where the wedding posset is said to put blushes in the bride's cheeks.

111 **throw their caps** celebrate, as modern collegians throw their caps in the air at graduation. The physician imagines himself lauded by his old college for performing the impossible – making a manufacturer of soap constipated (*costive*, 112), since they usually suffered from the opposite ailment. Cf. *Quiet Life*, 5.1.60: 'I may turn *Soap-boyler*, I have a loose body' (Webster, 3.114).

103 caroche] *(Caroach)*; Coach *Q4*

Here the dance, consisting of eight Madmen with music
answerable thereunto, after which

BOSOLA, *like an old man, enters.* *derait*

DUCHESS
Is he mad too?

SERVANT   Pray question him. I'll leave you.
                              [*Exeunt Servant and Madmen.*]

BOSOLA
I am come to make thy tomb.

DUCHESS   Ha? My tomb?   115
Thou speakst as if I lay upon my deathbed,
Gasping for breath. Dost thou perceive me sick?

BOSOLA
Yes, and the more dangerously since thy sickness is
    insensible.

DUCHESS
Thou art not mad, sure. Dost know me?   *been stripped*

BOSOLA   Yes.   *of everything*

DUCHESS   Who am I?

BOSOLA   Thou art a box of wormseed – at best, but a   120
    when you die you become
    worm food

113.1–2 *music ... thereunto* appropriate
   music (for a dance by madmen); the
   musical score has not survived.
113.3 *like* disguised as; perhaps Bosola
   bears the robe and sickle associated
   with Death. He later describes himself as a 'tomb-maker' in the sense
   of 'gravedigger'; cf. the sexton who
   is a gravedigger in *Hamlet* (5.1). The
   sexton's duties would typically involve
   digging graves and ringing church bells,
   as Bosola rings his smaller bell below at
   170 and ff. Q4 specifies that he enters
   '*like an Old Bell-Man*', or town watch-
   man, who typically also carried a bell.

He must also wear a mask, because the
   Duchess does not recognize him.
114 SD Since the exit of the madmen
   is not specified in Q1, a few of them
   could remain onstage to eavesdrop on
   part or all of the dialogue that follows.
118 As a verse line, this is a hexameter
   crowded with extra unaccented syllables; it could alternatively be understood as prose, like Bosola's following
   speech (120ff.).
120 **Thou ... wormseed** Bosola likens
   the Duchess's body to a mere container
   for seeds that will 'germinate' into maggots when her body putrefies after death;

113.1 *the ... Madmen*] *is a Dance of Mad-Men,* | *Q4*   113.3 *man*] *Bell-Man,* | *Q4*   114–15] *Q1 lines*
to? / you. / tombe. / tombe? /   114] *om. Q4*   too] *(to)*   SD] *Dyce*   119] *Q1 lines* me? / I? /

salvatory of green mummy. What's this flesh? A little
crudded milk, fantastical puff-paste. Our bodies are
weaker than those paper prisons boys use to keep
flies in; more contemptible, since ours is to preserve
earthworms. Didst thou ever see a lark in a cage? Such   125
is the soul in the body: this world is like her little turf
of grass; and the heaven o'er our heads, like her looking
glass, only gives us a miserable knowledge of the small
compass of our prison.

DUCHESS

Am not I thy Duchess?

BOSOLA   Thou art some great woman, sure,   130
for riot begins to sit on thy forehead, clad in grey hairs,
twenty years sooner than on a merry milkmaid's. Thou
sleepest worse than if a mouse should be forced to take

---

wormseed could also be a plant used to
cure intestinal worms (Brown).

121 **salvatory . . . mummy** box for
a medicine prepared from mummified corpses; presumably the mummy
is *green* because the Duchess is not
yet dead. Cf. Donne's misogynist
characterization of women in 'Love's
Alchemy', 24, as 'mummy possessed'.

122 **crudded milk** implying the body is
composed of thickened milk refined in
the womb. 'Crudded' and 'curded' were
alternative forms of the word. Cf. Donne,
The Second Anniversary: 'This curded
milke, this poore unlettered whelpe, /
My body'; and Job, 10.10: 'Hast thou
not powred me out as mylke? and turned
me to cruds like chese?'
    fantastical puff-paste puff pastry
designed into outlandish shapes, as
was popular during the period; it was
visually striking but extremely fragile.

124–5 **preserve earthworms** Cf. *wormseed* at 120 above – the body as a mere
container for that which will eventually consume it.

125–9 **Didst . . . prison** That the body
is a prison for the soul was proverbial; cf. Fig. 10, p. 47, and Dent,
B497*. The image of the lark in a
cage relates to earlier bird imagery
in the scene (13n.) but is used here
of the plight of the soul on earth, for
whom the whole created universe is
nothing but a cage. Webster imagines a birdcage standing on a lawn
and fitted out with a mirror, so that
the imprisoned soul, imagined as
feminine (*her*, 126, 127), is trapped
between earth and heaven – the
world is the *turf of grass* beneath her
and the heavens are a mere *looking
glass* above her.

129 **compass** dimensions

131 **riot** high living, excess – implying
that an aristocratic lifestyle causes pre-
mature ageing

132–4 **Thou . . . ear**   Cf.   *2H4*
3.1.30: 'Uneasy lies the head that
wears a crown.'

133–4 **mouse . . . ear** proverbial for a
dangerous situation; cf. Dent, M1231.

---

122 crudded] *(cruded); ;* curded *Q2*   125 ever] never *Q2*   130] *this edn; prose Q1*   133 sleepest]
(sleep'st)

up her lodging in a cat's ear. A little infant that breeds
its teeth, should it lie with thee, would cry out as if thou   135
wert the more unquiet bedfellow.

DUCHESS

I am Duchess of Malfi still. — *totally defiant*

BOSOLA

That makes thy sleeps so broken:
'Glories, like glow-worms, afar off shine bright, *sententia*
But looked to near have neither heat nor light.'   140

DUCHESS

Thou art very plain.

BOSOLA

My trade is to flatter the dead, not the living.
I am a tomb-maker.

DUCHESS   And thou com'st to make my tomb?

BOSOLA

Yes.

DUCHESS   Let me be a little merry:
Of what stuff wilt thou make it?   145

BOSOLA

Nay, resolve me first of what fashion.

DUCHESS

Why, do we grow fantastical in our deathbed?

134–5 **breeds its teeth** is teething, and
therefore sleeps poorly
136 **unquiet bedfellow** Cf. Cariola's earlier teasing reference to the Duchess's
disquiet as a bedfellow (3.2.12–13).
137 This is the play's most famous line,
an assertion of the Duchess's continuing identity, inseparable from her title,
as well as heroic stoicism in the face of
persecution.
138 This repeats 132–4: her high rank is
responsible for what Bosola imagines
to be her sleepless state.
139 **Glories** exalted status; halos or

beams of light, especially heavenly
light. 'Like a glow worm' was proverbial (Dent, G142.1). Cf. *White Devil*,
5.1.38–9, where Webster repeats himself verbatim.
140 **looked to near** looked at closely;
looked at too closely
145 **stuff** material
146 **of what fashion** in what style (see
149–55n. below)
147 **fantastical** The Duchess turns
Bosola's word from 122 back to him,
implying it is rather late for extreme
fantasies or extravagances.

134 her] his *Q2*   139–40 'Glories . . . light.'] ("Glories . . . light.)   140 to] too *Q2;* on *Q4*   143–4]
Q1 lines tombe-maker. / tombe? / Yes. / merry, /

Do we affect fashion in the grave?

BOSOLA

Most ambitiously. Princes' images on their tombs
Do not lie, as they were wont, seeming to pray   150
Up to heaven; but with their hands under their cheeks,
As if they died of the toothache. They are not carved
With their eyes fixed upon the stars, but as
Their minds were wholly bent upon the world –
The selfsame way they seem to turn their faces.   155

DUCHESS

Let me know fully, therefore, the effect
Of this thy dismal preparation,
This talk, fit for a charnel.   – *acceptance or death groom he*

BOSOLA   Now I shall.
Here is a present from your princely brothers;
And may it arrive welcome, for it brings   160
Last benefit, last sorrow.

[*Enter*] EXECUTIONERS [*carrying*] *a coffin, cords and a bell.*

DUCHESS   Let me see it.
I have so much obedience in my blood,
I wish it in their veins to do them good.

149–55 refers to a new fashion in tomb design. The older style was for the image of the deceased to be lying on its back praying up to heaven (see the tomb of Elizabeth I, Fig. 6, p. 40); the new style was for the image of the deceased to lie on its side gazing at onlookers and supporting the head on one hand – the so-called 'toothache' position (see the 1610 tomb of Elizabeth Drury, Fig. 7, p. 41).

150 **wont** accustomed to (in the past)
153 **as** as if
154 **bent upon** occupied with
156 **effect** purpose

157 **preparation** pronounced as five syllables
161 SD   Following Q4, some editors specify this entrance at 159, which creates a longer delay before the Duchess's response. Brennan suggests that the coffin is initially shrouded and uncovered by Bosola only at 164, which would account for the women's delayed reaction.
   cords rope
163 **their** the Duchess's brothers' (her speech counters their earlier ravings about her 'corrupted' blood)

153–4] Lucas; *Q1 lines* as their / world, /   158] *Q1 lines* charnell? / shall, /   161] *Q1 lines* sorrow. / it, /   SD] Dyce (subst.); Executioners, | *0 SD Q1; A Coffin, Cords, and a Bell.* | *opp. 159–61 Q1*

BOSOLA

This is your last presence chamber.

CARIOLA

Oh, my sweet lady!

DUCHESS   Peace! It affrights not me.   165

BOSOLA

I am the common bellman

That usually is sent to condemned persons

The night before they suffer.

DUCHESS   Even now thou saidst

Thou wast a tomb-maker.

BOSOLA   'Twas to bring you

By degrees to mortification. Listen: [*Rings the bell.*]   170

Hark, now everything is still –

The screech owl and the whistler shrill,

Call upon our dame aloud

[Handwritten marginal note:] utterly noble in this death scene, given a realistic structure, death only thing which has order in the play

---

164 **This** Bosola could indicate either the
room they are in or the coffin itself.
In an 1850 production one of the
executioners '*uncovers and exhibits the
coffin-lid*' to show her her last 'chamber' (*Acting Copy*, 42).

165 **Peace!** Silence!

166 At this point, Bosola may pick up
the bell brought in by the executioners (Lucas); bellmen traditionally carried bells they would ring at intervals
to assure the populace that all was
well. Beginning in 1605, London bellmen were enlisted to put condemned
Newgate prisoners 'in minde of their
mortalitie' by ringing a hand bell at
midnight 'under Newe-gate, the Night
after their Condemnation' (Nixon, sig.
C4). A John Webster who was almost
certainly the playwright's father was
among the sponsors of the endowment
that created this custom.

168 **suffer** are executed

170 **mortification** alienation from
worldly things appropriate for one
facing death

170 SD Bosola (as bellman) may ring
his bell to punctuate elements of the
speech that follows; cf. *Devil's Law-
Case*, 2.3.61ff., where bells are heard
and two bellmen enter and ring their
bells before Leonora's gate to remind
those present of mortality (Webster,
2.106).

172 **whistler** bird (the whimbrel), whose
call was believed to presage death;
cf. 'The Whistler shrill, that who so
heares, doth dy' (*FQ*, 2.12.36; Brown).

173 **our dame** the Duchess, but Bosola's
possessive suggests she has assumed
a more universal role as a figure of
mortification; *our dame* suggests the
French *Notre Dame*, 'Our Lady', i.e.
the Virgin Mary.

165] *Q1 lines* Lady, / me. /   168–9] *Q1 lines* suffer: / said'st, / tombe-maker? / you /   168 Even] I
Q4   170 SD] *Q4 (subst.)*   171–88] *ital. Q1*   172 screech owl] *(Scritch-Owle)*

And bid her quickly don her shroud.
Much you had of land and rent; 175
Your length in clay's now competent.
A long war disturbed your mind;
Here your perfect peace is signed.
~~Of what is't fools make such vain keeping?~~
Sin their conception, their birth weeping, 180
Their life a general mist of error,
Their death a hideous storm of terror. *Original*
Strew your hair with powders sweet, *Sin*
Don clean linen, bathe your feet,
And, the foul fiend more to check, 185
A crucifix let bless your neck.
'Tis now full tide 'tween night and day;
End your groan and come away.

174 **don her shroud** as the dying some-times did while still alive; cf. John Donne, who, according to Walton, had himself painted in his shroud and kept the picture at his bedside as a *memento mori*. The command is a macabre echo of epithalamia or wedding songs, in which the bride was admonished to get dressed for her wedding (see also pp. 27–8); cf. *Penitential Psalms*, 208, where the poet, addressing God, describes his suffering on earth as 'My bridell chamber, wedded to thy will'.

176 **length in clay** grave
competent sufficient

177 **war** against France, who repeatedly invaded Italy during the Duchess's time; war against the passions or against her duty to her brothers

178 **peace is signed** you have attained peace (imagined as a recently completed treaty)

179 **make . . . keeping** so foolishly strive to hold on to

180 **Sin their conception** According to standard Protestant doctrine (inter-preting Exodus, 20.5, 'visiting the iniquitie of the fathers upon the chil-dren, upon the third *generacion* and upon the fourth of them that hate me'), the taint of original sin was passed from parents to child at the moment of conception.
birth weeping commonplace: the infant's cry at birth was interpreted as a lament for entering into the sinful world.

183 Cf. 3.2.58–9, where the Duchess con-templates hair powder as a way of hiding her age.

186 **let** allow to

187 **full . . . day** midnight; modern sta-tistics confirm that deaths occur with particular frequency at the waning of the tide or in the early hours of the morning, as Bosola seems to consider appropriate.

188 **come away** The phrase carries iron-ic overtones, since it was familiar from ballads and love songs, as in the song by John Dowland (1563–1626), 'Come away, come sweet love'; it was also used in epithalamia of the period to urge the bride to her bridal bed (Brown).

180 Sin] *Lin* | *Q2* 182 terror] *error* | *Q2* 184 bathe] *(bath)*

CARIOLA

Hence villains, tyrants, murderers! Alas,
What will you do with my lady? Call for help!   190

DUCHESS

To whom? To our next neighbours? They are madfolks.

BOSOLA

Remove that noise.   [*Executioners seize Cariola.*]

DUCHESS   Farewell, Cariola.
In my last will I have not much to give.
A-many hungry guests have fed upon me;
Thine will be a poor reversion.

CARIOLA   I will die with her.   195

DUCHESS

I pray thee, look thou giv'st my little boy
Some syrup for his cold, and let the girl
Say her prayers ere she sleep.   [*Cariola is forced off.*]
                    Now – what you please. What death?

BOSOLA

Strangling. Here are your executioners.

DUCHESS

I forgive them.   200
The apoplexy, catarrh or cough o'th' lungs

---

191 **next** nearest

194 **A-many** many (colloquialism)
  fed upon me been fed at my expense (as part of the normal running of an aristocratic household), but also suggests cannibalism or Eucharistic sacrifice: cf. 229 below.

195 **reversion** office attained through the death of its previous holder, used here wryly of the Duchess's diminished estate, as if it were to be inherited by Cariola

196–8 **I . . . sleep** Either the Duchess now recognizes that the figures of her dead children were mere effigies or she has

forgotten their deaths. But see 342, where her joyous reaction to the news that her family is still alive suggests that she had previously considered them dead.

197 **syrup** As Wall suggests, *syrup*, in addition to being used to treat minor ailments, was part of the ritual of death at the time, given to the dying to help make death *sweet* (2.1.66) by domesticating it.

201 **apoplexy** stroke
  catarrh respiratory infection; cerebral haemorrhage
  cough o'th' lungs pneumonia or tuberculosis

192] *Q1 lines* noyse. / *Cariola*, /   SD] *Gunby*   195] *Q1 lines* reuersion. / her. /   198] *this edn; Q1 lines* please, / death? /   SD] *Q4 opp. 197*   201 lungs] *(loongs)*

283

Would do as much as they do.

BOSOLA

Doth not death fright you?

DUCHESS   Who would be afraid on't,

Knowing to meet such excellent company

In th'other world?

BOSOLA   Yet methinks   205

The manner of your death should much afflict you.

This cord should terrify you.

DUCHESS   Not a whit.

What would it pleasure me to have my throat cut

With diamonds, or to be smothered

With cassia, or to be shot to death with pearls?   210

I know death hath ten thousand several doors

For men to take their exits; and 'tis found

They go on such strange geometrical hinges,

You may open them both ways. Any way, for heaven

sake,

So I were out of your whispering. Tell my brothers   215

---

203 **on't** of it
204–5 **Knowing . . . world** Socrates expressed the same sentiment as he was about to die at the hands of the Athenian executioners (Plato, *Apology*, 1.422); contrast 17–20, where the Duchess asked Cariola about the possibility of meeting loved ones in the afterlife as if unsure of the answer.
209 **diamonds** pronounced as three syllables
smothered smotherèd; cf. *Fifty Sermons*, 235, referring to dangerous men who are worse than lycanthropes or 'devouring wolves' because they betray you by pretending to be your confessor or by pretending to confess to you: 'This whisperer . . . strangles

thee with scarfes of silk, he smothers thee with the down of Phoenixes, he stifles thee with a perfume of Ambar.'
211–12 **death . . . exits** Senecan commonplace that was proverbial by Webster's day (Dent, D140*)
213–14 **They . . . ways** They are swinging doors; the same material goods (diamonds, cassia, pearls, 209–10) that are brought into human life to sustain it can also lead us out of life. The doors also 'swing' in the sense that their closing on life is simultaneously an opening to the afterlife.
215 **whispering** gossip, espionage (suggesting the Duchess may now recognize Bosola beneath his disguise)

203] *Q1 lines* you? / on't? /   205] *Q1 lines* world. / thinkes, /   207 a whit] at all *Q4*   211–15 I . . . whispering] *om. Q4*

That I perceive death, now I am well awake,
Best gift is they can give or I can take.
I would fain put off my last woman's fault –
I'd not be tedious to you.

EXECUTIONER We are ready

DUCHESS

Dispose my breath how please you, but my body   220
Bestow upon my women, will you?

EXECUTIONER Yes.

DUCHESS

Pull and pull strongly; for your able strength
Must pull down heaven upon me.
Yet stay – heaven gates are not so highly arched
As princes' palaces; they that enter there   225
Must go upon their knees.   [*Kneels.*]
                    Come, violent death –
Serve for mandragora to make me sleep.
Go tell my brothers, when I am laid out,
They then may feed in quiet.   (*They strangle her.*)

BOSOLA Where's the waiting-woman?

[handwritten: reference to parasites Bosola perv slovenly morals]

216 **awake** in a spiritual sense. The Q1 spelling 'a wake' yields a pun: the Duchess is already participating in her own funeral wake.
218 **woman's fault** Women were proverbially held to be too talkative; cf. Dent, W676: 'A Woman's tongue is the last thing about her that dies.'
220 **Dispose** take order for
224–6 **heaven . . . knees** based on the Christian commonplace that humility is required for salvation; one of many echoes recalling the scene of her marriage, in which the Duchess asked Antonio to 'raise' himself from

his humility to marry her (1.2.327–30)
227 **mandragora** mandrake, used as a narcotic; cf. Ferdinand's claim to have been maddened by a mandrake (2.5.2), and Cleopatra's request for mandragora as a sleep potion (*AC* 1.5.4–5).
229 **feed in quiet** enjoy their meals peacefully; feed off her body without interruption (like the *hungry guests* at 194). Cf. the body of Christ as sacrificial feast.
229 SD Frequently in performance the Duchess puts the cords, or noose, around her own neck.

216 awake] *(*a wake*)* 218 woman's fault] *(*womans-fault*)* 219] *Q1 lines* you. / ready. / 225 princes'] Princely *Q2* 226 SD] *Q4 (subst.) opp. 225* 229] *Q1 lines* quiet. / woman? / SD] *opp. 228–9* quiet *Q1*

Fetch her. Some other strangle the children.					230

[*Exit Executioners.*]

[EXECUTIONER *brings in* CARIOLA.]

Look you: there sleeps your mistress.

CARIOLA								Oh, you are damned

Perpetually for this! My turn is next.

Is't not so ordered?

BOSOLA					Yes, and I am glad

You are so well prepared for't.

CARIOLA					You are deceived, sir.

I am not prepared for't. I will not die.					235

I will first come to my answer and know how

I have offended.

BOSOLA					Come, dispatch her! –

You kept her counsel; now you shall keep ours.

CARIOLA

I will not die. I must not: I am contracted

To a young gentleman.

---

230 **other** could be either singular or plural

230 SD1, SD2 Editors vary markedly in the number of executioners specified as exiting or bringing back Cariola, and in whether or not the executioners strangle the children onstage, adding to the horror of this chaotic scene. McLuskie and Uglow suggest that in the original Globe and Blackfriars productions the children could have been placed in the discovery space and killed there (McLuskie and Uglow, 169). Or the executioners may have 'killed' their wax figures instead, echoing the earlier discovery of the '*artificial figures*' at 4.1.54.1. In 19th-century

productions, the deaths of Cariola and the children were generally cut.

231 **sleeps** as in the 'sleep of death', but suggesting the possibility that the Duchess may yet be alive

you are damned Cariola's *you* could encompass both Bosola and the executioners; Q2's 'thou' (see t.n.) makes Bosola the sole recipient of her curse.

236 **come . . . answer** defend myself against a formal accusation

239–40 **I am . . . gentleman** Cariola's seemingly irrational plea may be based on the hope that, if they believe she has a man available to avenge her, the executioners will be less likely to take her life.

230 SD1] *Brennan* SD2] *Lucas (subst.);* Enter *Cariola.* | *Q4* 231] *Q1 lines* mistris. / damn'd / you are] thou art *Q2* 233 and] *om. Q2* 234] *Q1 lines* for't. / Sir, / 236–7] *this edn; Q1 lines* know / her: / 236 first] *om. Q2* answer] Tryal *Q4* 240] *Q1 lines* Gentle-man. / Ring. /

EXECUTIONER   Here's your wedding ring.   240
    [*Shows a noose.*]

CARIOLA
    Let me but speak with the duke. I'll discover
    Treason to his person.

BOSOLA   Delays! Throttle her.

EXECUTIONER
    She bites and scratches.

CARIOLA   If you kill me now
    I am damned. I have not been at confession
    This two years.

BOSOLA   When?

CARIOLA   I am quick with child!

BOSOLA   Why then   245
    Your credit's saved.   [*They strangle her.*]
                    Bear her into th' next room.
    Let this lie still. [*Exeunt Executioners carrying Cariola's body.*]

    [*Enter* FERDINAND.]

241–2 **discover . . . person** reveal a (fic-
    titious) plot against Ferdinand's life
243 **bites and scratches** The colons
    after both verbs in Q1 (see t.n.) may
    indicate pauses in the executioner's
    speech while he copes with Cariola's
    attempts to escape.
243–5 **If . . . years** In England, the
    condemned were not executed until
    they had received the opportunity
    for absolution. Cf. the Duke's protest
    against the execution of the unrepent-
    ant Barnardine in *MM* 4.3.67–8: 'to
    transport him in the mind he is / Were
    damnable.'
245 **When?** could indicate either shock

at Cariola's long absence from the
    confessional or a testy comment to
    the executioners on their delay in dis-
    patching her
    quick with child A pregnant woman
    was spared execution until after the
    birth of her child.
246 **credit** reputation
247 **this lie still** the Duchess's body
    remain here
247 SD2 The speed of Ferdinand's entry
    suggests he may have been observ-
    ing – possibly from a place visible
    to the audience but concealed from
    those onstage: cf. 4.1.29 SD1n., 4.1.52
    SD2n. and 4.1.109–10n.

SD] *Brennan (subst.)*   242–3] *Q1 lines* person. / throttle-her. / scratches: / now /   243 bites and
scratches] *(*bites: and scratches:*)*   245] *Q1 lines* When, / child. / then, /   When?] *Q2;* When. *Q1;*
When! *Brennan*   246 SD] *Dyce (subst.)*   247–50] *this edn; Q1 lines* dead? / what / pitty, / offended?
/ death / pittied. / Constantly. / weepe? /   247 SD1] *Dyce² (subst.)*   SD2] *Q4;* Ferdinand. | *0 SD
Q1*   247 you'd] *(*You'll'd*)*

FERDINAND   Is she dead?

BOSOLA   She is what you'd have her.

But here begin your pity.

     [*Opens the traverse and*] *shows the Children strangled.*

                 Alas, how have these offended?

FERDINAND

The death of young wolves is never to be pitied.

BOSOLA

Fix your eye here.

FERDINAND   Constantly.

BOSOLA   Do you not weep?   250

Other sins only speak; murder shrieks out.

The element of water moistens the earth,

But blood flies upwards and bedews the heavens.

FERDINAND

Cover her face. Mine eyes dazzle; she died young.

BOSOLA

I think not so. Her infelicity   255

Seemed to have years too many.

---

248 SD Opening the traverse to show Ferdinand the bodies is not specified in Q1 (see t.n.), but if so performed would nicely turn the tables on Ferdinand's tableau for the Duchess in the previous scene (4.1.54 SD). If the children were killed behind the traverse in the discovery space in Globe and Blackfriars productions, as suggested by McLuskie and Uglow, their bodies were already in position (see 230 SD1, SD2n.). Or, if the children's bodies are simply lying at the front of the stage, Bosola need only point at them.

249 **death . . . wolves** proverbial 'The death of a young wolf does never come too soon' (Dent, D145); suggests that Ferdinand thinks of the children's father as a wolf or werewolf, in another unconscious suggestion of incest if he is begin-

ning to think of himself as a wolf.

250 **Constantly** steadfastly, without flinching

251 **murder shrieks out** Cf. Genesis, 4.10: after Cain had murdered Abel, God said, 'The voice of thy brother's blood crieth unto me from the ground.'

254 This line, which consists of three independent clauses, is one of the most famous in the play but has caused difficulty for actors and is sometimes broken up onstage by action between each of the sentences (McLuskie and Uglow, 169).

dazzle are blinded by light, as though he is viewing the sun, perhaps through tears

young The historical Duchess was around 34 at the time of her death.

256 **have . . . many** continue too long

248–9] *om. in performance Q4*   248 SD *Opens . . . and*] *Brennan (subst.)*   *shows . . . strangled*] *opp. 248 Q1*   250] *Q1 lines* Constantly. / weepe? /   256] *Q1 lines* many. / Twinnes: /

FERDINAND   She and I were twins,
And, should I die this instant, I had lived
Her time to a minute.
BOSOLA   It seems she was born first.
You have bloodily approved the ancient truth
That kindred commonly do worse agree   260
Than remote strangers.
FERDINAND   Let me see her face again.
Why didst not thou pity her? What an excellent
Honest man mightest thou have been
If thou hadst borne her to some sanctuary!
Or, bold in a good cause, opposed thyself,   265
With thy advanced sword above thy head,
Between her innocence and my revenge.
I bade thee, when I was distracted of my wits,
Go kill my dearest friend, and thou hast done't.
For let me but examine well the cause: 270
What was the meanness of her match to me?
Only, I must confess, I had a hope,
Had she continued widow, to have gained
An infinite mass of treasure by her death.
And that was the main cause – her marriage –   275
That drew a stream of gall quite through my heart.

[Handwritten margin notes: "showed some real regret and sorrow"; "idea that he hasn't thought through why he killed her"]

257–8 i.e. if she was born a few minutes
    before he was and he dies a few min-
    utes after her, their lives will have been
    the same length.
259 **approved** confirmed
260 **worse** less well
263 **mightest** Although the Q1 read-
    ing is 'might'st' (t.n.) the metre calls
    for a disyllabic word – unless, as at
    other points, Ferdinand's rough diction
    implies extreme perturbation of mind.
266 **advanced** advancèd

273–4 Assuming the Duchess had no
    other heir, Ferdinand and his brother
    the Cardinal would have been next of
    kin. Here, as throughout most of the
    play, her son by her first husband is
    overlooked, but Ferdinand's explana-
    tion is in any case specious.
276 **stream of gall** black bile from the
    liver, which Ferdinand claims has
    overflowed into his heart, causing his
    extreme melancholy; cf. 2–3n. above
    and 2.3.74–5 and n.

258] *Q1 lines* Mynute. / first: /   261] *Q1 lines* strangers. / againe; /   263 mightest] *(*might'st*)*   267
innocence] innocency *Q2* 268 bade] bid *Q4* 269 done't] *(*don't*)* 275 that] what *Q2*

For thee, as we observe in tragedies
That a good actor many times is cursed
For playing a villain's part, I hate thee for't;
And for my sake say, thou hast done much ill, well.   280

BOSOLA

Let me quicken your memory; for I perceive
You are falling into ingratitude. I challenge
The reward due to my service.

FERDINAND

I'll tell thee what I'll give thee.

BOSOLA   Do.

FERDINAND   I'll give thee
A pardon for this murder.

BOSOLA   Ha?

FERDINAND   Yes, and 'tis   285
The largest bounty I can study to do thee.
By what authority didst thou execute
This bloody sentence?

BOSOLA   By yours.

FERDINAND   Mine? Was I her judge?
Did any ceremonial form of law
Doom her to not-being? Did a complete jury   290
Deliver her conviction up i'th' court?
Where shalt thou find this judgement registered
Unless in hell? See – like a bloody fool
Th' hast forfeited thy life, and thou shalt die for't.

277–9 In early performances the role of Ferdinand was taken by the renowned Richard Burbage, chief actor of the King's Men, who frequently played villains, as in this play, and whose lines here would therefore apply to himself.

280 **ill** evil

281 **quicken** revive, stimulate

286 **bounty** gift, favour
   study endeavour

289–91 i.e. she was not properly tried by a jury and condemned before she was executed.

292–3 **Where . . . hell** Only in hell would this be considered justice.

284–5] *this edn; Q1 lines* tell thee, / Doe: / pardon / murther: / 'tis /   288] *Q1 lines* yours / Iudge? / sentence] service *Q2*

BOSOLA

> The office of justice is perverted quite 295
> When one thief hangs another. Who shall dare
> To reveal this?

FERDINAND   Oh, I'll tell thee:

> The wolf shall find her grave and scrape it up –
> Not to devour the corpse, but to discover
> The horrid murder.

BOSOLA   You, not I, shall quake for't. 300

FERDINAND

> Leave me.

BOSOLA   I will first receive my pension.

FERDINAND

> You are a villain.

BOSOLA   When your ingratitude

> Is judge, I am so.

FERDINAND   O horror!

> That not the fear of him which binds the devils
> Can prescribe man obedience. 305
> Never look upon me more.

BOSOLA   Why, fare thee well.

> Your brother and yourself are worthy men.
> You have a pair of hearts are hollow graves,

295–6 **The . . . another** Cf. *Appius and Virginia*, 4.1.240–1 (Webster, 2.558); and Guevara, 3.9, sig. H6ᵛ: 'For much is the office of justice perverted when one thiefe hangeth an other.'

299 **devour the corpse** Cf. the Duchess's earlier remark about her brothers' feeding on her (229).
discover reveal, uncover; cf. *White Devil*, 5.4.97–8, 'But keepe the wolfe far thence, that's foe to men, / For with his nailes hee'l dig them up agen.'

300 **quake** tremble in fear; shake as you hang from the gallows

301 **pension** payment (for services rendered to Ferdinand)

304–5 Not even the fear of God, who can force obedience from devils (or which compels even devils), can make humans obey. Or Ferdinand may mean fear of himself, in which case, in his increasing madness, he now believes that he has power over devils.

306 **Never . . . more** Cf. Ferdinand's earlier words to the Duchess: 'I will never see thee more' (3.2.139).

308 **are** that are

300–2] *Sampson; Q1 lines* murther. / me: / Pention. / villaine: / Ingratitude /

Rotten and rotting others; and your vengeance,
Like two chained bullets, still goes arm in arm.   310
You may be brothers: for treason, like the plague,
Doth take much in a blood. I stand like one
That long hath ta'en a sweet and golden dream:
I am angry with myself now that I wake.

FERDINAND

Get thee into some unknown part o'th' world,   315
That I may never see thee.

BOSOLA   Let me know
Wherefore I should be thus neglected? Sir,
I served your tyranny, and rather strove
To satisfy yourself than all the world;
And, though I loathed the evil, yet I loved   320
You that did counsel it, and rather sought
To appear a true servant than an honest man.

[marginal handwritten note: — wants to be honest but wants wealth and status]

FERDINAND

I'll go hunt the badger by owl-light.
'Tis a deed of darkness.   *Exit.*

BOSOLA

He's much distracted. Off, my painted honour!   325

---

310 **chained bullets** cannon-balls linked
   by a chain so they can be fired together and cause maximum damage in a
   densely crowded area
   arm in arm Bosola now sees the
   resemblance between Ferdinand's perfidy and that of the Cardinal he complained of in 1.1.
311 **may** may well; are indeed
312 **Doth . . . blood** runs in families
313 **ta'en** entered into; adopted as his
   own
317 **Wherefore** for what reason
318–22 Cf. *Arcadia*, book 2, ch. 10, 211–
   12: Tydeus and Telenor, serving a
   tyrant, 'willingly held out the course,
   rather to satisfie him, then al the
   world; and rather to be good friends,

then good men: so as though they did
   not like the evill he did, yet they liked
   him that did the evill.'
323 **by owl-light** in the evening or moon-
   lit night, the preferred time for catching badgers, according to Turberville,
   190
325 **painted honour** Lucas, rejecting the
   disguise, thinks this is metaphorical –
   some badge of office or allegiance that
   Bosola now perceives as specious and
   wishes to divest himself of; if he is still
   masked, however, he may at this point, as
   in the 1980 Manchester Royal Exchange
   production, tear off his mask, which is
   painted because it is false and hypocritical, and he wishes finally to be himself
   (McLuskie and Uglow, 173).

310 two chained] *(two-chain'd); to chain'd Q4*

While with vain hopes our faculties we tire,
We seem to sweat in ice and freeze in fire.
What would I do, were this to do again?
I would not change my peace of conscience
For all the wealth of Europe.   [*Goes to the Duchess.*]
                She stirs! Here's life. –   330
Return, fair soul, from darkness, and lead mine
Out of this sensible hell. – She's warm, she breathes! – *hope*
Upon thy pale lips I will melt my heart *for the*
To store them with fresh colour. – Who's there? *Duchess*
Some cordial drink! – Alas, I dare not call.   335
So pity would destroy pity. Her eye opes,
And heaven in it seems to ope, that late was shut,
To take me up to mercy. – *if she's alive, then she*
will get mercy, worry that
he would go to hell

DUCHESS
    Antonio –
BOSOLA   Yes, madam, he is living.

first thing she thinks of is even she loves

326 **faculties we tire** We exhaust ourselves (by hoping for things that can never come true); we dress or 'attire' ourselves (in vain hopes).

327 commonplace of Petrarchan love poetry; see below, 330–4, which can almost be read as a love scene, at least on Bosola's part.

328 **to do** to be done

330 SD Gunby specifies here '*Duchess moves*'. If she makes a large enough gesture, Bosola could see her move from some distance, but he may be standing above her, and the audience may initially be unsure whether he is seeing a motion or imagining it.

330–42 **She . . . atonement** Cf. the parallel scene in *Oth* 5.2.115–23, where Desdemona similarly revives briefly from strangulation to utter her dying words.

332 **sensible** palpable, perceptible

334 Some editors specify that Bosola kisses the Duchess here, to *store* her lips *with fresh colour* by transferring the warmth of his own. Given that the executioner had earlier promised to give her body to her women so that it would not be mistreated by men (220–1), a kiss at this point would probably appear intrusive.

335 **cordial** restorative

335–6 **I . . . destroy pity** If I call I will simply bring back Ferdinand, who will destroy her.

336 **opes** opens

337 **late** just now, lately

338–9 Alternatively, these can be understood as 'squint' lines: the Duchess's *Antonio* can either complete Bosola's previous line at 338 or introduce his speech at 339 to make it a complete pentameter line. Her metrical 'fulfilling' of his lines can be seen as parallel to her effect on his spirit.

328 to] *om. Q4*   330 SD] *this edn*   334 colour.] colour. *Kisses her.* | *Gunby*   337 ope] open *Q4*
339] *Q1 lines* Antonio. / liuing. /

The dead bodies you saw were but feigned statues. 340
He's reconciled to your brothers. The Pope hath
  wrought
The atonement.

DUCHESS   Mercy! *She dies.*

BOSOLA
Oh, she's gone again. There the cords of life broke.
O sacred innocence that sweetly sleeps
On turtles' feathers! Whilst a guilty conscience 345
Is a black register wherein is writ
All our good deeds and bad, a perspective
That shows us hell. That we cannot be suffered
To do good when we have a mind to it!
This is manly sorrow.
These tears, I am very certain, never grew 350
In my mother's milk. My estate is sunk
Below the degree of fear.
Where were these penitent fountains while she was
  living?

340 **feigned** feignèd
341–2 Does the Duchess's *Mercy* register a joyful response to the news
  that her family is alive, which she
  may already have realized (196–8), or
  only a reaction to Bosola's white lies
  about Antonio's *atonement* (reconciliation) with her brothers? Alternatively,
  Lucas contends that she is pleading for
  mercy, still trying to save her own life.
343 **cords . . . broke** death imagined as
  the severing of a thread or cord (perhaps like the cord of life woven and cut
  by the three fates of classical myth); cf.
  KL 5.3.215–16: 'the strings of life /
  Began to crack.'
345 **turtles'** turtle doves', associated with
  marital fidelity; cf. the doves and kisses
  of 3.2.20–1.

346 **register** record book
347 **perspective** viewing point in a physical sense; point of view or prospect in
  a mental sense: good deeds provide
  the moral perspective that shows evil
  deeds to be damnable.
348 **That we . . . suffered** It is unfortunate that we can't be permitted.
350–2 **This . . . milk** Cf. Macduff's grief
  over the death of his family: 'But I must
  also feel it as a man' (*Mac* 4.3.221).
352 **mother's milk** imagined as a source
  of effeminacy
352–3 **My estate . . . fear** I am so low
  that I can't even feel fear. Cf. *Arcadia*,
  book 2, ch. 10, 208: 'our state is soncke
  below the degree of feare.'
354 **penitent fountains** Bosola's weeping eyes

342] *Q1 lines* attonement. / Mercy. /   352–3 My estate . . . fear] *om. Q4*   353–4] *this edn; Q1 lines*
were / liuing? /

Oh, they were frozen up! Here is a sight   355
As direful to my soul as is the sword
Unto a wretch hath slain his father. Come,
I'll bear thee hence
And execute thy last will: that's deliver
Thy body to the reverend dispose   360
Of some good women. That the cruel tyrant
Shall not deny me. Then I'll post to Milan,
Where somewhat I will speedily enact
Worth my dejection.   *Exit [with the Duchess's body].*

[handwritten annotations: "good and bad, people do not prosper" / "one Cant good their he can do, bring duchess' body to good women"]

5.1   *[Enter]* ANTONIO *[and]* DELIO.

ANTONIO
What think you of my hope of reconcilement *[handwritten: "not likely, foolish"]*
To the Aragonian brethren?
DELIO   I misdoubt it,
For, though they have sent their letters of safe conduct
For your repair to Milan, they appear
But nets to entrap you. The Marquess of Pescara,   5
Under whom you hold certain land in 'cheat,

356 **direful** dreadful
357 **hath** that has
360 **reverend dispose** respectful preparation for burial
363 **somewhat** something
364 **Worth** worthy of, in accordance with
(suggesting suicide or revenge)
5.1 Location: Milan, where Antonio has
fled after parting from the Duchess.
See 3.5.57 and 4.1.135, where
Ferdinand reports that Antonio 'Lurks
about Milan' and implies that he will

send Bosola there to kill Antonio.
2 **misdoubt** distrust, have misgivings
about
3 **letters . . . conduct** pass allowing
Antonio to travel between southern
Italy and Milan
4 **repair** travel
they the letters
6 **'cheat** escheat, meaning that they
automatically become Pescara's if
Antonio dies without heirs or has been
convicted of treason or felony

355 Here is] Here's *Q4* 357–8] *Dyce; one line Q1* 359 last] *om. Q2* 363 speedily enact] put in Act
Q4 364 SD] *Q4 (subst.)* 5.1] (ACTVS V. SCENA I.) 0 SD] *Q4; Antonio, Delio, Pescara, Iulia.
| Q1* 6 land in 'cheat] Lands in *Escheat | Q4*

Much 'gainst his noble nature hath been moved
To seize those lands; and some of his dependants
Are at this instant making it their suit
To be invested in your revenues.   10
I cannot think they mean well to your life
That do deprive you of your means of life –
Your living.

ANTONIO   You are still an heretic
To any safety I can shape myself.

DELIO

Here comes the marquess. I will make myself   15
Petitioner for some part of your land,
To know whether it is flying.

ANTONIO   I pray, do.

[Enter] PESCARA.

DELIO

Sir, I have a suit to you.

PESCARA   To me?

DELIO

An easy one: there is the citadel of St Bennet,
With some demesnes, of late in the possession   20
Of Antonio Bologna. Please you bestow them on me.

7 **moved** pressured
8 **dependants** followers
10 **be invested in** become legally entitled
   to
11–13 **I . . . living** Cf. Shylock's complaint in *MV* 4.1.372–3: 'you take my
   life / When you do take the means
   whereby I live.'
13 **heretic** unbeliever
14 **shape** fashion for
17 **whether** could be either 'whether', as
   in Q1, in which case Delio is attempting to establish that Antonio's land
   is indeed up for grabs, or 'whither'

(where to) as in Q2, in which case
Delio's aim would instead be to find
out to whom the land is being offered.
Beginning with Sampson and Lucas,
most editors specify at this point that
Antonio withdraws so that he is not
visible to Pescara; however, he may
well be visible to the audience, and it
could add to the power of the scene to
have the other characters nonchalantly
discuss Antonio in his presence.
19 **Bennet** Benedict
20 **demesnes** surrounding lands
21 **Please you** may it please you to

17 SD] *Q4; Pescara,* | *0 SD Q1*   19] *this edn; Q1 lines* one: / *Bennet,* /

PESCARA

    You are my friend, but this is such a suit

    Nor fit for me to give nor you to take.

DELIO

    No, sir?

PESCARA   I will give you ample reason for't

    Soon in private. Here's the Cardinal's mistress.   25

[Enter] JULIA.

JULIA

    My lord, I am grown your poor petitioner,

    And should be an ill beggar had I not

    A great man's letter here, the Cardinal's,

    To court you in my favour.

PESCARA *[Reads the letter.]*   He entreats for you

    The citadel of St Bennet that belonged   30

    To the banished Bologna.

JULIA   Yes.

PESCARA   I could not

    Have thought of a friend I could rather pleasure with it.

    'Tis yours.

JULIA   Sir, I thank you.

---

25 **Cardinal's mistress** The relationship between the Cardinal and Julia, which she tried to conceal at 2.4.48–50, is now open knowledge. Although it was no doubt shocking to English Protestant sensibilities in early audiences (see 2.4.0 SDn.), similar relationships were commonplace among the young aristocratic cardinals in Italy of the early 16th century, who were known for their amorousness and lack of ecclesiastical gravity (see pp. 23–4). The historical Cardinal did in fact have a mistress named Giulia (see List of Roles, 10n.).

26 **am grown** have become

27–8 **should . . . letter** i.e. (with false modesty) if I had to ask on my own I would manage it badly, but I have a letter to support my petition.

31–6 **I . . . greater** The courtly artificiality of the exchange between Julia and Pescara suggests extreme politeness and perhaps also a degree of coldness: contrast Pescara's speech to Delio explaining the gift at 40ff.

33 a partial line shared between two speakers; the missing theatrical 'beats' implied by the short lines may be filled in performance by the formal transfer of the deed.

24] *Q1 lines* sir? / for't, /   25 SD] *Q4; Iulia.* | *0 SD Q1*   29] *Q1 lines* fauour / you /   SD] *Lucas (subst.)*   31–3] *this edn; Q1 lines* Yes: / could / yours: / you: /   32 could] wou'd *Q4*

And he shall know how doubly I am engaged,
Both in your gift and speediness of giving,   35
Which makes your grant the greater.   *Exit.*

ANTONIO   How they fortify
Themselves with my ruin!

DELIO   Sir, I am little bound
To you.

PESCARA   Why?

DELIO   Because you denied this suit
To me and gave't to such a creature.

PESCARA
Do you know what it was?   40
It was Antonio's land, not forfeited
By course of law, but ravished from his throat
By the Cardinal's entreaty. It were not fit
I should bestow so main a piece of wrong
Upon my friend. 'Tis a gratification   45
Only due to a strumpet, for it is injustice.
Shall I sprinkle the pure blood of innocents
To make those followers I call my friends
Look ruddier upon me? I am glad
This land, ta'en from the owner by such wrong,   50
Returns again unto so foul an use
As salary for his lust. Learn, good Delio,
To ask noble things of me, and you shall find
I'll be a noble giver.

[handwritten marginal annotations]

34–6 **he . . . greater** proverbial: 'He that gives quickly gives twice' (Dent, G125).
36 **fortify** make strong, bolster up
42 **ravished . . . throat** torn from him as though by attack dogs (or wolves)
43 **were not fit** would not be appropriate
44 **main** flagrant, significant
45–6 **gratification . . . injustice** implying that Julia's prostitution is a breach of law best rewarded by another

47 **blood of innocents** or blood of innocence (both would have sounded similar onstage), referring to Antonio and his family, who have done no wrong but have been 'sacrificed' through the loss of their land
49 **ruddier** more sanguinely, with more warmth of friendship (playing on the idea that the *blood of innocents* would have reddened his followers' complexions)

36–9] *this edn; Q1 lines* greater. / fortefie / am / Why. / gau't / creature. /   51 an] a *Q4*

298

DELIO   You instruct me well.

ANTONIO

Why here's a man, now, would fright impudence   55
From sauciest beggars!

PESCARA   Prince Ferdinand's come to Milan
Sick, as they give out, of an apoplexy.
But some say 'tis a frenzy. I am going
To visit him.   *Exit.*

ANTONIO   'Tis a noble old fellow!

DELIO

What course do you mean to take, Antonio?   60

ANTONIO

This night I mean to venture all my fortune,
Which is no more than a poor lingering life,
To the Cardinal's worst of malice: I have got
Private access to his chamber, and intend
To visit him about the mid of night,   65
As once his brother did our noble Duchess.
It may be that the sudden apprehension
Of danger – for I'll go in mine own shape –
When he shall see it, freight with love and duty,
May draw the poison out of him and work   70
A friendly reconcilement. If it fail,
Yet it shall rid me of this infamous calling;
For better fall once, than be ever falling.

[Handwritten margin notes: "reconcilement or death" beside lines 64–65; "sentention" with brace beside lines 72–73]

---

55 **man** Pescara
55–6 **fright . . . From** scare impudence
  out of
58 **frenzy** mania held to be caused by
  inflammation of the brain
67 **apprehension** recognition
69 **freight** fraught; provided or abound-
  ing with
70 **draw . . . out** reduce the infection by
  causing it to come to the surface,

where it can be drained away (like
  discharge from a wound)
72 **calling** position in life; also suggests
  gossip or news that is *calling* out his
  loss of favour
73 Cf. Montaigne, 1.108: 'There is no
  man so base-minded, that loveth not
  rather to fall once, then ever to remaine
  in feare of falling' (Lucas).
  ever always

56] *Q1 lines* Beggers. / Millaine /   59] *Q1 lines* him. / fellow: /   62 lingering] *(*lingring*)*   64 intend]
I intend *Q4*   69 freight] *(*fraight*); fraught Brown*

DELIO

I'll second you in all danger and, howe'er,
My life keeps rank with yours.   75

ANTONIO

You are still my loved and best friend.   *Exeunt.*

5.2   [*Enter*] PESCARA [*and*] DOCTOR.

PESCARA

Now, doctor, may I visit your patient?

DOCTOR

If't please your lordship, but he's instantly
To take the air here in the gallery
By my direction.

PESCARA   Pray thee, what's his disease?

DOCTOR

A very pestilent disease, my lord,   5
They call *lycanthropia*.

PESCARA   What's that?

I need a dictionary to't.

DOCTOR   I'll tell you:

In those that are possessed with't there o'erflows
Such melancholy humour, they imagine

---

74 **second** support; serve as back-up in case of a duel
  howe'er come what may
75 **keeps rank with** marches along with; stays even with
76 **still** even now; always
5.2 Location: the Cardinal's palace in Milan
2 **instantly** immediately
3 **take the air** walk for health or pleasure. Evidently the gallery is imagined as open to the outside.
4 **Pray thee** could also be spelled 'Prithee'
6 *lycanthropia* disease or magical condi-

tion in which humans are transformed into werewolves (see Appendix 2 for a near-contemporary historical account). At the time it was considered an effect of melancholy: 'This disease . . . is a kinde of melancholie, but very black and vehement: for such as are toucht there-with, goe out of their houses in Februarie, counterfeit Wolves to a manner in all things, and all night doe nothing but runne into Church-yardes, and about graves, so as you shall presently discover in them a wonderfull alteration of the braine' (Goulart, 386).
7 **to't** to interpret it

---

74 howe'er] ((how ere)) **5.2**] *(SCENA. II.)* 0 SD] *Q4 (subst.); Pescara, a Doctor, Ferdinand, Cardinall, Malateste, Bosola, Iulia. | Q1* 4] *Q1 lines* direction. / disease? / 8 those] these *Q2*

Themselves to be transformed into wolves,   10
Steal forth to churchyards in the dead of night
And dig dead bodies up – as two nights since
One met the duke, 'bout midnight in a lane
Behind St Mark's church, with the leg of a man
Upon his shoulder; and he howled fearfully,   15
Said he was a wolf, only the difference
Was, a wolf's skin was hairy on the outside,
His on the inside; bade them take their swords,
Rip up his flesh, and try. Straight I was sent for,
And having ministered to him, found his grace   20
Very well recovered.

PESCARA   I am glad on't.

DOCTOR

Yet not without some fear
Of a relapse. If he grow to his fit again
I'll go a nearer way to work with him
Than ever Paracelsus dreamed of.   25
If they'll give me leave I'll buffet his madness out of
    him.
Stand aside – he comes.

---

10 **transformed** transformèd
14 **St Mark's church** Stow, *Survey*, does not record a church of this name within the City of London, but San Marco in Milan, originally built in the 13th century and extensively renovated in the 17th, is the second largest church in the city after the Duomo. For early audiences unfamiliar with Italy, however, *St Mark's* probably suggested the much more famous San Marco in Venice.
19 **try** test his statement by examining the inside of his skin; cf. Goulart's account of the lycanthrope, who car-

ries a 'whole thigh and the legge of a dead man' upon his shoulder and is 'hayrie within' like a wolf (Goulart, 386–7). Hair on the inside also suggests a hair shirt worn for penance (Gunby).
20 **ministered** attended
23 **grow** develop; revert
24 **nearer** more 'hands-on'
25 **Paracelsus** German medical expert (*c.* 1490–1541) who made pioneering use of chemical agents to cure human ailments. By claiming to outdo Paracelsus, the doctor is boasting that he will offer a very up-to-date cure.

17 wolf's] Woolves *Q2*   skin was] skin is *Q2*   18 bade] *(bad)*   23–5 If . . . of] *om. Q4*   24] *om. Q2*   25–6] *this edn; Q1 lines* If / him, /

[*Enter* FERDINAND,] CARDINAL, MALATESTE [*and*] BOSOLA.

FERDINAND   Leave me.

MALATESTE

Why doth your lordship love this solitariness?

FERDINAND

Eagles commonly fly alone.

They are crows, daws and starlings that flock together.   30

Look! What's that follows me?

MALATESTE   Nothing, my lord.

FERDINAND   Yes.

MALATESTE

'Tis your shadow.

FERDINAND   Stay it! Let it not haunt me.

MALATESTE

Impossible, if you move and the sun shine.

FERDINAND

I will throttle it!   [*Throws himself on the ground.*]

MALATESTE   Oh, my lord, you are angry with nothing!

FERDINAND

You are a fool. How is't possible   35

I should catch my shadow unless I fall upon't?

29–30 a statement about both Ferdinand's rank, since eagles were considered to be at the top of the hierarchy of birds, and also about the danger he can pose for others, since eagles are birds of prey

30 *Crows*, jackdaws (*daws*) and *starlings* are all noted for being sociable birds that gather together in flocks.

32 **Stay** stop

34 SD Since Pescara asks Ferdinand to rise at 39, Ferdinand apparently hurls himself to the ground at this point so

that he can *fall upon* his shadow (36) and physically attack it. Cf. Dent, S261*–2: 'to fight with' and 'to be afraid of one's shadow' were proverbial. Whitney, 32, associates this fear with guilt, showing a man with outstretched sword, terrified of his shadow. The accompanying verse explains that 'The wicked wretche, that mischiefe late hath wroughte / By murther, thefte, or other heynous crimes . . . standes in feare, of everie busshe, and brake, / Yea oftentimes, his shaddowe makes him quake.'

27 SD] *Q4 (subst.); Ferdinand, Cardinall, Malateste, Bosola. | 0 SD Q1* 28 love] use *Q2* 29–32] *this edn; Q1 lines* and / what's that, / Lord) / shadow. / me. /; *prose Dyce* 34–40] *this edn; Q1 lines* it. / nothing. / foole: / shadow / Hell, / you / persons / Lord. / Patience. / Vertue; /; *prose Dyce* 34 SD] *Q4*

When I go to hell, I mean to carry a bribe;
For, look you, good gifts evermore make way
For the worst persons.

PESCARA   Rise, good my lord.

FERDINAND

I am studying the art of patience.

PESCARA   'Tis a noble virtue.   40

FERDINAND

To drive six snails before me from this town
To Moscow, neither use goad nor whip to them,   *patience = Duchess*
But let them take their own time (the patientest man
I'th' world match me for an experiment!)
And I'll crawl after like a sheep-biter.

CARDINAL   Force him up.   45

FERDINAND

Use me well, you were best.
What I have done, I have done: I'll confess nothing.

DOCTOR

Now let me come to him. Are you mad, my lord?
Are you out of your princely wits?

FERDINAND   What's he?

PESCARA   Your doctor.

37–9 **When ... persons** Ferdinand associates catching his black shadow with
suffering death and damnation – a further suggestion of guilt (see 34 SDn.).

37 **bribe** payment to a jailor for good
treatment; in classical mythology, payment to Charon on behalf of departing
souls for transport across the river into
Hades (cf. 3.5.106–7)

38 **look you** you see

40 **patience ... virtue** Patience was one
of the four cardinal virtues, associated with fortitude, as shown by the
Duchess during her long ordeal in 4.2.

See also 3.5.71n.

41 **drive** herd, as one might herd cattle;
'To drive a snail' was proverbial for
futility (Dent, S581.11).

45 **sheep-biter** sheepdog (or perhaps a
wolf that is snapping at sheep)

46 **Use** treat
   best well advised

47 Echoes Lady Macbeth's 'what's done is
done' and her guilty acknowledgement
during her madness, 'What's done cannot be undone' (*Mac* 3.2.12, 5.1.64);
also Iago in *Oth* 5.2.300: 'Demand me
nothing. What you know, you know.'

43–5] *this edn; Q1 lines* world / after / vp. /; *prose Dyce*   43 patientest] *(*patientst*)*   48–54] *this
edn; Q1 lines* mad / wits? / Doctor. / eye / ciuill. / him, / brought / you / sun-burning. / eyes. /;
prose Dyce

FERDINAND

Let me have his beard sawed off, and his eyebrows   50
Filed more civil.

DOCTOR   – I must do mad tricks
With him, for that's the only way on't. –
I have brought your grace a salamander's skin
To keep you from sun-burning.

FERDINAND   I have cruel sore eyes.

DOCTOR

The white of a cockatrice's egg is present remedy.   55

FERDINAND

Let it be a new-laid one, you were best.
Hide me from him! Physicians are like kings –
They brook no contradiction.

DOCTOR   Now he begins to fear me;
Now let me alone with him.   [*Takes off his gown.*]

CARDINAL   How now, put off your gown?

50–1 could be either prose or verse, like many of the speeches that follow

51 **more civil** more neatly

52 **on't** to manage it

53–4 **salamander's . . . sun-burning** Salamanders were believed to have the ability to live in fire, and therefore to aid against burning; contrast Pescara's earlier observation (3.3.48–9) that Ferdinand carried a salamander in his eye 'To mock the eager violence of fire.'

54 **cruel . . . eyes** extremely sore eyes, perhaps from his earlier viewing of the Duchess's body (4.2.254)

55 **cockatrice's** basilisk's; cf. 3.2.85–6, where Ferdinand talks of 'chang[ing] / Eyes with a basilisk'; and Isaiah, 59.4–5, where those who 'bring forth iniquity' are said to 'hatch cockatrices' eggs, and . . . he that eateth of their eggs dieth.'

58 **brook** tolerate

59 SD Editors have varied widely in interpreting the doctor's action: does he take off his professional robe, as in most modern editions, so that he can 'get down to business' and embark on the cure of Ferdinand? In early performances, according to the Q1 list of Actors' Names (p. 118 and 119–20nn.), Ferdinand was played by the powerful actor Richard Burbage, and the doctor by the boy actor who also played Cariola; the disparity in size suggests that the doctor's attempted cure that follows was designed to be ludicrous rather than impressive. Onstage in 1707, as recorded in Q4's SD, the doctor removed his '*four Cloaks one after another*'; the scene that followed was full of slapstick and clearly played for laughs. Most of the scene, including the unseemly disrobing, was cut in 19th-century productions.

---

51 Filed] fill'd *Q2*   56 were] are *Q4*   58–9] *Q1 lines* contradiction. / me, / him. / gowne? /; *prose Dyce*   59 SD] *Lucas; puts off his four Cloaks one after another.* | *Q4*

DOCTOR

Let me have some forty urinals filled with rose-water.   60
He and I'll go pelt one another with them.
Now he begins to fear me. – Can you fetch a frisk, sir? –
Let him go, let him go, upon my peril!
I find by his eye he stands in awe of me.
I'll make him as tame as a dormouse.   65

FERDINAND

Can you fetch your frisks, sir?
I will stamp him into a cullis – flay off his skin
To cover one of the anatomies this rogue hath set
I'th' cold yonder, in Barber-Surgeons' Hall.
Hence, hence! You are all of you like beasts for sacrifice: 70
There's nothing left of you but tongue and belly,
Flattery and lechery.

PESCARA

Doctor, he did not fear you thoroughly!

Alternatively, as Brennan suggests, it could be Ferdinand who attempts to take off his gown in a further display of madness, until restrained by the Cardinal's *How now* (59).

62 **fetch a frisk** cut a caper

63 **let him go** Evidently some of the other characters are restraining Ferdinand.

65 **dormouse** Cf. the 'politic dormouse' at 1.2.199 – quiet but far from innocuous.

66 repeated in mockery of the doctor's question (62)

67 **cullis** sauce; broth made from meat (like the more recent phrase 'bloody pulp')

68–9 **anatomies . . . Hall** Anatomies were a new component of medical science at the period. In London the bodies of executed criminals were brought to Barber-Surgeons' Hall, near Cripplegate, to be dissected and preserved as specimens (Brown).

70–1 **beasts . . . belly** Cf. North, 797, describing an insolent orator who attempted to rule Athens and nearly wrecked her: 'after he was very old . . . there was nothing left of him, no more then of a beast sacrificed, but the tongue and belly' (Dent, *Webster*).

72 **lechery** Given the Q1 spelling (t.n.), this could also be a mocking reference to the doctor's cures as 'leachery', that is, the use of leeches for blood-letting.

73 Following Q4, which is based on stage practice *c*. 1707, some editors specify that this observation is precipitated by an assault on the doctor by Ferdinand after 70. Ferdinand may exit after 72 as in Q4, possibly in an angry huff; he may exit later with the Doctor (94 SD), which suggests that he is still to some degree under the doctor's control; or he may remain onstage during the conversation between Bosola

66–9] *this edn; Q1 lines* Cullice: / Anotomies, / hall: /; *prose Dyce*   67 flay] *(Flea)*   69 Barber-Surgeons'] *(Barber-Chyrurgeons)*   70 sacrifice:] sacrifice. *Throws the Doctor down and beats him.* | *Q4*   72 lechery.] *(leachery.);* Leachery. *Exit,* | *Q4*   73 thoroughly] *(throughly)*

DOCTOR

   True, I was somewhat too forward.

BOSOLA

   Mercy upon me, what a fatal judgement   75
   Hath fallen upon this Ferdinand!

PESCARA   Knows your grace

   What accident hath brought unto the prince
   This strange distraction?

CARDINAL

   – I must feign somewhat. – Thus they say it grew:
   You have heard it rumoured for these many years   80
   None of our family dies, but there is seen
   The shape of an old woman, which is given
   By tradition to us to have been murdered
   By her nephews for her riches. Such a figure
   One night, as the prince sat up late at's book,   85
   Appeared to him, when crying out for help,
   The gentlemen of 's chamber found his grace
   All on a cold sweat, altered much in face
   And language. Since which apparition,
   He hath grown worse and worse, and I much fear   90
   He cannot live.

BOSOLA   Sir, I would speak with you.

PESCARA

   We'll leave your grace,
   Wishing to the sick prince, our noble lord,

---

and the Cardinal, and leave only with the Cardinal (134 SD), which draws renewed attention to the unholy alliance between the two brothers even as the Cardinal glibly disavows knowledge of the Duchess's death.

75 **fatal judgement** implying that Ferdinand's madness is punishment for his crimes; Bosola's *Mercy upon me* may suggest that he fears the same fate

for himself (Gunby).

79 **I . . . somewhat** The Cardinal presumably says this aside, but with the possibility that he is overheard.
  somewhat something, to some degree

80–4 **You . . . riches** Cf. Goulart, 620, where the same story is told of an 'ancient familie at *Parma*'.

85 **at's book** reading

88 **All on** All in

76] *Q1 lines* Ferdinand? / grace /   91] *Q1 lines* liue. / you /

All health of mind and body.

CARDINAL   You are most welcome.

[Exeunt Pescara, Malateste and Doctor.]

– Are you come? So. – This fellow must not know   95
By any means I had intelligence
In our Duchess's death. For, though I counselled it,
The full of all th'engagement seemed to grow
From Ferdinand. – Now, sir, how fares our sister?
I do not think but sorrow makes her look   100
Like to an oft-dyed garment. She shall now
Taste comfort from me. Why do you look so wildly?
Oh, the fortune of your master here, the prince,
Dejects you; but be you of happy comfort:
If you'll do one thing for me I'll entreat,   105
Though he had a cold tombstone o'er his bones,
I'd make you what you would be.

BOSOLA   Anything:
Give it me in a breath, and let me fly to't.
They that think long, small expedition win –
For musing much o'th' end, cannot begin.   110

96–7 **had intelligence / In** knew about; helped to plan. The Cardinal goes on to disclaim responsibility for the precise method employed in the Duchess's death.

98 **full . . . engagement** complete plan

101 **Like . . . garment** i.e. pale and wan

102 **wildly** evidently in reaction to the Cardinal's (feigned) lack of knowledge of the Duchess's death. If Ferdinand is still onstage (see 73n.) then the Cardinal's *you* may refer to both Ferdinand and Bosola, who had previously appeared onstage together in tense conversation over the Duchess's body (4.2.247ff.).

103 **here** suggests that Ferdinand is still onstage, but could also be a more gener-

al recognition of Ferdinand's presence in Milan or in the Cardinal's palace

106 even if Ferdinand were already dead and buried; cf. Bosola's reference to both brothers as empty graves or rotting sepulchres at 4.2.308–9.

107 **would** wish to
Anything whatever Bosola would wish to be; whatever the Cardinal wants him to do

109–10 Cf. Hamlet's 'thinking too precisely on th'event' (*Ham* 4.4.40) that causes him to postpone action; and Alexander, *Julius Caesar*, 4.1, sig. Y4[r]: 'Who muse of many things, resolve of none, / And thinking of the end, cannot beginne' (Gunby).

94] *Q1 lines* body. / welcome: / SD] *Dyce* 97 Duchess's] Sister's *Q4* 98 th'engagement] th'agreement *Q2* 100–2 I . . . me] *om. Q4* 105 one] (on) 106 o'er] over *Q4* 107] *Q1 lines* be. / thing, / I'd] (I'll'd) you would] you should *Q2;* you'd *Q4* 108 it me] me it *Q2*

[*Enter*] JULIA.

Mistress

JULIA

Sir, will you come in to supper?

CARDINAL   I am busy; leave me.

JULIA

What an excellent shape hath that fellow!   *Exit.*

CARDINAL

'Tis thus: Antonio lurks here in Milan.
Enquire him out and kill him. While he lives
Our sister cannot marry, and I have thought   115
Of an excellent match for her. Do this and style me
Thy advancement.

BOSOLA   But by what means shall I find him out?

CARDINAL

There is a gentleman called Delio,
Here in the camp, that hath been long approved
His loyal friend. Set eye upon that fellow –   120
Follow him to mass. Maybe Antonio,   *no saith*
Although he do account religion
But a school-name, for fashion of the world
May accompany him. Or else go enquire out
Delio's confessor, and see if you can bribe   125
Him to reveal it. There are a thousand ways

110 SD Although Julia is listed in the
massed entry at the beginning of the
scene, her name appears last, suggesting
that she is the last to enter. Her matter-
of-fact attempt here to summon the
Cardinal to dinner seems to be the first
logical moment for her to come onstage.
112 **fellow** Bosola
114 **Enquire him out** Find out where he is.
116–17 **style . . . advancement** Consider
me to be your means of promotion.
119 **camp** military installation
    approved tried, tested; established

123 **school-name** empty words; the
Cardinal seems to regard Antonio's
breaches of social convention as sufficient proof that he must be an atheist.
124–6 **go . . . reveal it** In the Catholic
Church, the confidentiality of confession is, in theory, inviolable. The
Cardinal's suggestion that Bosola bribe
a priest to break the traditional seal
of the confessional suggests that this
high-ranking churchman has little
regard either for confession in itself or
for the priests who hear it.

110 SD] *Q4; Iulia.* | *0 SD Q1*   111] *Q1 lines* Supper? / me. /   117] *Q1 lines* aduancement. / out?
/   But] *om. Q2*   118 There is] There's *Q2*   121–4 Follow . . . him] *om. Q4*

A man might find to trace him: as to know
What fellows haunt the Jews for taking up
Great sums of money, for sure he's in want;
Or else to go to th' picture-makers, and learn   130
Who brought her picture lately. Some of these
Happily may take –
BOSOLA   Well, I'll not freeze i'th' business.
I would see that wretched thing, Antonio,
Above all sights i'th' world.
CARDINAL   Do, and be happy.

Exit [with Ferdinand].

BOSOLA
This fellow doth breed basilisks in's eyes: 135
He's nothing else but murder. Yet he seems
Not to have notice of the Duchess's death.
'Tis his cunning. I must follow his example.
There cannot be a surer way to trace
Than that of an old fox.

[Enter JULIA, aiming a pistol at BOSOLA.]

127 **as** such as
128–9 **What . . . money** what men go to the Jewish money-lenders to borrow large sums
131 **brought** i.e. dropped off her picture to be copied; sometimes emended to 'bought', but it seems unlikely that Antonio, even in his present troubles, would not already possess a miniature of his own wife.
132 **Happily** gladly; or 'haply', perhaps. The rest of the uncompleted thought may have been 'a bribe' – making *these* refer to the confessor, or the Jews or the picture-makers.
I'll . . . business I'll be quick about it
133–4 **I . . . world** Bosola's phras-

ing allows the Cardinal to think that Bosola wants to see Antonio in order to kill him, but Bosola's intentions have been suggested at 4.2.362–4 and he will later clarify them at 5.4.51–2.
135 **basilisks** Cf. 3.2.85–6 and n. The gaze of the basilisk caused death.
139 **surer . . . trace** more certain path to follow (echoing the Cardinal's *trace* at 127); cf. Dent, W164: 'There is no surer way to follow than that of the old fox.'
140 **old fox** the Cardinal, who is young in years but wily like a *fox* and *old* in political experience
140 SD The pistol is confirmed by 150 below; cf. 3.2.139 SD2, where Antonio similarly enters with a pistol drawn

127–32 as . . . take] *om. Q4*   131 brought] bought *Dyce*   132] *Q1 lines* take— / businesse, /   134] *Q1 lines* world. / happy. /   SD] *this edn; Exit.* | *Q1*   140–1] *Brown; Q1 lines* Fox. / now? / enough: /   140 SD] *Lucas (subst.); Enter Julia. Q4*

309

JULIA   So, sir, you are well met.   140
BOSOLA

  How now?

JULIA   Nay, the doors are fast enough.

  Now, sir, I will make you confess your treachery.

BOSOLA

  Treachery?

JULIA   Yes. Confess to me

  Which of my women 'twas you hired to put

  Love powder into my drink!

BOSOLA   Love powder?

JULIA   Yes,   145

  When I was at Malfi. Why should I fall in love

  With such a face else? I have already suffered

  For thee so much pain, the only remedy

  To do me good is to kill my longing.

BOSOLA

  Sure, your pistol holds nothing but perfumes or

    kissing comfits.   150

  Excellent lady, you have a pretty way on't

  To discover your longing! Come, come – I'll disarm you

  And arm you thus.   [*Embraces her.*]

                          Yet this is wondrous strange –

after Ferdinand's exit. In Q4 there is
no pistol: Bosola's line mentioning it is
cut; and in many productions much of
Julia's role in 5.2 is severely reduced or
eliminated. At the Manchester Royal
Exchange in 1980, Julia entered with
her pistol aimed, but sent a seductive
double message by wearing a diapha-
nous bodice that showed her breasts.
141 **fast** securely locked; evidently Bosola
  is looking for an escape.
145 **Love powder** aphrodisiac, designed

to induce sexual passion; cf. 3.1.65–9,
where Bosola insinuates that a similar *potion* has been used on the
Duchess.
147 **such a face** implies that Bosola is
  not good-looking enough to attract her
  without artificial help
149 **kill my longing** i.e. by sleeping with
  me (but with ominous overtones)
150 **kissing comfits** sugar confections
  that sweeten the breath
152 **discover** reveal

145–52] *this edn; Q1 lines* drinke? / powder? / *Malfy,* / else? / paine, / good, / longing. / holds /
Lady, / discouer / disarme you, /   150–8] *om. Q4*   153 SD] *Lucas opp. 153*

JULIA

    Compare thy form and my eyes together:
    You'll find my love no such great miracle.   155
    Now you'll say I am wanton. This nice modesty
    In ladies is but a troublesome familiar
    That haunts them.

BOSOLA

    Know you me? I am a blunt soldier –

JULIA   The better.

    Sure, there wants fire where there are no lively sparks   160
    Of roughness.

BOSOLA   – And I want compliment.

JULIA   Why, ignorance
    In courtship cannot make you do amiss
    If you have a heart to do well.

BOSOLA   You are very fair.

JULIA

    Nay, if you lay beauty to my charge,
    I must plead unguilty.

BOSOLA   Your bright eyes   165

154–5 i.e. your figure matches my eyes in attractiveness; contradicts 147, where she implies that she's too good a catch for Bosola. Cf. *Devil's Law-Case*, 2.1.242–4: 'Compare her beauty, and my youth together, / And you will find the faire effects of love / No myracle at all' (Webster, 2.100).

156 **Now . . . wanton** Julia may kiss Bosola at this point.
  nice too precise or punctilious

157 **familiar** demonic companion like those said to be nurtured by witches

158–9 These can also be understood as squint lines: Bosola's part-line both finishes Julia's *That haunts them* and introduces Julia's following part-line, which can then be seen as complet-ing Bosola's. He appears to think that Julia's *troublesome familiar* that *haunts* her (157–8) is a reference to himself; cf. 1.1.29, where he claims to *haunt* the Cardinal, and 1.2.176, where he claims to have become Ferdinand's *familiar*.

160–1 **Sure . . . roughness** You can't make a fire without something rough to create sparks.

161 **want compliment** am lacking in the polite graces

162–3 **do** Gunby suggests a pun on 'do' meaning 'fuck'.

165–6 **Your . . . sunbeams** Playing along with Julia's attempted seduction, Bosola combines two trite Petrarchan ideas from love poetry of the period: your eyes are wounding darts; your eyes blind

---

155–9] *this edn; Q1 lines* say, / Ladies / familiar, / them. / better, /   161–3] *Thorndike; Q1 lines* complement. / amisse, / well. / faire. /   165 unguilty] not Guilty *Q4*

Carry a quiver of darts in them sharper than sunbeams.

JULIA

You will mar me with commendation.

Put yourself to the charge of courting me,

Whereas now I woo you.

BOSOLA

    – I have it! I will work upon this creature.   170

Let us grow most amorously familiar.

If the great Cardinal now should see me thus,

Would he not count me a villain?

JULIA

No, he might count me a wanton,

Not lay a scruple of offence on you.   175

For if I see and steal a diamond

The fault is not i'th' stone, but in me the thief

That purloins it. I am sudden with you:

We that are great women of pleasure use

To cut off these uncertain wishes and unquiet longings,   180

And in an instant join the sweet delight

And the pretty excuse together. Had you been in th'

    street

Under my chamber window, even there

me like sunlight (cf. also Ferdinand's reaction to the Duchess at 4.2.254).

167 **mar me** spoil me
    commendation pronounced as five syllables

168–9 parallels the marriage scene (1.2.351ff.), where the Duchess protests that she is required to woo Antonio

168 **charge** trouble

169 **woo** The Q1 spelling 'woe' suggests a pun; cf. 1.2.352.

173 **count** consider

176–8 **if . . . purloins it** gender reversal of the usual courtly compliment, by which it is women who are compared

to precious jewels and men who take or 'purloin' them

178 **sudden** precipitous; hasty

179–82 **We . . . together** Cf. *Arcadia*, book 3, ch. 17, 452, where very similar language is used by Cecropia to explain why women love to be raped: they achieve thereby all of the pleasures of sex without the moral responsibility.

179 **great . . . pleasure** famous courtesans **use** make a practice

182–4 **Had . . . courted you** the situation in which common prostitutes, as opposed to 'great women of pleasure', solicit their customers

166] *this edn; Q1 lines* sharper / Sun-beames. /   169 woo] *(woe)*   174 a] *om. Q4*   176–8] *om. Q4*   179–80] *this edn; Q1 lines* off / longings, /   183] *om. Q2*

I should have courted you.

BOSOLA   Oh, you are an excellent lady!

JULIA

Bid me do somewhat for you presently   185
To express I love you.

BOSOLA   I will and, if you love me,
Fail not to effect it. The Cardinal is grown
Wondrous melancholy. Demand the cause;
Let him not put you off with feigned excuse.
Discover the main ground on't.

JULIA   Why would you know this?   190

BOSOLA

I have depended on him, and I hear
That he is fallen in some disgrace with the emperor.
If he be, like the mice that forsake falling houses,
I would shift to other dependence.

JULIA   You shall not need
Follow the wars – I'll be your maintenance.   195

BOSOLA

And I your loyal servant. But I cannot
Leave my calling.

JULIA   Not leave an ungrateful general
For the love of a sweet lady? You are like
Some cannot sleep in featherbeds but must have
Blocks for their pillows.

185 **somewhat** something
186 **express** show that
190 **ground on't** reason for it
191 **depended on him** been his depend-
ant or servant
192 **emperor** Charles V, with whom the
House of Aragon was allied against
France; see 3.3.1n. for the anachro-
nism of the reference.

193 proverbial: 'Mice quit a falling house'
(or sinking ship) (Dent, M1243*).
195 **Follow the wars** serve as a soldier
I'll . . . maintenance I'll support
you (which would create a parallel with the Duchess's support of
Antonio).
197 **calling** (military) profession
199 **Some** some who

184] *Q1 lines* you. / Lady. /   186–200] *this edn; Q1 lines* you. / me, / mellancholly, / off, / on't. /
this? / him, / disgrace / mice / shift / dependance. / warres, / maintenance. / seruant, / calling. /
an / Lady? / feather-beds, / pillowes. / Cunningly. /

BOSOLA   Will you do this?

JULIA   Cunningly.   200

BOSOLA

Tomorrow I'll expect th'intelligence.

JULIA

Tomorrow? Get you into my cabinet. *speaking in verse; elevated by medicines; intent*

You shall have it with you. Do not delay me,

No more than I do you. I am like one

That is condemned: I have my pardon promised   205

But I would see it sealed. Go, get you in.

You shall see me wind my tongue about his heart

Like a skein of silk.   [*Bosola goes behind the traverse.*]

[*Enter* CARDINAL *and* SERVANTS *at different doors.*]

CARDINAL

Where are you?

SERVANT   Here.

CARDINAL   Let none, upon your lives,

Have conference with the prince Ferdinand   210

202 **cabinet** private chamber (imagined as immediately offstage)

203 **have** take

204–6 **I am ... sealed** I have received a promise of sexual satisfaction but need to actually experience it (with a play on sealing a pardon and sex, imagined in Aristotelian terms, as the imprint of male form upon female matter).

206–8 **Go . . . silk** Though Julia orders Bosola offstage she still expects him to hear and *see* her conversation.

208 SD1 echoes the wedding scene (1.2), where it was Cariola who hid behind the *traverse* or *arras*; *traverse* echoes 4.1.54.1.

208 SD2 Alternatively, the Cardinal may come onstage and then call the servants (see t.n.). In some 19th-century productions, the Cardinal entered, '*followed by Servants*' (*Acting Copy*, 51).

209 SP2 The mass entrance to 5.2 does not include either '*Servant*' or '*Servants*', but the Cardinal's 'none, upon your lives' (209) suggests there are more than one. Q1's SP here, '*Seru.*', is likewise indeterminate; one could answer or several could speak together. The number of servants probably depended on the number of actors available; two was a common number of attendants.

208 SD1] *Brennan (subst); Exit* Bosola. *Q4; Exit Bosola, into her cabinet.* | *Lucas* SD2 *Enter ...* SERVANTS] *Dyce; Re-enter* Cardinal. *Dyce², with Enter* Servants *at 209   at different doors*] *this edn*   209] *Q1 lines* Here. / liues /   you] you all *Q4*   210 the] *om. Q4*

no one can speak to his

Unless I know it.   [*Exeunt Servants.*]
           In this distraction
He may reveal the murder.
Yond's my lingering consumption:
I am weary of her, and by any means
Would be quit off.

JULIA   How now, my lord? What ails you?   215

CARDINAL
     Nothing.

JULIA   Oh, you are much altered. Come,
I must be your secretary and remove
This lead from off your bosom. What's the matter?

CARDINAL
     I may not tell you.

JULIA   Are you so far in love with sorrow
You cannot part with part of it? Or think you   220
I cannot love your grace when you are sad
As well as merry? Or do you suspect
I, that have been a secret to your heart
These many winters, cannot be the same
Unto your tongue?

---

211 **distraction** pronounced as four syllables

213 **consumption** pronounced as four syllables; Julia is a wasting disease (like tuberculosis); she is a long-term drain on the Cardinal's revenues.

215 **quit off** rid of her

217 **secretary** in the Renaissance sense, where secretaries were the bearers of their master's most private business and closest secrets; Julia has been the Cardinal's *secret* (223).

218 **lead** heaviness of heart; suggests the lead weights that were pressed

on those accused of treason to exact confession. If the accused suffered in silence, his property was not confiscated to the state. Cf. 3.2.111–13, where Ferdinand suffers from a similar condition.

222–5 **Or . . . tongue?** If I have kept the secret of the love you have held in your heart, will I not keep the secret of your words? Julia attempts to counter the proverb 'A woman conceals what she knows not' (Dent, W649*), which the Cardinal summarizes in his next speech.

---

211 SD] *Dyce after 213*   213 lingering] *(lingring)*   215–17] *this edn; Q1 lines* Lord? / Nothing. / alterd: / remoue /   215 off] off her *Q4*   216–18 Come . . . bosom] *om. Q4*   219] *Q1 lines* you. / sorrow, /   Are you] You are *Q4*   225] *Q1 lines* tongue? / longing, /

CARDINAL   Satisfy thy longing.   225
 The only way to make thee keep my counsel
 Is not to tell thee.
JULIA   Tell your echo this –
 Or flatterers that like echoes still report
 What they hear, though most imperfect – and not me.
 For if that you be true unto yourself   230
 I'll know.
CARDINAL   Will you rack me?   *— torture him*
JULIA   No, judgement shall
 Draw it from you. It is an equal fault
 To tell one's secrets unto all or none.
CARDINAL
 The first argues folly –   *Card entering*
JULIA   But the last, tyranny.   *confession*
CARDINAL
 Very well. Why, imagine I have committed   235
 Some secret deed, which I desire the world
 May never hear of.
JULIA   Therefore may not I know it?
 You have concealed for me as great a sin
 As adultery. Sir, never was occasion

225–7 **Satisfy . . . thee** The Cardinal shifts his form of address from 'you' to the more intimate *thy* and *thee*; similar shifts happen at 243 and 262 below.

225 **Satisfy thy longing** Get over your desire to know.

227–9 **Tell . . . me** Echo and flatterers need to be admonished not to repeat what they hear (with a suggestion that such admonition is fruitless), but not Julia. She again counters proverbial depictions of women as unable to keep a secret (see 222–5n.). The image

anticipates the Echo in 5.3.

230–1 **if . . . know** Ironically, this tender statement of trust in the power of sincerity occurs as part of Julia's deception of the Cardinal.

231 **rack me** put me on the *rack*, an instrument of torture used to extract the truth from reluctant witnesses

234 **But . . . tyranny** i.e. a ruler or other authority figure who doesn't share his secrets with anyone is attempting to hide the fact that his rule is unjust.

237 **Therefore** for that reason

227–9 Tell . . . me] *om. in performance Q4* 230 be] are *Q4* unto] to *Q4* 231] *Q1 lines* me? / shall / 234] *Q1 lines* folly. / tyranny. / 237] *Q1 lines* of? / it? / 239 never was occasion] I beseech you *Q2*

For perfect trial of my constancy   240
Till now. Sir, I beseech you. *trial of her faithfulness*

CARDINAL   You'll repent it.

JULIA

Never.

CARDINAL

It hurries thee to ruin. I'll not tell thee.
Be well advised, and think what danger 'tis
To receive a prince's secrets. They that do   245
Had need have their breasts hooped with adamant
To contain them. I pray thee, yet be satisfied;
Examine thine own frailty. 'Tis more easy
To tie knots than unloose them. 'Tis a secret
That, like a lingering poison, may chance lie   250
Spread in thy veins and kill thee seven year hence.

JULIA

Now you dally with me.

CARDINAL   No more – thou shalt know it.
By my appointment the great Duchess of Malfi   *Admits*
And two of her young children, four nights since,
Were strangled.

JULIA   O heaven! Sir, what have you done?   255

CARDINAL

How now? How settles this? Think you your bosom
Will be a grave dark and obscure enough
For such a secret?

---

246 **adamant** strong metal: only metal bands encasing the breast (or heart) of the confidant will be able to hold in the prince's secrets. Cf. the same image in other dramatic contexts: *Bussy*, 3.2.224–6, 'if my hart was not hooped with adamant, the conceit of this would have burst it'; and *Antonio and Mellida*, 5.2.232.

249 **unloose** untie
250 **like . . . poison** The Cardinal imagines the secret's effect on Julia as similar to her 'consumptive' effect on him (213).
253 **appointment** arrangement
256 **How settles this?** How are you reacting?; Is it settling in?

241–2] *Q1 lines* you. / Neuer. /   247–9 I . . . them] *om. in performance Q4*   250 lingering] *(*lingring*)*   252] *Q1 lines* me. / it. /   255–60] *Q1 lines* strangled. / done? / your / enough / secret? / (sir.) / it. / booke. /

JULIA You have undone yourself, sir.

CARDINAL
Why?

JULIA It lies not in me to conceal it.

CARDINAL No?
Come I will swear you to't upon this book. 260
[*Holds up a Bible.*]

JULIA
Most religiously.

CARDINAL Kiss it. [*She kisses the Bible.*] *poison kills her*
Now you shall never utter it. Thy curiosity
Hath undone thee: thou'rt poisoned with that book.
Because I knew thou couldst not keep my counsel,
I have bound thee to't by death. 265
[*Bosola reveals himself.*]

BOSOLA
For pity sake, hold!

CARDINAL Ha, Bosola?

JULIA I forgive you
This equal piece of justice you have done:
For I betrayed your counsel to that fellow.
He overheard it; that was the cause I said
It lay not in me to conceal it.

BOSOLA Oh, foolish woman, 270
Couldst not thou have poisoned him?

---

260 SD The book is nowhere specified as a Bible in Q1, but a Bible would have maximum shock value and contribute to the play's anti-Catholic bias in its portrayal of the Cardinal (see pp. 24–5). Julia's phrase 'most religiously' supports this interpretation. Alternatively, the book could be the one the Cardinal goes on to read at the beginning of 5.5.

267 **equal** reciprocal
269 **cause** reason
270–1 **Oh ... him** That Bosola would utter this sentiment in the Cardinal's presence signals the open breach between them.

260 SD] *Weis (subst.)* 261 SD] *Brennan (subst.); She kisses the book. | Brown* 265–6] *Sampson; Q1 lines* death. / *Bosola?* / you, / 265 thee] *Q2;* the *Q1* SD] *this edn; Enter* Bosola. *Q4* 270–1] *Q1 lines* it. / woman, / him? / weaknesse, /

JULIA   'Tis weakness
  Too much to think what should have been done.
  I go I know not whither.   [*Dies.*]

CARDINAL
  Wherefore com'st thou hither?

BOSOLA
  That I might find a great man like yourself,   275
  Not out of his wits, as the lord Ferdinand,
  To remember my service.

CARDINAL   I'll have thee hewed in pieces.

BOSOLA
  Make not yourself such a promise of that life
  Which is not yours to dispose of.

CARDINAL   Who placed thee here?

BOSOLA
  Her lust, as she intended.

CARDINAL   Very well.   280
  Now you know me for your fellow murderer.

BOSOLA
  And wherefore should you lay fair marble colours
  Upon your rotten purposes to me?
  – Unless you imitate some that do plot great treasons,
  And, when they have done, go hide themselves i'th'
      graves   285

273 i.e. I do not know what is in store for me after death – a favourite Websterian phrase signalling an ungodly death or fear of it; cf. *White Devil*, 5.6.106, 243–4, Flamineo's 'Whither shall I go now?' and Vittoria's 'My soule . . . / Is driven I know not whither'; and *Devil's Law-Case*, 5.6.12, Romelio's 'I doe not well know whither I am going' (Webster, 2.164). Alternatively *whither* could be 'whether', as at 5.1.17, implying that she dies with an incomplete thought (though Q1 follows 'whether' with a full stop).

275 **like yourself** like you; in possession of your faculties
279 **Which . . . of** i.e. I'm my own man now.
282 **fair marble colours** a faux-finish – wood painted to resemble marble (popular in decorating of the baroque era)
285–6 cover up their deeds by killing those enlisted to perpetrate them; cf. *Penitential Psalms*, 'A Great Man', 62, 'Plots treason, and lies, hid in th'actors grave' (Brown).

273 SD] *Q4*   274 com'st] cam'st *Q4*   277] *Q1 lines* seruice. / peeces. /   279–81] *Sampson; Q1 lines* of. / here. / intended. / murderer. /

Of those were actors in't.

CARDINAL

No more. There is a fortune attends thee.

BOSOLA

Shall I go sue to Fortune any longer?
'Tis the fool's pilgrimage.

CARDINAL   I have honours in store for thee.

BOSOLA

There are a-many ways that conduct to seeming
    honour,   290
And some of them very dirty ones.

CARDINAL

Throw to the devil thy melancholy! The fire burns well:
What need we keep a stirring of't and make
A greater smother? Thou wilt kill Antonio?

BOSOLA

Yes.

CARDINAL   Take up that body.

BOSOLA   I think I shall   295
Shortly grow the common bier for churchyards.

CARDINAL

I will allow thee some dozen of attendants
To aid thee in the murder.

BOSOLA   Oh, by no means.

---

288 **Fortune** Bosola deliberately misin-
    terprets the Cardinal's offer of money
    as a reference to the goddess Fortune
    (cf. 3.5.94).
289 **fool's pilgrimage** fool's errand
290–1 Cf. *Gallant's*, sig. A4ᵛ, 'There are
    infinite wayes that conduct to seeming
    Honour, excluding Vertue; the end of
    them all is shame.'
290 **a-many** many (colloquial); cf. the

many doors of death (4.2.211) and the
thousand ways of tracing a fugitive
(126–7).
292–4 **The . . . smother?** i.e. why quar-
    rel with success?
294 **smother** stifling smoke
296 **common bier** movable stand used
    to carry corpses to the grave, *common*
    because the same one is used by all; *com-
    mon* also suggests social degradation.

286–7] *Brown; Q1 lines* more, / thee. /   288 to] a *Q2*   289–92] *this edn; Q1 lines* Pilgrimage. / thee.
/ seeming / ones. / diuell / well, /   290 a-many] many *Q2*   294 greater] great *Q2*   295] *Q1 lines*
body. / shall /   296 bier] *Q3;* Beare *Q1*   298] *Q1 lines* murther. / meanes, /

Physicians that apply horse-leeches to any rank swelling
use to cut off their tails, that the blood may run through   300
them the faster. Let me have no train when I go to shed
blood, lest it make me have a greater when I ride to the
gallows.

CARDINAL

Come to me after midnight to help to remove
That body to her own lodging. I'll give out   305
She died o'th' plague. 'Twill breed the less inquiry
After her death.

BOSOLA

Where's Castruccio, her husband?

CARDINAL   He's rode to Naples
To take possession of Antonio's citadel.

BOSOLA

Believe me, you have done a very happy turn.   310

CARDINAL

Fail not to come. There is the master key

299–303 Bosola (appropriately, considering his profession) suggests a comparison between himself and a leech. Like the cut tail on the leech (which was used for medicinal purposes and was able to draw more blood when cut because what it sucked in could flow out the other end), having the attendants the Cardinal proposes at 297 might help Bosola operate more efficiently in assassinating Antonio. But a *train* (group of attendants) would also hasten Bosola's death by making his crime more likely to be discovered and therefore lead to his execution, which would be attended by a *greater* train of observers than had the murder itself. (By this point, Bosola has no intention of carrying out the assassination of Antonio, so his elaborate explanation is only a smokescreen.)

304–5 **Come . . . lodging** The Cardinal revises his previous plan to have Bosola remove Julia's body immediately (295).

305 **give out** release the information that; spread the rumour that

309 **Antonio's citadel** St Bennet, which Pescara had given to Julia, Castruccio's wife (5.1.30–6)

310 **happy turn** good deed (since the Cardinal's letter had instigated the gift to Julia); possibly also an ironic comment on the murder of Julia, who might, if alive, have accused Bosola of attempting to win her away from the Cardinal

311 **There . . . key** another of the play's many repetitions with difference: cf. 3.1.81, where Bosola similarly procures a key for Ferdinand.

299–301 Physicians . . . faster] *om. Q4*   304–9] *this edn; Q1 lines* body / Plague; / death. / husband? / possession / Cittadell. /*; prose to 307 Brown*   308 rode] *(rod)*

Of our lodgings, and by that you may conceive
What trust I plant in you.

BOSOLA   You shall find me ready.

Exit [Cardinal].

Oh, poor Antonio! Though nothing be so needful
To thy estate as pity, yet I find   315
Nothing so dangerous. I must look to my footing.
In such slippery ice-pavements, men had need
To be frost-nailed well; they may break their necks else.
The precedent's here afore me: how this man
Bears up in blood, seems fearless! Why, 'tis well: 320
Security some men call the suburbs of hell –
Only a dead wall between. Well, good Antonio,
I'll seek thee out, and all my care shall be
To put thee into safety from the reach
Of these most cruel biters that have got   325
Some of thy blood already. It may be
I'll join with thee in a most just revenge.
The weakest arm is strong enough that strikes
With the sword of justice. Still, methinks the Duchess

---

315 **estate** condition
315–16 **yet . . . dangerous** The very measures Bosola might wish to take for Antonio's relief would endanger him (and Bosola).
316 **look . . . footing** be mindful of my actions
317 **ice-pavements** icy walkways (referring to the peril of Bosola's situation)
318 **be frost-nailed** wear hobnailed boots to protect against slipping
else otherwise
319 **precedent** either Julia, as an example of someone who fell, or the Cardinal, as an example of someone who bears up under adversity. The punctuation here reflects the latter interpretation.
afore before; if he refers to Julia, 'lying in front of'

this man the Cardinal
320 **Bears . . . blood** keeps up his courage
321–2 **Security . . . between** echoes a strongly Protestant sentiment about salvation: a sense of security, or self-satisfaction that one has been saved, is dangerous because it can easily lead to spiritual indolence and hence to damnation; cf. *Gallant's*, sig. B3ᵛ: 'Securitie is the very suburbes of Hell.'
322 **dead** unbroken; suggests a wall surrounding hell and separating the damned souls from those on their way to judgement
325 **cruel biters** Cf. Ferdinand's self-portrayal as a 'sheep-biter' (45).
326 **blood** i.e. his dead wife and children

313] *Q1 lines* you. / ready. /   SD] *opp.* in you *Q1*   316–19 I . . . me] *om. Q4*   321–2] *om. Q4*

Haunts me. There, there – 'tis nothing but my
   melancholy.   330
O penitence, let me truly taste thy cup,
That throws men down, only to raise them up.   *Exit.*

5.3   [*Enter*] ANTONIO, DELIO [*and*] ECHO [*unseen*].

DELIO

Yond's the Cardinal's window. This fortification
Grew from the ruins of an ancient abbey;

329 **Still** constantly, continually; at the
same time.

329–30 **methinks . . . me** foreshadows the
following scene, 5.3; basing themselves
on Q4's SD '*Starts*' (t.n.), some editors
call for the Duchess's spirit to appear to
Bosola, in which case *There, there*, rather
than self-soothing, could be his attempt
to locate the ghost (cf. *Ham* 1.1.140).

331–2 The *cup* of repentance (suggesting
the sacrament of communion) hum-
bles men but spiritually exalts them.
Another seemingly aphoristic closing
to a major speech and to a scene;
however, this one is not typographi-
cally identified by italics or quotation
marks in Q1.

332 SD Some editors specify that Bosola
exits with the body of Julia, which
nicely echoes the end of act 4, where
he exits with the body of the Duchess.
However, the Cardinal's explicit plan
was for Bosola to return and remove
the body *after midnight* (304). Possibly,
at Blackfriars and the Globe, the body
was removed in the break between acts.

5.3 Location: Milan

0 SD Q1 lists Echo among the characters
in the entrance here as '*Eccho, (from
the Dutchesse Graue.)*', suggesting that
the Duchess's grave may be visible
onstage. See also List of Roles, 1n.
and 17n. She may enter here unseen

along with Antonio and Delio, perhaps
from a different door. Alternatively,
she could enter at 19, or remain a dis-
embodied voice from offstage or from
within the curtained discovery space.
In early productions the Duchess may
have appeared above her grave in white
grave clothes when Antonio says he
sees a *face* (see 44 and n.). There is no
reason to suppose the Duchess would
be buried in Milan, since she died in
Amalfi. Nevertheless, the reference to
dead stones (35) may refer to her grave,
as well as to the *ruins* (2), which were
probably not represented onstage in
early productions, but formed a striking visual element of the scene in
19th- and early 20th-century stagings
and illustrations (see Fig. 14, p. 99).

1–4 **Yond's . . . cloister** This suggests
that the scene takes place behind the
Cardinal's palace, which is a walled castle (*fortification*) built out of the stones
from a ruined abbey. The history of
the building recapitulates the Cardinal's
career, from churchman to soldier. For
English audiences, the castle built out
of a ruined abbey would have evoked
the ecclesiastical ruins left scattered in
the landscape after Henry VIII's dis-
solution of the monasteries, many of
which became building materials for
16th-century noble houses.

329] *Starts.* | *opp.* Duchess *Q4*   332 raise] rise *Q2*   **5.3**] (SCENA. III.*)*   0 SD *Enter . . .* ECHO]
Dyce (subst.*); Antonio, Delio, Eccho, (from the Dutchesse Graue.)* | *Q1*   unseen] *this edn*   1 Yond's]
That's *Q4*

And to yond side o'th' river lies a wall,
Piece of a cloister, which in my opinion
Gives the best echo that you ever heard –   5
So hollow and so dismal, and withal
So plain in the distinction of our words
That many have supposed it is a spirit
That answers.

ANTONIO   I do love these ancient ruins.
We never tread upon them but we set   10
Our foot upon some reverend history.
And questionless, here in this open court,
Which now lies naked to the injuries
Of stormy weather, some men lie interred
Loved the church so well, and gave so largely to't,   15
They thought it should have canopied their bones
Till doomsday. But all things have their end:
Churches and cities, which have diseases like to men,
Must have like death that we have.

ECHO   'Like death that we have.'

---

3 **river** probably the Po, which runs near Milan and is connected to it by a number of channels engineered by Leonardo da Vinci in the late 15th century
6 **withal** at the same time, along with that
9 **ancient** old but not necessarily classical
10–11 Cf. Montaigne, 3.597, adapting Cicero on Rome: '*which way soever wee walke, wee sette our foote upon some Historie*' (Lucas).
11 **reverend** revered, worthy of respect
12 **open court** uncovered courtyard (once the nave and chancel of the abbey)
13 **naked** exposed
14–17 **some . . . doomsday** Those interred inside the church as opposed

to the churchyard tended to be the wealthiest and most prominent members of the community and paid extra to have their graves located there. They believed so strongly in the stability of the church that they thought their bones would be safely sheltered (*canopied*) until the end of the world (*doomsday*), when all graves would open and the dead and living would meet together for the Last Judgement.
15 **largely** generously
17 **all . . . end** proverbial: 'Everything has an end' (Dent, E120*).
19 **like** a similar
Like . . . have If Echo is the Duchess's voice (see 0 SDn.), she can be understood to mean 'a death like mine and

9] *Q1 lines* answeres. / ruynes: /   14 men] *om. Q2*   interred] *(*Enterr'd*)*   19+] *Echo's speeches ital. Q1*

DELIO

Now the echo hath caught you.

ANTONIO   It groaned, methought, and gave   20

A very deadly accent.

ECHO   'Deadly accent.'

DELIO

I told you 'twas a pretty one. You may make it

A huntsman or a falconer, a musician

Or a thing of sorrow.

ECHO   'A thing of sorrow.'

ANTONIO

Ay, sure that suits it best.

ECHO   'That suits it best.'   25

ANTONIO

'Tis very like my wife's voice.

ECHO   'I, wife's voice.'

DELIO

Come, let's us walk farther from't.

I would not have you go to th' Cardinal's tonight.

Do not.

ECHO   'Do not.'

DELIO

Wisdom doth not more moderate wasting sorrow   30

the children's'. This and all Echo's words are italicized in Q1. They are placed in quotations here to set them apart and show their similarity to the 'echoing' aphorisms that frequently conclude speeches and scenes in the play. There were echo scenes in classical plays such as *Thesmophoriazusae*, which parodied the echo scene in a lost play by Euripides. Cf. also the familiar story of Echo and Narcissus from Ovid, 3.339–510.

21 **deadly** death-like

23 All of these in a rural setting might make sounds that could be mistaken for an echo.

26 **I** could also be 'Ay', but *I* suggests the Duchess is revealing herself through the Echo.

27 **let's us** let's (colloquial)

30–1 **Wisdom . . . time** i.e. wisdom is not better than time when it comes to dealing with grief. Cf. proverbial 'Time heals all wounds' or 'cures all disease' (Dent, T325).

30 **wasting** progressively debilitating

19–21] *Q1 lines* haue. / *haue.* / you: / gaue / Accent? / *Accent.* /   24–6] *Q1 lines* Sorrow. / *Sorrow.* / best. / *best.* / voyce. / *wifes-voyce.* /   26 my wife's] *(*my wiues*)*   28 go] *Q1b;* too *Q1a; om. Q2*   29] *Q1 lines* not. / *not.* /

Than time. Take time for't; be mindful of thy safety.

ECHO   'Be mindful of thy safety.'

ANTONIO

Necessity compels me. Make scrutiny

Throughout the passes of your own life; you'll find it

Impossible to fly your fate.

ECHO   'Oh, fly your fate.'

DELIO

Hark! The dead stones seem to have pity on you,   35

And give you good counsel.

ANTONIO

Echo, I will not talk with thee,

For thou art a dead thing.

ECHO   'Thou art a dead thing.'

ANTONIO

My Duchess is asleep now,

And her little ones, I hope sweetly. O Heaven,   40

Shall I never see her more?

ECHO   'Never see her more.'

ANTONIO

I marked not one repetition of the echo

But that, and on the sudden a clear light

---

31 **Be . . . safety** As in earlier cases, Echo's response here is treated as part of the same line as the speech she is responding to, even though the result is a metrically overloaded line.

33 **passes** events, passages (Q4's reading)

34 **Impossible . . . fate** proverbial: 'it is impossible to avoid fate' (Dent, F83*).

34 SP *Although Q1 omits the SP here, the italics in Q1 make it clear that this speech is also Echo's.

34 As frequently in echo verse of the period, the echo here works better for

the eye than for the ear, since the 'o' in *to* is pronounced differently from Echo's *Oh*.

Oh . . . fate Here Echo modulates into prophecy, seeming to foretell Antonio's death.

35 **dead stones** imagines Echo as coming from inanimate rock (she continues to be unseen)

41 **Shall . . . more** Cf. Antonio's words at 3.5.82: 'If I do never see thee more'.

42 **marked** took particular note of

43 **on the sudden** suddenly, unexpectedly

31–4] *this edn; Q1 lines* safety. / *safety.* / me: / passes / impossible / fate. / *fate.* /   33 passes] passages *Q4*   34 SP] *Q4*   38] *Q1 lines* Thing. / *Thing.* /   41] *Q1 lines* more? / *more:* /

Presented me a face folded in sorrow.

DELIO

Your fancy, merely.

ANTONIO   Come, I'll be out of this ague,   45

For to live thus is not indeed to live.

It is a mockery and abuse of life.

I will not henceforth save myself by halves:

Lose all or nothing!

DELIO   Your own virtue save you!

I'll fetch your eldest son and second you.   50

It may be that the sight of his own blood,

Spread in so sweet a figure, may beget

The more compassion. However, fare you well.

Though in our miseries Fortune have a part,

---

44 **Presented** made visible to
face . . . sorrow evidently the
Duchess's face, showing the ravages
of her still-recent tragedies. At this
point the Duchess's *face* may appear
visibly onstage, as in *Lady's Tragedy*,
4.4.42, where a SD calls for the ghost
of a lady to appear amidst bright light
in front of her open tomb. In 19th- and
20th-century productions the Duchess
sometimes appeared in a ghostly light,
as in the Manchester Royal Exchange
production (1980), or as a shadow
thrown across the stage, as in Poel's
version in 1892 (McLuskie and Uglow,
195). As Delio claims, this is *fancy*
(45): the vision, even if visible to the
audience, would be understood as seen
only by Antonio.
folded wrapped up (figuratively)
45–9 **Come . . . nothing** the same sentiment Antonio has already expressed
at 5.1.71–3
45 **ague** trembling associated with fear
and anxiety
46–7 Cf. Serres, 1050: a life 'deprived of
the Kings grace and favour . . . is no

Life, it is to languish and to abuse Life'
(Dent, *Webster*).
48 **by halves** with half measures, luke-
warmly; cf. Montaigne, 2.359: 'I will
neither feare, nor save my selfe by
halfes.'
49 **Your** may your
51 **his** the Cardinal's
52 **Spread** revealed, displayed fully
53–6 **However . . . own** Apparently
wishing to give Antonio the final word,
editors since Lucas have followed
Sampson's suggestion and assigned
these lines, beginning with *However*, to
Antonio (see t.n.). In Q1 there is a page
break after *compassion*, but no sign that
a SP indicating a change in speaker
has been omitted. The catchword is,
appropriately, 'How' for 'However'.
Rather than reflecting Antonio's stoic
response to his own particular situation, the lines can be understood as
Delio's more general comment to the
effect that 'Though Fortune can cause
bad things to happen to us she can't
dictate our response to them.'
53 **However** either way, however it goes

45] *Q1 lines* meerely. / Ague; /   49] *Q1 lines* nothing. / you: /   Lose] *(loose)*   52 in] into *Q2*   53]
Dyce; Q1 lines compassion. / well: /   compassion. However] compassion. ANTONIO However *Lucas*

327

Yet in our noble sufferings she hath none.   55
Contempt of pain – that we may call our own.   *Exeunt.*

5.4   [*Enter*] CARDINAL, PESCARA, MALATESTE,
                RODERIGO [*and*] GRISOLAN.

CARDINAL
  You shall not watch tonight by the sick prince.
  His grace is very well recovered.
MALATESTE
  Good my lord, suffer us.
CARDINAL   Oh, by no means.
  The noise and change of object in his eye
  Doth more distract him. I pray, all to bed,   5
  And, though you hear him in his violent fit,
  Do not rise, I entreat you.
PESCARA   So, sir, we shall not.
CARDINAL
  Nay, I must have you promise
  Upon your honours, for I was enjoined to't
  By himself, and he seemed to urge it sensibly.   10
PESCARA
  Let our honours bind this trifle.
CARDINAL
  Nor any of your followers.
MALATESTE   Neither.

5.4 Location: the Cardinal's palace in Milan
2 **recovered** recoverèd
3 **suffer** allow
10 **sensibly** vehemently; in a rational manner
11 **bind … trifle** be bound by this small matter
12 **Neither.** No, neither will our *followers* rise.

---

55 sufferings] (suffrings) 56 SD] (*Exe.*) 5.4] (SCENA. IIII.) 0 SD] *Dyce; Cardinall, Pescara, Malateste, Rodorigo, Grisolan, Bosola, Ferdinand, Antonio, Seruant.* | *Q1; Enter* Cardinal, Malateste, Pescara *Q4* 3] *Q1 lines* vs. / meanes: / 7] *Q1 lines* you. / not, / 11–12] *Q1 lines* trifle. / followers. / Neither. / 11 our] *Q2;* out *Q1*

CARDINAL

It may be, to make trial of your promise,
When he's asleep myself will rise and feign
Some of his mad tricks, and cry out for help   15
And feign myself in danger.

MALATESTE   If your throat were cutting,

I'd not come at you, now I have protested
Against it.

CARDINAL   Why, I thank you.

GRISOLAN   'Twas a foul storm tonight.

RODERIGO

The lord Ferdinand's chamber shook like an osier.

MALATESTE

'Twas nothing but pure kindness in the devil   20
To rock his own child.   *Exeunt [all but the Cardinal].*

CARDINAL

The reason why I would not suffer these
About my brother is because at midnight
I may with better privacy convey
Julia's body to her own lodging. Oh, my conscience!   25
I would pray now, but the devil takes away my heart
For having any confidence in prayer.
About this hour, I appointed Bosola

[Enter] BOSOLA *[unseen].*

13 **make . . . of** test
16 **cutting** being cut
17 **now** now that
19 **osier** species of willow (*Salix vimina-lis*), with thin flexible stems
21 **rock . . . child** rock Ferdinand as though in a cradle
22–3 **suffer these / About** allow these people to be near

23 **because** so that
24–5 **I . . . lodging** as planned, with Bosola's help, 5.2.304–5
28 SD Editors vary widely in when they have Bosola appear – early enough to hear the Cardinal's threat but not so early that the Cardinal detects him. *Enter . . . unseen* parallels Ferdinand's entry at 3.2.59.

16–18] *this edn; Q1 lines* danger. / cutting, / it. / you. / night. /   18–21 'Twas . . . child] *om. Q4*   21
SD *Exeunt*] *after 18* you *Q4   all . . . Cardinal] Lucas (subst.)*   28 SD] *Dyce (subst.) after 30* dies;
Bosola, | 0 SD Q1; Enter Bosola *behind | Gibbons after 27*

329

To fetch the body. When he hath served my turn,
He dies.   *Exit.*

BOSOLA   Ha? 'Twas the Cardinal's voice.   30
I heard him name 'Bosola' and my death.

[*Enter*] FERDINAND.

Listen – I hear one's footing.

FERDINAND
Strangling is a very quiet death.

BOSOLA
Nay then, I see I must stand upon my guard.

FERDINAND
What say to that? Whisper softly: do you agree to't?   35
So it must be done i'th' dark. The Cardinal
Would not for a thousand pounds the doctor should
see it.   *Exit.*

BOSOLA
My death is plotted. Here's the consequence of murder.
'We value not desert, nor Christian breath,
When we know black deeds must be cured with death.'   40

32 **one's footing** someone's footsteps
35–6 **What . . . dark** Does Ferdinand imagine himself to be speaking to Bosola about Antonio's death, or is he aware of the Cardinal's plot on Bosola and speaking of that? Bosola, who knows of the Cardinal's plot on his life (31), seems to assume the latter and is mostly concerned about his own immediate danger (38).
35 **What say** what do you say (as Q3 and Q4); what should be said
37 **the doctor** It is unclear why Ferdinand would worry more about the doctor than about other potential witnesses.

Perhaps the doctor's efforts to instil respect for his own authority succeeded better with Ferdinand than was apparent at the time (5.2.58–73).
40 **black . . . death** Evil deeds can only be *cured* (rectified) through further evil; evil deeds can only be rectified by the death of the perpetrator. The former of the two possible interpretations was a Senecan commonplace; cf. *Malcontent*, 5.3.15, 'Black deed only through black deed safely flies', and the proverb, 'Crimes are made secure by greater crimes' (Dent, C826*).

30–2] *this edn; Q1 lines* dies. / name, / footing. /   30 He dies] *after 32* footing *Q4*   31 SD] *Dyce after 32* footing; *Ferdinand,* | *0 SD Q1; Enter* Bosola, Ferdinand. *Q4*   32 Listen] hist *Q4*   33 quiet] *Q2;* quiein *Q1*   35 say] *Q2;* say' *Q1;* say you *Q3*   39–40 'We . . . death.'] (,,*We . . . death.); om. Q4*

[*Enter*] ANTONIO [*and*] SERVANT.

SERVANT

Here stay, sir, and be confident, I pray.

I'll fetch you a dark lantern.   *Exit.*

ANTONIO

Could I take him at his prayers, there were hope of

    pardon.

BOSOLA

Fall right, my sword!   [*Stabs Antonio.*]

I'll not give thee so much leisure as to pray.   45

ANTONIO

Oh, I am gone! Thou hast ended a long suit

In a minute.

BOSOLA   What art thou?

ANTONIO   A most wretched thing *attend*

That only have thy benefit in death,   *at rest*

To appear myself.

[*Enter* SERVANT *with a light.*]

---

42 **dark lantern** Cf. 2.3.0 SDn.

43 Antonio may kneel at the Cardinal's usual prie-dieu (prayer desk with a low bench for kneeling) as he says these words, which would increase the chance of his being mistaken for the Cardinal. Although the darkness of the scene would have been a stage fiction in performances at the Globe and Blackfriars, where there was no way of darkening the stage, the servant's exit to get a light (42) would have cued early audiences that the scene was happening in darkness. One of the 1850 acting versions specifies that Antonio is stabbed offstage; the other specifies that Bosola stabs Antonio '*mistaking him for the Cardinal*'. Alternatively,

Bosola may mistake Antonio for an assassin hired by the Cardinal (28–30) and understand his words 'Could I take him at his prayers' as plotting Bosola's murder.

45 **to pray** suggests Antonio is kneeling; or Bosola may be denying him the customary time for brief penance before killing him; cf. 4.2.243–5n. and 5.5.37, 'Pray, and be sudden.'

46 **long suit** long proceedings to recover Antonio's property; life itself, imagined as an unrelenting struggle for justice

47–9 **A most . . . myself** You have done me a benefit by causing my death, in that I can now appear the wretched thing that I am, or in that I no longer need to hide myself to evade capture.

---

40 SD] *Q4 (subst.); Antonio, Seruant.* | *0 SD Q1*   43] *this edn; Q1 lines* prayers, / pardon. /   44 SD] *Lucas (subst.)*   45 thee] you *Q4*   47] *Q1 lines* mynut. / thou? / thing, / minute] *(mynut)*   48 thy] this *Q4*   49–50] *Q1 lines* selfe. / Sir? / *Bosola?* / misfortune. /   49 SD] *Q4*

SERVANT   Where are you, sir?

ANTONIO

Very near my home. Bosola?

SERVANT   Oh, misfortune!   50

BOSOLA

Smother thy pity; thou art dead else. Antonio?
The man I would have saved 'bove mine own life?
We are merely the stars' tennis balls, struck and banded
Which way please them. O good Antonio,
I'll whisper one thing in thy dying ear   55
Shall make thy heart break quickly. Thy fair Duchess
And two sweet children –

ANTONIO   Their very names
Kindle a little life in me.

BOSOLA   – Are murdered!

ANTONIO

Some men have wished to die
At the hearing of sad tidings. I am glad   60
That I shall do't in sadness. I would not now
Wish my wounds balmed nor healed, for I have no use
To put my life to. In all our quest of greatness,
Like wanton boys whose pastime is their care,
We follow after bubbles blown in th'air.   65
Pleasure of life – what is't? Only the good hours

---

50 **Very . . . home** i.e. close to death
50–1 **Bosola? . . . Antonio?** Gunby suggests the two men can finally recognize each other because the servant has brought in the light. See 43n.
51 **else** otherwise
53–4 **We . . . them** commonplace, already marked as such in Renaissance editions of Plautus (Dent, *Webster*)
    banded bandied, knocked about
55–8 Contrast Bosola's offering of false assurances to the dying Duchess (4.2.339–42).

61 **do't** i.e. die
    sadness earnest (playing on *sad*, 60)
62 **balmed** treated with soothing ointments
64–5 commonplace for the futility of human striving; cf. Fig. 9, p. 46.
64 **wanton . . . care** carefree boys who need only concern themselves with games
66–7 **good . . . ague** the peaceful periods in a fever with ups and downs (like malaria); cf. Hall, *Epistles*, 1.2, 14: 'All these earthly delights . . . are but as a good day betweene two agues.'

53–4 We . . . them] *om. Q4*   53 struck] *(strooke)*   57–8] *Q1 lines* Children, / names / me. / murderd! /

Of an ague, merely a preparative
To rest, to endure vexation. I do not ask
The process of my death. Only commend me
To Delio.

BOSOLA   Break, heart!

ANTONIO

And let my son fly the courts of princes.   [*Dies.*]   70

BOSOLA

Thou seemst to have loved Antonio.

SERVANT   I brought him hither
To have reconciled him to the Cardinal.

BOSOLA

I do not ask thee that.
Take him up if thou tender thine own life,   75
And bear him where the lady Julia
Was wont to lodge. – Oh, my fate moves swift!
I have this Cardinal in the forge already;
Now I'll bring him to th' hammer. Oh, direful
    misprision!
I will not imitate things glorious,   80
No more than base. I'll be mine own example.

67–8 **preparative . . . vexation** preparation for death, which may bring *rest* or
further troubles; or, more negatively,
the *good hours* only give the strength to
undergo further sufferings, in this case
after death.

69 **process** story; explanation of how it
happened

71 Cf. Vittoria's dying words in *White
Devil*, 5.6.256: 'O happy they that
never saw the Court.'
fly fly from

74 **that** for a reconciliation (which would
be advantageous for Antonio's surviving son)

75 **tender** value

76–7 **bear . . . lodge** Presumably Julia's
body has already been moved to her
'lodging'. Bosola may want all the
bodies stowed in the same place for
convenience in disposing of them.

78 **forge** blacksmith's fire; cf. proverbial
'Strike while the iron is hot' (Dent,
I94).

79 **direful misprision** dreadful misper-
ception (the mistaking of Antonio for
the Cardinal)

80–1 Cf. Flamineo's similar sentiment
in *White Devil*, 5.6.251–3: 'I doe not
looke / Who went before, nor who
shall follow mee; / Noe, at my selfe I
will begin and end.'

67–8] *this edn; Q1 lines* rest, / aske /   70] *Q1 lines* Delio. / heart: /   71 SD] *Dyce*   72] *Q1 lines*
Antonio? / hether, /   hither] *Q2;* hether *Q1*   73 to] with *Q2*   79–83 Oh . . . bearest] *om. Q4*

– On, on, and look thou represent, for silence,
The thing thou bearest.   *Exeunt [with Antonio's body].*

5.5   [*Enter*] CARDINAL *with a book.*

CARDINAL

I am puzzled in a question about hell.
He says in hell there's one material fire,
And yet it shall not burn all men alike.
Lay him by.   [*Puts down the book.*]
    How tedious is a guilty conscience!
When I look into the fishponds in my garden,   5
Methinks I see a thing armed with a rake
That seems to strike at me.

[*Enter*] BOSOLA.

82 **represent** emulate (spoken to the servant, but also perhaps to himself)

5.5 Location: the Cardinal's palace in Milan. The precise space is fluid. The Cardinal's speech (1–7) suggests that he is meditating in his own private study or library, perhaps the same room in which 5.4 took place. However, the servant, who had been directed at 5.4.75–7 to carry Antonio's body to Julia's chamber, enters with the body at 31 SD2, which suggests that he thinks the space he has entered is her chamber. Alternatively, the servant may disobey Bosola's orders and deliver Antonio's body to the Cardinal's study in order to show him the victim, unaware that the Cardinal himself had sought Antonio's death. Cf. 5.4.72–3, where the servant states that he brought Antonio to the Cardinal's palace with the hope of effecting their reconciliation.

2 **He** the Cardinal's theological authority, probably Luis de Granada, whose *Spiritual and Heavenly Exercises* were available in English from 1598. Granada uses the unusual phrase 'materiall fire' and says of the damned, 'they have the same fire, and yet it doth not burne al the damned that be therein alike' (Granada, sig. I10; Dent, *Webster*).

4 **tedious** boring (indicating cynicism); painful (indicating spiritual torment)

6 **thing . . . rake** a demon or perhaps Death with his scythe (foreshadowing Bosola's entrance immediately after), or even the Cardinal's own unrecognized reflection. This is the first point at which the Cardinal has seemed touched by the guilt-induced madness that has disabled his brother. In Webster's probable source, a similar apparition appears to a man three days before his death by sword (Lavater, 61).

83 SD] *Gunby (subst.)*   5.5] *(SCENA. V.)*   0 SD] *Q4; Cardinall (with a Booke) Bosola, Pescara, Malateste, Roderigo, Ferdinand, Delio, Seruant with Antonio's body. | Q1*   4 SD] *this edn*   5 fishponds] Fish-pond *Q4*   7–8] *Gunby; one line Q1*   7 SD] *after 10* fear *Q4; Bosola, | 0 SD Q1*

Now, art thou come? Thou look'st ghastly.
There sits in thy face some great determination,
Mixed with some fear.

BOSOLA   Thus it lightens into action: 10
I am come to kill thee.

CARDINAL   Ha? Help! Our guard!

BOSOLA
Thou art deceived. They are out of thy howling.

CARDINAL
Hold, and I will faithfully divide
Revenues with thee.—

BOSOLA   Thy prayers and proffers
Are both unseasonable.

CARDINAL   Raise the watch!   15
We are betrayed!

BOSOLA   I have confined your flight.
I'll suffer your retreat to Julia's chamber
But no further.

CARDINAL   Help! We are betrayed!

[*Enter above*] PESCARA, MALATESTE, RODERIGO
[*and* GRISOLAN].

10 **lightens** springs, kindles
12 suggests Bosola may have slaughtered
   the guards already
   out of beyond range of
14 **proffers** offers, proposals
17 **Julia's chamber** where her body
   awaits disposal
18 SD Grisolan is omitted from the mass
   entrance at 0 SD in Q1, but he speaks
   at 23–4. If he is not brought onstage
   with the other courtiers, his single

speech could be assigned to Roderigo.
Q4, which reflects 1707 performances,
calls for the courtiers to be above (see
t.n.) on the stage balcony, where they
can hear Bosola and the Cardinal but
not see them. Since both the Globe
and Blackfriars theatres had balconies,
the same arrangement of the scene was
probably used in early performances.
Pescara's *down to him* (29) implies that
he will descend.

10–12] *Gunby; Q1 lines* feare. / Action: / thee. / Guard. / deceiu'd: / howling. / 10 Thus . . .
action] *after 11* kill thee *Q4* 13 and] *om. Q2* 14–16] *Brown; Q1 lines* thee. / proffers / vnseasonable.
/ betraid. / flight: / 17 retreat] *(retreyt)* 18–20] *Q1 lines* further. / betraid. / Listen: / rescew. /
counterfeyting. / Cardinall. / he: / 18 further] farther *Q4* SD] *Dyce (subst.); Pescara, Malateste,
Roderigo, | 0 SD Q1; Enter Malateste, Roderigo, Pescara, above. | Q4*

MALATESTE   Listen!

CARDINAL

My dukedom for rescue!

RODERIGO   Fie upon his counterfeiting!

MALATESTE

Why, 'tis not the Cardinal.

RODERIGO   Yes, yes – 'tis he.   20

But I'll see him hanged ere I'll go down to him.

CARDINAL

Here's a plot upon me! I am assaulted! I am lost

Unless some rescue!

GRISOLAN   He doth this pretty well,

But it will not serve to laugh me out of mine honour.

CARDINAL

The sword's at my throat!

RODERIGO   You would not bawl so loud then.   25

MALATESTE

Come, come – let's go to bed. He told us thus much

    aforehand.

PESCARA

He wished you should not come at him, but believe't,

The accent of the voice sounds not in jest.

I'll down to him, howsoever, and with engines

Force ope the doors.   [*Exit Pescara above.*]

RODERIGO   Let's follow him aloof,   30

---

19 **My . . . rescue** Cf. *R3* 5.4, where
Catesby and the embattled Richard
III repeatedly call for rescue. This is
the first of the scene's echoes of *R3*,
which intensify upon the entrance of
Ferdinand at 45.

counterfeiting since the Cardinal had
earlier said he might feign distress just
to test their oath not to interrupt him
(5.4.13–18)

20 **Why . . . Cardinal** As usual Malateste
is out of touch. Cf. the Duchess's earlier description of him as mere 'sugar
candy' at 3.1.42 and the soldiers' ridi-
cule of him at 3.3.12ff.

23 **doth . . . well** is a fairly good actor

24 **honour** since he had sworn an oath
not to go to the Cardinal

29 **engines** machines, tools

30 **ope** open

19 rescue] a rescue *Q4*   his] this *Q4*   23] *Q1 lines* rescew. / well: /   25] *Q1 lines* throat: / then.
/   30] *Q1 lines* doores. / aloofe, /   SD] *Dyce (subst.)*

And note how the Cardinal will laugh at him.

> [*Exeunt above Malateste, Roderigo and Grisolan.*]

> [*Enter*] SERVANT *with Antonio's body.*

BOSOLA

There's for you first,
'Cause you shall not unbarricade the door
To let in rescue.   *He kills the Servant.*

CARDINAL

What cause hast thou to pursue my life?

BOSOLA   Look there!   35

CARDINAL

Antonio?

BOSOLA   Slain by my hand unwittingly.

Pray, and be sudden. When thou killed'st thy sister
Thou took'st from Justice her most equal balance,
And left her naught but her sword.

---

31 SD2 Alternatively, the servant may
enter with Bosola at 7, as in some
modern editions (see t.n.), in which
case he stands onstage for several minutes with a body that mysteriously
goes unremarked. Note the Cardinal's
evident surprise on seeing Antonio at
36–9. Either timing for the entrance
presents difficulties.

33–4 Evidently Bosola fears that the servant, misinterpreting the situation, will
try to get help for the Cardinal. See
5.5n.

33 **'Cause** so that

37 **sudden** quick about it; Bosola shows
punctiliousness in allowing the
Cardinal time to pray. To urge a victim
to his or her prayers is a formulaic
stage warning of impending death. Cf.
Leonine in *Per* 4.1.64, 'Come, say your
prayers', and Othello's demand that
Desdemona pray before she is killed

because he 'would not kill thy soul'
(*Oth* 5.2.32). Contrast Bosola's earlier
behaviour towards Antonio, 5.4.45 and
n. Cf. also Hamlet, who refused to kill
Claudius when he was at prayer (*Ham*
3.3.73ff.).

thou From this point onwards,
Bosola addresses the Cardinal with
the familiar (and disrespectful) *thou*
instead of the more respectful 'you'
that he used even with the servant
above at 32.

killed'st thy sister Cf. 5.2.281, where
the Cardinal acknowledges himself
Bosola's 'fellow murderer'.

38–9 Justice was typically depicted with
scales in one hand and a sword in
the other. In killing the Duchess, the
Cardinal took away equity or mercy
(imagined as Justice's scales); he can
therefore expect only the sword for
himself.

---

31 SD1] *Dyce*   SD2] *this edn; Seruant with Antonio's body.* | *0 SD Q1; after* BOSOLA *7 SD
Dyce*   32–6] *Q1 lines* doore / rescew. / life? / there: / *Antonio? /* vnwittingly: /

CARDINAL   Oh, mercy!

BOSOLA

Now it seems thy greatness was only outward: 40
For thou fallest faster of thyself than calamity
Can drive thee. I'll not waste longer time.   [*Stabs him.*]
                                                              There!

CARDINAL

Thou hast hurt me!

BOSOLA   Again!

CARDINAL   Shall I die like a leveret
Without any resistance? Help! Help! Help!
I am slain!

                    [*Enter*] FERDINAND.

FERDINAND   Th'alarum? Give me a fresh horse.   45
Rally the vanguard or the day is lost.
Yield, yield! I give you the honour of arms,
Shake my sword over you. Will you yield?

40–2 thy . . . thee Cf. the similar language in Webster's *Characters*, 'An Intruder into Favour' (Webster, 3.467); and *Arcadia*, book 2, ch. 29, 332: the base-born '*Antiphilus*, that had no greatnesse but outwarde, that taken away, was readie to fall faster then calamitie could thrust him.'

40 **outward** external

41 **of thyself** on your own

43 **leveret** rabbit (hence defenceless)

44 **resistance** which the Cardinal, strangely for one who has given up the cloth for the sword, expects to come from others rather than to provide for himself. Since he is at home in a private room, he may not have a weapon close at hand.

45 **Th'alarum . . . horse** Ferdinand thinks he hears a military call to action and springs into battle. Cf. *R3* 5.4.7: 'My kingdom for a horse!' Both Richard III and Ferdinand were played by Richard Burbage: in fact, Burbage was so strongly identified with the role that people at the time sometimes referred to Richard III as 'Burbage' (Gurr, *Playgoing*, 126). This close association has interesting metadramatic implications: perhaps, as Gibbons suggests, mad Ferdinand thinks he is acting the part of Richard in Shakespeare's play.

46 **vanguard** advance troops (in this case imaginary)

47–8 Ferdinand thinks he is taking the Cardinal prisoner.

47 **honour of arms** the honourable treatment due to a prisoner of quality

---

39] *Q1 lines* sword. / mercy. /   her sword] the sword *Q2*   41 fallest] (fall'st*)*   42 SD] *Q4 after* There.   43] *Q1 lines* me: / Againe: / Leuoret /   45] *Q1 lines* slaine. / horse: /   SD] *Q4; Ferdinand,* | *0 SD Q1*   45 Th'alarum] Th'alarm *Q4*   46 vanguard] *Q4;* vaunt-guard *Q1*

CARDINAL

Help me! I am your brother.

FERDINAND   The devil!

My brother fight upon the adverse party?   50

There flies your ransom!

(*He wounds the Cardinal and in the scuffle gives Bosola his
death wound.*)

CARDINAL   Oh, justice!

I suffer now for what hath former been.

'Sorrow is held the eldest child of sin.'

*now he gets what
he deserved*

FERDINAND   Now you're brave fellows! Caesar's fortune

was harder than Pompey's: Caesar died in the arms of   55

prosperity, Pompey at the feet of disgrace. You both

died in the field. The pain's nothing; pain many times

is taken away with the apprehension of greater, as the

toothache with the sight of a barber that comes to pull

it out. There's philosophy for you.   60

BOSOLA

Now my revenge is perfect: sink, thou main cause

Of my undoing! The last part of my life

---

49 **your . . . devil** Ferdinand responds
to the Cardinal's plea for recognition
with an oath, but it comes out as a
description of the Cardinal, echoing
1.1.45–7 and the 'character' of him at
1.2.102–4.

50–1 Since, in Ferdinand's mad reason-
ing, the Cardinal has revealed himself
as a brother, his perfidy in fighting for
the opposing side does not merit the
honour of arms and he will therefore be
killed, not ransomed.

52 Just as we killed our sister, I now die at
the hand of a brother.

53 Cf. *White Devil*, 5.4.20: 'I have heard
griefe nam'd the eldest child of sinne.'

54–60 printed as a mixture of short and

long lines in Q1, all beginning with
capital letters but all apparently prose

55 **harder** more difficult

55–6 **Caesar . . . disgrace** Cf. *Heptameron*,
sig. H2ʳ, where a similar illustration
appears in a chapter on the 'inconvenience of rash marriages'. Caesar
died in *prosperity* since he was slain
during peacetime by his fellow sen-
ators. Pompey the Great, rival to
Caesar, died in *disgrace* because he
died obscurely in Egypt after his
military defeat.

56 **You both** the Cardinal and Bosola

59–60 **toothache . . . out** Barbers, or
'barber-surgeons', performed many of
the tasks of modern-day dentists.

49] *Q1 lines* brother. / diuell? /   51] *Q1 lines* ransome. / Iustice: /   SD] *opp. 50–1 Q1   death*] *Deaths*
| *Q4*   53 'Sorrow . . . sin.'] ('Sorrow . . . sin.*)   is held] hath reacht *Q4*   54–60] *Dyce; Q1 lines* fel-
lows: / Pompey: / prosperity, / *followed by prose*

339

Hath done me best service.

> *He [gives] Ferdinand [his death wound].*

FERDINAND

Give me some wet hay; I am broken-winded.
I do account this world but a dog kennel.   65
I will vault credit and affect high pleasures
Beyond death.

BOSOLA   He seems

To come to himself now he's so near the bottom.

FERDINAND

My sister, oh, my sister – there's the cause on't.
'Whether we fall by ambition, blood or lust,   70
Like diamonds we are cut with our own dust.' [*Dies.*]

CARDINAL

Thou hast thy payment too.

BOSOLA

Yes, I hold my weary soul in my teeth:
'Tis ready to part from me. I do glory

---

63 SD Most editors follow Q1's SD and have Ferdinand 'die' here, but he goes on to utter seven more lines.

64 Ferdinand believes himself to be a horse.
broken-winded unable to breathe properly, a malady of horses

66–7 **I . . . death** Ferdinand imagines the afterlife as an even more opulent version of his life at court.

66 **vault credit** exceed credibility (by his imagined heroic feats)

67 a part-line shared between two speakers; on the effect of these part-lines, which imply a theatrical pause between the two speeches, see p. 79.

68 **To . . . himself** to be his old self (spoken in trenchant irony)

69 **on't** of all the preceding disasters

71 Everyone is his own worst enemy;

but Ferdinand, specifically, has been destroyed by the Duchess, whom he sees as an aspect of himself (his *own dust*). Cf. Nashe, *Christ's Tears over Jerusalem* (1593), in Nashe, 2.9, dedication: '*An easie matter is it for anie man to cutte me (like a Diamond) with mine owne dust*' (D&S); and the proverb 'Diamonds cut diamonds' (Dent, D323).

72 **payment** death; ironically, the Cardinal, who had so long withheld rewards, finally sees Bosola 'paid' for all his efforts.

73 **I . . . teeth** i.e. I'm barely clinging to life: a Renaissance commonplace based on Seneca and implying that Bosola's soul is ready to fly out of his body but has to be held back because he wants to explain his actions before he can allow himself to die.

---

63 SD] *this edn; He kills Ferdinand.* | *Q1*   67–8] *this edn; Q1 lines* death. / bottom. /   67 Beyond death] *om. Q2*   70 'Whether] ("*Whether*); Whether *Q3*   71 Like . . . dust.'] ('*Like . . . dust.*); Like . . . dust. *Q3*   SD] *Dyce*

That thou, which stood'st like a huge pyramid   75
Begun upon a large and ample base,
Shalt end in a little point – a kind of nothing.

[*Enter below* PESCARA, MALATESTE, RODERIGO
and GRISOLAN.]

PESCARA

How now, my lord?

MALATESTE   Oh, sad disaster!

RODERIGO   How comes this?

BOSOLA

Revenge for the Duchess of Malfi, murdered
By the Aragonian brethren; for Antonio,   80
Slain by his hand; for lustful Julia,
Poisoned by this man; and lastly, for myself,
That was an actor in the main of all,
Much 'gainst mine own good nature, yet i'th' end
Neglected.

PESCARA   How now, my lord?

CARDINAL   Look to my brother.   85

76 **base** the wealth and power of the House of Aragon and of the Catholic Church

77 **point** the tip of the pyramid
kind of nothing equivalent to zero. More frequently in the period, the *point* of the pyramid was used to suggest the pinnacle of greatness, as in *Whore*, preface, where the reign of Elizabeth I is called a pyramid that '*stands yet so high, and so sharply pointed into the clouds, that the Art of no pen is able to reach it*'.

79 **murdered** murderèd

81 **his** often emended to 'this', the Q4 reading, which removes the moral ambiguity; *his* could indicate either of the Aragonian brothers, and suggests that Bosola still fails to take responsibility for the actions he undertook at their behest.

82 **this man** the Cardinal (to call him *man* indicates disrespect of the Cardinal's station; cf. 37n., *thou*)

83 **actor . . . all** main plotter (with metadramatic implications)

84 **Much . . . nature** Bosola now sees himself as having acted against his own fundamental probity in serving as spy and assassin for the Aragonian brothers. Cf. 1.1.76–7, where Antonio said of Bosola, 'This foul melancholy / Will poison all his goodness'.

85 **How now** addressed to the Cardinal

77 SD] *Dyce (subst.); Enter* Pescara, &c. *Q4*   78] *Q1 lines* Lord?) / disastre. / this? /   Oh, sad disaster] *om. Q4*   81 his] this *Q4*   85] *Q1 lines* Neglected.) / Lord?) / brother: /   How . . . lord] *om. Q4*

He gave us these large wounds as we were struggling
Here i'th' rushes. And now, I pray, let me
Be laid by and never thought of.   [*Dies.*]

PESCARA

How fatally, it seems, he did withstand
His own rescue! ~ *plot backfired*

MALATESTE   Thou wretched thing of blood,   90
How came Antonio by his death?

BOSOLA

In a mist; I know not how –
Such a mistake as I have often seen
In a play. Oh, I am gone.
We are only like dead walls or vaulted graves   95
That, ruined, yields no echo. Fare you well.
It may be pain but no harm to me to die   *nd content*
In so good a quarrel. Oh, this gloomy world –
In what a shadow or deep pit of darkness
Doth, womanish and fearful, mankind live!   100
Let worthy minds ne'er stagger in distrust

87 **Here i'th' rushes** on the floor; rooms
(and the stage in theatres) were strewn
with rushes to sweeten the air.

87–8 **let . . . of** in marked contrast to the
opulent funeral a high magnate would
ordinarily expect. As the illustrations
reproduced in Amendola make clear,
every major event in the Aragonese
family was commemorated with elaborate public ceremony. Q4 adds an 'Oh',
a death groan, after the Cardinal's final
words (88 t.n).

88 **laid by** as the Cardinal had earlier set
aside his book (4)

89 **withstand** hold off, prevent

90 **thing of blood** Malateste's address to
Bosola suggests that he is bloody from
his wounds, but also that he is inher-

ently bloodthirsty, a killer. Cf. *Cor*
2.2.109–10, where the blood-covered
warrior Coriolanus is described as a
'thing of blood, whose every motion
/ Was tim'd with dying cries'.

92 **In a mist** Cf. the dying Flamineo's
'I am in a mist' (*White Devil*, 5.6.255)
and Bosola's own description of life as
a 'mist of error' (4.2.181).

95 **dead walls** Cf. 5.2.322, where only a
dead wall (a wall without breaks) stood
between Bosola and hell.

96 **ruined . . . echo** unlike the Duchess,
whose 'echo' reverberates through 5.3

98 **quarrel** cause

101–2 Cf. Cordelia in *KL* 5.3.3–4: 'We
are not the first / Who with best meaning have incurred the worst.'

88 of.] of: Oh? *Q4*   SD] *Q4*   90] *Q1 lines* rescew? / blood, /   95–103] *om. in performance Q4*

To suffer death or shame for what is just.
Mine is another voyage.   [*Dies.*]

PESCARA

The noble Delio, as I came to th' palace,
Told me of Antonio's being here, and showed me   105
A pretty gentleman, his son and heir.

[*Enter*] DELIO [*with Antonio's son*].

MALATESTE

Oh, sir, you come too late.

DELIO   I heard so, and was armed
For't ere I came. Let us make noble use
Of this great ruin, and join all our force
To establish this young hopeful gentleman   110
In's mother's right. These wretched, eminent things
Leave no more fame behind 'em than should one
Fall in a frost and leave his print in snow —
As soon as the sun shines, it ever melts
Both form and matter. I have ever thought   115
Nature doth nothing so great for great men
As when she's pleased to make them lords of truth.

---

103 i.e. I am going to hell, with the
unjust; or perhaps Bosola imagines
himself back in the galleys, still a slave
to the Aragonian brethren.
107 **armed** mentally prepared
110–11 **establish . . . right**   settle
Antonio's son as Duke of Amalfi and
perhaps also as heir of the House of
Aragon (here as before at 4.2.273–4,
the Duchess's son by her first husband

has dropped out of sight)
112 **should one** if one should
114 **it ever** the sun always
116–17 implies that rectitude is predes-
tined (ordained by *Nature*), rather
than individually achieved; cf. *Arcadia*,
book 2, ch. 7, 190: 'Nature having done
so much for them in nothing, as that it
made them Lords of truth, whereon
all the other goods were builded'.

103 SD] *Q4*   106 SD] *Dyce (subst.); Delio,* | *0 SD Q1*   107–8] *this edn; Q1 lines* late. / *and* / vse
/   111–15 These . . . matter] *om. in performance Q4*

'Integrity of life is fame's best friend,
Which nobly beyond death shall crown the end.'   *Exeunt.*

FINIS

[handwritten: You will only be remembered for what you do — opens and]

118–19 Contradicts Bosola's dying words implying that one can behave worthily and still die in disgrace (101–2). Delio's comment extolling *Integrity of life* recalls Horace's famous ode, 1.22, *Integer vitae*, which begins, 'He who is upright of life and free from crime does not need the javelin or bow of the Moor', but goes on to imply that the upright need not fear the wolf – a sentiment the play, with its portrait of Ferdinand's lycanthropy, is far from confirming (see p. 51).

118 **fame's** reputation's
119 **crown the end** exalt the end of life. 'The end crowns all' was proverbial (Dent, E116*); cf. also *White Devil*, 5.6, epilogue.

118–19] *ital. Q1* 'Integrity . . . end.'] *("Integrity . . . end.); Integrity . . . end. | Q3*

APPENDIX 1

The second Tome
of the Palace of Pleasure,
conteyning store of goodly Histories,
Tragicall matters, and other **Mo-
rall argument, very re-**
quisite for delighte
and profit.

Chosen and selected out of
divers good and commen-
dable Authors:

By William Painter, Clerke of the
Ordinance and Armarie
ANNO. 1567.

Imprinted at London, in
Pater Noster Rowe, by Henry
Bynneman, for Nicholas
England.

The Duchesse of Malfi.

¶ The Infortunate mariage of a Gentleman, called ANTONIO BOLOGNA, with the Duchesse of MALFI, and the pitifull death of them bothe.[1]

The .xxiii. Novel.

The greater Honor and authoritie men have in this world, & the greater their estimation is, the more sensible & notorious are the faultes by them committed, & the greater is their slander. In lyke manner more difficult it is for that man to tolerate and sustaine Fortune, which [170][2] all the dayes of his life hathe lived at his ease, if by chaunce hee fall into any great necessitie, than for hym which never felt but woe, mishappe, and adversitie. *Dyonisius* the Tyrant of *Sicilia*, felte greater payne when hee was expelled his kingdome, than *Milo* did, being banished from *Rome*. For so muche as the one was a Sovereign Lord, the sonne of a King, a Justiciarie on earth, and the other but a simple Citizen of a Citie, wherein the people had Lawes, and the lawes of Magistrates had in reverence. So likewyse the fall of a high and loftie Tree, maketh a greater noyse, than that whiche is lowe and little. Highe Towers and stately Palaces of Princes be seene further off, than the poore Cabans and homely shephierds Sheepecotes. The Walles of loftie Cities salute the viewers of the same farther of, than the simple caves, which the poore doe dig belowe the Mountaine rocks. Wherefore it behoveth the Noble, and such as have charge of Common wealth, to live an honest lyfe, and beare their port up-ryght, that none have cause to take ill example upon dyscourse of their deedes and naughtie life. And above all, that modestie ought

---

1 In this transcription, as elsewhere in the edition, u/v and i/j are normalized to modern usage; similarly, contractions are expanded, black-letter type appears in ordinary
   roman type, and roman and italic departures from the text's usual black-letter type
   are both indicated by italic.
2 This and the subsequent numbers indicate the ends of folios in the original text.

to be kept by women, whome as their race, Noble birth, authoritie and name, maketh them more famous, even so their vertue, honestie, chastitie, and continencie more praise worthy. And behovefull it is, that like as they wishe to be honoured above all other, so their life do make them worthy of that honour, without disgracing their name by deede or woorde, or blemishing that brightnesse which may commende the same. I greatly feare that all the Princely factes, the exploits and conquests done by the *Babylonian* Queen *Semyramis*, never was recommended with such praise, as hir vice had shame, in records by those which left remembrance of ancient acts. [170v] Thus I say, bicause a woman being as it were the Image of sweetenesse, curtesie & shamefastnesse, so soone as she steppeth out of the right tracte, and leaveth the smel of hir duetie and modestie, bisides the denigration of hir honor, thrusteth hir self into infinite troubles and causeth the ruine of such which should be honored and praised, if womens allurement solicited them not to follie. I wil not here indevor my self to seeke for examples of *Samson*, *Salomon* or other, which suffred themselves fondly to be abused by women: and who by meane of them be tumbled into great faults, and have incurred greater perils. Contenting my self to recite a right pitifull Historie done almost in our time, when the French under the leading of that notable captaine, *Gaston de Foix*, vanquished the force of *Spaine* and *Naples* at the journey of *Ravenna* in the time of the French king called *Lewes* the twelfth, who married the Lady *Marie*, daughter to king *Henry* the seventh, and sister to the victorious Prince of worthy memory king *Henry* the eight, wife (after the death of the sayd *Lewes*) to the puissant Gentleman *Charles*, late Duke of *Suffolke*.

In that very time then lived a Gentleman of *Naples*, called *Antonio Bologna*, who having bene Master of houshould to *Federicke* of *Aragon*, sometime King of *Naples*, after the French had expelled those of *Aragon* out of that Citie, the sayde *Bologna* retired into Fraunce, & thereby recovered the goods, which hee possessed in his countrey. The Gentleman bisides that he was valiant of his persone, a good man of warre, & wel estemed amongs the best, had a passing numbre of good graces, which made him to be beloved & cherished of every wight: & for riding & managing of great horse, he had not his fellow in *Italy*: he could also play exceeding well and trim upon the Lute, whose faining voyce so [171] well agreed therunto, that the most melancholike persons wold forget their heavinesse, upon hearing of his heavenly noise: and bisides these qualities, hee was of personage comely, and of good proportion. To be short, Nature having travailed and dispoyled hir Treasure house for inriching of him, he had by Arte gotten that, which made him most happy & worthy of praise, which was, the knowledge of good letters, wherin hee was so well trained, as by talke and dispute thereof, he made those to blushe that were of that state and profession. *Antonio Bologna* having left *Federicke* of *Aragon* in Fraunce, who expulsed out of *Naples* was retired to king *Lewes*, went home to his house to live at rest and to avoyd trouble, forgetting the delicates of Courtes and houses of great men, to be the only husband of his owne revenue. But what? It is impossible to eschue that which the heavens have determined upon us: and lesse the unhappe, whych seemeth to followe us, as it were naturally proceeding from our mothers wombe: In such wise as many times, he which seemeth the wisest man, guided by misfortune, hasteth himself wyth stouping head to fall headlong into his deathe & ruine. Even so it chaunced to this *Neapolitane* Gentleman: for in the very same place where he attained his advancement, he received also his diminution and decay, and by that house which preferred hym to what he had, he was deprived, both of his estate and life: the discourse whereof you shall understand. I have tolde you already, that this Gentleman was Maister of the King of *Naples* houshold, & being a gentle person, a good Courtier, wel trained up, and wise for government of himself in the Court and in the service of Princes, the Duchesse of *Malfi* thought to intreat him that hee would serve hir, in that office which he served the king. This [171v] Duchesse was of the house of *Aragon*, & sister to the Cardinal of *Aragon*, which then was a rich & puissant personage. Being thus resolved, was wel assured that she was not deceived: for so much as she was persuaded, that *Bologna* was devoutly affected to the house of *Aragon*, as one brought up there from a childe. Wherfore sending for him home to his house, she used unto him these, or like words: 'Master *Bologna*, sith your ill fortune, nay rather the unhap of our whole house is such, as your good Lord & master hath forgon his state & dignitie, and that you therwithall have lost a good Master, wythout other recompence but the praise which every man giveth you for your good service, I have thought good to intreat you to do me the honor, as to take charge of the government of my house, & to use the same, as you did that of the king your master. I know well that the office is to unworthy for your calling: notwithstanding you be not ignoraunt what I am, and how neere to him in bloud, to whom you be so faithfull and loving a servaunt: & albeit that I am no Queene, endued with great revenue, yet with that little I have, I bear a Princely heart: & such as you by experience do knowe what I have done, and daily do to those which depart my service, recompensing them according to their paine & travaile: magnificence is observed as well in the Courts of poore Princes, as in the stately Palaces of great Kings and monarches. I do remembre that I have red of a certain noble gentleman, a *Persian* borne, called *Ariobarzanes*, who used great examples of curtesie & stoutnes towards king *Artaxerxes*, wherwith the king wondred at his magnificence, & confessed himself to be vanquished: you shall take advise of this request, & I in the mean time do think you will not refuse the same, as well for that my demaund is just, as also being assured, that our house & race is so well imprinted in your heart, as it is impossible that the me- [172] mory therof can be defaced.' The gentleman hearing the courteous demaund of the Duchesse, knowing himself how deeply bound he was to the name of *Aragon*, & led by some unknowen provocation to his great yll luck, answered hir in this wise: 'I wold to god madame, that with so good reason & equitie I were able to make denial of

349

your commaundement, as justly you require the same: wherfore for the bounden duety which I owe to the name & memorie of the house of *Aragon*, I make promise that I shall not only sustain the travail, but also the daunger of my life, daily ready to be offred for your service: but I feele in minde I know not what, which commaundeth me to withdraw my self to live alone at home at my house, & to be content with the little I have, forgoing the sumptuouse charge of Princes houses, which life would be wel liked of my self, were it not for the feare that you madame shold be discontented with my refusal, & that you shold conceive, that I disdained your offred charge, or contempne your Court for respect of the great Office I bare in the Court of the King, my Lord & Master. For I cannot receive more honor, than to serve hir, which is of that stock & royall race. Therefore at all adventures I am resolved to obey your wil, & humbly to satisfy the duty of the charge wherin it pleaseth you to imploy me, more to pleasure you for avoiding of displeasure: then for desire I have to live an honorable life in the greatest princes house of the world, sith I am discharged from him in whose name resteth my comfort & only stay, thinking to have lived a solitary life, & to passe my yeres in rest, except it were in the pore abilitie of my service to that house, wherunto I am bound continually to be a faithful servaunt. Thus Madame, you see me to be the rediest man of the world, to fulfill the request, and accomplish such other service wherin it shall please you to imploy me.' [172v] The Duchesse thanked him very heartily, and gave him charge of all hir housholde traine, commaunding eche person to do him such reverence as to hir self, and to obey him as the chief of all hir familie. This Lady was a widow, but a passing faire Gentlewoman, fine and very yong, having a yong sonne under hir guard & keping, left by the deceased Duke hir husband, togither with the Duchie, the inheritaunce of hir childe. Now consider hir personage being such, hir easy life and delicate bringing up, and daily seeing the youthely trade and maner of Courtiers life, whether she felt hir self prickt with any desire, which burned hir heart the more incessantly, as the flames were hidden & covert: from the outward shew whereof she stayd hir self so well as she could. But she following best advise, rather esteemed the proofe of mariage, than to burne with so little fire, or to incurre the exchange of lovers, as many unshamefast strumpets do, which be rather given over, than satisfied with pleasure of love. And to say the truthe, they be not guided by wisdomes lore, which suffer a maiden ripe for mariage to be long unwedded, or yong wife long to live in widdowes state, what assurance so ever they make of their chaste and stayed life. For bookes be so full of such enterprises, and houses stored with examples of such stolne and secrete practises, as there neede no further proofe for assurance of our cause, the same of it self being so plaine and manifest. And a great follie it is to build the fantasies of chastitie, amid the follies of worldly pleasures. I will not goe about to make those matters impossible, ne yet wil judge at large, but that there be some maidens & wives, which wisely can conteine themselves amongs the troupe of amorous sutors. But what? the experience is very hard, and the proofe no lesse daungerous, & perhaunce [173] in a moment the minde of some perverted, whych all their living dayes have closed their eares from the wordes of those that have made offer of loving service, we neede not run to forayne Histories, ne yet to seeke records that be auncient, sith we may see the daily effects of the like, practized in Noble houses, and Courtes of Kings and Princes. That this is true, example of this fair Duchesse, who was moved with that desire which pricketh others that be of Flesh and bone. This Lady waxed very weary of lying alone, & grieved hir heart to be without a match, specially in the night, when the secrete silence and darknesse of the same presented before the eies of hir minde, the Image of the pleasure which she felt in the life time of hir deceased Lord and husband, whereof now feeling hir selfe despoiled, she felt a continuall combat, and durst not attempte that which she desired most, but eschued the thing wherof hir minde liked best. 'Alas (said she) is it possible after the taste of the value of honest obedience which the wife oweth unto hir husband, that I should desire to suffer the heat which burneth & altereth the martired minds of those that subdue them selves to love? Can such attempt pierce the heart of me to become amorous by forgetting & straying from the limittes of honest life? But what desire is this? I have a certaine unacquainted lust, & yet very well know not what it is that moveth me, and to whome I shall vow the spoile thereof. I am truely more fonde and foolish than ever *Narcissus* was, for there is neither shadow nor voyce, upon which I can well stay my sight, nor yet simple Imagination of any worldly man, whereupon I can arrest the conceipt of my unstayed heart, and the desires which provoke my mind. *Pygmalion* loved once a Marble piller, and I have but one desire, the coloure wherof is more [173v] pale than death. There is nothyng which can give the same so much as one spot of vermilion rud. If I do discover these appetites to any wight, perhaps they will mock me for my labor, and for all the beautie & Noble birth that is in me, they wil make no conscience to deeme me for their jesting stock, & to solace themselves with rehersall of my fond conceits. But sith there is no enimie in the field, & that but simple suspition doth assaile us, we must breake of the same, and deface the entier remembrance of the lightnesse of my braine. It appertaineth unto me to shew my self, as issued forth of the Noble house of *Aragon*. To me it doeth belong to take heede how I erre or degenerate from the royall bloud wherof I came.' In this sort that fair widow and yong Princess fantasied in the nyght upon the discourse of hir appetites. But when the day was come, seeing the great multitude of the *Neapolitan* Lords & gentlemen which marched up & downe the Citie, eying and beholding their best beloved, or using talk of mirth with them whose servaunts they were, al that which she thought upon in the night, vanished so sone as the flame of burned straw, or the pouder of the Canon shot, & purposed for any respect to live no longer in that sort, but promised the conquest of some friend that was lustie and discreete. But the difficultie rested in that she knew not, upon whom to fixe hir love, fearing to be slaundered, and also that the light disposition and maner of most part of youth wer to be suspected, in such wise as giving over all them whych vauted upon their Gennets, Turkey Palfreis, & other Coursers along the Citie of *Naples*, she purposed to take repast of other Venison, than of that fond & wanton troupe. So hir mishap began already to spin the threede which choked the aire and breath of hir unhappie life. Ye have heard before that M. *Bologna* was [174] one of the wisest & most perfect gentlemen that the land of *Naples* that tyme brought forth, & for his beautie, proportion, galantnesse, valiance, & good grace, without comparison. His favor was so sweete and pleasant, as they which kept him companie, had somwhat to do to abstain their affection. Who then could blame this faire Princesse, if (pressed with desire of matche, to remove the ticklish instigations of hir wanton flesh, and having in hir presence a man so wise) she did set hir minde on him, or fantasie to mary him? wold not that partie for calming of his thirst & hunger, being set at the table before sundry sorts of delicate viands, ease his hunger? Me think the person doth greatly forget himself, which having handfast upon occasion, suffreth the same to vanish & flie away, sith it is wel knowne that she being bald behinde, hath no place to sease upon, when desire moveth us to lay hold upon hir. Which was the cause that the Duchesse becam extremely in love with the master of hir house. In such wise as before al men, she spared not to praise the great perfections wherwith he was enriched, whom she desired to be altogether hirs. And so she was inamored, that it was as possible to see the night to be void of darknesse, as the Duchesse without the presence of hir *Bologna*, or else by talk of words to set forth his praise, the continual remembrance of whome (for that she loved him as hir self) was hir only minds repast. The gentleman that was ful wise, & had at other times felt the great force of the passion which procedeth from extreme love, immediatly did mark the countenance of the Duchesse, & perceived the same so nere, as unfainedly he knew that very ardently the Ladie was in love with him: & albeit he saw the inequality & difference betwene them both, she being sorted out of the royal bloud, yet knowing love to have no respect to state or dignity, determined to folow his fortune, & to serve hir [174v] which so lovingly shewed hir self to him. Then sodainly reproving his fonde conceit, hee sayd unto himself: 'What follie is that I enterprise, to the great prejudice and perill of mine honor and life? Ought the wisdom of a Gentleman to straie and wandre through the assaults of an appetite rising of sensuality, and that reason give place to that which doeth participate with brute beastes deprived of all reason by subduing the mynde to the affections of the body? No no, a vertuous man ought to let shine in him self the force of the generositie of his mynde. This is not to live according to the spirite, when pleasure shall make us forget our duetie and savegard of our Conscience. The reputation of a wise Gentleman resteth not onely to be valiant, and skilfull in feates of armes, or in service of the Noble: But nedefull it is for him by discretion to make himselfe prayse worthy, and by vanquishing of him self to open the gate to fame, whereby he may everlastingly make himselfe glorious to all posteritie. Love pricketh and provoketh the spirit to do wel, I do confesse, but that affection ought to be addressed to some vertuous end, tending to mariage, for otherwise that vertuous image shall be soyled with the villanie of beastly pleasure. Alas said he, how easie it is to dispute, when the thing is absent, which can bothe force and violently assaile the bulwarks of most constant hearts. I full well doe see the trothe, and doe feele the thing that is good, and know what behoveth me to follow: but when I view that divine beautie of my Ladie, hir graces, wisdome, behavior and curtesie, when I see hir to cast so loving an eie upon me, that she useth so great familiaritie, that she forgetteth the greatnesse of hir house to abase hir self for my respect: how is it possible that I should be so foolish to dispise a duetie so rare and pre- [175] cious, and to set light by that which the Noblest would pursue with all reverence and indevor? Shall I be so much voide of wisedome to suffer the yong Princesse, to

see hir self contempned of me, to convert hir love to teares, by
setting hir mynde upon an other, to seeke mine overthrow? Who
knoweth not the furie of a woman? specially of the Noble dame,
by seeing hir self despised? No, no, she loveth me, and I will be
hir servaunt, and use the fortune proffred. Shal I be the first
simple Gentleman that hath married or loved a Princesse? Is it
not more honourable for me to settle my minde upon a place so
highe, than upon some simple wenche by whome I shall neither
attaine profit, or advauncement? *Baldouine* of *Flaunders*, did not
hee a Noble enterprise when he caried away *Judith* the daughter
of the *French* King, as she was passing upon the seas into
England, to be married to the king of that Countrey? I am neither Pirat nor adventurer, for that the Ladie loveth me. What
wrong doe I then to any person by yelding love againe? Is not she
at libertie? To whome ought she to make accompt of hir dedes &
doings, but to God alone and to hir owne conscience? I will love
hir, and cary like affection for the love which I know & see that
she beareth unto me, being assured that the same is directed to
good end, and that a woman so wise as she is, will not commit a
fault so filthy, as to blemish and spot hir honor.' Thus *Bologna*
framed the plot to intertaine the Duchesse (albeit hir love alredy
was fully bent upon him) and fortified him self against all mishap
and perillous chaunce that might succeede, as ordinarily you see
that lovers conceive all things for their advauntage, & fantasie
dreames agreable to that which they most desire, resembling the
mad and Bedlem persons, which have before their eies, the figured [175v] fansies which cause the conceit of their furie, and
stay themselves upon the vision of that, which most troubleth
their offended brain. On the other side, the Duchesse was in no
lesse care of hir lover, the wil of whom was hid & secrete, which
more did vexe & torment hir, than the fire of love that burned
hir so fervently. She could not tell what way to hold, to do him
understand hir heart & affection. She feared to discover the same
unto him, doubting either of some fond & rigorous answer, or of
reveling of hir mind to him, whose presence pleased hir more

than all the men of the world. 'Alas said she, am I happed into so strange misery, that with mine own mouth I must make request to him, which with al humilitie ought to offer me his service? Shall a Ladie of such bloud as I am, be constrained to sue, wher all other be required by importunat instance of their suters? Ah love, love, what so ever he was that clothed thee with such puissance, I dare say he was the cruel enimie of mans fredom. It is impossible that thou hadst thy being in heaven, sith the clemencie & courteous influence of the same, investeth man with better benefits, than to suffer hir nourse children to be intreated with such rigor. He lieth which sayth that *Venus* is thy mother, for the sweetenesse & good grace that resteth in that pitifull Goddesse, who taketh no pleasure to see lovers perced with so egre travails as that which afflicteth my heart. It was some fierce cogitation of *Saturne*, that brought thee forth, & sent thee into the world to breake the ease of them which live at rest without any passion or grief. Pardon me Love, if I blaspheme thy majestie, for the stresse and endlesse grief wherein I am plunged, maketh me thus to rove at large, & the doubts which I conceive, do take away the health and soundnesse of my mind, the little experience in thy schole causeth this amaze in me, to be solicited with desire that [176] countersayeth the duetie, honor, and reputation of my state: the partie whome I love, is a Gentleman, vertuous, valiant, sage, & of good grace. In this there is no cause to blame Love of blindnesse, for all the inequalitie of our houses, apparant upon the first sight and shew of the same. But from whence issue the Monarches, Princes & greater Lords, but from the naturall and common mosse of earth, wherof other men doe come? what maketh these differences betwene those that love eche other, if not the sottish opinion which we conceive of greatnesse, and preheminence: as though naturall affections be like to that ordained by the fantasie of men in their lawes extreme. And what greater right have Princes to joyn with a simple gentlewoman, than the Princesse to mary a Gentleman, and such as *Anthonio Bologna* is, in whome heaven & nature have forgotten nothing to make him equall with them which marche amongs the greatest. I thinke we be the daily slaves of the fond and cruell fantasie of those Tyraunts, which say they have puissance over us: and that straining our will to their tirannie, we be still bound to the chaine like the galley slave. No no, *Bologna* shall be my husband, for of a friend I purpose to make him my loyall and lawfull husband, meaning therby not to offend God & men togither, & pretend to live without offense of conscience, wherby my soule shall not be hindred for any thing I do, by marying him whom I so straungely love. I am sure not to be deceived in Love. He loveth me so much or more as I do him, but he dareth not disclose the same, fearing to be refused & cast off with shame. Thus two united wils, & two hearts tied togithers with equal knot cannot choose but bring forth fruites worthie of such societie. Let men say what they list, I will do none otherwise than my head and mind have alredy framed. [176v] Semblably I neede not make accompt to any persone for my fact, my body, and reputation being in ful libertie and freedome. The bond of mariage made, shall cover the fault which men would deeme, & leaving mine estate, I shall do no wrong but to the greatnesse of my house, which maketh me amongs men right honorable. But these honors be nothing worth, where the minde is voide of contentation, and where the heart prickt forward by desire leaveth the body and mind rest-lesse without quiet.' Thus the Duchesse founded hir enterprise, determining to mary hir housholde Maister, seeking for occasion and time, meete for disclosing of the same, & albeit that a cer-taine naturall shamefastnesse, which of custome accompanieth Ladies, did close hir mouth, and made hir to deferre for a cer-taine time the effect of hir resolved minde. Yet in the end vanquished with love and impacience, she was forced to breake of silence, and to assure hir self in him, rejecting feare conceived of shame, to make hir waie to pleasure, which she lusted more than mariage, the same serving hir, but for a Maske and cover-ture to hide hir follies & shamelesse lusts, for which she did the penance that hir follie deserved. For no colorable dede or

deceitful trompery can serve the excuse of any notable wickednesse. She then throughly persuaded in hir intent, dreamyng
and thinking of nought else, but upon the imbracement of hir
Bologna, ended and determined hir conceits & pretended follies:
and upon a time sent for him up into hir chamber, as commonly
she did for the affaires and matters of hir house, and taking him
a side unto a window, having prospect into a garden, she knew
not how to begin hir talk: (for the heart being seased, the minde
troubled, and the wittes out of course, the tongue failed to doe
his office,) in such wise, as of long time she [177] was unable to
speake one onely woord. Hee surprised with like affection, was
more astonned by seeing the alteration of his Ladie. So the two
Lovers stoode still like Images beholding one another, without
any moving at all, until the Ladie the hardiest of them bothe, as
feeling the most vehement and greatest grief, tooke *Bologna* by
the hand, and dissembling what she thought, used this or such
like language: 'If any other bisides your self (Gentleman) should
understand the secretes which now I purpose to disclose, I doubt
what speeche were necessary to colour my woords: But being
assured of your discretion and wisdom, and with what perfection
nature hath indued you, and Arte, having accomplished that in
you, which nature did begin to work, as one bred and brought up
in the royall Court of the second *Alphonse*, of *Ferdinando* and
Federick of *Aragon* my cousins, I wil make no doubt at all to
manifest to you the hidden secretes of my heart, being well persuaded that, when you shall both heare and savor my reasons,
and tast the light which I bring forthe for me, easily you may
judge that mine advise cannot be other, than just and reasonable.
But if your conceits shall straye from that which I shal speak, &
deeme not good of that which I determine, I shall be forced to
thinke & say that they which esteeme you wise & sage, and to be
a man of good and ready wit, be marvelously deceived.
Notwithstanding my heart foretelleth that it is impossible for
maister *Bologna*, to wandre so farre from equitie, but that by and
by he wil enter the lystes, & discerne the white from black, and

358

the wrong from that which is just and right. For so much as hitherto I never saw thing done by you, which preposterated or perverted the good judgement that all the world esteemeth to shine in you, the same well manifested & declared by your tongue, the [177v] right judge of the mind: you know and see how I am a widow through the death of that noble Gentleman of good remembrance, the Duke my Lord & husband: you be not ignoraunt also, that I have lived and governed my self in such wise in my widow state, as there is no man so hard and severe of judgement, that can blason reproche of me in that which appertaineth to the honesty & reputation of such a Ladie as I am, bearing my port so right, as my conscience yeldeth no remorse, supposing that no man hath wherewith to bite & accuse me. Touching the order of the goods of the Duke my sonne, I have used them with such diligence and discretion, as bisides the dettes which I have discharged sithens the death of my Lord, I have purchased a goodly Manor in *Calabria*, and have annexed the same to the Dukedom of his heire: and at this day doe not owe one pennie to any creditor that lent mony to the Duke, which he toke up to furnish the charges in the warres, which he sustained in the service of the Kings our soveraine Lords in the late warres for the kingdome of *Naples*. I have as I suppose by this meanes stopped the slaunderous mouth, and given cause unto my sonne, during his life to accompt himself bound unto his mother. Now having till this time lived for other, and made my self subject more than Nature could beare, I am entended to chaunge both my life and condition. I have till thys time run, travailed, & removed to the Castels & Lordships of the Dukedome, to *Naples* and other places, being in mind to tary as I am a widow. But what? new affaires and new councel hath possest my mind. I have travailed and pained my self inough, I have too long abidden a widowes life, I am determined therefore to provide a husband, who by loving me, shal honor & cherish me, according to the love which I shal bear to him, [178] & my desert. For to love a man without mariage, God defend my heart should ever think, & shall rather die a hundred thousand deathes, than a desire so wicked shald soile my conscience, knowing well that a woman which setteth hir honor to sale, is lesse than nothing, & deserveth not that the common aire shold breathe upon hir, for all the reverence that men do beare or make them. I accuse no person, albeit that many noble women have their forheds marked, with the blame of dishonest life, & being honored of some, be neverthelesse the common fable of the people. To the intent then that such mishap happen not to me, & perceiving my self unable stil thus to live, being yong as I am, & (God be thanked) neither deformed nor yet painted, I had rather be the loving wife of a simple feere, than the Concubine of a king or great Prince. And what? is the mightie Monarche able to wash away the fault of his wife which hath abandoned him contrary to the duty & honesty which the undefiled bed requireth? no les then Princesses that whilom trespassed with those which wer of baser stuffe than themselves. *Messalina* with hir imperial robe could not so wel cover hir faults, but that the Historians do defame hir with the name & title of a common woman. *Faustina* the wife of the sage Monarch *Marcus Aurelius*, gained lyke report by rendring hir self to others pleasure, bisides hir lawful spouse. To mary my self to one that is mine equall, it is impossible, for so much as there is no Lord in all this Countrey meete for my degree, but is to olde of age, the rest being dead in these later warres. To mary a husband that yet is but a child, is follie extreeme, for the inconveniences which daily chaunce therby, & the evil intreatie that Ladies do receive when they come to age, & their nature waxe cold, by reson wherof, imbracements be not so favorable, & their husbands glutted with ordinary meat use to run in exchange. [178v] Wherefore I am resolved without respite or delay, to choose some wel qualitied and renoumed Gentleman, that hath more vertue than richesse, of good Fame and brute, to the intent I may make him my Lord, espouse, and husband. For I cannot imploy my love upon treasure, which may be taken away, where richesse of the minde do faile, and shall be better content to see an honest Gentleman with little revenue to be praised and commended of every man for his good deedes, than a rich carle curssed and detested of all the world. Thus much I say, and it is the summe of all my secretes, wherin I pray your Councell and advise. I know that some wil be offended wyth my choise, & the Lords my brothers, specially the Cardinall will think it straunge, and receive the same with ill digesture, that muche a do shall I have to be agreed with them and to remove the grief which they shall conceive against me for this mine enterprise: wherefore I would the same should secretely be kept, until without perill and daunger either of my self or of him, whome I pretende to mary, I may publish and manifest, not my love but the mariage which I hope in God shall soon be consummate and accomplished with one, whome I doe love better than my self, and who as I full well do know, doeth love me better than his owne proper life.' Maister *Bologna*, which till then harkned to the Oration of the Duchesse without moving, feeling himself touched so neere, and hearing that his Ladie had made hir approche for mariage, stode stil astonned, his tongue not able to frame one word, only fantasied a thousand *Chimeraes* in the aire, and formed like numbre of imaginations in his minde, not able to conjecture what hee was, to whome the Duchesse had vowed hir love, & the possession of hir beauty. He could not thinke that this joy was prepared for himself for that [179] his Ladie spake no woord of him, and he lesse durst open his mouth, and yet was wel assured that she loved him beyond measure. Notwithstanding knowing the ficklenesse and unstable heart of women, he sayd unto himself that she would chaunge hir minde, for seing him to be so great a Cowarde, as not to offer hys service to a Ladie by whome he saw himself so manie times bothe wantonly looked upon, & intertained with some secresie more than familiar. The Duchesse which was a fine and subtile dame, seeing hir friend rapt with the passion, and standing stil unmoveable through feare, pale & amazed, as if hee had bene accused and condempned to die, knew by that countenaunce & astonishment of *Bologna*, that she was perfectly beloved of him: and so mean-ing not to suffer hym any longer to continue in that amaze, ne yet to further fear him, wyth hir dissembled and fained mariage of any other but with him, she toke him by the hand, and beholding him with a wanton and luring eye, (in such sort as the curious Philosophers themselves would awake, if such a Lampe and torch did shine within their studies,) she sayde thus unto hym: 'Seignor *Anthonio*, I pray you be of good cheere, & torment not your self for any thing that I have said: I know well, and of long time have perceyved what good and faithfull love you beare me, & with what affection you have served me, sithens first you used my companie. Thinke me not to be so ignorant, but that I know ful wel by outward signes, what secretes be hid in the inner heart: and that conjectures many times doe give me true and certaine knowledge of concealed things. And am not so foolish to thinke you to be so undiscrete, but that you have marked my countenaunce & maner, and therby have knowen that I have bene more affectioned to you, than to any other. For that cause (sayd [179v] she, straining him by the hand very lovingly, & with cherefull coloure in hir face) I sweare unto you, & doe promise that if you so thinke meete, it shall be none other but your self whom I wil have, & desire to take to husband and lawfull spouse, assuring my self so much of you, as the love which so long time hath ben hidden & covered in our hearts, shal appeare by so evident proofe, as only death shal end & undoe the same.' The gentleman hearing such sodain talk, & the assurance of that which he most wished for, albeit he saw the daunger extreeme wherunto he launched himself by espousing this great Ladie, & the enimies he shold get by entring such aliance: notwithstand-ing building upon vaine hope, and thinking at length that the choler of the *Aragon* brother would passe away if they under-stoode the mariage, determined to pursue the purpose, & not to refuse that great preferment, being so prodigally offred, for which cause he answered his Lady in this maner. 'If it were in my power madame, to bring to passe that, which I desire for your service by acknowledging of the benifits & favors which you depart unto me, as my mind presenteth thanks for the same, I wold think my self the happiest Gentleman that lyveth, & you the best served Princesse of the world. For one better beloved (I dare presume to say, and so long as I live wil affirm) is not to be found. If til this time I delayed to open that which now I discover unto you, I beseeche you Madame to impute it to the greatnesse of your estate, and to the duetie of my calling & office in your house, being not seemely for a servant to talk of such secretes with his Ladie and mistresse. And truely the pain which I have indured to holde my peace, and to hide my griefe, hath bene more noysome to me than one hundred thousand like sorowes together, although it had ben lawfull to have revealed them to some [180] trusty friend: I do not deny madame, but of long time you did perceive my follie and presumption, by addressing my minde so high, as to the *Aragon* bloud, and to such a Princesse as you be. And who can beguile the eye of a Lover, specially of hir, whose Paragon for good minde, wisedom & gentlenesse is not? And I confesse to you bisides, that I have most evidently perceived how certain love hath lodged in your gracious heart, wherwith you bare me greater affection, than you did to any other within the compasse of your familie. But what? Great Ladies hearts be fraught with secretes & conceits of other effects, than the minds of simple women, which caused me to hope for none other guerdon of my loyal & faithfull affection, than death, & the same very short, Sith that litle hope accompanied with great, nay rather extreme passion, is not able to give sufficient force, both to suffer & to stablish my heart with constancie. Now for so much as of your motion, grace, curtesie & liberalitie the same is offred, & that it pleaseth you to accept me for yours, I humbly beseche you to dispose of me not as husband, but of one which is, & shalbe your servaunt for ever, & such as is more ready to obey, than you to commaund. It resteth now Madame, to consider how, & in what wise our affairs are to be directed, that things being in assurance, you may so live without peril and brute of slaunderous tongues, as your good fame & honest port may continue without spot or blemish.'

Beholde the first Acte of the Tragedie, and the provision of the fare which afterwardes sent them bothe to their grave, who immediately gave their mutuall faith: and the houre was assigned the next day, that the fair Princesse shold be in hir chamber alone, attended upon with one only Gentlewoman which had ben brought up with the Duchesse from hir cradle, & was made [180v] privie to the heavy mariage of those two lovers which was consummate in hir presence. And for the present time they passed the same in words, for ratification wherof they went to bed togither. But the pain in the end was greater than the pleasure, and had ben better for them bothe, yea and also for the third, that they had shewed them selves so wyse in the deede, as discrete in keping silence of that which was done. For albeit their mariage was secrete, and therby politikely governed them selves in their stelthes and robberies of love, and that *Bologna* more oft held the state of the steward of the house by day, than of Lord of the same, and by night supplied that place, yet in the end, the thing was perceived which they desired to be closely kept. And as it is impossible to till and culture a fertile ground, but that the same must yelde some frute, even so the Duchesse after many pleasures (being ripe and plentiful) became with child, which at the first astonned the maried couple: neverthelesse the same so well was provided for, as the first childbedde was kept secrete, and none did know thereof. The childe was nourced in the towne, and the father desired to have him named *Federick*, for remembraunce of the parents of his wife. Now fortune which lieth in daily waite and ambushment, & liketh not that men shold long loiter in pleasure and passetime, being envious of such prosperity, cramped so the legges of our two lovers, as they must needes change their game, and learne some other practise: for so much as the Duchesse being great with childe again, and delivered of a girle, the businesse of the same was not so secretely done, but that it was discovered. And it suffised not that the brute was noised through *Naples*, but that the sound flew further off. As eche man doth know that rumor hath many mouthes, who with the multi- [181] tude of his tongues and Trumps, proclaimeth in divers and sundry places, the things which chaunce in al the regions of the earth. Even so that babling foole, caried the newes of that second childbed to the eares of the Cardinall of *Aragon* the Duchesse brother, being then at *Rome*. Think what joy and pleasure the *Aragon* brothers had, by hearing the report of their sisters facte. I dare presume to say, that albeit they were extremely wroth with this happened slaunder, & with the dishonest fame whych the Duchesse had gotten throughout *Italie*, yet farre greater was their sorrow & grief, for that they did not know what hee was, that so courteously was allied to their house, and in their love had increased their ligneage. And therfore swelling wyth despite, & rapt with furie to see themselves so defamed by one of their bloud, they purposed by all meanes whatsoever it cost them, to know the lucky lover that had so wel tilled the Duchesse their sisters field. Thus desirous to remove that shame from before their eyes, and to be revenged of a wrong so notable, they sent espial round about, and scoutes to *Naples*, to view and spy the behavior & talk of the Duchesse, to settle some certaine judgement of him, whych stealingly was become their brother in law. The Duchesse Court being in thys trouble, shee dyd continually perceive in hir house, hir brothers men to mark hir countenance, and to note those that came thither to visite hir, & to whom she used greatest familiaritie, bicause it is impossible but that the fire, although it be raked under the ashes, must give some heat. And albeit the two lovers used eche others companie, without shewing any signe of their affection, yet they purposed to chaunge their estate for a time, by yelding truce to their pleasures. Yea, & although *Bologna* was a wise and provident personage, [181v] fearing to be surprised upon the fact, or that the Gentlewoman of the Chamber corrupted with Money, or forced by feare, shold pronounce any matter to his hinderance or disavantage, determined to absent himself from *Naples*, yet not so sodainly but that hee made the Duchesse his faithfull Ladie & companion privie of his intent. And as they were secretely in their chamber togither, hee used these or such like woords: 'Madame, albeit the right good intent and unstained conscience, is free from fault, yet the judgement of men hath further relation to the exterior apparance, than to vertues force and innocencie it self, as ignorant of the secrets of the thought: and so in things that be wel done, we must of necessitie fall into the sentence of those, whom beastly affection ravisheth more, than ruled reason. You see the solempne watch and garde which the servaunts of the Lords your brothers do within your house, & the suspicion which they have conceived by reason of your second childbed, & by what meanes they labor truely to know how your affaires proceede, and things do passe. I feare not death where your service may be advaunced, but if herein the maiden of your chamber be not secrete, if she be corrupted, and if she kepe not close that which she ought to do, it is not ignorant to you that it is the losse of my life, and shall die suspected to be a whoremonger & varlet, even I, (I say) shall incurre that perill, which am your true and lawfull husband. Thys separation chaunceth not by Justice or desert, sith the cause is too righteous for us: but rather your brethren will procure my death, when I shall thinke the same in greatest assurance. If I had to do but with one or two, I wold not change the place, ne march one step from *Naples*, but be assured, that a great band, and the same wel armed will set upon me. I pray you madame suffer me to re-[182] tire for a time, for I am assured that when I am absent, they will never soile their hands, or imbrue their sweards in your bloud. If I doubted any thing at al of perill touching your owne person, I had rather a hundred hundred times die in your companie, than live to see you no more. But out of doubt I am, that if the things were discovered, & they knew you to be begotten with childe by me, you should be safe, where I shold sustaine the penaunce of the fact, committed without fault or sinne. And therfore I am determined to goe from *Naples*, to order mine affaires, and to cause my Revenue to be brought to the place of mine abode, and from thence to *Ancona*, until it pleaseth God to mitigate the rage of your brethren, and recover their good wils to consent to our mariage. But I meane not to doe or conclude any thing without your advise. And if this intent doe not like you, give me councell Madame, what I were best to doe, that both in life and death you may knowe your faithfull servaunt and loving husband is ready to obey and please you.' This good Ladie hearing hir husbands discourse, uncertain what to doe, wept bitterly, as wel for grief to lose his presence, as for that she felt hir self with child the third time. The sighes and teares, the sobbes and heavie lookes, which she threwe forth upon hir sorowfull husband, gave sufficient witnesse of hir paine and grief. And if none had heard hir, I thinke hir playntes woulde have well expressed hir inwarde smarte of minde. But like a wise Ladie, seeing the alleaged reasons of hir husband, licensed him, although against hir minde, not without utterance of these few words, before hee went out of hir Chamber: 'Deare husband, if I were so well assured of the affection of my brethren, as I am of my maides fidelitie, I would entreat [182v] you not to leave me alone: specially in the case I am, being with childe. But knowing that to be just & true which you have sayd, I am content to force my wil for a certaine time, that hereafter we may live at rest together, joyning our selves in the companie of our children and familie, voide of those troubles, which great Courts ordinarily beare within the compasse of their Palaces. Of one thing I must intreat you, that so often as you can by trustie messenger, you send me woord & intelligence of your health and state, bicause the same shal bryng unto me greater pleasure & contentation, than the welfare of mine owne: and bicause also, upon such occurrentes as shall chaunce, I may provyde for mine owne affaires, the suretie of my self, and of our children.' In saying so, she embraced him very amorously, and he kissed hir wyth so great sorrow and grief of heart, as the soule thought in that extasie out of his body to take hir flight, sorowful beyond mesure so to leve hir whome he loved, for the great curtesies and honor which he had received at hir hands. In the end, fearing that the *Aragon* espials wold come and perceive them in those privities, *Bologna* tooke his leave, and bad hys Ladie and spouse Farewell.

And thus was the second Acte of this Tragicall Historie, to see a fugitife husband secretely to mary, especially hir, upon whom he ought not so much as to loke but with feare and reverence. Beholde here (O ye foolish lovers) a Glasse of your lightnesse, and ye women, the course of your fonde behavior. It behoveth not the wise sodainly to execute their first motions and desires of their heart, for so much as they may be assured that pleasure is pursued so neare with a repentance so sharp to be suffred, and hard to be digested, as their voluptuousnesse shall utterly discontent them. True it is, that [183] mariages be done in Heaven, and performed in earth, but that saying may not be applied to fooles, which governe themselves by carnall desires, whose scope is but pleasure, & the reward many times equal to their follie. Shall I be of opinion that a housholde servaunt ought to sollicite, nay rather suborne the daughter of his Lord without punishment, or that a vile and abject person dare to mount upon a Princes bed? No no, pollicie requireth order in all, and eche wight ought to be matched according to their qualitie, without making a pastime of it to cover our follies, & know not of what force love and desteny be, except the same be resisted. A goodly thing it is to love, but where reason loseth his place, love is without his effect, and the sequele rage & madnesse. Leave we the discourse of those which beleve that they be constrained to folowe the force of their minde, and may easily subdue themselves to the lawes of vertue and honesty, like one that thrusteth his head into a sack, and thinks he can not get out, such people do please themselves in their losse, and think all well that is noisom to their health, daily folowing their contrarie. Come we againe then to sir *Bologna*, who after he had left his wife in hir Castell, went to *Naples*, and having sessed a rent upon his landes, and levied a good summe of money, he repaired to *Ancona*, a

Citie of the patrimonie of the *Romane* Church, whither he caried his two children, which he had of the Duchesse, causing the same to be brought up with such diligence and care, as is to be thought a father wel affectioned to his wife would doe, and who delighted to see a braunche of the tree, that to him was the best beloved fruit of the world. There he hired a house for his train, and for those that waited upon his wife, who in the meane time was in great care, & could not tell of what woode to make hir [183v] arowes, perceiving that hir belly began to swell and grow to the time of hir deliverie, seeing that from day to day, hir brothers servaunts were at hir back, voide of councel and advise, if one evening she had not spoken to the Gentlewoman of hir chamber, touching the douts and peril wherin she was, not knowing how she might be delivered from the same. That maiden was gentle & of a good minde and stomake, and loved hir mistresse very derely, & seeing hir so amazed and tormenting hir self to death, minding to fray hir no further, ne to reprove hir of hir fault, which could not be amended, but rather to provide for the daunger wherunto she had hedlong cast hir self, gave hir this advise: 'How now Madame (said she,) is that wisdom which from your childhode hath bene so familiar in you, dislodged from your brest in time, when it ought chiefly to rest for incountring of those mishaps that are comming upon us? Thinke you to avoid the dangers, by thus tormenting your self, except you set your hands to the work, thereby to give the repulse to adverse fortune? I have heard you many times speake of the constancie & force of minde, which ought to shine in the dedes of Princesses, more clerely than amongs those dames of baser house, & which ought to make them appere like the sunne amid the litle starres. And yet I see you now astonned, as though you had never forseene, that adversitie chaunceth so wel to catch the great within his clouches, as the base & simple sort. Is it but now, that you have called to remembraunce, that which might insue your mariage with sir *Bologna*? Did hys only presence assure you against the waits of fortune, & was it the thought of paines, feares &

frights, which now turmoileth your dolorous mind? Ought you
thus to vexe your self, when nede it is to think how to save both
your honor, and the frute within your intrailes? [184] If your
sorow be so great over sir *Bologna*, and if you feare your childbed
wil be descried, why seeke you not meanes to attempt some voyage, for covering of the fact, to beguile the eyes of them which so
diligently do watch you? Doth your heart faile you in that matter? Whereof do you dreame? Why sweat and freat you before
you make me answer?' 'Ah sweete heart (answered the Duchesse,)
if thou feltest the paine which I do suffer, thy tongue wold not
be so much at will, as thou shewest it now to be for reprofe of my
smal constancie. I do sorow specially for the causes which thou
alleagest, and above all, for that I know wel, that if my brethren
had never so litle intelligence of my being with child, I were
undone & my life at an end, and peradventure poore wench,
thou shouldest beare the penaunce for my sinne. But what way
can I take, that stil these candles may not give light, and I may
be voided of the traine which ought to wayt upon my brethren?
I thinke if I should descend into Hel, they would know, whither
any shadowe there were in love with me. Now gesse if I should
travaile the Realme, or retire to any other place, whither they
wold leave me at peace? Nothing lesse, sith they would sodainly
suspect, that the cause of my departure proceeded of desire to
live at libertie, to dallie wyth him, whome they suspect to be
other than my lawfull husbande. And it may be as they be wicked
and suspicious, and will doubt of my greatnesse, so shall I be
farre more infortunate by travailyng, than here in miserie amidde
myne anguishe: and you the rest that be keepers of my Councell,
shall fal into greater daunger, upon whome no doubt they wil be
revenged, and flesh themselves for your unhappy waiting and
attendance upon us.' 'Madame said the bolde maiden, be not
afraide, and follow mine advise. [184v] For I hope that it shall be
the meanes both to see your spouse, & to rid those troublesome
verlets out of your house, & in like manner safely to deliver you
into good assuraunce.' 'Say your minde sayd the Ladie, for it

may be, that I will governe my self according to the same.' 'Mine advise is then, sayd the Gentlewoman, to let your houshold understand, that you have made a vow to visite the holy Temple of our Lady of *Loretto*, (a famous place of Pilgrimage in *Italie*) and that you commaund your traine to make themselves ready to waite upon you for accomplishment of your devotion, & from thence you shall take your journey to sojorne at *Ancona*, whither before you depart, you shall send your moveables and plate, with such money as you shall think necessarie. And afterwardes God will performe the rest, and through his holy mercy will guide & direct all your affaires.' The Duchesse hearing the mayden speake those woords, and amazed of hir sodaine invention, could not forbeare to embrace and kisse hir, blessing the houre wherin she was borne, and that ever she chaunced into hir companie, to whome afterwardes she sayd. 'My wench, I had well determined to give over mine estate and noble porte, joyfully to live like a simple Gentlewoman with my deare and welbeloved husband, but I could not devise how I should conveniently departe this Countrey wythout suspition of some follie: and sith that thou hast so well instructed me for bringing the same to passe, I promise thee that so diligently thy councel shal be performed, as I see the same to be right good and necessarie. For rather had I see my husband, being alone without title of Duchesse or great Lady, than to live without him beautified with the graces and foolish names of honor and preheminence.' This devised plot was no soner grounded, but she gave such order for exe- [185] cution of the same, & brought it to passe wyth such dexteritie, as the Ladie in lesse than .viii. dayes had conveyed and sent the most part of hir moveables, and specially the chiefest and best to *Ancona*, taking in the meane time hir way towards *Loretto* after she had bruted hir solempne vow made for that Pilgrimage. It was not sufficient for this foolish woman to take a husband, more to glut hir libidinous appetite, than for other occasion, except she added to hir sinne, an other execrable impietie, making holy places and dueties of devotion, to be as it were the ministers of hir follie. But let us consider the force of Lovers rage, which so soone as it hath seased upon the minds of men, we see how marvelious be the effects thereof, and with what straint and puissaunce that madnesse subdueth the wise and strongest worldlings. Who wold think that a great Ladie wold have abandoned hir estate, hir goods and childe, would have misprised hir honor and reputation, to folow like a vagabond, a pore and simple Gentleman, and him bisides that was the houshold servaunt of hir Court? And yet you see this great and mightie Duchesse trot & run after the male, like a female Wolfe or Lionesse (when they goe to sault,) and forget the Noble bloud of *Aragon* wherof she was descended, to couple hir self almost with the simplest person of all the trimmest Gentlemen of *Naples*. But turne we not the example of follies, to be a matter of consequence: for if one or two become bankrupt of their honor, it foloweth not good Ladies, that their facte should serve for a matche to your deserts, & much lesse a patron for you to folow. These Histories be not written to train and trap you, to pursue the thousand thousand slippery sleightes of Loves gallantise, but rather carefully to warn you to behold the semblable faultes, and to serve for a drugge to discharge [185v] the poyson which gnaweth and fretteth the integritie and soundnesse of the soule. The wise & skilfull Apothecary or compositor of drugges, dresseth Vipers flesh to purge the patient from hote corrupted bloude, which conceiveth and engendreth Leprosie within his body. In like manner, the fonde love, & wicked ribauldrie of *Semiramis, Pasiphae, Messalina, Faustina*, and *Romida* is shewed in wryt, that every of you should feare to be numbred and recorded amongs such common and dishonorable women. You Princes and great Lordes read the follies of *Paris*, the adulteries of *Hercules*, the daintie and effeminate life of *Sardanapalus*, the tirannie of *Phalaris Busiris*, or *Dionysius* of *Scicile*, and see the History of *Tiberius, Nero Caligula, Domitian* and *Heliogabalus*, & spare not to numbre them amongs our wanton youthes which soile themselves with such villanies more filthily than the swine do in the durt. Al this intendeth it an instruction for your youth to follow the infection and whoredome of those monsteres. Better it were all those bokes were drenched in bottomlesse depth of seas, than christian life by their meanes shold be corrupted: but the example of the wicked is induced for to eschue & avoid them as the life of the good & honest is remembred to frame & addresse our behavior in this world to be praise worthy & commended. Otherwise the holinesse of sacred writ shold serve for an argument to the unthrifty & luxurious to confirm & approve their beastly & licencious wickednesse. Come we again then to our purpose: the good Pilgrime of *Loretto* went forth hir voyage to atchieve hir devotions, & to visite the Saint for whose Reliques she was departed the Countrey of the Duke hir sonne. When she had done hir suffrages at *Loretto*, hir people thought that the voyage was at an end, & that she wold have returned again into hir Countrey. But she [186] said unto them: that sith she was so neere *Ancona*, being but .xv. miles off, she would not returne before she had seen that auncient & goodly city, which divers Histories do greatly recommend, as wel for the antiquitie, as for the pleasant seat therof. All were of hir advise, & went to see the antiquities of *Ancona*, & she to renue the pleasures which she had before begon with hir *Bologna*, who was advertised of all hir determination, resting now like a God, possessed with the jewels & richesse of the Duchesse, & had taken a faire palace in the great streat of the Citie, by the gate wherof the train of his Ladie must passe. The Harbinger of the Duchesse posted before to take up lodging for the traine: but *Bologna* offred unto him his Palace for the Lady. So *Bologna* which was already welbeloved in *Ancona*, and entred new amitie and great acquaintance with the Gentlemen of the Citie, with a goodly troupe of them, went forth to meete his wife, to whome he presented his house, and besought hir that she and hir traine would vouchsafe to lodge with him. She received the same very thankfully, and withdrew hir self unto his house, who conducted hir thither, not as a Husband, but like hym that was hir humble and affectionate servaunt. But what needeth much discourse of woordes? The Duchesse knowing that it was impossible but eche man must be privie to hir facte, and know what secretes hath passed betweene hir and hir Husband, to the ende that no other opinion of hir Childebed should be conceyved, but that which was good and honest, and done since the accomplishment of the mariage, the morrowe after hir arrivall to *Ancona*, assembled all hir traine in the Hall, of purpose no longer to keepe secrete that syr *Bologna* was hir Husbande, and that already she had had two Children by him, and againe was great with childe. [186v] And when they were come together after dinner, in the presence of hir husband, she spake unto them these words: 'Gentlemen, and al ye my trusty and loving servants, highe time it is to manifest to every of you, the thing which hath ben done before the face, and in the presence of him who knoweth the most obscure & hydden secrets of our thoughts. And needefull it is not to kepe silent that which is neither evill done ne hurtfull to any person. If things could be kept secrete and still remaine unknown, except they were declared by the doers of them, yet would not I commit the wrong in concealing that, which to discover unto you doth greatly delite me, and delivereth my mind from exceeding grief, in such wise as if the flames of my desire could breake out with such violence, as the fire hath taken heat within my mind, ye shold see the smoke mount up with greater smoulder than that which the mount *Gibel* doeth vomit forth at certaine seasons of the yeare. And to the intent I may not keepe you long in this suspect, this secrete fire within my heart, and that which I will cause to flame in open aire, is a certain opinion which I conceive for a mariage by me made certaine yeares past, at what time I chose and wedded a husband to my fantasie and liking, desirous no longer to live in widow state, and unwilling to doe the thing that should prejudice & hurt my conscience. The same is done, and yet in one thing I have offended, which is by long keeping secrete the performed mariage: for the wicked brute dispearsed through the realme by reason of my childbed, one yere past, hath displeased some, howbeit my conscience receiveth comfort, for that the same is free from fault or blot. Now know ye therfore what he is, whome I acknowledge for my Lord and spouse, and who it is that lawfully hath me espoused in the presence of this Gen-[187] tlewoman whom you see, which is the witnesse of our Nuptials & accorde of mariage. This gentleman here present *Antonio Bologna*, is he to whom I have sworn and given my faith, and hee againe to me hath ingaged his owne. He it is whom I accompt for my spouse and husband, (& with whome hence-forth) I meane to rest and continue. In consideration wherof, if there be any heere amongs you all, that shall mislike of my choise, & is willing to wait upon my sonne the Duke, I meane not to let them of their intent, praying them faithfully to serve him and to be carefull of his person, and to be unto him so honest and loyall, as they have bene to me so long as I was their mistresse. But if any of you desire stil to make your abode with me, and to be partakers of my wealth and woe, I wil so entertain him, as hee shall have good cause to be contented, if not, depart ye hence to *Malfi*, and the steward shall provide for either of you according to your degree: for touching my self I do minde no more to be termed an infamous Duchesse: rather had I be honored with the title of a simple Gentlewoman, or with that estate which she can have that hath an honest husband, and with whom she holdeth faithfull and loyall companie, than reverenced with the glory of a Princesse, subject to the despite of slaunderous tongues. Ye know (said she to *Bologna*) what hath passed betwene us, and God is the witnesse of the integritie of my Conscience, where-fore I pray you bring forth our children, that eche man may beholde the fruites raised of our alliance.' Having spoken those words, and the children brought forth into the hall, all the com-panie stode stil so astonned with that new successe and tale, as though hornes sodainely had started forth their heads, and rested unmoveable and amazed, like the great marble piller of *Rome* called *Pasquile*, [187v] for so much as they never thought, ne conjectured that *Bologna* was the successor of the Duke of *Malfi* in his mariage bed.

This was the preparative of the *Catastrophe* & bloudie end of this Tragedie. For of all the Duchesse servaunts, there was not one that was willing to continue with their auncient mistresse, who with the faithful maiden of hir chamber remained at *Ancona*, enjoying the joyful embracements of hir husband, in al such pleasure & delights as they doe, which having lived in feare, be set at liberty, & out of al suspition, plunged in a sea of joy, & fleting in the quiet calme of al passetime, where *Bologna* had none other care, but how to please his best beloved, & she studied nothing else but how to love and obey him, as the wife ought to do hir husband. But this faire weather lasted not long, for although the joyes of men do not long endure, and wast in litle time, yet delights of lovers be lesse firme & stedfast, & passe away almost in one moment of an hour. Now the servaunts of the Duchesse which were retired, and durst tary no longer with hir, fearing the fury of the Cardinal of *Aragon* brother to the Ladie, the very day they departed from *Ancona*, devised amongs themselves that one of them shold ride in post to *Rome*, to advertise the Cardinal of the Ladies mariage, to the intent that the *Aragon* brethren shold conceive no cause to accuse them of felonie & treason. That determination spedily was accomplished, one posting towards *Rome*, and the rest galloping to the Countrey and Castels of the Duke. These newes reported to the Cardinal & his brother, it may be considered how grievously they toke the same, & for that they were not able to digest them with modestie, the yongest of the brethren, yelled forth a thousand cursses & despites, against the simple sexe of womankind. [188] 'Ha said the Prince (transported with choler, & driven in to deadly furie,) what law is able to punish or restrain the foolish indiscretion of a woman, that yeldeth hir self to hir own desires? What shame is able to bridle & withdrawe hir from hir minde & madnesse? Or with what feare is it possible to snaffle them from execution of their filthinesse? There is no beast be he never so wilde, but man sometime may tame, and bring to his lure and order. The force and diligence of man is able to make milde the strong and proud, and to overtake the swiftest beast and foule, or otherwise to attaine the highest and deepest thing of the world: but this incarnate divelish beast the woman, no force can surmount hir, no swiftnesse can approche hir mobilitie, no good mind can prevent hir sleights and deceites, they seeme to be procreated and borne against all order of nature, and to live without law, which governeth all other things indued wyth some reason and understanding. But what a great abhomination is this, that a Gentlewoman of such a house as ours is, hath forgotten hir estate, and the greatnesse of hir aliance, besides the nobilitie of hir deceased husband, with the hope of the towarde youth of the Duke hir sonne and our Nephew. Ah false and vile bitch, I sweare by the almightie God and by his blessed wounds, that if I can catch thee, and that wicked knave thy chosen mate, I will pipe ye both such a galiarde, as ye never felt the lyke joy and mirthe. I will make ye daunce such a bloudy bargenet, as your whorish heate for ever shall be cooled. What abuse have they committed under title of mariage, which was so secretely done, as their Children do witnesse their filthy embracements, but their promise of faith was made in open aire, and serveth for a cloke and visarde for their most filthy whoredome? [188v] And what if mariage was concluded, be we of so little respect, as the carion beast would not vouchsafe to advertise us of hir entent? Or is *Bologna* a man worthy to be allied or mingled with the royall bloud of *Aragon* and *Castille*? No no, be hee never so good a Gentleman, his race agreeth not with kingly state. But I make to God a vowe, that never will I take one sound and restfull sleepe, untill I have dispatched that infamous fact from our bloud, and that the caitife whoremonger be used according to his desert.' The Cardinall also was out of quiet, grinding his teeth togither, chattering for the Jacke an Apes *Pater noster*, promising no better usage to their *Bologna* than his yonger brother did. And the better to intrap them both (without further sturre for

that time) they sent to the Lord *Gismondo Gonsago* the Cardinal
of *Mantua* then Legate for Pope *Julius* the second at *Ancona*, at
whose hands they enjoyed such friendship, as *Bologna* and all his
familie were commaunded spedily to avoide the Citie. But for al
that the Legate was able to do, of long time he could not prevaile.
Bologna had so great intelligence within *Ancona*. Neverthelesse
whiles he differred his departure, hee caused the most part of his
train, his children & goods to be conveyed to *Siena*, an auncient
Citie of *Thoscane*, which for the state and liberties, had long time
bene at warres with the *Florentines*, in such wise as the very same
day that newes came to *Bologna* that he shold departe the Citie
within .xv. dayes, hee was ready, and mounted on horseback to
take his flight to *Siena*, which brake for sorrow the hearts of the
Aragon brethren, seeing that they were deceived and frustrate of
their intent, bicause they purposed by the way to apprehend
Bologna, and to cut him in pieces. But what? the time of his hard
luck was not yet expired, and so the marche [189] from *Ancona*,
served not for the Theatre of those two infortunate lovers overthrow, who certain moneths lived in peace in *Thoscane*. The
Cardinal night nor day did sleepe, and his brother stil did wayt
to performe his othe of revenge. And seeing their enimie out of
feare, they dispatched a post to *Alfonso Castruccio*, the Cardinall
of *Siena*, that he might entreat the Lord *Borghese*, chief of the
seignorie there, that their sister and *Bologna* should be banished
the Countrey and limits of that Citie, which with small sute was
brought to passe. These two infortunate, husband and wife,
were chased from al places, and so unlucky as whilom *Acasta*
was, or *Oedipus*, after his fathers death and incestuous mariage
with his mother, uncertain to what Saint to vow themselves, and
to what place to take their flight. In the end they determined to
goe to *Venice*, and to take their flight to *Ramagna*, there to
imbarke themselves for to retire to the savegarde of the Citie,
environned with the sea *Adriaticum*, the richest in *Europa*. But
the poore soules made their reconing there without their hoste,
failing half the price of their banket. For being upon the territo-

rie of *Forly*, one of the train a farre off, did see a troupe of horsemen galloping towardes their company, which by their countenaunce shewed no signe of peace or amitie at all, which made them consider that it was some ambush of their enimies. The *Neapolitan* Gentleman seeing the onset bending upon them, began to fear death, not for that he cared at all for his mishap and ruine, but his heart began to cleave for heavinesse to see his wife and litle children ready to be murdered, and serve for the passetime of the *Aragon* brethrens eyes, for whose sakes he knew himself already predestinate to die, and that for despite of him, and to accelerate his death by the overthrow of his, he was assu-
[189v] red that they wold kil his children before his face & presence. But what is there to be done, where counsell & meanes to escape do faile? Ful of teares therfore, astonishment & fear, he expected death so cruel as man could devise, & was alredy determined to suffer the same with good corage, for any thing that the Duchesse could say unto him. He might well have saved himself & his eldest sonne by flight, being both wel mounted upon two good Turkey horsses, which ran so fast, as the quarrel discharged forth of a crosbow. But he loved too much his wife & children, and wold keepe them companie both in life and death. In the end the good Ladie sayd unto him: 'sir for all the joyes & pleasures which you can doe me, for Gods sake save your self & the little infant next you, who can wel indure the galloping of the horse. For sure I am, that you being out of our companie, we shal not neede to fear any hurt. But if you do tary, you wil be the cause of the ruine and overthrow of us all, & receive therby no profit or advauntage: take this purse therfore, & save your self, attending better Fortune in time to come.' The poore gentleman *Bologna* knowing that his wife had pronounced reason, & perceiving that it was impossible from that time forth that she or hir traine could escape their hands, taking leave of hir, & kissing his children not forgetting the money which she offred unto him, willed his servants to save themselves by such meanes as they thought best. So giving spurrs unto his horse, he began to flee

amaine, and his eldest sonne seeing his father gone, began to followe in like sorte. And so for that time they two were saved by
breaking of the intended yll luck like to light upon them. And in
a place to rescue himself at *Venice*, hee turned another way, & in
great journeys arrived at *Millan*. In the meane time the horsemen were approched neere the Duchesse, [190] who seeing that
Bologna had saved himself, very courteously began to speake
unto the Ladie, were it that the *Aragon* brethren had given them
that charge, or feared that the Ladie wold trouble them with hir
importunate cries & lamentations. One therfore amongs them
sayd unto hir: 'Madame, we be commaunded by the Lordes your
brethren, to conducte you home unto your house, that you may
receive again the government of the Duchie, and the order of the
Duke your sonne, & doe marvell very much at your folly, for
giving your self thus to wander the Countrey after a man of so
small reputation as *Bologna* is, who when he hath glutted his
lusting lecherous mind with the comelinesse of your Noble personage, wil despoil you of your goods & honor, and then take his
legs into some strange countrey.' The simple Ladie, albeit griev-
ous it was unto hir to heare such speech of hir husband, yet held
hir peace and dissembled what she thought, glad and well contented with the curtesy done unto hir, fearing before that they
came to kill hir, and thought hir self already discharged, hoping
upon their courteous dealings, that she and hir Children from
that time forth should live in good assuraunce. But she was
greatly deceyved, and knew within shorte space after, the good
will hir brethren bare unto hir. For so soone as these gallants had
conducted hir into the kingdome of *Naples*, to one of the Castels
of hir sonne, she was committed to prison with hir children, and
she also that was the secretarie of hir infortunate mariage. Till
this time Fortune was contented to proceede with indifferent
quiet against those Lovers, but henceforth ye shall heare the
issue of their little prosperous love, and how pleasure having
blinded them, never forsoke them untill it had given them
the overthrow. [190v] It booteth not heere to recite fables or

histories, contenting my self that ladies do read without too many weping teares, the pitiful end of that miserable princesse, who seeing hir self a prisoner in the companie of hir litle children and welbeloved Maiden, paciently lived in hope to see hir brethren appaised, comforting hir self for the escape of hir husband out of the hands of his mortal foes. But hir assurance was changed into an horrible feare, & hir hope to no expectation of suretie, when certain dayes after hir imprisonment, hir Gaoler came in, and sayd unto hir: 'Madame I do advise you henceforth to consider upon your conscience, for so much as I suppose that even this very day your life shall be taken from you.' I leave for you to thinke what horrour and traunce assailed the feeble heart of this pore Lady, and with what eares she received those cruell newes, but hir cries and mones together with hir sighes and lamentations, declared with what cheere she received that advertisement. 'Alas (sayd she) is it possible that my brethren should so farre forget themselves, as for a fact nothing prejudiciall unto them, cruelly to put to death their innocent sister, and to imbrue the memory of their fact, in the bloud of one which never did offend them? Must I against all right and equitie be put to death before the Judge or Magistrate have made trial of my life, & known the unrighteousnesse of my cause? Ah God most righteous, and bountiful father, beholde the malice of my brethren, and the tyrannous crueltie of those which wrongfully doe seeke my bloud. Is it a sinne to mary? Is it a fault to flie and avoide the sinne of whoredome? What lawes be these, where mariage bed and joyned matrimony is pursued with like severitie, as murder, theft and advoutrie? And what Christianitie in a Cardinall, to shed the bloud which he ought [191] to defend? What profession is this, to assaile the innocent by the hie way side, in place to punish theeves and murderers? O Lord God thou art just, & dost al things righteously, I see well that I have trespassed against thy Majestie in some other notorious crime than by mariage: I most humbly therfore beseeche thee to have compassion upon me, and to pardon mine offenses, accepting the confession and repentance of me thine humble servaunt for satisfaction of my sinnes, which it pleased thee to wash away in the precious bloud of thy sonne our Savior, that being so purified, I might appere at the holy banket in thy glorious kingdome.' When she had thus finished hir prayer, two or three of the ministers which had taken hir bisides *Forly*, came in, and sayd unto hir: 'Now Madame make ready your self to goe to God, for beholde your houre is come.' 'Praised be that God (sayd she) for the wealth and woe which it pleaseth him to send us. But I beseeche you my friendes to have pitie upon these lyttle children and innocent creatures. Let them not feele the smarte which I am assured my brethren beare against their poore unhappie father.' 'Well well Madame sayd they, we will convey them to such a place, as they shal not want.' 'I also recommend unto you (quod she) this poore maiden, and entreat hir wel, in consideration of hir good service done to the infortunate Duchesse of *Malfi*.' As she had ended those woords, the two Ruffians did put a corde about hir neck, and strangled hir. The mayden seeing the piteous tragedie commensed upon hir mistresse, cried out a main, and cursed the cruell malice of those tormenters, and besought God to be witnesse of the same, and crying out upon his divine Majestie, she besought him to bend his judgement against them which causelesse (being no Magistrates,) hadde killed such innocent creatures. [191v] 'Reason it is (said one of the tyrants) that thou be partaker of the joy of thy mistresse innocencie, sith thou hast bene so faithfull a minister, and messanger of hir follies.' And sodainly caught hir by the hair of the head, & in stead of a carcanet placed a roape about hir necke. 'How now (quod she,) is this the promised faith which you made unto my Ladie?' But those woords flew into the air with hir soule, in companie of the miserable Duchesse.

But hearken now the most sorowfull scene of all the tragedie. The litle children which had seene all the furious game done upon their mother and hir maide, as nature provoked them, or as some presage of their mishap led them therunto, kneled upon their knees before those tyrants, and embracing their legs, wailed in such wise, as I think that any other, except a pitilesse heart spoiled of all humanitie, wold have had compassion. And impossible it was for them to unfold the embracements of those innocent creatures, which seemed to forethink their death by the wilde lokes and countenance of those roisters. Wherby I think that needes it must be confessed, that nature hath in hir self, and upon us imprinted some signe of divination, and specially at the hour and time of death, in such wise as the very beasts feele some conceits, although they see neither sword nor staffe, and indevor to avoyde the cruell passage of a thing so fearful, as the separation of two things so neerely united, even the body and soule, which for the motion that chaunceth at the very instant, sheweth how nature is constrained in that monstruous separation, & more than horrible overthrow. But who can appease a heart determined to do evil, & hath sworn the death of another forced therunto by some special commaundement? The *Aragon* brethren ment hereby nothing else, but to roote [192] out the whole name & race of *Bologna*. And therfore the two ministers of iniquitie did like murder & slaughter upon those two tender babes, as they committed upon their mother, not without some motion of horror, for doing of an act so detestable. Behold here how far the crueltie of man extendeth, when it coveteth nothing else but vengeance, and marke what excessive choler the minde of them produceth, which suffer themselves to be forced & overwhelmed with furie. Leave we apart the crueltie of *Euchrates*, the sonne of the king of *Bactria*, & of *Phraates* the sonne of the *Persian* Prince, of *Timon* of *Athens*, & of an infinite numbre of those which were rulers and governers of the Empire of *Rome*: and let us match with these *Aragon* brethren, one *Vitoldus* Duke of *Lituania*, the crueltie of whom, constrained his own subjects to hang themselves, for fear least they shold fall into his furious & bloudy hands. We may confesse also these brutal brethren to be more butcherly than ever *Otho* erle of *Monferrato*, & prince of *Urbin* was, who caused a yeoman of his chamber to be wrapped in a sheete poudred with sulpher & brimston, & afterwards kindled with a candle, was scalded & consumed to death, bicause only he waked not at an hour by him apointed. Let us not excuse them also from some affinity with *Maufredus* the sonne of *Henry* the second Emperor, who smoldered his own father, being an old man, between ii. coverleds. These former furies might have some excuse to cover their crueltie, but these had no other cause but a certain beastly madnesse which moved them to kil those litle children their nevews, who by no meanes could prejudice or anoy the duke of *Malfi* or his title, in the succession of his Duchie, the mother having withdrawn hir goods, & was assigned hir dowry: but a wicked hart must needes bring forth semblable works according to his malice. [192v] In the time of these murders, the infortunate Lover kept himself at *Millan* wyth his sonne *Federick*, and vowed himself to the Lord *Silvio Savello*, who that time besieged the Castell of *Millan*, in the behalf of *Maximilian Sforcia*, which in the end he conquered and recovered by composition with the French within. But that charge being atchieved, the generall *Savello* marched from thence to *Cremona* with his campe, whither *Bologna* durst not folow, but repaired to the Marquize of *Bitonte*, in which time the *Aragon* brethren so wrought, as his goods were confiscate at *Naples*, and he driven to his shifts to use the golden Duckates which the Duchesse gave him to relieve him self at *Millan*, whose Death althoughe it was advertised by many, yet hee coulde not be persuaded to beleve the same, for that divers which went about to betray him, and feared he should flie from *Millan*, kept his beake in the water, (as the Proverbe is,) and assured him both of the life & welfare of his spouse, and that shortly his brethren in law wold be reconciled, bicause that many Noble men favored him well, and desired his returne home to his Countrey. Fed and filled with that vaine hope, he remained more than a yeare at *Millan*, frequenting the companie, and well entertained of the richest Marchants and Gentlemen of the Citie: and above all other, he had familiar accesse to the house of the Ladie *Hippolita Bentivoglia*, where upon a day after dinner, taking his Lute in hand, wheron he could exceedingly wel play, he began to sing a certain Sonnet, which he had composed upon the discourse of his misfortune, the tenor whereof is this. [193]

The song of *Antonio Bologna*,

the husband of the Duchesse of *Malfi*.

If love, the death, or tract of time, have measured my distresse,
   Or if my beating sorrowes may my languor well expresse:
Then love come sone to visit me, which most my heart desires,
   And so my dolor findes some ease, through flames of fansies fires.
The time runnes out his rolling course, for to prolong mine ease,
   To thend I shall enjoy my love, and heart himself appease.
A cruell Darte brings happy death, my soule then rest shall finde:
   And sleping body under tombe, shall dreame time out of minde.
And yet the Love, the time, nor Death, lokes not how I decrease:
   Nor giveth eare to any thing of this my wofull peace.
Full farre I am from my good happe, or halfe the joy I crave,
   wherby I change my state with teares, & draw full nere my grave.
The courteous Gods that gives me life, nowe moves the Planets all:
   For to arrest my groning ghost, and hence my sprite to call.
Yet from them still I am separd, by things unequall here,
   Not ment the Gods may be unjust, that bredes my changing chere.
For they provide by their foresight, that none shall doe me harme:
   But she whose blasing beuty bright, hath brought me in a charm.
My mistresse hath the powre alone, to rid me from this woe:
   whose thrall I am, for whome I die, to whome my sprite shall goe.
Away my soule, go from the griefs, that thee oppresseth still,
   And let thy dolor witnesse beare, how much I want my will.
For since that love and death himself, delights in guiltlesse bloud,
   Let time transport my troubled sprite, where destny semeth good.

His song ended, the poore Gentleman could not forbeare from pouring forth his luke warme teares, which aboundantly ran downe his heavie face, and his panting sighes truely discovered the alteration of his mind, which moved eche wight of that assembly to pitie his [193v] mournefull state: and one specially of small acquaintaunce, and yet knew the devises which the *Aragon* brethren had trained and conspired against him: that unacquainted Gentleman his name was *Delio*, one very well learned and of trimme invention, and very excellently hath endited in the *Italian* vulgar tongue. Who knowing the Gentleman to be husbande to the deceased Duchesse of *Malfi* came unto him, & taking him aside, sayd: 'Sir, albeit I have no great acquaintance with you, this being the first time that ever I saw you, to my remembrance, so it is, that vertue hath such force, and maketh gentle mindes so amorous of their like, as when they doe beholde eche other, they feele themselves coupled as it were in a bande of minds, that impossible it is to divide the same. Now knowing what you be, and the good and commendable qualities in you, I compte it my duetie to reveale that which may chaunce to breede you damage. Know you then, that I of late was in companie with a Noble man of *Naples*, which is in this Citie, banded with a certaine companie of horsemen, who tolde me that hee had a speciall charge to kill you, and therfore prayed me (as he seemed) to require you not to come in his sight, to the intent hee might not be constrained to doe that, which should offende his Conscience, and grieve the same all the dayes of his life. Moreover I have worse tidings to tell you, which are, that the Duchesse your wife is deade by violent hand in prison, and the moste parte of them that were in hir companie. Besides this assure your self, that if you doe not take heede to that which this *Neapolitane* captaine hathe differred, other will doe and execute the same. This much I have thought good to tell you, bicause it woulde verie much grieve me, that a Gentleman so excellent as you be, [194] should be murdered in that miserable wise, and would deeme my selfe unworthy of life, if knowing these practises I should dissemble the same.' Wherunto *Bologna* answered: 'Syr *Delio* I am greatly bounde unto you, and give you heartie thankes for the good will you beare me. But of the conspiracie of the brethren of *Aragon*, and the death of my Ladie, you be deceyved, and some have given you wrong intelligence. For within these two dayes I received letters from *Naples*, wherein I am advertised, that the right honorable and reverende Cardinall and his brother be almost appeased, and that my goodes shall be rendred againe, and my deare wife restored.' 'Ah syr sayd *Delio*, how you be beguiled and fedde with follies, and nourished with sleights of Courte. Assure your self that they which wryte these trifles, make such shamefull sale of you, as the Butcher doeth of his flesh in the shambles, and so wickedly betray you, as impossible it is to invent a Treason more detestable: but bethinke you well thereof.' When he had sayde so, hee tooke his leave, and joyned himself in companie of fine and pregnant wittes, there assembled togither. In the meane tyme, the cruell spryte of the *Aragon* brethren were not yet appeased with the former murders, but needes must finish the last acte of *Bologna* his Tragedie by losse of his life, to keepe his wife and Children companie, so well in an other worlde, as hee was united with them in Love in this fraile and transitorie passage. The *Neapolitan* gentleman before spoken of by *Delio*, which had taken an enterprise to satisfie the barbarous Cardinal, to berieve his Countreyman of life, having changed his minde, and differring from day to day to sorte the same to effect, which hee had taken in hande, it chaunced that a *Lombarde* [194v] of larger conscience than the other, invegled with Covetousnesse, and hired for readie money, practised the death of the Duchesse pore husband. This bloudy beast was called *Daniel de Bozola* that had charge of a certaine bande of footemen in *Millan*. This newe *Judas* and assured manqueller, within certaine dayes after, knowing that *Bologna* oftentimes repaired to heare service at the Church and covent of *S. Fraunces*, secretly conveyed himself in ambush, hard bisides the church of *S. James* whether he came, (being accompanied with a certaine troupe of souldioures) to assaile the infortunate *Bologna*, who was sooner slaine than hee was able to thinke upon defense, & whose mishap was such, that he which killed him had good leisure to save himself by reason of the little pursuite made after him. Beholde heere the Noble facte of a Cardinall, and what saver it hath of Christian puritie, to commit a slaughter for a facte done many yeares past upon a poore Gentleman which never thought him hurte. Is this the sweete observation of the Apostles, of whom they vaunt themselves to be the successors and folowers? And yet we cannot finde nor reade, that the Apostles, or those that stept in their trace, hired Ruffians and Murderers to cut the throtes of them which did them hurt. But what? It was in the time of *Julius* the second, who was more marshall than christian, and loved better to shed bloud than give blessing to the people. Such ende had the infortunate mariage of him, which ought to have contented himself with that degree and honor that hee had acquired by his deedes and glory of his vertues, so much by eche wight recommended. We ought never to clime higher than our force permitteth, ne yet surmount the bounds of duety, and lesse suffer our selves to be haled fondly forth with desire of brutal sensualitie. The sinne [195] being of such nature, that hee never giveth over the partie whome he mastereth, until he hath brought him to the shame of some Notable follie. You see the miserable discourse of a Princesse love, that was not very wise, and of a gentleman that had forgotten his estate, which ought to serve for a loking glasse to them which be over hardie in making of enterprises, and doe not measure their abilitie with the greatnesse of their attemptes: where they ought to maintaine themselves in reputation, and beare the title of wel advised:

foreseeing their ruine to be example to all posteritie, as may be seene
by the death of *Bologna*, and of all them which sprang of him,
and of his infortunate spouse his Ladie
and mistresse.
But we have discoursed inoughe hereof, sith
diversitie of other Histories doe call us
to bring the same in place, which
were not much more happie
than those, whose Historie
ye have already
tasted.

APPENDIX 2

A CONTEMPORARY WEREWOLF

A true Discourse.
Declaring the damnable life
and death of one Stubbe Peeter, a most
wicked Sorcerer, who in the likenes of a
Woolfe, committed many murders, continuing this
divelish practise 25. yeeres, killing and de-
vouring Men, Woomen, and
Children.
Who for the same fact was ta-
ken and executed the 31. of October
last past in the Towne of Bedbur
neer the Cittie of *Collin*
in *Germany.*

Trulye translated out of the high Duch.
according to the Copie printed in Collin,
brought over into England by George
Bores ordinary poste, the xi. daye of
this present Moneth of June 1590,
who did both see and heare the same.

AT LONDON

Printed for Edward Venge, and are to be *solde in* Fleet-street *at
the signe of the* Vine.

[1]

¶ A most true Discourse,
declaring the life and death of one
Stubbe Peeter, being a most
wicked Sorcerer.

THose whome the Lord dooth leave to followe the Imagination of their own hartes, dispising his proffered grace, in the end through the hardnes of hart and contempt of his fatherly mercy, they enter the right path to perdicion and destruction of body and soule for ever: as in this present historie in perfect sorte may be seene, the strangenes whereof, together with the cruelties committed, and the long time therin continued, may drive many in doubt whether the same be truth or no, and the ratherfore that sundry falce & fabulous mat- [2]¹ ters have heertofore passed in print, which hath wrought much incredulitie in the harts of all men generally, insomuch that now a daies fewe thinges doo escape be it never so certain, but that it is embased by the tearm of a lye or falce reporte.² In the reading of this story, therfore I doo first request reformation of opinion, next patience to peruse it, because it is published for examples sake, and lastly to censure thereof as reason and wisdome dooth think convenient, considering the subtilty that Sathan useth to work the soules destruction, and the great matters which the accursed practise of Sorcery dooth effect, the fruites whereof is death and destruction for ever, and yet in all ages practised by the reprobate and wicked of the earth, some in one sort, and some in another even as the Devill giveth promise to perfourme. But of all other that ever lived, none was comparable unto this helhound, whose tiranny and cruelty did well declare he

---

1   This and the subsequent numbers indicate the ends of pages in the original publication.

2   In this transcription, as elsewhere in the edition, u/v and i/j are normalized to modern usage; similarly, contractions are expanded, black-letter type appears in ordinary roman type, and roman and italic departures from the text's usual black-letter type are both indicated by italic.

was of his Father the devill, who was a murderer from the beginning, whose life and death and most bloody practises the discourse following dooth make just reporte. [3] In the townes of *Cperadt* and *Bedbur* neer unto *Collin* in high *Germany*, there was continually brought up and nourished one *Stubbe Peeter*, who from his youth was greatly inclined to evill, and the practising of wicked Artes even from twelve yeers of age till twentye, and so forwardes till his dying daye, insomuch that surfeiting in the Damnable desire of magick, negromancye, and sorcery, acquainting him selfe with many infernall spirites and feendes, insomuch that forgetting the God that made him, and that Saviour that shed his blood for mans redemption: In the end, careles of salvation gave both soule and body to the devil for ever, for small carnall pleasure in this life, that he might be famous and spoken of on earth, though he lost heaven thereby. The Devill who hath a readye eare to listen to the lewde motions of cursed men, promised to give unto him whatsoever his hart desired during his mortall life: wherupon this vilde wretch neither desired riches nor promotion, nor was his fancy satisfied with any externall or outward pleasure, but having a tirannous hart, and a most cruell [4] bloody minde, he only requested that at his plesure he might woork his mallice on men, Women, and children, in the shape of some beast, wherby he might live without dread or danger of life, and unknowen to be the executor of any bloody enterprise, which he meant to commit: The Devill who sawe him a fit instruement to perfourm mischeefe as a wicked feend pleased with the desire of wrong and destruction, gave unto him a girdle which being put about him, he was straight transfourmed into the likenes of a greedy devouring Woolf, strong and mighty, with eyes great and large, which in the night sparkeled like unto brandes of fire, a mouth great and wide, with most sharpe and cruell teeth, A huge body, and mightye pawes: And no sooner should he put off the same girdle, but presently he should appeere in his former shape, according to the proportion of a man, as if he had never beene changed.

Stubbe Peeter heerwith was exceedingly well pleased, and the shape fitted his fancye and agreed best with his nature, being inclined to blood and crueltye, therfore satisfied [5] with this strange and divelish gifte, for that it was not troublesome nor great in cariage, but that it might be hidden in a small room, he proceeded to the execution of sundry most hainous and vilde murders, for if any person displeased him, he would incontinent thirst for revenge, and no sooner should they or any of theirs walke abroad in the feeldes or about the Cittie, but in the shape of a Woolfe he would presentlye incounter them, and never rest till he had pluckt out their throates and teare their joyntes a sunder: And after he had gotten a taste heerof, he tooke such pleasure and delight in shedding of blood, that he would night and day walke the Feelds, and work extreame cruelties. And sundry times he would goe through the Streetes of *Collin,* *Bedbur,* and *Cperadt,* in comely habit, and very civilly as one well knowen to all the inhabitants therabout, & oftentimes was he saluted of those whose freendes and children he had buchered, though nothing suspected for the same. In these places, I say, he would walke up & down, and if he could spye either Maide, Wife or childe, that his [6] eyes liked or his hart lusted after, he would waite their issuing out of the Cittie or town, if he could by any meanes get them alone, he would in the feeldes ravishe them, and after in his Woolvish likenes cruelly murder them: yea often it came to passe that as he walked abroad in the feeldes, if he chaunste to spye a companye of maydens playing together, or else a milking of their Kine, in his Woolvishe shape he would incontinent runne among them, and while the rest escaped by flight, he would be sure to laye holde of one, and after his filthy lust fulfilled, he would murder her presentlye, beside, if he had liked or knowne any of them, look who he had a minde unto, her he would pursue, whether she were before or behinde, and take her from the rest, for such was his swiftnes of foot while he continued a woolf: that he would outrunne the swiftest greyhound in that Countrye: and so muche he had practised this wickednes, that the whole Province was feared by the cruelty of this bloody and devouring Woolfe. Thus continuing his divelishe and damnable deedes within the compas of fewe yeeres, he had [7] murdered thirteene yong Children, and two goodly yong women bigge with Child, tearing the Children out of their wombes, in most bloody and savedge sorte, and after eate their hartes panting hotte and rawe, which he accounted dainty morsells & best agreeing to his Appetite.

Moreover he used many times to kill Lambes and Kiddes and such like beastes, feeding on the same most usually raw and bloody, as if he had beene a naturall Woolfe indeed, so that all men mistrusted nothing lesse then this his divelish Sorcerie.

He had at that time living a faire yong Damosell to his Daughter, after whom he also lusted most unnaturallye, and cruellye committed most wicked inceste with her, a most groce and vilde sinne, far surmounting Adultrye or Fornication, though the least of the three dooth drive the soule into hell fier, except hartye repentance, and the great mercy of God. This Daughter of his he begot when he was not altogither so wickedlye given, who was called by the name of *Stubbe Beell*, whose beautye and good grace was such as deserved commen- [8] dacions of all those that knewe her: And such was his inordinate lust and filthye desire toward her, that he begat a Childe by her, dayly using her as his Concubine, but as an insaciate and filthy beast, given over to woork evil, with greedines he also lay by his owne Sister, frequenting her company long time even according as the wickednes of his hart lead him: Moreover being on a time sent for to a Gossip of his there to make merry and good cheere, ere he thence departed he so wunne the woman by his faire and flattering speech, and so much prevailed, that ere he departed the house: he lay by her, and ever after had her companye at his commaund, this woman had to name *Katherine Trompin*, a woman of tall and comely stature of exceeding good favour and one that was well esteemed among her neighbours. But his lewde and inordinat lust being not satisfied with the company of many Concubines, nor his wicked fancye contented with the beauty of any woman, at length the devill sent unto him a wicked spirit in the similitude and likenes of a woman, so faire of face and comelye of perso- [9] nage, that she resembled rather some heavenly *Hellin* then any mortall creature, so farre her beauty exceeded the cheifest sorte of women, and with her as with his harts delight, he kept company the space of seven yeeres, though in the end she proved and was found indeed no other then a she Devil, notwithstanding, this lewd sinne of lecherye did not any thing asswage his cruell and bloody minde, but continuing an insatiable bloodsucker, so great was the joye he took therin, that he accounted no day spent in pleasure wherin he had not shed some blood not respecting so much who he did murder, as how to murder and destroy them, as the matter ensuing dooth manifest, which may stand for a speciall note of a cruell and hard hart. For having a proper youth to his sonne, begotten in the flower and strength of his age, the firste fruite of his bodye, in whome he took such joye, that he did commonly call him his *Hartes ease*, yet so farre his delight in murder exceeded the joye he took in his only Sonne, that thirsting after his blood, on a time he inticed him into the feeldes, and from thence into a Forrest hard [10] by, where making excuse to stay about the necessaries of nature, while the yong man went on forward, incontinent in the shape and likenes of a Wolfe he encountred his owne Sonne, and there most cruelly slewe him, which doon, he presently eat the brains out of his head as a most saverie and dainty delycious meane to staunch his greedye apetite: the most monstrous act that ever man heard off, for never was knowen a wretch from nature so far degenerate.

Long time he continued this vilde and villanous life, sometime in the likenes of a Woolfe, sometime in the habit of a man, sometime in the Townes and Citties, and sometimes in the Woods and thickettes to them adjoyning, whereas the duche coppye maketh mention, he on a time mette with two men and one woman, whom he greatly desired to murder, and the better to bring his divelish purpose to effect, doubting by them to be overmatched and knowing one of them by name, he used this pollicie to bring them to their end. In subtill sorte he convayed himselfe far before them in their way and craftely couched out of their sight, [11] but as soone as they approched neere the place where he lay, he called one of them by his name, the partye hearing him selfe called once or twice by his name, supposing it was some familier friend that in jesting sorte stood out of his sight, went from his companye towarde the place from whence the voice proceeded, of purpose to see who it was, but he was no sooner entred within the danger of this transformed man, but incontinent he was murdered in the place, the rest of his company staying for him, expecting still his returne, but finding his stay over long: the other man lefte the woman, and went to looke him, by which means the second man was also murdered, the woman then seeing neither of both returne againe, in hart suspected that some evill had fallen upon them, and therfore with all the power she had, she sought to save her selfe by flight, though it nothing prevailed, for good soule she was also soone overtaken by this light footed Woolfe, whom when he had first deflowred, he after most cruelly murdered, the men were after found mangled in the wood, but the womans body was never af-[12] ter seene, for she the caitife had most ravenouslye devoured, whose fleshe he esteemed both sweet and dainty in taste.

Thus this damnable *Stubbe Peeter* lived the tearme of five and twenty yeeres, unsuspected to be Author of so many cruell and unnaturall murders, in which time he had destroyed and spoyled an unknowen number of Men, Women, and Children, sheepe, Lambes, and Goates: and other Catttell, for when he could not through the warines of people drawe men, Women, or Children in his danger, then like a cruell and tirannous beast he would woorke his cruelty on brut beasts in most savadge sort, and did act more mischeefe and cruelty then would be credible, although high *Germany* hath been forced to taste the trueth thereof.

By which meanes the inhabitantes of *Collin*, *Bedbur* and *Cperadt*, seeing themselves so greevously endaungered, plagued, and molested by this greedy & cruel Woolfe, who wrought continuall harme and mischeefe, insomuch that few or none durst travell to or from those places without good provision of defence, and all for feare of this [13] devouring and fierce woolf, for oftentimes the Inhabitants found the Armes & legges of dead Men, Women, and Children, scattered up and down the feelds to their great greefe and vexation of hart, knowing the same to be doone by that strange and cruell Woolfe, whome by no meanes they could take or overcome, so that if any man or woman mist their Childe, they were out of hope ever to see it again alive, mistrusting straight that the Woolfe had destroyed it.

And heere is to be noted a most strange thing which setteth foorth the great power and mercifull providence of God to the comfort of eache Christian hart. There were not long agoe certain small Children playing in a Medowe together hard by the town, where also some store of kine were feeding, many of them having yong calves sucking upon them: and sodainly among these Children comes this vilde Woolfe running and caught a prittie fine Girle by the choller, with intent to pull out her throat, but such was the will of God, that he could not pearce the choller of the Childes coate, being high and very well stiffened & close claspt about her neck, and therwith all the sodaine great [14] crye of the rest of the children which escaped, so amazed the cattell feeding by, that being fearfull to be robbed of their young, they altogether came running against the Woolfe with such force that he was presently compelled to let goe his holde and to run away to escape the danger of their hornes, by which meanes the Childe was preserved from death, and God be thanked remains living at this day.

And that this thing is true, Maister *Tice Artine* a Brewer dwelling at *Puddlewharfe*, in *London*, beeing a man of that Country borne, and one of good reputation and account, is able to justifie, who is neere Kinsman to this Childe, and hath from thence twice received Letters conserning the same, and for that the firste Letter did rather drive him into wondering at the act then yeelding credit therunto, he had shortlye after at request of his writing another letter sent him, wherby he was more fully satisfied, and divers other persons of great credit in *London* hath in like sorte received letters from their freends to the like effect.

Likewise in the townes of *Germany* aforesaid continuall praier was used unto [15] god that it would please him to deliver them from the danger of this greedy Woolfe.

And although they had practised all the meanes that men could devise to take this ravenous beast, yet untill the Lord had determined his fall, they could not in any wise prevaile: notwithstanding they daylye continued their purpose, and daylye sought to intrap him, and for that intent continually maintained great mastyes and Dogges of muche strength to hunt & chase the beast whersoever they could finde him. In the end it pleased God as they were in readines and provided to meete with him, that they should espye him in his woolvishe likenes, at what time they beset him round about, and moste circumspectlye set their Dogges upon him, in such sort that there was no means to escape, at which advantage they never could get him before, but as the Lord delivered *Goliah* into the handes of *David*, so was this Woolfe brought in danger of these men, who seeing as I saide before no way to escape the imminent danger, being hardly pursued at the heeles presently he slipt his girdle from about him, wherby the shape of a Woolfe cleane avoi- [16] ded, and he appeered presently in his true shape & likenes, having in his hand a staffe as one walking toward the Cittie, but the hunters whose eyes was stedfastly bent upon the beast, and seeing him in the same place metamorphosed contrary to their expectation: it wrought a wonderfull amazement in their mindes, and had it not beene that they knewe the man so soone as they sawe him, they had surely taken the same to have beene some Devill in a mans likenes, but for as much as they knewe him to be an auncient dweller in the Towne, they came unto him, and talking with him they brought him by communication home to his owne house, and finding him to be the man indeede, and no delusion [text reads 'selusion'] or phantasticall motion, they had him incontinent before the Majestrates to be examined.

Thus being apprehended, he was shortly after put to the racke in the Towne of *Bedbur*, but fearing the torture, he volluntarilye confessed his whole life, and made knowen the villanies which he had committed for the space of xxv. yeeres, also he confessed how by Sorcery he procured of the Devill a Girdle, which beeing put on, he [17] forthwith became a Woolfe, which Girdle at his apprehension he confest he cast it off in a certain Vallye and there left it, which when the Majestrates heard, they sent to the Vallye for it, but at their comming found nothing at al, for it may be supposed that it was gone to the devil from whence it came, so that it was not to be found. For the Devil having brought the wretch to al the shame he could, left him to indure the torments which his deedes deserved.

After he had some space beene imprisoned, the majestrates found out through due examination of the matter, that his daughter *Stubbe Beell* and his Gossip *Katherine Trompin*, were both accessarye to divers murders committed, who for the same as also for their leaud life otherwise committed, was arraigned, and with *Stubbe Peeter* condempned, and their severall Judgementes pronounced the 28 of October 1589. in this manor, that is to saye: *Stubbe Peeter* as principall mallefactor, was judged first to have his body laide on a wheele, and with red hotte burning pincers in ten several places to have the flesh puld off from the bones, after that, his legges and Armes to [18] be broken with a woodden Axe or Hatchet, afterward to have his head strook from his body, then to have his carkasse burnde to Ashes.

Also his Daughter and his Gossip were judged to be burned quicke to Ashes, the same time and day with the carkasse of the aforesaid *Stubbe Peeter*, And on the 31. of the same moneth, they suffered death accordingly in the town of *Bedbur* in the presence of many peeres & princes of *Germany*.

Thus Gentle Reader have I set down the true discourse of this wicked man *Stub Peeter*, which I desire to be a warning to all Sorcerers and Witches, which unlawfully followe their owne divelish imagination to the utter ruine and destruction of their soules eternally, from which wicked and damnable practice, I beseech God keepe all good men, and from the crueltye of their wicked hartes. Amen.

AFter the execution, there was by the advice of the Majestrates of the town of *Bedbur* a high pole set up and stronglye framed, which first went through the wheele wheron he was broken, whereunto also it [19] was fastened, after that a little above the Wheele the likenes of a Woolfe was framed in wood, to shewe unto all men the shape wherein he executed those crueltyes. Over that on the top of the stake the sorcerers head it selfe was set up, and round about the Wheele there hung as it were sixteen peeces of wood about a yarde in length which represented the sixteene persons that was perfectly knowen to be murdered by him. And the same ordained to stand there for a continuall monument to all insuing ages, what murders by *Stub Peeter* was committed, with the order of his Judgement, as this picture [i.e., the tableau of the wolf and wheel] doth more plainelye expresse.

Witnesses that this is

true.

Tyse Artyne.

William Brewar.

Adolf Staedt.

George Bores.

With divers others that have seen the same.

APPENDIX 3

MUSICAL SETTING FOR THE MADMAN'S SONG, 'O LET US HOWL' (4.2.60–71)

O Let Us Howle

This eerie song is sung by one of the madmen just before they give their wildly irrational speeches and then dance before the Duchess of Malfi in 4.2. The musical setting for 'O let us howl' exists in three manuscripts of which the British Library copy transcribed here (BL Add. MS 29481), though by no means the earliest, since it dates from the 1630s or later, is the most valuable in that it includes elaborate ornamentation of the kind that a vocalist in the early seventeenth century would typically improvise in performance. The song setting is almost certainly by Robert Johnson (*c.* 1582–1633), to whom it is attributed in one of the manuscripts; Johnson was a prolific composer for the Jacobean theatre and for the King's Men in particular. Onstage at Blackfriars, the song would have been accompanied by the musical consort or 'Act' that played before the performance and between acts of the play; the same was probably true at the Globe theatre, which at the time of *Malfi*'s first run of performances was already adopting musical practices that had been initiated at Blackfriars (Taylor and Jowett). The text of the play tells us that the song onstage was sung to a '*dismal kind of music*' (4.2.59 SD); this instrumental accompaniment has not survived.

The song is in G-dorian, a typical key and mode for consort songs of the period. As was sometimes the practice at the time, it makes daring use of chromatics to indicate madness: note the oscillation between B flat and B natural on 'howle' in measures 3–4 and again on 'howle' between F and F sharp in measure 6, which invite the singer to repeatedly imitate the sound of a wolf's howl. It is noteworthy, however, that in most song texts of the period it is the dementia of women rather than the dementia of men that is 'signalled through chromatic excess' (McClary, 81). In this as in several other elements of the play, Webster reverses standard gender associations of the period: despite Ferdinand's efforts to drive her out of her wits through contagious association with the madmen, the Duchess remains sane and it is her brothers who sink into madness. Other significant examples of word painting in the song include the long sequence of 'bawling' notes in measure 19, which follow the singer's promise in the previous measure that the Madmen will 'bell and bawle' their parts. Similarly, at the end of the song, when the singer begins to imagine a transcendence of the horror of madness, 'our bodies beinge blest', the music modulates upwards in imitation.

The words of the song in this manuscript version vary at several points from the song text in Q1. In the printed text of

Malfi, the singer expects that his 'yerksome noise' will soon have had a deleterious effect upon the listening Duchess and Cariola: 'cloyed *your* ears / And corrosived *your* hearts' (4.2.66–7; emphasis added); in the manuscript version, the singer's 'noise' instead rebounds back upon himself and the other madmen, eating away at *'our* eares' and *'our* hearts'. In the final line of the song from *Malfi* Q1, the singer says that his choir will, like swans, 'die in love and rest'; in the manuscript version, they will instead 'die in peace and reste'. In keeping with its serene conclusion, the song as performed onstage probably ended in a Picardy cadence, modulating from G minor to G major on the final chord to suggest a resolution of the 'dismal' mood of earlier parts of the song. One of the manuscripts (New York Public Library Drexel MS 4175), which includes a standard lute accompaniment appropriate to performance in a domestic as opposed to a theatrical setting, preserves the Picardy cadence.

The idea of dying 'like swans' was frequently used in songs of the period as code language for sexual passion and the 'little death' of orgasm (Macy, Henze). The words of Webster's song can be found in several verse miscellanies independent of the play; in one of these, Folger Shakespeare Library, MS v.a.124, 43b, the song is titled 'Lovers deluded by their mistresses' (Stern). The association with sexuality may have originated in a copyist's experience of a performance of the play and suggests that Webster's madmen may have gestured towards the Duchess in sexually threatening or inviting ways during their 'antimasque' in 4.2. It also suggests a connection with Thomas Campion's *Lords' Masque*, performed at court on 14 February 1613, which included an antimasque of lovers and other frantics who danced an *'absolute medley of madness'* (Campion; Orgel and Strong, 1.241–52). The coincidence in time and subject between Campion's masque and the masque elements in 4.2 of Webster's play is suggestive. In Campion's masque, the dance of madmen moves from a *'mad measure'* to a *'very solemn air'* (Orgel and Strong, 1.243) that heals their disease just as the words and music of Webster's song modulate from mad howling to transcendence and peace. Some critics have gone so far as to suggest that the words of 'O let us howl' may have been Campion's rather than Webster's (Stern). Songs often migrated independently of the plays in which they were performed; we have seen this in the case of the 'ditty' sung before the Cardinal in Loreto at 3.4, which Webster made a point of disavowing. But Campion's printed description of his masque appears to include the words to all of the songs, and 'O let us howl' is not among them. If the resemblance between Campion's mad folk and Webster's is more than coincidental, it is likely that Webster deliberately echoed and travestied Campion's *Lords' Masque* as part of his play's satire on the excesses of the Jacobean court (see pp. 27–8).

My transcription of BL Add. MS 29481 follows the spelling and musical notation of the original manuscript with the exception of bar lines supplied between measures 27–8 and 28–9 and missing accidentals supplied in measures 3, 16 and 38. The B natural of measure 3 is essential to the 'mad' chromaticism discussed above; it exists in the New York Public Library manuscript of the song and was most likely omitted in the British Library version by a careless copyist. Additional evidence of carelessness comes in the fact that the song in the British Library manuscript is missing its last line, which the copyist had to squeeze on to the facing page at the end of another song. I am grateful to my colleague Cynthia Cyrus of the Blair School of Music for invaluable help and advice on music of the period and to Christine Smith for preparing the final version of the musical score.

ABBREVIATIONS AND REFERENCES

Place of publication is London unless otherwise stated. Quotations and references relating to *The Duchess of Malfi* are keyed to this edition. Works of Shakespeare are cited from the most recent Arden editions. *OED* references are to *OED²*. Biblical quotations are from the Geneva Bible (1560), unless otherwise noted.

ABBREVIATIONS

ABBREVIATIONS USED IN NOTES

*	precedes commentary notes involving readings altered from the text on which this edition is based (Q1)
( )	surrounding a reading in the textual notes, indicates original spelling, usually in the base text for the edition
conj.	conjectured by
MS	manuscript
n.	commentary note
om.	omitted
opp.	opposite
sig.	signature
SD	stage direction
SP	speech prefix
subst.	substantially
this edn	a reading adopted for the first time in this edition
t.n.	textual note

ABBREVIATIONS FOR SHAKESPEARE PLAYS

AC	*Antony and Cleopatra*
AYL	*As You Like It*
Cor	*Coriolanus*
Cym	*Cymbeline*
Ham	*Hamlet*
1H4	*King Henry IV, Part 1*

2H4	*King Henry IV, Part 2*
H5	*King Henry V*
3H6	*King Henry VI, Part 3*
H8	*King Henry VIII*
KL	*King Lear*
MA	*Much Ado about Nothing*
Mac	*Macbeth*
MM	*Measure for Measure*
MND	*A Midsummer Night's Dream*
MV	*The Merchant of Venice*
Oth	*Othello*
Per	*Pericles*
R2	*King Richard II*
R3	*King Richard III*
RJ	*Romeo and Juliet*
Tem	*The Tempest*
TGV	*The Two Gentlemen of Verona*
Tit	*Titus Andronicus*
TN	*Twelfth Night*
TNK	*The Two Noble Kinsmen*
TS	*The Taming of the Shrew*
WT	*The Winter's Tale*

REFERENCES

EDITIONS OF *THE DUCHESS OF MALFI* COLLATED

Bevington	*English Renaissance Drama*, ed. David Bevington et al. (2002)
Brennan	John Webster, *The Duchess of Malfi*, ed. Elizabeth M. Brennan, New Mermaids, 1st edn (1964)
Brown	John Webster, *The Duchess of Malfi*, ed. John Russell Brown, Revels Plays (Cambridge, Mass., 1964)
D&S	*The Selected Plays of John Webster*, ed. Jonathan Dollimore and Alan Sinfield, Plays by Renaissance and Restoration Dramatists (Cambridge, 1983)
Dyce	*The Works of John Webster*, ed. Alexander Dyce, 4 vols (1830)
Dyce²	*The Works of John Webster*, ed. Alexander Dyce, 2nd edn, 4 vols (1857)
Gibbons	John Webster, *The Duchess of Malfi*, ed. Brian Gibbons, New Mermaids, 4th edn (2001)

Gunby	John Webster, *The Duchess of Malfi*, ed. David Gunby, in *The Works of John Webster*, ed. David Gunby, David Carnegie and Macdonald P. Jackson, 3 vols (Cambridge, 1995–2007), vol. 1 (1995)
Hazlitt	*The Dramatic Works of John Webster*, ed. William Hazlitt, 4 vols (1857)
Lucas	*The Complete Works of John Webster*, ed. F. L. Lucas, 4 vols (1927)
Norton	*The Norton Anthology of English Literature*, vol. 1, ed. M. H. Abrams, 3rd edn (New York, 1974)
Q1	*The Tragedy of the Dutchesse of Malfy . . . Written by John Webster* (1623), STC 25176
Q2	*The Dutchess of Malfy. A Tragedy . . . Written by John Webster* (1640), STC 25177
Q3	*The Dutchess of Malfey: A Tragedy* (1678), Wing W1223
Q4	*The Unfortunate Dutchess of Malfy, or The Unnatural Brothers: A Tragedy . . . Written by Mr. Webster* (1708)
Sampson	*The White Devil and The Duchess of Malfi by John Webster*, ed. Martin W. Sampson (Boston, Mass., 1904)
Thorndike	*Masterpieces of the English Drama: Webster and Tourneur*, ed. Ashley H. Thorndike (New York, 1912)
Weis	John Webster, *The Duchess of Malfi and Other Plays*, ed. René Weis (Oxford, 1996)

OTHER WORKS CITED

Acting Copy	*The Duchess of Malfi: A Tragedy, in Five Acts, adapted from John Webster* (no date, *c.* 1850)
Adams	Thomas Adams, *The Works of Thomas Adams* (1630), STC 104
Alexander	William Alexander, Earl of Stirling, *Alexandrian Tragedy* and *Julius Caesar*, in *Monarchic Tragedies* (1607), STC 344
Allman	Eileen Allman, *Jacobean Revenge Tragedy and the Politics of Virtue* (1999)
Amendola	Barbara Banks Amendola, *The Mystery of the Duchess of Malfi* (Thrupp, Stroud, Gloucestershire, 2002)
Antonio and Mellida	John Marston, *The History of Antonio and Mellida* (1602), STC 17473, in Marston
Apology	Thomas Heywood, *An Apology for Actors* (1612), STC 13309
Appius and Virginia	[John Webster and Thomas Heywood,] *Appius and Virginia: A Tragedy* (1625–6), Wing W1215, in Webster

Arcadia	Philip Sidney, *Prose Works I: Arcadia*, ed. Albert Feuillerat, 4 vols (Cambridge, 1963)
Artaud	Antonin Artaud, *The Theatre and its Double*, trans. Mary Caroline Richards (New York, 1958)
Astrophil and Stella	Philip Sidney, *Astrophil and Stella* (1598), in *The Poems of Sir Philip Sidney*, ed. William A. Ringler, Jr (Oxford, 1962)
Atheist's Tragedy	Cyril Tourneur, *The Atheist's Tragedy: or, The Honest Man's Revenge* (1611), STC 24146
Bacon, *Apophthegms*	Francis Bacon, *Apophthegms* (1624), in *Works of Francis Bacon*, ed. James Spedding et al., 15 vols (Cambridge, 1863)
Bacon, *Essays*	Francis Bacon, *Essays or Counsels, Civil and Moral*, ed. Michael Kiernan (Cambridge, Mass., 1985)
Bacon, *Sylva*	Francis Bacon, *Sylva Sylvarum* (1626), STC 1168
Bandello	Matteo Bandello, *La prima parte de le novelle*, ed. Delmo Maestri (Alessandria, 1992), novella 26, 248–57
Barnavelt	[John Fletcher and Philip Massinger,] *The Tragedy of John van Olden Barnavelt*, BL Add. MS 18653, in Beaumont and Fletcher
Barthes	Roland Barthes, 'From work to text', in Harari, 73–81
Batman	Steven Batman, *Batman upon Bartholome his Book De proprietatibus rerum* (1582), STC 1538
Beaumont and Fletcher	*The Dramatic Works in the Beaumont and Fletcher Canon*, gen. ed. Fredson Bowers, 10 vols (Cambridge, 1966–96)
Belleforest	François de Belleforest, *Histoires tragiques*, vol. 2 (1565)
Bentley	G. E. Bentley, *The Jacobean and Caroline Stage*, vol. 2: *Dramatic Companies and Players* (Oxford, 1941)
Berry	Ralph Berry, *The Art of John Webster* (Oxford, 1972)
Bible	*The Geneva Bible, a Facsimile of the 1560 Edition*, ed. Lloyd E. Berry (Madison, Wis., 1969)
Bible, King James version	Cited only where specified in the notes
Blayney	Peter W. M. Blayney, *The Texts of* King Lear *and their Origin*, vol. 1: *Nicholas Okes and the First Quarto* (Cambridge, 1982)
Bodin	Jean Bodin, *The Six Books of a Commonweal*, trans. Richard Knolles (1606), STC 3193

Boklund	Gunnar Boklund, *The Duchess of Malfi: Sources, Themes, Characters* (1962)
Bonduca	[John Fletcher,] *The Tragedy of Bonduca*, Wing B1581, in Beaumont and Fletcher
Bradbrook	Muriel C. Bradbrook, *John Webster: Citizen and Dramatist* (New York, 1980)
Brecht	Bertolt Brecht, *The Duchess of Malfi* (1943), ed. A. R. Braunmuller, in *Collected Plays*, ed. Ralph Manheim and John Willett, vol. 7 (1974), 329–449
Brooke	Rupert Brooke, *John Webster and the Elizabethan Drama* (New York, 1916)
Brown, 'Printing' 1	John Russell Brown, 'The printing of John Webster's plays (I)', *Studies in Bibliography*, 6 (1954), 117–41
Brown, 'Printing' 2	John Russell Brown, 'The printing of John Webster's plays (II)', *Studies in Bibliography*, 8 (1956), 114–29
Burton	Robert Burton, *The Anatomy of Melancholy*, ed. Floyd Dell and Paul Jordan-Smith (New York, 1927)
Bushnell	Rebecca W. Bushnell, *Tragedies of Tyrants: Political Thought and Theatre in the English Renaissance* (1990)
Busino	*The Journals of Two Travellers in Elizabethan and Early Stuart England: Thomas Platter and Horatio Busino*, ed. Peter Razzell (1995)
Bussy	George Chapman, *Bussy D'Ambois* (1607), STC 4966, in Chapman
Caesar's Fall	[John Webster, Thomas Dekker, Michael Drayton, Thomas Middleton and Anthony Munday,] *Caesar's Fall* (1602), lost play
Calbi	Maurizio Calbi, *Approximate Bodies: Gender and Power in Early Modern Drama and Anatomy* (2005)
Callaghan	Dympna Callaghan (ed.), *The Duchess of Malfi: Contemporary Critical Essays* (2000)
Camden, *Britannia*	William Camden, *Britain*, trans. Philemon Holland (1610), STC 4509
Camden, *Remains*	William Camden, *Remains of a Greater Work, concerning Britain* (1605), STC 4521
Campion	Thomas Campion, *A Relation of the Late Royal Entertainment . . . Whereunto is annexed the Description, Speeches and Songs of the Lords Mask . . .* (1613), STC 4545
Castiglione	Baldesar Castiglione, *The Book of the Courtier*, trans. Charles S. Singleton (New York, 1959)
Cecil	David Cecil, 'Comment', in Holdsworth, 66–8

Certain Elegies   Henry Fitzgeffrey, *Certain Elegies, Done by Sundry Excellent Wits* (1618), STC 10945.3

Chambers   E. K. Chambers, 'The disintegration of Shakespeare', Annual Shakespeare Lecture, 1924, in *Proceedings of the British Academy 1924–1925* ([1925]), 89–108

Changeling   [William Rowley and Thomas Middleton,] *The Changeling* (1622), Wing M1980, in Middleton

Chapman   George Chapman, *The Tragedies*, ed. Thomas Marc Parrott, 2 vols (New York, 1961)

Chaucer   Geoffrey Chaucer, *The Riverside Chaucer*, ed. Larry D. Benson, 3rd edn (New York, 1987)

Clement   Jennifer Clement, personal communication, 2007

Coddon   Karin S. Coddon, '*The Duchess of Malfi*: tyranny and spectacle in Jacobean drama', in Callaghan, 25–45

Column   John Webster, *A Monumental Column* (1613), in Webster

Cotgrave   Randle Cotgrave, *Dictionary of the French and English Tongues* (1611), STC 5830; and (1632), STC 5831

Cuckold   [John Webster, William Rowley and Thomas Heywood,] *A Cure for a Cuckold: A Pleasant Comedy* (1624), Wing W1220, in Webster

Custom   [John Fletcher and Philip Massinger,] *The Custom of the Country*, Wing B1581, in Beaumont and Fletcher

Dallington   Robert Dallington, *The View of France* (1604), STC 6202

Dekker   Thomas Dekker, *Dramatic Works*, ed. Fredson Bowers, 4 vols (Cambridge, 1953–61)

Dent   R. W. Dent, *Proverbial Language in English Drama Exclusive of Shakespeare, 1495–1616* (1984)

Dent, *Webster*   R. W. Dent, *John Webster's Borrowing* (1960)

Dever   Carolyn Dever, personal communication, based on her research with the unpublished diaries of 'Michael Field' at the British Library, BL Add. MS 46776–804

Devil's Law-Case   John Webster, *The Devil's Law-Case; or, When Women go to Law, the Devil is full of Business: A New Tragicomedy* (1617–19; published 1623), STC 25173, in Webster

Dollimore   Jonathan Dollimore, *Radical Tragedy: Religion, Ideology and Power in the Drama of Shakespeare and his Contemporaries* (1984; 3rd edn 2004)

Donne   John Donne, *The Major Works*, ed. John Carey (Oxford, 1990)

Dowland   *Lute Songs of John Dowland*, ed. David Nadal (New York, 1997)

Eastward Ho	[George Chapman, Ben Jonson and John Marston,] *Eastward Ho* (1605), STC 4970, in George Chapman, *The Comedies*, ed. Thomas Marc Parrott, 2 vols (New York, 1961)
Edmond	Mary Edmond, 'In search of John Webster', *Times Literary Supplement*, 24 December 1976
EEBO	Early English Books Online, URL: http://eebo.chadwyck.com
Ekeblad	Inga-Stina Ekeblad, 'The "impure art" of John Webster', in Rabkin, 49–64
Eliot, *Elizabethan Essays*	T. S. Eliot, *Elizabethan Essays* (New York, 1964)
Eliot, 'Metaphysical'	T. S. Eliot, 'The metaphysical poets' (1921), in Frank Kermode (ed.), *Selected Prose of T. S. Eliot* (1975), 59–67
Eliot, *Waste Land*	T. S. Eliot, *The Waste Land* (1922)
Elizabeth I	Elizabeth I, *Collected Works*, ed. Leah S. Marcus, Janel Mueller and Mary Beth Rose (Chicago, 2000)
Elyot	Thomas Elyot, *The Image of Governance* (1541), STC 7664
Empson	William Empson, 'Mine eyes dazzle', in Rabkin, 90–5
Enterline	Lynn Enterline, *The Tears of Narcissus: Melancholia and Masculinity in Early Modern Writing* (Stanford, Calif., 1995), 242–403
Erne	Lukas Erne, *Shakespeare as Literary Dramatist* (Cambridge, 2003)
Every Man Out	Ben Jonson, *Every Man Out of His Humour* (1600), STC 14767 in Jonson
Fair Maid	[John Fletcher, John Webster, John Ford and Philip Massinger,] *The Fair Maid of the Inn* (licensed 1626), Wing B1581, in Beaumont and Fletcher
Faustus	Christopher Marlowe, *The Tragical History of the Life and Death of Doctor Faustus* (1604), STC 17429, 17432, ed. David Bevington and Eric Rasmussen, Revels Plays (Manchester, 1993)
Fifty Sermons	John Donne, *Fifty Sermons Preached by that Learned and Reverend Divine, John Donne* (1649), Wing D1862
Florio	John Florio, *Queen Anna's New World of Words, or Dictionary of the Italian and English Tongues* (1611)
Forker	Charles R. Forker, *The Skull beneath the Skin: The Achievement of John Webster* (Carbondale, Ill., 1986)
Foucault	Michel Foucault, 'What is an author?' in Harari, 141–60
Fountain	Richard Linche (trans.), *The Fountain of Ancient Fiction* (1599), STC 4691

411

Foxe   John Foxe, *Acts and Monuments* [Foxe's *Book of Martyrs*] (1563), STC 11222

FQ   Edmund Spenser, *The Faerie Queene*, ed. J. C. Smith, 2 vols (Oxford, 1909)

Gallant's   Thomas Adams, *The Gallant's Burden, a Sermon Preached ... 1612* (1614), STC 118

Game at Chess Thomas Middleton, *A Game at Chess* (1625), Folger Library MS V.a.231 and STC 17882, in Middleton

Garcia   Luciano Garcia, 'The Duchess of Malfi and *El mayordomo de la duquesa de Amalfi* revisited: some differences in literary convention and cultural horizon', in José Manuel González (ed.), *Spanish Studies in Shakespeare and his Contemporaries* (Newark, NJ, 2006), 299–310

Godfrey   Torquato Tasso, *Godfrey of Bulloigne, or The Recovery of Jerusalem*, trans. Edward Fairfax (1600), STC 23698

Goldberg   Dena Goldberg, *Between Worlds: A Study of the Plays of John Webster* (Waterloo, Ont., 1987)

Gossett   William Shakespeare, *Pericles*, ed. Suzanne Gossett, Arden Shakespeare (2004)

Goulart   Simon Goulart, *Admirable and Memorable Histories Containing the Wonders of Our Time*, trans. Edward Grimeston (1607), STC 12135

Governance   Thomas Elyot, *The Image of Governance* (1541), STC 7664

Granada   Luis de Granada, *Granados Spiritual and Heavenly Exercises*, trans. Francis Meres (1598), STC 16920

Graves   R. B. Graves, *Lighting the Shakespearean Stage 1567–1642* (Carbondale, Ill., 1999)

Greg   W. W. Greg, *A Bibliography of the English Printed Drama to the Restoration*, 4 vols (1939–59)

Guazzo   Stefano Guazzo, *Civil Conversation*, trans. George Pettie (1581), STC 12422

Guevara   Antonio de Guevara, *Dial of Princes*, trans. Thomas North (1557), STC 12427

Gurr, *Company* Andrew Gurr, *The Shakespeare Company, 1594–1642* (Cambridge, 2004)

Gurr, *Playgoing* Andrew Gurr, *Playgoing in Shakespeare's London*, 3rd edn (Cambridge, 2004)

Hageman and   Elizabeth H. Hageman and Katherine Conway (eds),
   Conway   *Resurrecting Elizabeth I in Seventeenth-Century England* (Madison, NJ, 2007)

Hall, *Characters* Joseph Hall, *Characters of Virtues and Vices* (1608), STC 12648

Hall, *Epistles*	Joseph Hall, *Epistles* (1608), STC 12662
Harari	Josué V. Harari (ed.), *Textual Strategies* (Ithaca, NY, 1979), 73–81
Henderson and McManus	Katherine Henderson and Barbara F. McManus, *Half Humankind: Contexts and Texts of the Controversy about Women in England 1540–1640* (Urbana, Ill., 1985)
Henze	Catherine A. Henze, 'How music matters: some songs of Robert Johnson in the plays of Beaumont and Fletcher', *Comparative Drama*, 34 (2000), 1–32
Heptameron	George Whetstone, *Heptameron of Civil Discourses* (1582), STC 25337
Herrick	*Complete Poetry of Robert Herrick*, ed. J. Max Patrick (New York, 1968)
Hill	Christopher Hill, *Society and Puritanism in Pre-Revolutionary England* (1958; repr. New York, 1997)
Hogg	James Hogg, 'Court satire in John Webster's *White Devil*', in James Hogg (ed.), *Jacobean Drama as Social Criticism* (Salzburg, 1995), 147–63
Holdsworth	R. V. Holdsworth (ed.), *Webster,* The White Devil *and* The Duchess of Malfi*: A Casebook* (1975)
Homer	Homer, *The Iliad*, trans. Richmond Lattimore (1951)
Hope	Jonathan Hope, *Shakespeare's Grammar* (2003)
Horace	Horace, *Odes and Epodes*, ed. Niall Rudd, Loeb Classical Library (2004)
Horne	R. H. Horne, *The Duchess of Malfi: A Tragedy in Five Acts by John Webster, 1612* (1850)
Howard-Hill	Trevor Howard-Hill, *Ralph Crane and Some Shakespeare First Folio Comedies* (Charlottesville, Va., 1972)
Humorous Lieutenant	[John Fletcher,] *The Humorous Lieutenant*, also known as *The Noble Enemies* and *Demetrius and Enanthe*, Wing B1581, in Beaumont and Fletcher
Hyland	Peter Hyland, 'Re-membering Gloriana: *The Revenger's Tragedy*', in Hageman and Conway, 82–94
If You Know 1	Thomas Heywood, *If You Know Not Me, You Know Nobody: Or, The Troubles of Queen Elizabeth* (1605), STC 13328
If You Know 2	Thomas Heywood, *The Second Part of If You Know Not Me, You Know Nobody, With The Building of the Royal Exchange: And The Famous Victory of Queen Elizabeth, in the Year 1588* (1606), STC 13336
Ignatius	John Donne, *Ignatius His Conclave* (1611), ed. T. S. Healy (Oxford, 1969)

Illis	L. Illis, 'On porphyria and the aetiology of werewolves', *Proceedings of the Royal Society of Medicine*, 57 (1964), 23–6; repr. in Otten, 195–9
Insatiate Countess	[John Marston and William Barksted,] *The Insatiate Countess, a Tragedy* (1613), STC 17476, ed. Giorgio Melchiori, Revels Plays (Manchester, 1984)
Island Princess	[John Fletcher,] *The Island Princess: A Tragicomedy*, Wing B1581, in Beaumont and Fletcher
Jellerson	Donald Jellerson, personal communication, 2007
Jonson	Ben Jonson, *Works*, ed. C. H. Herford and Percy and Evelyn Simpson, 11 vols (Oxford, 1925–52); plays authored by Jonson alone are not listed separately by title in this list
Kathman, 'Boy actors'	David Kathman, 'How old were Shakespeare's boy actors?', *Shakespeare Survey*, 58 (2005), 220–46
Kathman, 'Freemen'	David Kathman, 'Grocers, goldsmiths, and drapers: freemen and apprentices in the Elizabethan theater', *Shakespeare Quarterly*, 55 (2004), 1–49
Klapisch-Zuber	Christiane Klapisch-Zuber, *Women, Family, and Ritual in Renaissance Italy*, trans. Lydia G. Cochrane (Chicago, 1985)
Knight of Malta	[John Fletcher, Nathan Field and Philip Massinger,] *The Knight of Malta*, Wing B1581, in Beaumont and Fletcher
Lady's Tragedy	[Thomas Middleton,] untitled (acted 1611), BL MS Lansdowne 807, fols 29–56, in Middleton (also known as *The Second Maiden's Tragedy*, the title on the MS's acting license, fol. 56)
Lamb	Charles Lamb, *Specimens of English Dramatic Poets* (1808), ed. William Macdonald, 2 vols (1903)
Larkin and Hughes	*Stuart Royal Proclamations*, vol. 1: *Royal Proclamations of King James I*, ed. James F. Larkin and Paul L. Hughes (Oxford, 1973)
Lavater	Ludwig [Lewes] Lavater, *Of Ghosts and Spirits* (1572), STC 15320
Lever	J. W. Lever, *The Tragedy of State* (1971)
Levin	Carole Levin, *'The Heart and Stomach of a King': Elizabeth I and the Politics of Sex and Power* (Philadelphia, 1994)
Loraux	Nicole Loraux, *Tragic Ways of Killing a Woman*, trans. Anthony Forster (1987)
Luckyj	Christina Luckyj, *A Winter's Snake: Dramatic Form in the Tragedies of John Webster* (1989)

Lukács	Georg Lukács, *History and Class Consciousness: Studies in Marxist Dialectics*, trans. Rodney Livingstone (Cambridge, Mass., 1971)
McClary	Susan McClary, *Feminine Endings: Music, Gender and Sexuality* (2002)
MacDonald	Michael MacDonald, *Mystical Bedlam: Madness, Anxiety, and Healing in Seventeenth-Century England* (1981)
Machiavelli, *History*	Niccolò Machiavelli, *The History of Florence and of the Affairs of Italy*, introduction by Felix Gilbert (1960)
Machiavelli, *Prince*	Niccolò Machiavelli, *The Prince and Selected Discourses*, trans. Daniel Donno (New York, 1966; repr. 1971)
McLuskie and Uglow	Kathleen McLuskie and Jennifer Uglow (eds), *Plays in Performance: The Duchess of Malfi by John Webster* (Bristol, 1989)
Macy	Laura Macy, 'Speaking of sex: metaphor and performance in the Italian madrigal', *Journal of Musicology*, 14 (1996), 1–34
Mad World	Thomas Middleton, *A Mad World, My Masters* (1605), STC 17888, in Middleton
Maguire	Nancy Klein Maguire, *Regicide and Restoration: English Tragicomedy, 1660–1671* (Cambridge, 1992)
Mahon	Derek Mahon, *Collected Poems* (Oldcastle, Ireland, 1999)
Maid's Tragedy	[Francis Beaumont and John Fletcher,] *The Maid's Tragedy* (1611), STC 1676 and 1678, in Beaumont and Fletcher
Malcontent	John Marston, *The Malcontent* (1604), STC 17479, in Marston
Marcus, *Puzzling*	Leah S. Marcus, *Puzzling Shakespeare: Local Reading and its Discontents* (1988)
Marcus, 'Textual'	Leah S. Marcus, 'Textual scholarship', in David G. Nicholls (ed.), *Introduction to Scholarship in Modern Languages and Literatures* (New York, 2007), 143–59
Marcus, *Unediting*	Leah S. Marcus, *Unediting the Renaissance: Shakespeare, Marlowe, Milton* (1996)
Marston	*Selected Plays of John Marston*, ed. Macdonald P. Jackson and Michael Neill (Cambridge, 1986)
Marvell	*Andrew Marvell*, ed. Frank Kermode and Keith Walker (Oxford, 1990)
Massinger	*The Plays and Poems of Philip Massinger*, ed. Philip Edwards and Colin Gibson, 5 vols (Oxford, 1986)
Match Me	Thomas Dekker, *A Tragicomedy: Called, Match Me in London* (1631), STC 6529, in Dekker

Matthieu   Pierre Matthieu, *The Heroic Life And Deplorable Death of the Most Christian King Henry the Fourth*, trans. Edward Grimeston (1612), STC 17661

Middleton   *Thomas Middleton: The Collected Works*, gen. eds Gary Taylor and John Lavagnino, 2 vols (Oxford, 2007)

Milton   John Milton, *Complete Poems and Major Prose*, ed. Merritt Y. Hughes (Indianapolis, 1957)

Montaigne   Michel de Montaigne, *Essays*, trans. John Florio (1603), STC 18041

Moore   Don D. Moore, *John Webster and his Critics 1617–1964*, Louisiana State University Studies Humanities Series 17 (Baton Rouge, La., 1966)

Mouzell   Rachel Speght, *A Mouzell for Melastomus, the Cynical Baiter of, and Foul-Mouthed Barker against Eva's Sex* (1617), STC 23058

Mullaney   Steven Mullaney, 'Mourning and misogyny: *Hamlet, The Revenger's Tragedy*, and the Final Progress of Elizabeth I, 1600–1607', in Newman, 238–60

Murray   Peter B. Murray, *A Study of John Webster* (The Hague, 1969)

Nashe   *The Works of Thomas Nashe*, ed. Ronald B. McKerrow, 5 vols (Oxford, 1958)

Neill   Michael Neill, *Issues of Death: Mortality and Identity in English Renaissance Tragedy* (Oxford, 1997)

Newman   Robert Newman (ed.), *Centuries' Ends, Narrative Means* (Stanford, Calif., 1996)

Nice Valour   [Thomas Middleton,] *The Nice Valour; or, The Passionate Madman* (1622), Wing B1581, in Middleton

Nixon   Anthony Nixon, *London's Dove* (1612), STC 18588

North   Plutarch, *The Lives*, trans. Thomas North (1579), STC 20065

Northward Ho!   [Thomas Dekker and John Webster,] *Northward Ho!* (1607), STC 6539, in Dekker

OED   *Oxford English Dictionary*, 2nd edn (Oxford, 1989)

Orgel and Strong Stephen Orgel and Roy Strong, *Inigo Jones: The Theatre of the Stuart Court*, 2 vols (1973)

Otten   Charlotte F. Otten (ed.), *A Lycanthropy Reader: Werewolves in Western Culture* (Syracuse, NY, 1986)

Overbury   Thomas Overbury, *New and Choice Characters* (1615), STC 18908

Ovid   Ovid, *Metamorphoses*, trans. Frank Justus Miller, 3rd edn, 2 vols, Loeb Classical Library (1984)

Painter	William Painter, *The Second Tome of the Palace of Pleasure* (1567), STC 19124
Paradise Regained	John Milton, *Paradise Regained* (1671), Wing M2152
Paster	Gail Kern Paster, *Humoring the Body: Emotions and the Shakespearean Stage* (Chicago, 2004)
Peacham	Henry Peacham, *The Compleat Gentleman* (1622), STC 19502
Penitential Psalms	George Chapman, *Seven Penitential Psalms* (1612), in *Poems*, ed. Phyllis Brooks Bartlett (1941)
Pepys	*The Diary of Samuel Pepys*, ed. Robert Latham and William Matthews, 11 vols (Berkeley, Calif., 1970)
Philaster	Francis Beaumont and John Fletcher, *Philaster, or, Love Lies a-Bleeding* (1608–10), STC 1681.5, ed. Suzanne Gossett, Arden Early Modern Drama (2009)
Phillippy	Patricia Phillippy, *Women, Death and Literature in Post-Reformation England* (Cambridge, 2002)
Phoenix	Thomas Middleton, *The Phoenix* (1607), STC 17892, in Middleton
Picture	Philip Massinger, *The Picture: A Tragaecomaedie* (1630), STC 17640, in Massinger
Plato	*The Dialogues of Plato*, trans. B. Jowett, 2 vols (New York, 1937)
Pliny	Pliny the Elder, *The History of the World, Commonly Called The Natural History of C. Plinius Secundus*, trans. Philemon Holland (1601), STC 20029
Plutarch	See North
Potter	Lois Potter, 'Realism versus nightmare: problems of staging *The Duchess of Malfi*', in Price, 170–89
Potts	Thomas Potts, *Wonderful Discovery of Witches* (1613), STC 20138
Price	Joseph G. Price (ed.), *The Triple Bond: Plays, Mostly Shakespearean, in Performance* (University Park, Pa., 1975)
Quarles	Francis Quarles, *Emblems* (1643), Wing 77
Quarrel	[Thomas Middleton and William Rowley,] *A Fair Quarrel* (performed 1615–17), STC 17911, in Middleton
Quiet Life	[John Webster and Thomas Middleton,] *Anything for a Quiet Life: A Comedy* (*c.* 1621), Wing M1979, in Webster
Rabkin	Norman Rabkin (ed.), *Twentieth Century Interpretations of The Duchess of Malfi: A Collection of Critical Essays* (Englewood Cliffs, NJ, 1968)
Rebhorn	Wayne A. Rebhorn, 'Circle, sword and the futile quest: the nightmare world of Webster's *Duchess of Malfi*', *Cahiers Elisabéthains*, 27 (1985), 54–66

Revenge of Bussy	George Chapman, *The Revenge of Bussy D'Ambois* (1613), STC 4989, in Chapman
Revenger	[Thomas Middleton,] *The Revenger's Tragedy* (1607), STC 24149, in Middleton
Ridler	Anne Ridler, *Collected Poems* (Manchester, 1994)
Roaring Girl	[Thomas Middleton and Thomas Dekker,] *The Roaring Girl; or Moll Cut-Purse* (1611), STC 17908, in Dekker
Roman Actor	Philip Massinger, *The Roman Actor: A Tragedy* (1629), STC 17642, in Massinger
Rose	Mary Beth Rose, *The Expense of Spirit: Love and Sexuality in English Renaissance Drama* (1988)
Rowe	Katherine Rowe, *Dead Hands: Fictions of Agency, Renaissance to Modern* (Stanford, Calif., 1999)
Sadler	John Sadler, *The Sick Woman's Private Looking-Glass*, 2nd edn (1636), STC 21544
Scot	Reginald Scot, *Discovery of Witchcraft* (1584), STC 21864
Second Maiden's Tragedy	See *Lady's Tragedy*
Seneca	Seneca, *De Beneficiis*, in *Moral Essays*, trans. John W. Basore, 3 vols, Loeb Classical Library (New York, 1928–35)
Serres	Jean [Jhon] de Serres and Pierre Matthieu, *A General Inventory of the History of France*, trans. Edward Grimeston (1607), STC 22244
Shepherd	Simon Shepherd, *Amazons and Warrior Women: Varieties of Feminism in Seventeenth-Century Drama* (New York, 1981)
Shoemaker's Holiday	[Thomas Dekker,] *The Shoemaker's Holiday; or, The Gentle Craft with the Humorous Life of Simon Eyre, Shoemaker, and Lord Mayor of London* (1600), STC 6523, in Dekker
Sidky	H. Sidky, *Witchcraft, Lycanthropy, Drugs and Disease: An Anthropological Study of the European Witch-Hunts* (New York, 1997)
Sinfield	Alan Sinfield, *Literature in Protestant England 1560–1660* (1983)
Smith	G. C. Moore Smith (ed.), *William Heminges's Elegy on Randolph's Finger* (Oxford, 1923)
Snyder	Gary Snyder, *Turtle Island* (New York, 1974)
Spanish Viceroy	[John Fletcher and Philip Massinger,] *The Spanish Viceroy*, lost play

STC	*Short-Title Catalogue of Books Printed in England, Scotland, and Ireland and of English Books Printed Abroad, 1475–1640*, 2nd edn, ed. W. A. Jackson, S. F. Ferguson and Katharine F. Pantzer (Oxford, 1986–91) (All titles listed here with STC numbers are available online through EEBO, Early English Books Online.)
Steen	Sara Jayne Steen, 'The crime of marriage: Arbella Stuart and *The Duchess of Malfi*', *Sixteenth-Century Journal*, 22 (1991), 61–76
Stephens	John Stephens, *Essays and Characters, Ironical and Instructive* (1615), STC 23250
Stern	Tiffany Stern, *Documents of Performance in Early Modern England* (Cambridge, forthcoming)
Stow, *Annals*	John Stow, *Annals of England* (1592), STC 23334
Stow, *Survey*	John Stow, *Survey of London* (1598), STC 23341
Sweet	James H. Sweet, 'The Iberian roots of American racist thought', *William and Mary Quarterly*, 54, 1 (1997), 143–66
Swetnam	Joseph Swetnam, *The Arraignment of Lewd, Idle, Froward, and Unconstant Women* (1615)
Swinburne	Algernon Charles Swinburne, *Swinburne as Critic*, ed. Clyde K. Hyder (1972)
Tate, A.	Allen Tate, *Collected Poems 1919–1976* (New York, 1977)
Tate, N.	Nahum Tate, *The History of King Lear, acted at the Duke's Theatre* (1681), Wing S2918
Taylor and Jowett	Gary Taylor and John Jowett, *Shakespeare Reshaped, 1606–1623* (Oxford, 1993)
Theobald	Lewis Theobald, *The Fatal Secret, a Tragedy* (1735)
Thesmophoriazusae	Aristophanes, *Thesmophoriazusae*, ed. Colin Austin and S. Douglas Olson (Oxford, 2004)
Thomas	Keith Thomas, *Religion and the Decline of Magic* (Harmondsworth, England, 1971)
Tilley	Morris Palmer Tilley, *Dictionary of the Proverbs in England in the Sixteenth and Seventeenth Centuries* (Ann Arbor, Mich., 1950).
Times	*The Times Digital Archive*, 179 (Gale, Cengage, 2009)
Turberville	George Turberville, *Book of Hunting* (1576; facsimile edn Oxford, 1908)
Virgil	Virgil, *Works*, trans. H. Rushton Fairclough and G. P. Goold, rev. edn, 2 vols (Cambridge, Mass., 1999)
Wadsworth, 'American'	Frank W. Wadsworth, 'Webster, Horne and Mrs Stowe: American performances of *The Duchess of Malfi*', *Theatre Survey*, 11 (1970), 151–66

Wadsworth, 'Revivals'	Frank W. Wadsworth, 'Some nineteenth-century revivals of *The Duchess of Malfi*', *Theatre Survey*, 8 (1967), 67–83
Wadsworth, 'Shorn'	Frank W. Wadsworth, '"Shorn and abated": British performances of *The Duchess of Malfi*', *Theatre Survey*, 10 (1969), 89–104
Wall	Wendy Wall, '"Just a spoonful of sugar": syrup and domesticity in early modern England', *Modern Philology*, 104 (2006), 149–72
Wallace	David Wallace, *Chaucerian Polity: Absolutist Lineages and Associational Forms in England and Italy* (Stanford, Calif., 1997)
Walton	Izaak Walton, *The Lives of John Donne, Sir Henry Wotton, Richard Hooker, George Herbert, and Robert Sanderson*, ed. George Saintsbury (1927)
Warlock	Peter Warlock, 'The shrouding of the Duchess of Malfi', in *The Choral Music of Peter Warlock*, vol. 7 (1995)
Watkins	John Watkins, *Representing Elizabeth in Stuart England: Literature, History, Sovereignty* (Cambridge, 2002)
Webster	*The Works of John Webster*, ed. David Gunby, David Carnegie, Antony Hammond and Macdonald P. Jackson, 3 vols (Cambridge, 1995–2007)
Westward Ho	[Thomas Dekker and John Webster,] *Westward Ho* (1607), STC 6540, in Dekker
Whigham	Frank Whigham, *Seizures of the Will in Early Modern English Drama* (Cambridge, 1996)
White Devil	*The White Devil* (1612), STC 25178, in Webster
Whitney	Geoffrey Whitney, *A Choice of Emblems* (1586), STC 25438
Whore	Thomas Dekker, *The Whore of Babylon* (1607), STC 6532, in Dekker
Widow Waking	[John Webster, Thomas Dekker, John Ford and William Rowley,] *Keep the Widow Waking* (1624), lost play
Wing	*Short-Title Catalogue of Books Published in England, Scotland, Ireland, Wales, and British America, and of English Books Printed in Other Countries, 1641–1700*, ed. Donald Wing, 2nd edn, 4 vols (New York, 1972–98) (All titles listed here with a 'Wing' number are available online through EEBO, Early English Books Online.)
Wright	Thomas Wright, *The Passions of the Mind in General*, ed. Thomas O. Sloan (1604; repr. Urbana, Ill., 1971)
Wyatt	[Thomas Dekker and John Webster,] *The Famous History of Sir Thomas Wyatt* (1607), STC 6537, in Dekker

INDEX

This index covers the Introduction, commentary and appendices. It does not include the textual notes or the names of literary characters outside *Malfi*. For characters in *Malfi*, it records major references but not incidental ones. References to the commentary are given by page number only; references to Q1 in the commentary are omitted because they occur too frequently.